Maestros of the Pen

NORTHEASTERN UNIVERSITY 1898–1998

Music advisor to Northeastern University Press

GUNTHER SCHULLER

A HISTORY OF

CLASSICAL MUSIC

CRITICISM IN AMERICA

BY

Mark N. Grant

ERIC FRIEDHEIM, *Consulting Editor*

NORTHEASTERN UNIVERSITY PRESS

Boston

Northeastern University Press

Copyright 1998 by Mark N. Grant

Library of Congress Cataloging-in-Publication Data

Grant, Mark N., date
    Maestros of the pen : a history of classical music criticism in
America / by Mark N. Grant ; Eric Friedheim, consulting editor.
       p.   cm.
    Includes bibliographical references and index.
    ISBN 1-55553-363-9 (cloth : alk. paper)
    1. Musical criticism—United States. 2. Music—United States—
History and criticism. 3. Music—United States—Philosophy and
aesthetics. I. Friedheim, Eric. II. Title.
ML3915.G73   1998
781.6'8'0973—DC21   98-28959
                       MN

Designed by Gary Gore

Composed in Minion by G&S Typesetters, Austin, Texas. Printed and bound by Maple Press, York, Pennsylvania. The paper is Maple Antique, an acid-free sheet.

MANUFACTURED IN THE UNITED STATES OF AMERICA
02 01 00 99 98   5 4 3 2 1

*To my wife, Edith Hall Friedheim—*E F

To the memory of Leonard Altman,
who would have enjoyed reading this book,

A N D

*To the ever-living spirit of Nicolas Slonimsky—*M N G

Acknowledgments

THE AUTHOR gratefully acknowledges permission to reproduce excerpts from the following copyrighted materials:

Aaron Copland, letter from Aaron Copland to Nicolas Slonimsky dated February 10, 1927. Reprinted by permission of the Aaron Copland Fund for Music, Inc., the copyright holder.

Henry Pleasants, *The Agony of Modern Music.* Copyright © 1955 by Henry Pleasants. Reprinted by permission of John Hawkins & Associates, Inc.

John Rockwell, *All American Music.* Copyright © 1983 by John Rockwell. Reprinted, New York: Da Capo Press, 1997. Used by permission of the author.

Arnold Schoenberg, 1948 letter from Arnold Schoenberg to Olin Downes, published in the December 12, 1948, *New York Times.* Used by permission of Belmont Music Publishers, Pacific Palisades, Calif. 90272.

Oscar Thompson, "An American School of Criticism: The Legacy Left by W. J. Henderson, Richard Aldrich, and Their Colleagues of the Old Guard," *Musical Quarterly* 23 (July 1937), pp. 428–39. Reprinted by permission of Oxford University Press.

Material from the published and unpublished letters of Olin Downes is reprinted by permission of the Hargrett Rare Book and Manuscript Library, University of Georgia Libraries.

Material from Samuel Lipman's book *Music after Modernism* appearing on pages 312 to 314 is copyright © 1985 by Basic Books, Inc. Reprinted by permission of HarperCollins Publishers, Inc.

Material from the published writings of H. L. Mencken is reprinted by permission of the Enoch Pratt Free Library of Baltimore, Maryland, in accordance with the terms of the will of H. L. Mencken.

viii   Material from the writings of Winthrop Sargeant is reprinted by permission of Jane S. Sargeant, executrix of the estate of Winthrop Sargeant.

Material from the writings of Deems Taylor is reprinted by permission of Joan Kennedy Taylor, literary executor of the estate of Deems Taylor.

Material from the letters and published writings of Virgil Thomson is reprinted by permission of the Virgil Thomson Foundation, Ltd., the copyright holder.

The author gratefully acknowledges the assistance of Jay Sullivan for the Minna Lederman photograph, Thomas A. DeLong for the Deems Taylor photograph, Stewart Manville of the International Percy Grainger Society for the Henry T. Finck photograph, Suzanne Eggleston of the Yale Music Library, Martin Feinstein for the loan of his 1993 manuscript, and Michael Kagan for archival photography.

Contents

Illustrations

MONEY was not the main object. If it were, very few people would be music critics. In spite of the prestige wielded in the musical world by the New York critics, only a few of them, even today, earn as much as a Philharmonic fiddler. Critics, I soon found, were, like artists, dedicated men. They pretended to hate their work, which kept them up at all hours making late deadlines. They grumbled about their low pay, which often forced them to take odd extra jobs teaching or ghostwriting. But I never met one of them who really wanted to be anything but a critic. There was a delicious sense of importance and responsibility about striding to an aisle seat at Carnegie or Town Hall or the Metropolitan and sitting in solemn judgment on the work of an artist. . . . Being a critic, you left early to write your review, rushing up the aisle with an expression of dignified concern on your face. The rest of the audience was there for mere enjoyment. Not you. You were an important part of the act. . . . You took your work very seriously, for the fate of the artist depended, to some extent, on what you wrote. You tried to be scrupulously fair. You wielded power, and you were conscious of the responsibilities that went with it.

Like the members of the Philharmonic, you inhabited a microcosm. You lived in concert halls. You associated mainly with other critics. Your social life—what there was of it—consisted in visiting, during the intermission, with your colleagues and their wives. You talked, as well as wrote, criticism. You developed a tendency to consider the whole art of music as having one fundamental purpose: to be judged and evaluated. You were never without an opinion. You delighted in being asked what it was, and you always aired it with solemnity as if a good deal of the state of civilization depended on its correctness. You never associated with musicians. Most of them hated you anyway, and you bore this hatred with considerable pride, as a proof of your objectivity and incorruptibility. You knew that friendship for an artist would immediately cast suspicion on your opinions about his work. For this reason, you avoided parties to which you were invited, shunned press agents religiously, and practically never ventured backstage. Few critics knew what went on behind the scenes at Town Hall or the

Metropolitan Opera House. Few understood, or had any interest in, the psychology, personality or tribulations of the artist they wrote about. Human considerations were irrelevant. . . . You become able to form opinions, in a few minutes' time, on the capacities of almost any artist or composer. Your enjoyment of music becomes almost purely analytical. With the memory of a hundred other artists in mind, you would watch for certain key phrases, for certain high notes, for a singer's aplomb in tackling different registers of his voice, for the elegance or lack of it with which a violinist attacked a specific detail, and form your opinion accordingly. . . . It was difficult to avoid a growing sense of your own omniscience. . . . Nobody ever contradicted you, at least not to your face. Artists were afraid to, lest you take a dislike to them.

. . . New York music critics were likely to have the sort of one-way personality characteristic of lecturers, preachers, professors and other people who are always on the dominating end of discourse. Conversationally, they were apt to be monologists. They seldom listened to anybody. They were always propounding opinions. I remember one of them whose pontifical habits were so deeply ingrained that an inquiry whether the pea soup at Luchow's restaurant was up to snuff would produce a huge display of hemming and hawing followed by a ponderous and carefully considered pronouncement.

—WINTHROP SARGEANT, *Geniuses, Goddesses, and People*

Overture

*The trade of critic, in literature, music, and the drama, is the
most degraded of all trades.*
—MARK TWAIN, *Autobiography*

The immoral profession of musical criticism must be abolished.
—RICHARD WAGNER, 1848

*The average pressman [is a] . . . peculiar blend of smartness and
fatuity.*
—DANIEL GREGORY MASON, *Music in My Time*

Music critics are not merely the most unbeloved of the music world's *dramatis personae*; they are possibly, of all critics, the least esteemed by the artists about whom they write. True, critics in all the arts are sometimes despised because of their power, real or perceived; still, Clement Greenberg and Meyer Schapiro were not contemptuously dismissed by the painters and sculptors they wrote about; Edmund Wilson and Alfred Kazin were not relegated to lower Dantean hell rings by the novelists and poets they reviewed. And while there are, remarkably, two legitimate theaters in New York City named for drama critics (the Brooks Atkinson and the Walter Kerr), even Jean Sibelius, himself the object of un-critic-like hero worship by the leading American music critic of his era (the *New York Times*'s Olin Downes), stated, "Never pay any attention to what critics say. . . . Remember, a statue has never been set up in honor of a critic!"[1]

Why are music critics viewed less as friends of the art than other critics? The *New York Herald Tribune*'s music critic of the 1920s and 1930s, Lawrence Gilman, perhaps best answers the question by capsulizing the personal attributes necessary for entering this problematic profession:

> the constitution of a traffic policeman . . . the nervous system of a coal
> heaver . . . the hide of a rhinoceros . . . a measure of philosophy adequate
> to survive the realization that you can claim no disinterested friends in

that professional world, which views you either as a ruthless destroyer or as a useful builder of reputation . . . a willingness to accept the fact that your praise of artists will be regarded as their due, and your dispraise as the natural result of ignorance, animus, dyspepsia, or all three.[2]

To these endemic problems, one may add the intractable, intrinsic difficulties of putting thought about music into words, to which the composer (and critic) Hector Berlioz amusingly testified:

I have often sat up all night over my scores, and have spent eight hours at a time labouring at instrumentation, without once changing my position; but I have to fight myself to begin to write a page of prose, and about the tenth line or so I get up, walk about the room, look out into the street, take up a book, and strive by any means to overcome the weariness and fatigue which instantly overpowers me. I have to return to the charge eight or ten times before I can finish an article for the *Journal des Débats,* and it takes me quite two days to write one, even when I like the subject and am interested by it. And then, what erasures, and what scrawls! You should see my first draft! Musical composition comes naturally to me, and is a delight; but prose-writing is a labour.[3]

Even further, one may add to this that music critics, like bartenders, run the risk of losing the taste for their favorite poison. Both Virgil Thomson and Winthrop Sargeant in their memoir volumes attested that after years of nightly toil at the opera or symphony they had become inured to hearing music and no longer enjoyed it.

However thankless their task may be, music critics are an undetachable link in the professional music world's great chain of being. Every composer, conductor, and performer at one time or another believes that his career has been helped or hindered by them; every musician seeking to make a career freely employs critics' quotes in her publicity material. Many professional musicians casually despise newspaper reviewers, even though many reviewers are or have been professional musicians themselves. Audiences, listeners, and amateur music makers all at one time or another have read the critics and have had their thinking affected by them. Professional musicians frequently have a can't-live-with-them, can't-live-without-them attitude toward newspaper reviewers. Above and beyond this, however, hovers another, frequently unasked question: Are the critics ever real players in the larger currents of music history? Opine, pontificate, educate they do, but do they ever really influence music practice and appreciation as do the composers, conductors, and performers they review and criticize?

Critics have rarely been respectfully and dispassionately examined as a legitimate constituent element of the total musical community—or of any arts community. The only recent book that addresses such a question is Lehman Engel's *The Critics*, which, however, deals with New York drama critics, not music critics. One reason for this lacuna is the logistical difficulty of even searching out the critics' writings, much less determining their social or cultural influence. As Winton Dean writes in the entry on criticism in the *New Grove Dictionary of Music and Musicians*, "A comprehensive history of music criticism has been seldom attempted and perhaps never achieved. It would require endless research into books, pamphlets, prefaces and the files of old newspapers and periodicals." Seventy-five years ago, much the same was said by Otto Kinkeldey in his foreword to the collected reviews of Richard Aldrich, at that time the *New York Times*'s chief music critic.[4] The late scholar Vera Brodsky Lawrence, in attempting to seek out New York newspaper reviews of the 1840s and 1850s, was "shocked to discover that virtually no scholarly literature existed to which I might turn for the information I needed. The immense existing body of scholarship devoted to just about every aspect of the burgeoning American nineteenth century—social, cultural, political, industrial, technological . . . more strangely omitted any parallel investigation of its music."[5]

Thus an encyclopedically comprehensive survey of American music critics and their influence would encompass too many critics and reviewers, too many newspapers and periodicals, too many thousands of pages of prose in newspaper archives, and too many different cities and local spheres of influence to be rendered justice in the space afforded us between these covers. Perhaps another such book or books will be written someday. Till then *Maestros of the Pen* may serve as a compact documentary history that sketches the highlights, paints the much-caricatured critics in full human colors, and begins to explore the complex questions of whether music critics have ever exerted influence on the history of musical practice and taste in America. The only way to reduce such a sprawling historical canvas into a compact frame is to illustrate the whole through selected parts. So the scope of this inquiry has been circumscribed largely by Boston and New York, as the main trends adopted in other cities were inaugurated there. Also, the critics of the last thirty years are for the most part given a more shortwinded treatment than their forebears, xviii since the question of lasting influence is obviously impossible to answer; any failure to mention individual critics does not bespeak a judgment of their merit.

This book takes a broad view of what constitutes the history of classical music criticism in America. The subject is not confined to the people who write newspaper reviews. Rather, it extends to how men and women of letters wrote and thought about classical music, how their attitudes changed public attitudes toward classical music in America, and how the role of classical music appreciation in the general American intellectual and cultural tradition evolved. Thus some chapters deal with the newspaper critics, but others with ideas, controversies, the history of taste, and the changing role of classical music in American cultural life. I also write about the critics for the large and small magazines, the writers of music appreciation books, and the broadcasters; a sizable amount about the composers who were critics; a little about the professional literati who also wrote about classical music, and the classical music journalists who improbably became best-selling authors; a little about the Internet as a new medium for music criticism; and not a little about the general-purpose intellectuals and cultural critics who either wrote about music or whose omission to do so was glaring. I discuss the newspaper industry insofar as is necessary for clarity, but this is not a history of newspapers or newspaper critics: in American music criticism history, the little magazines with small circulation have sometimes been more influential than major-market newspapers with their mass circulations. I write equally of the salaried journeymen reviewers—whom James Gibbons Huneker dubbed the "critical chain gang"—and of the nonquotidian, intellectually rarefied critics to whom Henry James referred when he wrote, "The practice of 'reviewing' . . . in general has nothing in common with the art of criticism." I have tried to address the impact of music critics on the great unwashed masses as well as on the prestige elites and intellectuals; the total picture is out of balance without the one to complement the other. (I do leave out the musicologists, even though a few musicologists have served as journalistic critics and a few journalists have contributed to the musicology periodicals.)

A substantial part of the text consists of anatomizing the critics' writings, turning their own loupes back upon themselves and examining them as if they were the artists (some were), fixing them in a "formulated phrase . . . sprawling on a pin . . . pinned and wriggling on the wall," like T. S. Eliot's J. Alfred Prufrock. By thus dissecting their prose (Huneker would have called it "decomposition") one can learn who were the best musical analysts among them

as well as the best literary stylists. I attempt to show how styles of criticism   xix
evolved from vacuous gaseousness to reasoned commentary fairly early on in
the nineteenth century, at least in the major urban centers. I also look at the
devolution of literary style in American music criticism, from the "golden era"
of the late nineteenth and early twentieth centuries to the age of the dumbed-
down at the brink of the twenty-first.

Assessing the influence of music critics on the overall culture of the music
world is a vexing task. While the cultural repercussions of a Deems Taylor on
radio, or a Leonard Bernstein on television, are self-evident, the question of
whether a newspaper or magazine music critic ever consistently and concretely
influenced people to buy or not buy tickets, as do Broadway drama critics,
is difficult to tease out. The impact of *New York Times* music critics on the
music world would alone constitute a separate study, one that is largely side-
stepped here. *Maestros of the Pen* addresses the question of general influence
by asking, To what extent were the newspaper critics responsible for codifying
the canon of great composers for the public? Did the earlier critics correctly
predict the ultimate hierarchy of the canon? What was the relationship between paid publicity and professional criticism in classical music in this country? Did the critics themselves ever act as de facto publicists, or rather, were
the championships of individual critics ever single-handedly responsible for
changes adopted by the general taste?

Moreover, did turn-of-the-century American music critics as a group
miss the boat on modern music, or, from the hindsight of the postmodern era,
do they seem prescient? Were critics ever movers or shakers of repertory and
performance practice? Did music critics, indeed, ever have the power to make
or break careers of composers, conductors, singers, or instrumentalists, as did
theater and book critics—that is, did they get anybody fired or hired, as some
think Virgil Thomson got Koussevitsky hired in Boston and Barbirolli fired in
New York?

Further still, the troubling conundrums: Why do we find Emerson, Whitman, Poe, Sidney Lanier, and Washington Irving in the nineteenth century actively promoting classical music appreciation in their writings, but no comparable literary writers in the twentieth century so doing? Why, after cultural
synthesizers like Huneker and H. L. Mencken had championed the cause of
classical music, did Dwight Macdonald, Lewis Mumford, Kenneth Burke, and
other cultural critics give up on it? Why did classical music critics begin to lose
print space and salaries to popular music critics at the end of the twentieth century? Why don't composers take up the pen as music critics anymore in this

country, as they once did in great numbers? For that matter, why do practicing musicians so rarely double as music critics anymore in America, as they freely did in the nineteenth century?

In his provocative but tendentious 1988 book *Highbrow/Lowbrow: The Emergence of Cultural Hierarchy in America* (Harvard University Press), Lawrence W. Levine argues that toward the end of the nineteenth century, monied society, critics, and Euro-worshiping artists conspired to "sacralize" high culture—Shakespeare, legitimate theater, symphonic music, opera—and segregate it from the mass public who had earlier enjoyed it in the first part of the nineteenth century amid vulgar, vernacular culture and without intellectual explication. *Maestros of the Pen* vigorously argues the contrary. Evidence shows that from colonial days onward, a cultural hierarchy in America did indeed exist; it was the very same *bon ton* which Professor Levine cites as a late nineteenth-century excrescence who were the chief patrons of the opera and symphony in the early nineteenth century, though they consumed their culture with precious little understanding, as the nineteenth-century critic W. S. B. Mathews tellingly reports in chapter 1. It was in large part the music critics who helped turn the situation around, helping to educate the monied community leaders to build the concert halls and opera houses that enabled concert music and opera to be better understood and more widely appreciated than earlier in the nineteenth century. Mencken's withering denunciations of the "sahara of the Bozart" climate toward the arts that pervaded America throughout the nineteenth century and into the twentieth are, tellingly, omitted in Professor Levine's analysis.

On the other hand, whereas Mencken, a committed amateur musician, continued writing in his newspaper columns about classical music throughout his career, the twentieth-century cultural critic Gilbert Seldes, though he began his career writing music reviews for the *Philadelphia Evening Ledger* in 1914–15, quickly dropped reviewing symphony concerts for a then daring new approach: a high culture appreciation of popular music. That trend proved the sea change; while generalists like Huneker and Mencken had presupposed classical music as a bedrock constituent of culture, Seldes and other redefiners of culture—popularizers and "desacralizers"—inaugurated the end of classical music in the larger cultural tradition, as we shall see later in these pages.

Finally, I have tried to be entertaining as well as scholarly and serious, as classical music critics in America, despite the stereotypes, have by no means invariably been gradgrinds. Deems Taylor was once a vaudeville comic, James Huneker a writer of soft-core pornography, Rupert Hughes a millionaire

novelist and screenwriter who also wrote a biography of George Washington,   xxi
Irving Lowens an air traffic controller, Donal Henahan a fighter pilot, W. J.
Henderson the author of a text on navigation used by the military, Winthrop
Sargeant an ex-orchestra player who dabbled in Sanskrit, Carl Van Vechten a
photographer of the Harlem Renaissance, Harold Schonberg a chess connois-
seur, Virgil Thomson a subject of *New Yorker* cartoons. In the "six degrees of
separation" department, one is amused to learn that the critic Richard Grant
White was the father of the architect Stanford White, who was murdered by
Harry K. Thaw in 1906 over the chorus girl Evelyn Nesbit; that Deems Taylor's
first wife later had an affair with Gilbert Seldes, then married a Spanish fascist
and became the Nazi counterpart of Tokyo Rose, making Axis broadcasts from
Berlin as the infamous "Georgia Peach"; that Huneker's real-life relationship
with the Met diva Olive Fremstad may in some part have traveled into Willa
Cather's novel *The Song of the Lark*. Edgar J. Levey started as Henry T. Finck's
assistant at the *New York Evening Post* but then went into politics, becoming assistant comptroller of New York City, and the television investigative reporter
and radio commentator Daniel Schorr started in the business at eighteen as a
stringer for Olin Downes at the *New York Times*. The author of the first serious
article on Charles Ives in the *Musical Quarterly* (January 1933), Henry Bellamann (1882–1945), was also the author of the best-selling novel *Kings Row,*
which became the Warner Brothers motion picture that gave Ronald Reagan
his greatest movie role. Music critics come in all human varieties; many of the
good ones have themselves been successful musicians, and a surprising number have been composers.

   At the end of the twentieth century, in an embattled time for classical music, music critics may still be regarded grudgingly by many music lovers, but
perhaps a look back at what they did may help us look forward to find ways to
ensure the survival of classical music and its appreciation in this country as the
millennium approaches. (From Finck's camphor vials to Gilman's ear plugs to
Schonberg's stopwatch—perhaps the music critic of the twenty-first century
will carry some kind of vestpocket computer that will digitally record the concerts he attends!) "Reviewers, with some rare exceptions, are a most stupid and
malignant race," wrote Shelley. Into this breach of fear and loathing intrepidly
steps *Maestros of the Pen*.

Maestros of the Pen

The Birth of
Critic Bedlam

Gotham as the Wild, Wild West

*When I arrived in Baltimore in 1831 music was yet in its infancy
or cradle. Even in good society and among well educated people
nothing was appreciated beyond waltzes, marches and variations
on some familiar theme, or simple airs from some of Rossini's
operas.*
—JOHN F. PETRI, Leipzig-trained music teacher

*The condition of affairs thus simply characterized by Mr. Petri
was general throughout the country. In New York musical taste
was farther advanced at that time, but even in Europe the
taste was then, and continued to be for some years later, for much
the same kind of music as this described by him. It will be remembered that in 1831 only the earlier parts of the Beethoven music
had become known to the musical world outside the circle of most
advanced musicians in Vienna and a few other cities of Germany.
Schubert was entirely unknown, and Schumann, Mendelssohn,
and Chopin were only new composers, as yet unproved. . . .*
—W. S. B. MATHEWS, Chicago newspaper critic

These remarks, if anything, understate the predicament: for most non-upper-crust Americans at the
turn of the nineteenth century, the realm of music was described by an arc joining the hymns and chorales of churchgoing to Ulysses S. Grant's apocryphal remark, "I know two tunes; one is Yankee Doodle, and the other isn't." Said a senior colleague to the young New Englander W. S. B. Mathews when Mathews
first essayed his critical pen in midcentury, "My dear fellow, you will never get a
hearing in this country for your pretty talk about classical music; Americans do
not care for it. Come with us and praise the music which the average American
likes, and you will be happier, better paid and have a better time." [1]

4   Yet Mathews persevered, and in fact, well before his estimable career in postbellum Chicago journalism blossomed, there had burgeoned more than a few sprigs of "pretty talk about classical music." For all the rawness of the new country, both its concert performing life and its musical press had antecedents back to prerevolutionary days.

ᚙ *Concerts and the press of the 1700s*   In the eighteenth century four urban centers supported concert activity more than sporadically: Philadelphia (before 1800 a larger city than New York), New York, Boston, and Charleston, South Carolina. Oratorios of Handel and Haydn and symphonies of Haydn and Pleyel *(sic transit gloria mundi)* were the mainstays of the repertoire mustered by local orchestras in the period from the mid-1700s till the early 1800s. While opera in America did not really arrive until after the century's end, vocal music was represented on the programs of the eighteenth century by airs and duets from oratorios and operas, as well as by popular songs, catches, and glees. In Boston there was a greater emphasis on sacred music than elsewhere, but there as well as in the other cities, vocal and instrumental secular music could also be heard.

American audiences of the time frequently sampled the concerti and chamber music of such now nearly forgotten European composers as Martini, Stamitz, and Wanhal. The educated and socially privileged among them might even get to hear repeated performances of *The Battle of Prague* by Kotzwara, something called the Overture to *The Caliph of Bagdad,* and Steibelt's *Storm Rondo.* But they heard Bach infrequently, Mozart rarely, and Beethoven hardly at all; first performances of much of what we now recognize as the classical canon had to wait until the 1830s and 1840s. The first American performances even of Beethoven's *Eroica* and Mozart's "Jupiter" Symphonies did not take place until February 18, 1843, and January 15, 1844, respectively, in New York City.

The precursors of legitimate music criticism in American journalism were not commissioned reviews but rather squibs—notices of forthcoming concerts or society news items reporting on which dignitaries had been in attendance at musical soirees. The Library of Congress historiographer Oscar Sonneck thus cited as the first known American musical "review" the following, from the October 21–28, 1732, *South Carolina Gazette,* of Charleston: "On Wednesday Night there was a Concert for the Benefit of Mr. Salter, at which was a fine Appearance of good Company." Sonneck hastily appended that such curt observations of society attendance were not limited to gauche colonial journalism; he ruefully notes that the New York papers of his time had sent their society editors in greater numbers to the New York premiere of Wagner's *Parsifal* than their music critics.[2]

In those surviving published write-ups most closely resembling modern reviews, "the papers simply published a report offered by some prominent music lover among their subscribers," often signed under a Latinate pseudonym such as Philomusicus.[3] The "correspondents" who had been at the concerts would extol the virtues of the music they had heard, typically in terms florid, ethereal, and meaningless, because, according to Sonneck, "in olden times journalism moved more slowly and it made little difference to the public when they received the news as long as they received it in somewhat stilted and grandiloquent language."[4] On the other hand, Sonneck's researches disclosed that even in the early days intelligent criticism was not unknown, as the following excerpt from a review of a concert of sacred music held on May 4, 1786, in Philadelphia, appearing May 30, 1786, in the *Pennsylvania Packet*, suggests: "A succession of celebrated anthems . . . were performed with a precision and effort sufficient to enforce powers of harmony on the most untutored ears . . . a violin concerto . . . by Mr. Juhan, who not only displayed the most promising talents, but a taste and execution which did him present honor and gave acknowledged satisfaction."

∾ *Prelude to the
new century:
the immigrant tide*

The diaspora of Europeans to the newly formed United States after the War for Independence, the French Revolution, and the Napoleonic Wars included many well-trained musicians who greatly expanded the pool of performers and teachers in America. The immigrant wave had a double edge, however, paradoxically diluting the stateside population's appreciation of classical music, as the great preponderance of the new immigrants were uneducated, uninterested in attending concerts, and without the British- or French-patinated, socially pretentious, cosmopolitan airs that had often characterized colonial classical musicians and their listeners and had helped endow prerevolutionary music making with an air of the quasi-noble (both Thomas Jefferson and Benjamin Franklin, two aristocratic democrats, were accomplished musical amateurs). The point of disembarkation and settlement for most of these immigrants was New York, by 1790 the largest American city.

However, the mercantile classes of New York, who provided the ticket support for music and opera, were ready to entertain anything new and less in-

6   clined to be patient with tradition. "New York has always been behindhand, as compared with Boston and Philadelphia, in the cultivation of the higher branch of music," wrote W. S. B. Mathews in the 1880s, "though it was in advance in the encouragement given to the operatic form. . . . it was always more liberally disposed toward the more showy and frivolous uses of the musical art."[5] As the straitlaced elder capitals Boston and Philadelphia began ceding the limelight to their scrappy Gothamite kid sister, a tradition of music appreciation had to be built up again from scratch at the dawn of the nineteenth century in America's not-yet-greatest city.

ᴄᴡ *Even then, New*
York was the place   By 1800 New York City (which until 1875 consisted solely of the borough of Manhattan) was, with a population of sixty thousand, dirtier, noisier, and poorer—but livelier—than Philadelphia. But it was shortly to become the center of opera and symphony in America; the birthplace of the country's oldest orchestra; the laboratory for the country's first cheap, affordable daily newspapers; and the first urban ganglion of critical opinion about music expressed in the public prints to a mass audience in America. It was about to become the indispensable port of call to all visiting foreign artists; already by 1835 a New York periodical, the *American Music Journal,* could chauvinistically proclaim without fear of contradiction that "all [musical] talent must fail in America which is not imported via New-York and makes its debut in the city." *

As late as 1845 physical conditions in Manhattan were still crude. "The metropolitan city was then a provincial town of two-story houses, and the pigs ran through Broadway and ate the refuse," recalled the conductor Theodore Thomas in his autobiography. As for seating in concert venues, the critic Richard Grant White reminisced of one, "The floor was dirty and broken into holes; the seats were bare, backless benches. . . . The place was pervaded with evil smells; and, not uncommonly, in the midst of a performance, rats ran out of the holes in the floor and across into the orchestra. . . . The gallery was occupied by howling roughs."[6]

At first, the New York concert scene, too, was rough-hewn. Even with the influx of European performing talent, wrote a German musician who visited New York around the 1820s, most American orchestras of the time lacked

---

* Until at least the middle of the nineteenth century the hyphenated "New-York" was the standard spelling.

essential instruments and simply rode roughshod over their deficiencies of personnel by having certain instrumentalists double to cover the gaps, the concertmaster taking part in every solo, the trombone player doubling the cellos or even the violins, and other practices comical even by modern high school standards of cross-cuing. Orchestra groups, rehearsals, and concerts were pickup affairs. A New York Philharmonic Society was started and stopped three times before the effort that lasted began in earnest in 1842. Concerts were frequently olios combining serious lieder with bell ringers, yodelers, folksingers, and other examples of what would later become to be known as vaudeville.

But advances were rapid. By February 1828 in New York, now a city of two hundred thousand, five operas could be presented in one week: *The Castle of Andalusia, Der Freischütz, The Marriage of Figaro, Clari,* and *Artaterxes.* With the advent of better transportation and railroad facilities in the 1830s, a stream of virtuosi started entering the United States and touring the country. By the 1840s there were some two dozen regular venues for concert music in New York City, though nary an "official" music hall, like the later Carnegie. There were also some forty regular newspapers and periodicals in New York, though none had yet become an official journal of record for the arbitration of musical taste, as the *New York Times* would become in the late twentieth century.

"Beauty, fashion, and taste"

A veritable mantra occurring in almost every concert review in American newspapers before the 1840s (and sometimes after)* is the phrase "beauty, fashion, and taste" or its near equivalent, code words for "society crowd in the audience." Dropping the phrase was a who-what-when-where journalistic shibboleth for any early review, as in this comment after the first performances of Manuel García's opera troupe in New York in 1825 in the *New-York Evening Post* of November 30: "An assemblage of ladies so fashionable, so numerous, and so elegantly dressed, had probably never been witnessed in an American theater." Examples of similar paeans to the audience abound in the concert reviews of other cities' newspapers, but it was in New York that such "fashion" phraseologies became most entrenched, because they epitomized the New York problem: an audience preoccupied with superficial glitter, with what in late twentieth-century parlance

---

* It was still true as recently as the 1940s, when Virgil Thomson in the *Herald Tribune* wryly commented in a review of a concert of the music of Paul Bowles, "The audience was brilliant."

8 would be called "the beautiful people" and "making the scene," even if they didn't understand what they were seeing or hearing—a circumstance that encouraged many first performances but gave critics quite a load of educating to do. W. S. B. Mathews said that performances of Rossini's *Barber of Seville* and other Italian operas by the Manuel Garcia troupe in New York in the 1820s made no sense to the audiences: "The enthusiasm . . . had no real basis of life. It was not founded upon intelligent musical comprehension or appreciation of the beauties of the opera. The music appealed to no realizing sense of its emotional meaning. . . . the apparent success of the opera was in reality attributable to its novelty."[7] Some reporters doubling as music critics, themselves incapable of making sense of the novelty, used the "beauty and fashion" catchphrase to conceal their own lack of musical education or critical discernment.

The fact was, as Vera Brodsky Lawrence writes, opera venues in early nineteenth-century New York were social bourses first, temples of art secondarily:

> The match-making role played by the opera house (and the Philharmonic) in upper-caste nineteenth-century New York was a potent one. Nathaniel Parker Willis, who subdivided the Astor Place Opera House into strategic zones—the "Dowager's Shelf," the "Fop's Terrace," the "Approachables," "Apoplexy Row"—described the *parquette* at Astor Place as being "more a pen for bachelors in the market than anything else." . . . Correspondingly, the boxes provided a properly decorous showcase for the available belles of the town, and many a flirtatious intermission visit, discreetly chaperoned by "dragons on guard, stowed in the rear," eventuated in a fashionable wedding at Grace Church or Trinity.[8]

Apart from the pursuit of matrimony, there was "probably as much electioneering, stock-jobbing, and gossiping done [at the Astor Place Opera House] as . . . in any place in Wall Street. . . . In fact the lobbies of the Opera House are now a lounge for finishing up all business, politics, finance, gossip, and humbug of the day" (*New-York Herald*, January 30, 1848). Up to about 1835, adds Lawrence, "the New York public—always intensely pleasure-seeking, insatiable for novelty, and easily bored—were consistent only in their resistance to the deluge of 'superior' extraneous musics—the uplifting English oratorios, unfamiliar German symphonies, and unintelligible Italian operas—with which successive generations of musical missionaries insistently sought to 'improve' their delinquent musical tastes."[9]

To put it bluntly, New York before 1850 was a cultural Johnny-come-lately with parvenu pretensions; not the centripetal gold standard of cultural taste that it later became, but a hotbed of "showiness and frivolity," as the Chicagoan Mathews put it, of a preference for "spasmodic brilliancy" over the "higher musical lines" pursued by sedater audiences in Boston and Philadelphia.[10] Ironically, this was partly due not to the rabble but to the social "Upper Ten Thousand," who were key in the support of the arts in the city. The Upper Ten Thousand's power of the purse resided in its purchase of the subscriptions that financed most opera series and concerts. Single-price ticket admission, when it did (increasingly) occur, was affordable only to society people, posing a dilemma for music reviewers, who themselves were the beneficiaries of free tickets to concerts but who wished to educate the public musically and promote larger attendance. An unnamed and undated writer for the *Lyre,* a journal in New York, applauded the cause of charging one dollar for admission to an oratorio, thought by some correspondents to be too high:

> Every reflecting person will not think it a disproportionate charge, when the amount of talent and labor necessary to the production of a performance on a remarkable scale is impartially considered; and we look forward with fond anticipation to a period when efforts of this kind shall be duly appreciated, and a corresponding liberality be extended to those institutions which have for their object . . . the formation of a correct and refined taste throughout the community.

Frédéric Ritter, a nineteenth-century music historian, added his own commentary to the above: "Thus . . . the necessity of the promotion of 'refined musical taste' . . . for the cultivation of the higher class of compositions, [was] continually held up to the American people as an ideal goal."[11] Which leads to the basic economic question: How, indeed, could the public be brought along if they could neither afford the opera ticket nor the newspaper to read about it?

The newspaper business before 1830

Early American newspapers were published essentially for the upper strata of American society. Journalism historians have characterized them in type as either "political"—fiercely partisan four-sheeters full of editorials that would be libelous by today's standards—or "mercantile"—house organs for the Wall

10 Street community whose space was primarily taken up with notices and announcements rather than editorial copy and with advertising for the business community. From 50 to 90 percent of the column space of mercantile newspapers was devoted to advertising, which looked like modern classified ads, display advertising being a thing of the future. The metropolitan dailies of the pre-1830 period tended to a four-page format but gradually increased the number of columns within each page.

The readership of both political and mercantile papers was drawn almost wholly from the mercantile classes, who alone could afford the annual subscription price of about ten dollars in the early decades of the nineteenth century for a daily newspaper (normally published six times a week). As time went on some mercantile papers (e.g., the *Boston Daily Advertiser*) and some political ones (the *New-York Evening Post,* founded by Alexander Hamilton) became mixtures in type; the *Daily Advertiser* added editorial copy and the *Evening Post* started running reviews of books, drama, and art (particularly after the ascent of the poet-journalist William Cullen Bryant to its editorship in 1829). With most newspapers, music reviews were the last type of arts reviews to be added.

Subscriptions to most weekly newspapers were less expensive—$1.50 to $2.50 a year. However, the weekly *New-York Albion,* which described itself as a "British, Colonial, and Foreign Weekly Gazette" embodying "the News, Politics, and Literature of Europe, more particularly of Great Britain" with "Poetry, history, music and the Drama [receiving] distinct and proper attention," at a cost of six dollars a year probably was above the means of working-class and middle-class people. From the 1820s on the *Albion* printed regular music reviews before any of the daily New York papers did, though they often appeared under the rubric of "New York Theatricals." In keeping with its neocontinental self-description, the *Albion* frequently reprinted European articles whole (international laws of reciprocal copyright at the time were murky). In keeping with its New World brethren, however, the *Albion* made constant references in its music coverage to the "beauty and fashion" of the audiences. Nevertheless, looking back in the 1880s, W. S. B. Mathews described the newspaper as having been acknowledged "the greatest literary authority of the times."[12]

As with other early American newspapers, music reviews in the *Albion* were little more than uneducated news accounts of performers who appeared onstage, rather than critical reviews of the music or composer. Reviews appearing in the *Albion* prior to 1840 were limited to opera, and all were unsigned. The anonymous correspondents rarely if ever mentioned the conductors but sometimes mentioned the orchestra concertmaster (who in fact often was the conductor in that era).

A sense both of the *Albion*'s music coverage and of the crudities of opera performance at the time in New York can be gleaned from the following excerpt from the *Albion*, April 20, 1833, upon the New York City premiere of Mozart's *Magic Flute*. Note that the writer, in observing the interpolations of other composers' music into the opera, implies that visiting only two such interruptions on the opera was less vandalism than the norm:

> Mr. Horn's version of *The Magic Flute* was produced on Wednesday evening to a crowded house, and with complete success. A more beautiful and sterling selection of music has never been offered to the public of New York, and we must do the management the justice to say that every expense has been incurred, and every pains taken to give due effect to the piece. We do not think the Drama good, and think it might have been much more ably constructed, but it is, nevertheless, redeemed by the excellency of the music. . . . The first act is charming . . . throughout the whole of which the music is exceedingly beautiful. . . . The ensuing act tends greatly to attract the attention to less interesting personages. True, Sarastro the Magician (Mr. Horn) makes his appearance, and so long as the agency of this personage is directed to his victim it is in admirable keeping, but we are afterwards totally removed from the plot of the piece, and have to console ourselves with a beautiful ballad introduced by Mr. Horn, "Dark eyed one come hither to me," the poetry by Thomas Haynes Bayley, set to Auber's music. Mr. Horn has likewise set Mr. Hallack's fine lines from Marco Bozzaris, "Come to the Bridal Chamber, Death," and these are the only interpolations upon Mozart in the opera. . . .
>
> The scenery is really beautiful, the dresses rich and appropriate, and the stage business admirably managed. . . . We cannot conclude without adverting to the improvement in music which is daily perceptible in this country. Here is a complete opera containing a selection of music by one of the great masters the world ever produced—brought out in New York for the first time in a style that would not disgrace the first cities of Europe.

The *Albion* was not the only newspaper of influence at the time. By the early 1820s the *Evening Post* had a circulation of about two thousand. James Watson Webb and Mordecai Noah engineered the merger of the *Courier* with the *Enquirer* around 1830 to make it the largest paper in New York, with a circulation of about four thousand. When it got up to forty-five hundred the

12   *Courier and Enquirer* had the largest circulation in the country, at a time when the *London Times* and two or three Paris newspapers had fifteen to twenty thousand and the average circulation for an American newspaper was one thousand. By 1833, however, there were three times as many newspapers in the United States as in England or France, as well as a few hundred periodicals, most of the latter short-lived.

     ∾ *The first*
         penny papers   By the 1830s more than 90 percent of the bulk of the U.S. mail consisted of newspaper delivery, but the papers didn't always arrive at their destinations, because whenever stagecoaches got stuck in mud (a then-frequent occurrence in pre-paved America), the mailbags containing the newspapers were the cargo first cast out into the mire to lighten the load. Daily newspapers had always been sold by annual subscription; many publishers would not sell single copies at all, even though the most frequent cause of newspapers' going under had been nonpayment by subscribers. The situation was ripe for a great innovation. On September 3, 1833, the *New-York Sun* made its debut at the single-issue cost of one penny. It was the first newspaper in America to reach the masses of working people, and the beginning of the newspaper as a mass communications medium.

     In just a few months *Sun* circulation was up to five thousand; only a year later, the paper's managers claimed ten thousand, then fifteen thousand. Other publishers quickly took notice. On May 11, 1835, James Gordon Bennett brought out the first issue of the penny paper the *New-York Morning Herald*. The direct descendants of both the *Sun* and the *Herald* survived in New York until the 1960s, when labor unions and another technological innovation, television, finally got the better of them. But the penny papers of the 1830s fairly created the modern newspaper by establishing police blotter news beats and other aspects of sensationalism and tabloid journalism to help make the man in the street a confirmed newsprint consumer. So much for the hoi polloi; where, though, would the penny papers stand in relation to "taste and fashion," and to the arts?

     Here, providence had it both ways: the penny publisher Bennett himself was an arts enthusiast who had reviewed music and drama since 1827, when he had been associate editor of the *New-York Enquirer*. Bennett saw himself as an evangelist for the newspaper as all-encompassing witness to humanity, from Dickensian slum to opera house, as he wrote in an early editorial: "What is to

prevent a daily newspaper from being made the greatest organ of social life?
Books have had their day—the theatres have had their day—the temple of religion has had its day. A newspaper can be made to take the lead of all these in
the great movements of human thought and human civilization" (*New-York
Herald,* August 19, 1836). But Bennett was also a canny businessman out to beat
the competition. So the *Herald* went the *Sun* one better in its arts coverage: its
amusements column, which included musical events, was almost a daily feature. The *Herald*'s amusements columnists frequently advised readers to go to
operas, to get tickets early, and to support various cultural events, even though
many of its readers could ill afford these same amusements. The point was the
aspiration to cultural grandeur.

At least thirty-four dailies were begun in New York during the 1830s after
the *Sun*'s debut, and the combined circulation of the penny papers was enormous for the time, more than seventy thousand in the New York of the late
1830s, recruiting newspaper readers for the first time in history from the lower
economic classes. All of these papers had drama reviews and what Bennett
called "theatrical chit-chat"; but music reviews followed more slowly. News-
papering was still an urban frontier, and not until the 1840s did even the largest
papers have reporters for even local news items, let alone dedicated music critics. Journalists for the penny papers got little pay (in the early 1850s annual
salaries were as low as five hundred dollars).[13] The editor and publisher frequently was also the reporter in the early days, and the only union yet established was for the typographers. And standards and practices, not to say ethics,
were not yet quite modern, as we shall see a little later.

The first
music critic?

Even before the advent of the penny papers, back in the
1820s, one particular bylined correspondent may pos-
sibly be credited as the first truly musically astute critic to appear in New
York: the pseudonymous "Musœus" of the *New-York American.* This mysteri-
ous writer—almost certainly a European émigré, probably British, but whose
true identity is lost to history—first made himself known in a letter to the editor of the *American.* The published letter announced that he had attended rehearsals of the New York Philharmonic Society (a short-lived predecessor to
the eventual New York Philharmonic), had some constructive suggestions to
be made known about the efforts of the group, and requested a platform for
his views. His wish was granted and his first column appeared March 1, 1825.

14   Musœus's writings in the *American* evince a trained musician who understood scoring and instrumentation. On one occasion he wrote, "The beautiful overture to *Esther* by Handel lost its effect by too powerful a bass for the number of violins," and in another, reviewing a different choral work by Handel, he wrote, "Where are your oboes? Where your trombones, in addition to your want of numbers on the stringed instruments? These are indispensable to Handel's music." Writing on the occasion of the celebrated 1828 appearance in New York of Manuel Garcia's opera troupe and its performances of nine operas, Musœus credibly demonstrated his knowledge not only of opera but of several European opera houses. He covered the Garcia performances by writing in a nonpatronizing, gently educative way, attempting to instruct his readership in the elements of opera ("The *Opera* is divided into *Recitative* and *Air* . . . the *Aria di bravura* [is] composed chiefly to indulge the singer in a display of particular powers or compass of voice; generally speaking, these airs are mere traps for applause, but void of sentiment, or any one sensible quality").

        In the beginning Musœus was a generous and constructive critic. But gradually the power of his bully pulpit crept up on him. According to Vera Brodsky Lawrence, Musœus felt " 'the people of these States' were not yet sufficiently acquainted with the works of Handel and Haydn." This was an odd claim, as the critic had asserted that he had attended concerts by the various sacred music societies in Boston, New York, Philadelphia, and Baltimore, where, to be sure, Handel and Haydn had been performed to a fare-thee-well. Musœus submitted, however, that the style of this music was not "relished by the people. Only through the 'zealous endeavors of well-governed societies,' such as the Philharmonic, could a 'true taste . . . be introduced and cherished.' " [14] In this and other holier-than-thou ways, Musœus early took it upon himself to admonish the Philharmonic Society's board of directors on musical grounds. It appears that he may have been denied membership in the society and was exacting his revenge through the power of his poison pen. Or was it the other way around? In any event, it was not long before Musœus became a petty tyrant of a critic, thus establishing a New York City archetype (in iconography if not also in reality) that has held to this day.

ᑳ *Quirks of*
   early reviewers   As other writers less musicianly than Musœus took up
                            their pens to write about operas and concerts in New
York, they had many beginners' kinks to work out. Without either scores of the operas or symphonies in tow or any previous firsthand experience playing or

hearing the works for themselves, early reviewers had to evolve some strata-
gems to circumvent their own shortcomings. (Inasmuch as most early reviews
were unsigned, their writers had little public vanity to worry about. Scholars,
however, have been able to determine the authorship of many unbylined music reviews by inference from other evidence such as editorials and letters to
the editor naming the critic.)

One gambit already mentioned was to spew encomiums to the "beauty,
taste, and fashion" of the audience instead of talking about the music. Another
ploy was for the reviewer, rather than to attempt to analyze the performance
specifically, to revert to the generic disclaimer that a piece of music was "caviar
to the million" or that it required "impossibly cultivated listeners." [15] A varia-
tion of this technique entailed the reviewer's getting himself off the hook by either digressing to report on the audience and its composition of learned and
unlearned persons, or his pleading solidarity with his fellow patrons en masse,
as with this critic for the *New-York Knickerbocker* reviewing the first American
performance of *Fidelio* in 1839, sung in English by a visiting British company:
"Above our individual capacity to appreciate . . . we are not doing an injustice
to nineteen-twentieths of those who have listened to it with us, in believing
that it is also above their complete apprehension." A more diplomatic and less
petulant version of the same trick ran this way: "Musicians tell us that [*Fidelio*]
is a most masterly effort of genius, abounding in all the elements of a sublime,
lyrical opera" (probably attributable to Nathaniel Parker Willis [1806–67], coeditor of the *Corsair*). But the most tried and true method of critical circum-
locution was to wax lexiphanic, as in this W. C. Fieldsian review of the same
Fidelio performance:

> Oh! may you give your spirit up to him fearlessly! He will transport you
> to other worlds, and infuse a thousand strange and thrilling sensations—
> will cradle you in his arms until, in admiration of his strength, you forget
> how powerful you are, and when he has poured those notes into your
> ear, and you are filled with tremblings, as of golden wires half conscious
> of their own thrilling—he leaves you petrified, enchanted—in a silent
> dream where even the echoes have subsided. [16]

This approach, however, ran the risk of solecism: the *Evening Star*'s critic referred to *Fidelio* as "a work of sublime *maestoso.*" It also ran the risk of exposure by other, more knowledgeable critics: Henry C. Watson in fact accused
Richard Grant White in print of being musically ignorant but covering it up
with learned allusions.

16   It must be remembered that even well-educated people of the time had difficulty assimilating music we now regard as canonical. The New York City lawyer and musical amateur George Templeton Strong, as musically sophisticated a layman as any of his era, wrote in his diary of the first performance in America of Beethoven's Fifth Symphony in the 1840s, "generally unintelligible to me, except the Andante," [17] and among the fraternity of opinion of his time, critics included, he was far from alone in his assessment: in 1831, still early days for Beethoven in America, even an especially forward-looking and sympathetic critic could write of *The Mount of Olives,* part of which was performed by the Sacred Music Society at Saint Paul's in Boston on February 24, "Beethoven is an author of great originality,—his compositions are truly energetic, and filled with uncommon passages,—his modulation is abstruse, and every listener feels, at the *first bar,* that he is about to hear something new; his discords attract our attention."

ॐ *Henry C.*
Watson   The fifth decade of the nineteenth century brought to the fore the first qualified, competent music critic in the modern mold to achieve lasting eminence. Henry Cood Watson was born in London in 1815 to John Watson, chorusmaster of Covent Garden Opera House, where young Henry became a celebrated boy soprano in such operas as Weber's *Oberon.* When his voice broke the boy found his career as a singer suddenly ended. Vexed with a Werther-like attack of adolescent *Sturm und Drang,* he tried to escape from the calamity by becoming a sailor on a voyage to the Mediterranean. But a Richard Dana or Joseph Conrad he was not destined to become, and young Watson returned to terra firma in England, where he continued serious music schooling and literary studies for some years.

In 1840 the young man sailed to New York City with letters of introduction to the well-known newspapermen William Cullen Bryant, Horace Greeley, Park Benjamin, and George P. Morris. In short order he became the busiest music journalist in town, finding his first employment under Park Benjamin (1809–64), writing art and music criticism for both Benjamin's weekly magazine *New World* and his daily penny newspaper *Evening Signal,* founded the year before. (Benjamin was a journalist of "less than immaculate reputation" whose *New World* consisted mostly of "pirated works by the best English authors.") [18] In 1843 Watson also replaced the English critic Alexander D. Paterson at the *Albion,* when Paterson left that periodical to establish his own journal, the *Anglo American.*

Watson's résumé becomes dizzying at this point. In addition to working for the *New World, Evening Signal,* and *Albion,* he edits and writes for a short-lived journal of his own, the *Musical Chronicle,* from 1843, and in 1847 becomes editor of a weekly called the *American Musical Times.* He contributes to the weekly *New Mirror,* a paper devoted to literature and the arts edited by George P. Morris and Nathaniel P. Willis, as well as to the *Evening Mirror.* And with Charles Briggs and Edgar Allan Poe, Watson also cofounds the *Broadway Journal,* a short-lived arts periodical. All of these many hats Watson wore during the space of a few years in the 1840s.

Watson was probably the first American to make a living at music criticism, by virtue of his many simultaneous writing assignments and editorial positions. This, of course, was in a fledgling era in the newspaper industry before individual newspapers could pay enough to critics to hold them exclusively. It helped also that Watson was tireless, if not workaholic. In addition to music criticism, he found time throughout his life to write art criticism, do occasional news reporting, compose songs, write poetry, and, at various times, serve as editor in chief of *Frank Leslie's Illustrated Newspaper;* help found the American Musical Fund Society, a performance group; help organize the Mendelssohn Union; guest-lecture at receptions for famous singers such as Jenny Lind and Henrietta Sontag; author the libretto for William Vincent Wallace's opera *Lurline;* organize the Mendelssohn Memorial Concert, held at Castle Garden, attended by ten thousand; and so on, ad infinitum.

Upon his stepping up to the plate in New York at the *New World,* Watson—still a young man, and with the redoubled arrogance of youth and British superiority—announced, "We do intend to cleanse out this Augean accumulation and to establish in its place a healthy principle that shall revolutionize the state of music in this city" (*New World,* December 4, 1841). He thereupon wreaked his wrathful Herculean labors on almost everyone "except for members of the Watson family [George Loder, his brother-in-law, was a conductor of the New York Philharmonic] and certain favored English performers." [19] In a review of the Sacred Music Society, Watson reported the orchestra "scarcely played six consecutive bars correctly," the organ "throughout was very unskillfully played," "the Fagotti were out of tune, and so were the tympani"; and the conductor, U. C. Hill, had insufficient "influence" over the orchestra, a body that, like every other New York orchestra, was composed of nothing but would-be soloists, each of whom "burst away at the top of his power. This is wrong, radically wrong, and must be altered," stormed Watson.

Having forewarned his readership, Watson proceeded to hurl his pen like a baton at the players of orchestras. Yet for all the fury, there was something in

18   his approach the likes of which New York had not seen before. He reported what he heard in detail only a trained musician could muster and couched his emotional reactions in technically reasoned terms. His criticisms were as constructive as those of a teacher or conductor, trying to raise both performer and auditor to a higher level. Though a stylish writer, he always gave specific musical reasons for his observations rather than devolve into extraneous verbiage about the music's stimulating ineffable states of mental opiation. In short, he was the first modern music critic.

He was instructive and educative, but he didn't pull his punches. Of one concert of the new Philharmonic Society Watson wrote: "The chief fault the orchestra has exhibited . . . is a heavy, mechanical method of playing; there is a want of delicacy and general expression. . . . We seldom or ever see a simultaneous movement of the bow—when one is up the other is down. . . . as far as correct time and steady beating, [the conductor] did it ably; but we listened in vain for any of those delicate variations of light and shade—the positive *piano* which makes the positive *forte*." Commenting on an occasion in which a noted opera singer had transposed her part up from alto to mezzo range "to accommodate her compass," he noted that, with the concomitant transposition of the orchestral parts, this "breeds confusion in the orchestra, rendering it difficult and sometimes impossible for the particular wind instruments to execute with effect, or even in tune, the passages set down for them. Should this confusion be observed by the audience, the *singer* is never to blame, but all the indignation is vented upon the innocent orchestral performers." [20]

His insights into the contemporary composers of his day are sometimes astonishingly predictive of posterity's judgment, sometimes wide of the mark. As prognosticator, on Spohr's oratorio *The Last Judgment*: "It abounds with melody, although nine-tenths of its hearers would be inclined to dispute our assertion, and apparently with justice, for notwithstanding almost all the pieces bear a melody of great beauty, they fail to strike the ear at once, from the mass of rich harmonies by which they are encumbered." Spohr's music, Watson contended, was too densely wrought with modulations and transitions that jolted by their "seeming strangeness and remoteness." Then, too, Spohr's rhythmic monotony was "palling to the senses" (*Evening Mirror*, December 8, 1846).

On the other hand, Watson, in the *Albion*, asserted that Verdi's melodies "do not possess the catching popular qualities of a Bellini or a Donizetti . . . [they] seem as though they were written under restraint, that is, as though they were composed under the most impressive remembrances of the masters of his school who have gone before him. . . . like all the modern Italian writers, [he] is a victim to a passion for instruments of brass and percussion. . . . This love of noise is the curse of our modern writers; with the Italians it is mere noise without substance. . . . it will be a happy day for music when writers return to Mozart's simplicity! His music always had meaning, always bore the impress of the mind, he needed not the aid of drums and trumpets to cover up the want of thought" (*Albion*, March 6, 1847).

Watson was writing in an era when standards of public deportment and decorum had yet to evolve into Victorian gentility. A kind of frontier code of honor prevailed even among the educated classes in New York City. Years after Aaron Burr killed the *New-York Evening Post* founder Alexander Hamilton in a duel, duels between newspaper people were still occurring, and deaths were not unknown. William Cullen Bryant's predecessor at the *Evening Post* was severely beaten by a disgruntled reader; the editor, who himself had been the aggressor in other fights, suffered permanent disability and died young. Even urbane city types packed pistols or knives, and crowds were sometimes known to break into brawls over expressions of disagreement about popular theater performers. Perhaps the most notorious example of this was the Astor Place Riot of 1849. That year fans of the American tragedian Edwin Forrest stormed the Astor Place Theater, where his great rival, the English tragedian William Charles Macready, was performing. The militia was called out and about two dozen people were killed.

For their part, editorialists, columnists, and reviewers of the 1840s, while not reaching for their holsters, would liberally indulge invectives against their opponents in language unimaginably libelous by modern standards. It was inevitable that Watson's outspokenness would ruffle some feathers. In 1840 Watson wrote of a recital by a soprano named Mrs. Sutton, whom James Gordon Bennett had championed in the *Herald*. "Her style," wrote Watson on November 10 in the *Evening Signal*, "is of the worst Italian school, her execution in the ascending scale is very neat, but descending it is all jerked out, hard and uncultivated. Her articulation is far from distinct, and her shake is wide and not always upon the right note." In the *Herald* the following day, Bennett riposted that Mrs. Sutton had a "most distinct enunciation in the ascending or descending scale, chromatic or otherwise," and made choice aspersions on the character of Watson and the penny paper he wrote for. Watson parried witheringly in the *Evening Signal:*

A scurrilous print of this city assails us bitterly because of some of our recent musical comments. Who, we ask, ever read a musical *criticism* in that infamous and impotent journal? Its "criticisms" are mere announce-

20 ments and, as wholesale praise is not so likely to meet with condemnation as ignorant censure, it discreetly beslabbers. It is not amusing to hear a fellow presume to talk musically, who does not know the chromatic from the diatonic scale, who could not tell the differences between the chords *do* or *fa* from *sol,** and who is as ignorant of instruments of vibration as he is of the sentiments and habits of a gentleman? But we have wasted too many words upon the imbecile trash of this shallow pretender—this ignorant and presumptuous vagabond.

But others would have at Watson. The composer Anthony Philip Heinrich responded to a Watson review in an 1842 letter to the *Herald:* "You adopt the qualities of a chameleon. . . . it is well known that you bring a party to assist you in hissing public masterly performances. . . . You mistook the name of the instrument, viz., 'violincello,' instead of 'violoncello,' as the latter term is derived from violon, and not violin. . . . Can you even discern the key in which a composition is performed, and when a transition takes place, or *what do you know?*" [21]

Unfortunately, for all his intelligence and musical perspicacity, Watson freely indulged in the common practice of his time of tilting one's reactions according to the amount of newspaper advertising purchased by the concert presenter and the number of complimentary tickets proffered the reviewer. In 1841, according to Vera Brodsky Lawrence, he "issued a furious ultimatum, declaring his intention of punishing all concert-givers who did not advertise in the *New World* by withholding from them 'the influence of our notice. Our expectations are but just. We ask only a reciprocation of benefits.'† Watson particularly reprimanded those who discontinued their advertising in the *New World* after having received his commendation: 'These gentlemen no sooner see a just and appreciating criticism than they believe themselves secure, and withdraw at once their advertisements and in many cases their tickets' (*New World,* December 4, 1841)." [22]

Apparently Watson's reviews won him enough enemies that he was rebuffed in his early attempts to join the board of the New York Philharmonic Society, even though he had written favorably of many of their concerts. Denying that Watson had been officially blackballed, the secretary of the society nevertheless wrote to the editor of the *Courier and Enquirer,* "The great portion of the musical public must have seen sufficient indications of the paltry and

* Presumably Watson meant the tonic, subdominant, and dominant triads.
† Whether Watson and other critics actually received bonus income when extra advertising was purchased is not known.

contemptible feelings generally perceptible in the musical criticisms which occasionally appear in the *New World* not to allow their judgments to be misled
by the articles that appear in that paper."

Despite the barrage of odium from his victims, which continued off and
on for some years, Watson survived to become the first American newspaper
music critic to be regarded as the national "dean" of his profession. He continued seeking new journalistic pulpits, becoming chief music critic of the *New
York Tribune* from 1863 to 1867 and founding and editing the *American Art
Journal* in 1863. In his later years he pursued his multifarious undertakings virtually unabated, until death abruptly interrupted him in December 1875.

*Puffery and
bribery: Ole Bull,
Jenny Lind,
and other sagas*   In merely expecting "reciprocation of benefits," Henry
C. Watson was guilty probably of one of the lesser
breaches of professional decorum rife before 1850 in
newspaper arts journalism. The prepaid puff—black-
mail, really—was, startlingly to us moderns, a universal practice. This was
decades before the advent of Edward Bernays and sophisticated modern public relations, and long before becoming a member of a union for theatrical
press agents required a long apprenticeship. Nowadays a performer giving a
debut in New York City hires a professional publicist, but wouldn't dream of
asking the publicist to tender a bribe to the *New York Times* critic covering the
debut. But in the 1830s and 1840s, music critics, good and bad alike, all had
greased palms extended. If you didn't pay the blackmailer, you'd be guaran-
teeing yourself a bad review or no review. Yet the purchase of advertising or do-
nation of complimentary tickets was a necessary but not a sufficient condition
to prevent a bad notice: money was the quid pro quo for puffs.

Even with the innocuous practice of giving critics free tickets to concerts
(which has become universal down to the present day), there was a notorious
if short-lived exception. In the late 1840s a group of speculators built the Astor
Place Opera House and required newspaper critics to purchase subscriptions along with the general audience. Only two journalists did, Richard Grant
White and James Gordon Bennett. Most other critics deplored the practice,
and it was soon abandoned. Then, ironically, as the Astor Place Opera started
to fail financially in 1848, a writer for the *Herald* wrote that it was all the critics' fault, "presumptuous and ignorant, and who [wrote] nonsense upon the
notes, tones, semi-tones, and quarters of tones of an opera singer." More interested in attracting attention to themselves than to covering the precincts of

22   the opera, the critics, said this writer, had, in taking to abusing the artists personally, dampened public interest in the new Opera House.[23]

The all-pervasiveness of the paid puff in America was attested by an anonymous letter, dated New York, October 31, 1846, published in the *London Musical World* and reprinted in the *Boston Musical Gazette* on January 4, 1847:

> You are aware that Ole Bull, the violinist, made a large fortune in the United States. You are aware that it was not his talents which backed him throughout, but the skillful manner in which he made the American press serve his purpose. He fed, bribed, and flattered them all, from Mr. Bennett of the *Herald* to the most insignificant punster in the *Yankee Doodle.* It must have cost him a mint of money, but it answered his purpose; and with a talent little more than mediocre, he left the United States, after a sojourn of two or three years, crowned with fame and loaded with dollars. . . . The art of puffing was never so transcendently developed as by [the pianist] Leopold de Meyer. . . . by force of pecuniary agreements, throughout the press, De Meyer . . . traveled over the entire surface of the United States. . . . You would imagine that a man of De Meyer's unquestionable talent stood in no need of such charlatanic aid; but I can assure you it is absolutely necessary in America. . . . Nothing, indeed, can surpass the despicable corruptibility of the American press. For one line of truth there are a dozen lines of falsehood in almost every paper.

To which nearly half a century later the journalist Charles Taber Congdon added, "Far be it from me to undertake any criticism of [Bull's] performance; but as a historian, I may set down the fact that we made asses of ourselves; that we thought nonsense, talked nonsense, and printed nonsense about this Norwegian."[24]

Much of the same sort of nonsense was indulged toward Jenny Lind, the "Swedish nightingale," by New York newspapers. Critics wrote about Jenny Lind far in advance of her actual appearance as if they had already heard her for themselves.* Upon her arrival in New York the *Herald* printed four and a half columns on the front page of the September 2, 1850, issue. The following

---

*This kind of "extrasensory reviewing" was widely practiced by the early critics. Richard Grant White made frequent comparisons in his reviews to Liszt and other European musical dignitaries, but he could never have heard them at all, since he never set foot on the Continent, and was in England only in 1876.

day it discussed editorially the state of music in the country and the fine qualities of Lind's voice. Phineas Taylor Barnum, the godfather of modern hype, wrote a full column the following day on the secret of Lind's popularity and described her social activities of the preceding day. On September 11, 1850, the *Herald* published a review of one of her rehearsals, which had been open to the public, ending with the comment, "Tonight in Castle Garden will be the most exciting and enthusiastic scenes that were ever witnessed in this city." On September 12 the review of her concert was printed on the front page of the *Herald*.

To his credit, Henry Watson immediately decried the practice of Barnumesque hype: "The papers have stated at various times that such an artist had over three thousand people present, or such a one had over two thousand. These statements do very well as puffs, but in no instance have they been true. The Tabernacle, when crammed, will not hold over thirty-one or two hundred; it will not seat over twenty-two hundred—so that many of the monster audiences, if properly estimated, would dwindle down to fourteen or fifteen hundred, which number, by-the-bye, when reduced to dollars, greatly increases one's importance at one's bankers."[25] The clear-eyed Watson also decried the presence of claques at concerts.

That blackmailing the critics was a de facto reality did not mean that either party to the transaction condoned the practice overtly; to the contrary, each side piously and pharisaically disavowed the thought. Consider this incident: In 1840, the editor of the *Evening Star*, Mordecai M. Noah, and the editors of the *Courier and Enquirer*, Park Benjamin and James Watson Webb, viewing the success of James Gordon Bennett's *Herald,* now tops in the New York market, as a threat to their own papers' survival, attempted to engineer a public boycott of the *Herald* by bringing a vicious campaign of personal vilification in their editorials against Bennett. Not only did they call him every name in the book and violate every conceivable libel law and canon of taste, but they also charged with him with extorting money not just from musical performers but also from politicians and ordinary citizens who wanted decent treatment from the *Herald.*

In 1846, the shoe was on the other foot: a lawsuit backed by the *Herald* was brought by the singer John Templeton against a critic of the *Mirror* named McLachlan, alleging that Mr. McLachlan was a flagrantly usurious practitioner of the puffer's privilege. The upshot, as described by Vera Brodsky Lawrence:

Mercilessly assaulted by the *Herald*, the *Mirror* countered by scurrilously accusing Mrs. James Gordon Bennett, the wife of the *Herald's* editor—

the "Black Mail Editor," he was dubbed—not only of accepting from Leopold de Meyer "a diamond bracelet and watch of great value, [but] other small favors, 'secret, sweet, and precious.'" The same article reported that Bennett, always a prime target for his colleagues' abuse, had been offered "$200 or $300" to change the "sneering tone" of his criticisms of an unnamed acting star and his wife, who had already, it was claimed, provided Mrs. Bennett with "a passport to a private box in the theatre during their whole engagement." (*Mirror,* May 25, 1846)[26]

In yet another instance, James Gordon Bennett lost a libel suit brought against him by Edward Fry, the brother of composer-critic William Henry Fry. Bennett later wrote of "denunciations which have been pronounced by disappointed artists against the editor of this journal, and of all the ridiculous charges reiterated about black mail and other vulgar business. What is to be done? How is the press to be independent? How are the critics to notice artists if every ordinary remark is to bring out a remonstrance, leading the way to charges and constant annoyances to those who, like myself, very seldom, go to the theater or opera?"

Though later readers are left to puzzle out on what points in his protestations Bennett was being less than candid, at the very least one can conclude that even in the 1840s the perennial problem of performers disgruntled by bad reviews complaining to the newspapers was already old hat. Today polite demurrals to critical opinion are dutifully printed in letters to the editor, but in the 1840s they could take the form of all-out assaults on the freedom of the press. In 1847, when the *Courier and Enquirer*'s critic Richard Grant White wrote a particularly scathing review of the violinist Camillo Sivori, a group of prominent New York musicians took out an advertisement in various papers, including the *Mirror,* to protest:

We, the undersigned professors of music, having read an article in the *Courier and Enquirer* of Friday last, October 1, directed against Mr. Camillo Sivori, do not hesitate to pronounce it unjust in the highest degree. And while we do not cast the slightest reproach or imputation on the respectable conductors of that paper, we pronounce this article to have originated either from the profound ignorance of the writer in musical matters, or to have been deliberately written with a malicious view to injure that great artist.—William Scharfenberg, Charles Thibault, Michele Rapetti, Antonio Bagioli, Henry C. Timm, J. Fontana, D. G. Étienne, Julius Metz, and A. Boucher.

Bernard Ullmann, Sivori's manager, a notorious hype artist who had shamelessly written puff reviews for his own clients in America such as the celebrated Austrian pianist Henri Herz, informed the editor of the *Courier and Enquirer* that complimentary tickets would no longer be available to that newspaper, putatively because its music editor had failed to include the puff of the Sivori-Herz concert that was the obligatory rider to a paid advertisement. Then the *Tribune* published an editorial siding with the *Courier and Enquirer,* opining that White was merely responding appropriately to Ullmann's PR overkill, a pernicious practice, the *Tribune* stated, to be found only in the United States, where overpuffing was necessary because Americans didn't know what to think of anything until they were told.

After the affair blew over, at least one correspondent wickedly suggested that the whole controversy might have been deliberately instigated by Mr. Ullmann: as the saying goes, any publicity is good publicity.

Styles of
early criticism   As more newspapers were founded (notably, in New York, the *Tribune* in 1841 and the *Times* ten years later) and the older ones flourished, music criticism was evolving beyond the first blush of novelty. By the mid-1840s two distinct approaches to writing music criticism had begun to emerge. One was that of the impressionistic poet-rhapsodist, attempting through language to evoke for his readers something of the emotional quality of the sounds without resorting to vague gaseous expatiations. The other was that of the technical analyst: at his best patiently indoctrinating the untutored reader in the vast craft and lore of the art; at his worst engaging in pettifogging displays of pedantic one-upmanship. These two styles have vied with each other ever after in the annals of music criticism, but the lines were drawn back at the beginning.

Of the two critical styles, poetry versus mathematics, the critics sometimes had to adopt the former because they did not yet have access to either scores of the music they were reviewing or a large fund of memory of previous performances—a disproportionate number of the performances they had to review were first performances. Thus it was making virtue of a necessity that the American critics of this early period often deferred making any judgment, shrewdly saying they needed more than one hearing to evaluate the merit of a new piece.

Later, Henry Krehbiel, the Gaslight Era dean of New York music critics, in his oft-reprinted 1896 book *How to Listen to Music* referred to these two styles

26   as pedants versus rhapsodists, but he approved of "intelligent rhapsody." The rhapsodist critic tries to use poetic language and metaphor to recreate the gestalt of the live hearing experience, as when Nathaniel Parker Willis wrote that "thin muslin cadences lacked the aerial floss with which humidity clothes a cadence" (*Home Journal*, November 10, 1849). Even such a technically grounded reviewer as Watson, in order to be an effective critic, would feel free at times to depart from a strict accounting of the mechanics of music and use language more floridly than a late twentieth-century newspaper critic would dare.

On the other side is music journalism's version of the certified public accountant: ". . . she took an air *andantino*, or almost *andante*, instead of *allegretto* [, as the score indicated]" (Richard Grant White on the English soprano Anna Riviere Bishop). What most good critics, then and now, instinctively strive for is a balance between those two poles:

> It is impossible to imagine bolder and more melodious execution than Signor Bottesini's . . . zebraed with diabolical arpeggios and diapered with miraculous harmonies. . . . Such feats of execution, so difficult to execute on the violin, are twice as difficult on the counterbass, not only from the unmanageable size of the instrument, but because the length of the cords [strings] betray the least error of the fingers, the most delicate irregularities of the diatonic gamut. (Nathaniel P. Willis writing in the *Home Journal*, April 19, 1847, about the Italian double bass virtuoso Bottesini)

ꙮ *Early critical*
    wisdom   At this early juncture in American musical history there was no such thing as received wisdom. "Immortal" composers as we know them had not yet been designated. There was no consensus by the critical fraternity of what was good or bad; there was only a huge tureen of opinions, stirred every which way by every which cook.

Donizetti, a prolific hit opera composer of Europe, was received with mixed reviews, "his friends proclaiming him unrivalled, a chemical anagram compounded of all the essences of Mozart, Rossini, and Boieldieu, while his opponents have long opened upon him the vials of wrath, denouncing him as a plagiarist—a musical freebooter, and charging that all his beauties are grand larcenies committed on the whole commonwealth of song" (*Spirit*, March 11, 1844). Richard Grant White found Verdi's music to be full of "incongruous instrumentation . . . unpalatable melody . . . [its harmony] outré . . . strange . . .

and intolerable. . . . one cannot sit and listen to it without feeling a strong inclination to murder the composer." [27]

And what of the divine child Mozart? A yes-no:

The orchestra was one of the best we have ever heard in this country and
they delivered the magnificent conceptions of Mozart, the Raphael of
music, with all the fervor and delicacy he could have desired. The music,
however, is not of that striking and fervid character which induces enthusiasm. Its harmony is admirable but the audience accustomed to the
passionate airs of Bellini seemed to feel its want of expression. Seguin has
the better voice; it is a full, rich, natural bass somewhat injured by taking
snuff. (Review of Mozart's *Magic Flute* produced in Philadelphia by the
Seguin Troupe, Leopold Meignen conducting, on February 8, 1841, in
Musical Fund Hall, with a chorus of eighty and orchestra of sixty-four,
North American and Daily Advertiser, March 17, 1841)

An ignorant pan:

The music of the opera, like that of the German school generally, is
deficient in melodies suited to the popular ear. The instrumentation is
ponderous, heavily scored and intimately blended with the voice part, so
that it is only here and there that the vocalist can shine, except on time to
time. A fine musical organization such as the Italians naturally possess is
not enough to carry one through the concerted pieces. A knowledge of
music is requisite. (Review of Mozart's *Don Giovanni*, *New York Herald*,
February 6, 1850)

And an assessment so shrewdly far-reaching as to anticipate Alfred Einstein's
"daemonic" Mozart:

Delicate, graceful, chastely pure . . . an intensity in its pathos and a might-
iness in the emotions which it suggests, which are not usually attributed
to [Mozart], though he has a full claim to them. (Richard Grant White in
the *Courier and Enquirer*, April 27, 1846, writing of Mozart's Symphony
No. 40 in G Minor)

The archives of music journalism in pre-1850 America, along with the few
extant diaries of musical dilettantes (such as those of New Yorkers George
Templeton Strong and Philip Hone), are our only reliquaries of how orches-

28 tras actually played, how singers actually sounded. Few of these early examples delve into those subtleties of comparative interpretations of orchestral conductors routinely charted by the critics of the twentieth century, simply because the cult of the conductor hadn't yet evolved. Orchestral conducting didn't yet have a history, certainly not in America. And though the early critics do give us glimpses into the state of orchestral playing at the time, their value as yardsticks of contemporary norms of well-rehearsed playing is limited by the extent to which most of the surviving reviews are of first performances, for which some roughness of execution must be expected: "On this occasion . . . the orchestra was weak, and with all the efforts of its excellent leader, Mr. Hill [later first conductor of the New York Philharmonic], the instruments were frequently out of tune and out of time" (from a review by Charles Dinghley of the first American performance of Beethoven's Symphony No. 1, given in New York City on April 27, 1831, by the Musical Fund Society, *Euterpeiad* 2, no. 1).[28]

The beginnings of evangelism for an American musical culture   Despite their internecine squabbles, by the end of the 1840s the critical fraternity of New York's newspapers was collectively beginning to express a missionary sense of its duty as courier of the arts to the great unwashed. In the *Anglo American* in 1845 Alexander D. Paterson lamented the dependence of opera, and of music as a whole, upon the whimsy of the "Upper Ten Thousand." He vehemently stumped for his belief that for the art of music to be properly lodged in the culture of the average New Yorker, it was "necessary to teach the general public to know what they were listening to and how to listen to it." He began agitating in his columns for the creation of "a Music Hall, with lecture rooms, class rooms, a musical library of standard works, the appointment of a Principal, Professors of Senior and Junior Departments"— in other words, for a nineteenth-century Lincoln Center complete with Juilliard School. The latter suggestion was sixty years ahead of its fruition; the former, over one hundred.

Other critics took up the quill where Paterson's ink dried. Hermann S. Saroni stumped in the *Musical Times* in 1850 for the building of a major concert hall, deploring that concert presenters had to resort to theaters and other inappropriate venues. "Philadelphia has its Musical Fund Hall, Boston its Melodeon. . . . it is strange that so many of our capitalists should suffer such a chance to escape them. Hundreds and thousands of dollars are paid annually to the Tabernacle, when a proper music room would command double the prices, not to mention the lasting benefit conferred upon the city by such praiseworthy enterprises." Largely as a result of Saroni's urgings, Metropolitan Hall was built in 1850.

At about this same time, the critics also began to campaign for a heightened appreciation of native-born American talent to counter the decadent and vacuous obeisance to European talent that had characterized pleasure-seeking but ignorant moneyed New Yorkers. Saroni, himself German-born, wrote in the *Musical Times* in capital letters, upon reporting the European concert successes of the American composer-pianist Louis Moreau Gottschalk, "WHEN WILL AMERICAN TALENT BE ENCOURAGED IN THIS COUNTRY?" Gradually, bit by bit, American composers started to get a sympathetic boost from the critics, a conscious bootstrap assist in the face of the uphill fight for them merely to get performances. At its premiere, Richard Grant White found the American composer George Bristow's Concert Overture, op. 3, "graceful and withall full of meaning," even if the score was "generally overloaded with wind" and the rhythm "somewhat wearisome from the recurrence of a period of four phrases with perfect cadences. Interrupted periods are necessary to prevent weariness in a long composition" (*Courier and Enquirer,* January 16, 1847). The comments by Watson in the *Albion* were similarly critical, but accentuating the positive: "He possesses much talent and promises much in future compositions. . . . It is too noisily instrumented, and wanting in individuality, but there are some charming points and good effects" (January 16, 1847).

But the most important task yet to be accomplished in the campaign to raise the public consciousness for the art of music was to raise the level of professional criticism. Upon assuming the post of music editor of the *Mirror,* Watson on September 5, 1846, wrote:

> Not more than two or three of our papers consider music of sufficient importance to pay for the aid of a competent writer, consequently the doers-up of the city items, or the law, or police reporters, are entrusted with the supervision of a science of which they are almost, if not entirely, ignorant. . . . Music needs the assistance of the press . . . it needs the help of those who can and will awaken the attention of the public at large, and direct, by judicious praise or deserved censure, the taste of the many. . . . We maintain that the prevailing tone of musical criticism tends to degrade music, both as a science and an art. . . . Its professors are noticed in that

30   elegant school of eulogistic hyperbole which is also used when describing Mlle. Fanny, the ape, and Mr. Jocko, the baboon. . . . it is of this that musicians justly complain; they deem that a science that demands for its accomplishment so many years of earnest study is worthy of serious attention, and should receive careful and well-considered criticism.

Of course, Watson was silently elbowing the reader that then and thereafter this kind of serious criticism would be found only in the pages of *his* newspaper, the *Mirror*. But in so self-puffing he was also a journalistic John the Baptist, pointing with prophetic accuracy toward the future of the profession whose path he himself had blazed.

Emerson, Whitman, and
John Sullivan Dwight

Hitching Wagons
to a Euterpean Star

[Music] takes us out of the actual and whispers to us dim secrets that startle our wonder as to who we are. . . . All the great interrogatories, like questioning angels, float in on its waves of sound.
—RALPH WALDO EMERSON, writing in his journal, 1838

I allowed the Italians the highest musical disposition but thought they carried their applause beyond their real appreciation. In a little while, however, by frequenting of operas and accustoming myself to the novelty of their music, I began to find a fondness for it stealing on myself and I now hurry to the opera with as much eagerness as an Italian.
—WASHINGTON IRVING, writing in his journal in Europe

From the retrospect of the late twentieth century, it is easy to see that magazine music journalism and criticism have had at least as much influence on the history of musical taste in America as have the daily newspapers, even though the number of magazine readers is dwarfed by the circulations of the major-market newspapers. This influence derives from the abiding tenet of American society (at least until very recently) that elite culture is something available to all and for all to aspire to appreciate. This public philosophy undergirds much of culture and arts funding to this day; without it, museums wouldn't exist. In a democracy, the culture of the cultivated elite is allowed to bear an influence incommensurate with its numbers because that influence is made publicly available to all, and all society's members are encouraged to participate and edify themselves (though of course the price of admission can be an obstacle).

32   But where did this cultural article of faith in high art as a public good originate? A strong argument can be made that the music magazines of the 1830s and 1840s were the first public organs in this country to articulate public exhortations for the neo-Athenian good of the cultural life, especially those published in that American Athens, Boston. Only later did these editorial attitudes find their way into other regions of the country and into American folklore.

Specialized magazines have always to some extent preached to the converted, and classical music magazines then and now are specialized magazines. But the 1840s forerunners of *Musical America* and *High Fidelity* had to do more than preach to the converted; they had to establish that there was a cause worth preaching, and then try to proselytize the great unwashed American to the cause. They were missionaries spreading the gospel of high culture to a new country with little or no native high culture. Though daily newspaper music critics such as Henry Watson in New York wrote of high culture to a diverse urban readership of thousands, most of their writings were reviews of actual concerts. But, unlike Watson and his colleagues, the authors of articles in the early music magazines never had to bend their tastes to the greased palm. Also, the newspapers afforded little space for the "think piece," the reviewer's expanded speculations on the value of music and on art as a whole. This function was taken over by the Boston magazines; by the belles-lettrists and social philosophers of the day who pulpiteered in print for the art of music; by some of the great literary writers of the time, pitching for their sister art; and most of all by one great visionary who practiced his trade mainly in Boston, the critic John Sullivan Dwight.

The attraction of so many literary writers of the nineteenth century to classical music is a striking phenomenon and a theme we will return to. Their writing on music goes far beyond merely summoning à la Wordsworth and Coleridge the poetic fancies of shepherds piping and such; it embraces outright advocacy, rather as though painters suddenly started writing editorials for playwrights, or vice versa.

ᘿ *The magazine in*
      pre-1850 America   The newspaper, not the magazine, was the sole mass
                              medium among periodicals for most of the 1800s, at
least until the latter years of the century, when such publications as *Harper's Weekly,* the *Saturday Evening Post,* and the *Atlantic Monthly* started to attain mass circulation. In the republic's early years, the magazine business, as with newspapers, was more brier patch than cultivated garden. For even the most

prominent magazines, circulation in the early nineteenth century rarely exceeded more than several hundred. Few magazines survived more than a few years. Contributors of articles were poorly paid if at all. Article authorship was usually anonymous, bylines not appearing regularly until after 1850. Authors had little control over their material; the editor's blue pencil tended to overrule and rewrite everything despotically. Editors and publishers freely pirated material from other publications in their own; the reciprocities of copyright law were not yet observed.

Efforts at magazines devoted to music go back to 1786, when for one year something called the *American Musical Magazine* was published in New Haven, Connecticut (but it contained printed music, not critical reviews or essays). In October 1800 a different *American Musical Magazine* appeared in Northampton, Massachusetts, publishing until January 1801. A few other musical periodicals appeared in Philadelphia in the first years of the 1800s, but there was no real musical magazine in America until after 1825, and even afterward there was little of distinction. The *Musical Magazine* of New York, published by Ezra Collier and edited by Thomas Hastings, proclaimed to its readers in its first number, May 1835, that though there had been "musical intelligencers before, a monthly magazine appropriated to all the important branches of theoretical and practical music will, to say the least, be regarded as something new." It published two annual volumes and then ceased.

The editor of the *Musical Magazine*, Thomas Hastings (1784–1872), has the distinction of publishing probably the first text in American musical criticism, an 1822 "Dissertation on Musical Taste." But Hastings was extremely pious and had little truck with secular concerts. As late as 1835 he wrote of his shock in hearing some opera and oratorio; it was all too vulgar for him. Yet in the short-lived *Musical Magazine* he wrote with eminent reasonableness in the July 1835 issue: "Musical taste is a thing that can never be suddenly superinduced, it is the result of gradual and continuous effort. It comes to maturity like the slow process of vegetation."[1]

∾ *Music and music journalism in Boston*   Although New York City was to overtake it as a cosmopolitan culture capital after 1850, Boston, in the early years of the nineteenth century, matched strides with Gotham both in civic musical development and in journalism about the euterpean art (as the ornate language of the time dubbed it — one early, short-lived New England musical periodical was called the *Euterpeiad*). According to

34   W. S. B. Mathews, the first real symphonic ensemble in America to play great music of European composers regularly was that formed in Boston by the German oboist Gottlieb Graupner in 1810 and lasting to 1824, a "Philharmonic Society" (a generic title given to innumerable short-lived groups in various cities during those times). Graupner had played in Haydn's orchestra in London, and his Bostonians, primarily European émigrés like himself, played mostly Haydn symphonies (Beethoven was as yet a more advanced taste). The modern Boston Symphony Orchestra was not founded until 1881.

Graupner, together with Thomas Smith Webb and Asa Peabody, also organized America's first enduring performing ensemble, the Boston Handel and Haydn Society, founded in 1815 and still going strong under the direction of Christopher Hogwood in the late 1990s. The Handel and Haydn Society performed oratorios and liturgical music by Haydn, Beethoven, Handel, Mozart, and others, with an emphasis in its early years on the two charter perennials, Handel's *Messiah* and Haydn's *Creation*. Other oratorio and sacred music societies quickly cropped up not only in Boston but in other American cities as well; however, with the eventual coast-to-coast proliferation of resident symphony orchestras over the ensuing century, and the eclipse of liturgical choral music by the symphonic repertoire, most urban sacred music societies eventually faded away. Only the Handel and Haydn Society has stayed the course, prestige intact.

With the introduction of music study into the public school curriculum of Boston in the 1830s, the time seemed auspicious for new efforts at starting musical magazines. And so began *Hach's Musical Magazine,* edited by H. Theodor Hach and T. B. Hayward. Hach, a cellist, teacher of music, and writer who had arrived from Germany as recently as 1837, spoke fluent English. *Hach's Musical Magazine* was in part an eclectic compilation of reprints, using material from English sources and many translations, especially from the German. Notable among such reprints were the English critic Henry F. Chorley's writings on Beethoven's later works, such as the late piano sonatas and string quartets then thought (and still regarded as) recondite. Though *Hach's* lasted only three years, Hayward, with a new partner, George J. Webb, started the monthly *Musical Cabinet* in the same city.

An idea of Hach's strong authority as musician and critic can be gleaned from his review of a pickup orchestra's performance of Beethoven's *Fidelio* Overture, which Hach found to be

one of those compositions which are difficult to understand unless performed by a master Orchestra, like that of the Paris Opera; and we do not wonder if, although our orchestra played it in the best style, some among the audience were not satisfied with the piece. One mistake . . . might have been prevented. In the duet of the two clarinets in the first Adagio there was no second clarinet, and the first had to play its four measures alone, of course, injuring the effect and the author's intentions that the two clarinets should answer the previous duet of two horns. (*Hach's Musical Magazine*, February 18, 1841)

Throughout the three years of his magazine Hach, according to the scholar Ora Frishberg Saloman, "advocated increased presentations of large-scale instrumental music, an improvement in string playing, knowledge of music acquired through concert performances and historical essays, and the promotion of higher standards of taste. He urged the Boston Academy of Music to 'get up an orchestra of its own.' When it expanded its operations into the instrumental field, he congratulated the Academy and offered suggestions; some of these were not always feasible to implement, such as the addition of time to regular weekly rehearsals."[2]

ᴄ∾ *Emerson and the*
transcendentalists   Many of Boston's intelligentsia and musical elite in the
on music   1830s and 1840s were active in the Harvard Musical Association, which presented chamber music concerts performed by its members, many of whom were Harvard graduates. In addition, the association's lecture presentations functioned as an incubator for ideas about public policy on music that would find their way into the Boston music magazines. In an address to the association in the 1840s, Christopher P. Cranch, a Harvard graduate and flutist who became a prolific contributor to the music magazines of the 1840s, perfectly summarizes both the state of music in America at the time and the mindset of those influential Boston-bred literary intellectuals and musicians who were about to take up their pens to do something about it as the so-called transcendentalists:

We must all agree that in the science and art of music we Americans are as yet scarcely pupils, and, of course, far enough from being masters. Our lamentable ignorance in the scientific principles of music, as well as our want of delicate susceptibility to the best works of musical composers, renders all comparisons of ourselves with Germany, Italy, and other countries of Europe, altogether unnecessary. We are, in fact, barely beginning to wake up as from a lethargy, and join in sympathy with the great musical culture on the other side of the Atlantic. Take the most cultivated and refined population of cities like Boston, New York, Philadelphia, and it will be seen that, even in the most crowded houses which a celebrated performer or a celebrated work will attract, the proportion of those who really appreciate the music is very small. Where thousands rush in to enjoy a novelty, or while away time, or at best have their ears tickled by imitations of bagpipes and flageolets on the violin, or to hear a singer tax invention and strength of lungs and flexibility of larynx to produce a cadenza more crowded with notes and of longer duration than ordinary, there may perhaps be a hundred who go with a simple, hearty love, and a cultivated taste, for the composer's works. . . . Men and women, and young misses at school, who have pianofortes of their own, and all the songs of Russell, Dempster, and the Hutchinsons on the tips of their tongues, set themselves up as the critics of Handel and Beethoven, and talk and yawn and go out in the midst of their sublimest choruses or symphonies.*[3]

As a music critic Cranch was, alas, an extreme version of the school of the florid, as can be seen in his review of the New York premiere of Beethoven's Seventh Symphony:

Here we have the man, not only free and strong at the very outset, like Hercules, victorious even in his cradle, but he becomes a winged, radiant God, he spurns the earth, he mounts upwards, in beautiful, victorious flights, and gazes with eagle eyes upon the sun. The explanation given in the Programme, which supposes this work to tell the story of Orpheus and Eurydice, does not satisfy us; and yet, having heard it [the symphony] but once, we feel at a loss to find an interpretation which would do it justice. (*Harbinger*, January 17, 24, 31, 1845)

These gossamer effusions took their cue, however, not so much from poetic flights of fancy as from the then-burgeoning New England transcendentalist movement, of which the *Harbinger* was a house organ. A secular offspring of Unitarianism, transcendentalism held that man had intuitive knowledge that "transcends" the reality-based information of the senses. The scientism, rationalism, and materialism of the Enlightenment were rejected in

---

*To which Frédéric Ritter, quoting this in 1890, appended, "My candid reader must confess that much of this picture can yet be justly applied, in a great measure, to our present situation."

favor of intuition and the personal experience of God within each individual, rather than in the context of church rituals. Transcendentalism's greatest exponent, Ralph Waldo Emerson, eventually resigned his Unitarian pastorate to spread the transcendentalist "gospel" as an itinerant lecturer on the lyceum circuit, as well as to keep up a lifelong stream of books containing essays and poetry. But it was as lyceum lecturer—lay minister, really—that he made his primary income.

The transcendentalists, among the earliest religious rebels in American culture, were also among its earliest arts boosters. At the same time that they were shucking the rituals of religion, like the flower children of the 1960s, they were also finding "religion" anew in their worship of the fine arts, particularly music. They published eight literary magazines between 1835 and 1850, and seven of the eight devoted at least one issue exclusively to classical music; in all there were 183 articles published about the euterpean art. Chief among these magazines were the *Dial* in the first half of the 1840s, edited by Emerson and Margaret Fuller, and the *Harbinger* in the second half of the 1840s, edited by George Ripley, the founder of Brook Farm, an experiment in communal living. Ripley was also the editor of the first American editions of many classics of European philosophy and literature in translation and, in his later years, became a leading literary critic, establishing the first book review department on an American newspaper at the *New York Tribune.*

Before the New England transcendentalists, the United States was a country where psalmody, hymnody, and other choral liturgical music formed the defining pillars of the concert repertoire, and the foregone assumption (except for those radical New York critics!) was that concert music existed for the religious belief it upheld, rather than for the emotional values inherent in the music. As W. S. B. Mathews later put it, "the error [was] of supposing the highest and the broadest function of music to be that of exemplifying gospel teachings, rather than its real mission. . . . music, the highest language of the emotions, cannot be cut down to the pattern of any creed or dogma, but lives to brighten and beautify every aspect, every instinct, every ambition and every aspiration and sentiment of the nobler elements of human life." [4] For the transcendentalists, great European music such as the Beethoven symphonies *was* the direct expression of ineffable spiritual states. When the dean of the transcendentalist music critics, J. S. Dwight, later established through his journalism the cult of Beethoven worship in America, he was definitively telling American culture that secular instrumental music, not liturgical-based choral music, was art, not amusement.

Emerson was the guru to such literary eminences as James Russell Lowell,

38 Henry David Thoreau, and Henry James Sr., and it was he, ironically, that set
the tone for the group's exaltation of music. The irony was that Emerson himself was utterly illiterate in music theory and made no pretense of being anything but tone-deaf. Yet in spite of his protestations and lack of musical tu-
toring, he clearly responded to, and even loved, classical music. He kept an
aeolian harp in the study of his home in Concord, Massachusetts, right near
the circular desk where he wrote his essays, lectures, and poetry. "I think sometimes—could I only have music on my own terms—could I live in a great city,
and know where I could go whenever I wished the ablution and inundation of
musical waves—that were a bath and a medicine," he wrote.[5] After attending
a performance of Handel's *Messiah* in 1843, Emerson entered in his journal:

> I walked in the bright paths of sound, and like it best when the long con-
> tinuance of a chorus had made the ear insensible to the music, made it as
> if there was none; then I was quite solitary and at ease in the melodious
> uproar. Once or twice in the solos, when well sung, I could play tricks, as
> I like to do, with my eyes, darken the whole house and brighten and
> transfigure the central singer, and enjoy the enchantment.[6]

Emerson used the *Dial* to elaborate his thoughts about the art of music in
"Thoughts on Art," in which he first presented the Emersonian proverb that
"the laws of each art are convertible into the laws of every other." If Emerson
was envious of those who made music and understood it better than he, it was
because he was sufficiently moved by hearing music to elevate it, as Schopenhauer did, to the top rung of all art forms in its ability to express the divinity
he himself could seek only through the printed and spoken word: "I am a poet
in the sense of a perceiver and dear lover of the harmonies that are in the soul
and in matter," as he wrote to his bride-to-be in 1835.[7] What Emerson was referring to, according to Irving Lowens, was the "root concept of the Transcen-
dental attitude toward music," that "if words were to be regarded as the language of thought, then music must be regarded as the language of feeling. The
unfortunate person who was unable to sense the uniquely communicative nature of music was debarred from comprehension of some of life's deepest mysteries. Not everything could be said in words."[8]

Emerson was only one of several transcendentalists who contributed articles about music to the *Dial* and the *Harbinger*. One of the most prolific was
Charles Anderson Dana (1819–97), known better to history as assistant secretary of war under Lincoln and editor of the *New York Sun* later in the century.

The young Dana, an intelligent music lover who had picked up what little he knew about music's technical construction from conversations at Brook Farm, where he lived in the early 1840s, was the author of seven articles in the *Harbinger* covering the 1847–48 Italian opera season in New York. Another Brook Farm literary aspirant turned music journalist for the *Harbinger* was George William Curtis (1824–92), in later years a literary heavyweight through his occupancy of *Harper's Magazine's* "Easy Chair" and his editorial work on *Harper's Weekly.* Wrote an overheated twenty-something Curtis of Beethoven's Seventh Symphony, "The mystery seems to be developing itself, where the earnest-seeking solemnly consecrates itself to success; and the Minuet and Finale conclude—the soaring, mocking, hellish laughter of fiends and demons of the air, at baffled curiosity and blighted hope."[9]

The other transcendentalist music writers were also impressively catholic in their interests. Margaret Fuller, American letters' first great feminist, a literary critic and English translator of *Conversations with Goethe,* wrote five of the eight articles about music that appeared in the *Dial,* including a fifty-five-page biographical essay, "Lives of the Great Composers, Haydn, Mozart, Handel, Bach, Beethoven" (*Dial* 2 [October 1841]). Another correspondent, Elam Ives, was one of the few trained musicians who wrote for the transcendentalist journals, including the *Harbinger.* The *Harbinger* also printed articles about music by Christopher Cranch, Albert Brisbane, Parke Godwin, and William Wetmore Story, who was primarily known as a sculptor. Perhaps at no other juncture in our country's history have the literati and culturati as a group taken such a committed interest in the promotion of the art of classical music.

John Sullivan Dwight, arch-deacon of music

The *Dial* and *Harbinger* contributor who did the most to bring the precepts of transcendentalism into the mainstream of American musical journalism was, like Emerson, an ordained minister who had forsaken the pulpit of a small congregation for the larger canvas of culturally aspirant Americans en masse. He was John Sullivan Dwight (1813–93), the Boston-born son of a Harvard graduate who had himself, too, studied for the ministry only to resign the cloth to become a medical doctor. Young Dwight attended Harvard College, where he played the piano and the clarinet in the campus chamber music groups, the Arionic and Pierian Sodalities, and upon graduation he organized the alumni of the Pierian Sodality into what became the Harvard Musical Association.

40 This is an early example of how music critics (which Dwight was then yet to become) have at times been responsible for the organization of major musical performing ensembles; the Harvard Musical Association was for decades Boston's leading chamber music society.

Dwight also excelled in both the classics and German and went on to Harvard Divinity School, graduating in 1836. His dissertation, "The Proper Character of Poetry and Music for Public Worship," was later published in the *Christian Examiner*. Upon graduation from divinity school Dwight would occupy himself translating poems of Schiller and Goethe, playing Beethoven piano sonatas, and freelancing articles on music to various publications (including *Hach*'s), all the while pursuing an on-again, off-again career as a Unitarian minister around Boston.

In 1841 Emerson, ten years older than Dwight, thought Dwight "a good, susceptible and yearning soul,"[10] and when Emerson resigned from his pulpit in East Lexington he recommended Dwight as his successor. Dwight preached there as a guest on a number of Sundays, but the congregation decided to look elsewhere for a permanent replacement. By that time Dwight had gained a pulpit of his own, at the Second Congregational Church in Northampton, Massachusetts, but he, like Emerson before him, was beginning to experience doubts about the value of church ritual and formal worship. The feeling between minister and congregants evidently was mutual; by the time Dwight's contract as pastor in Northampton was up after the first year it was not renewed.

This dismissal was fortuitous for posterity. George Ripley had started Brook Farm that year, and when Dwight left the ministry in November 1841 he promptly went to live there, where he gave piano lessons, taught Latin, participated in the communal efforts at manual labor, and began to write more prolifically than ever before about music for the *Dial* and later for the *Harbinger*. Dwight stayed at Brook Farm till it was closed for good in 1847.

Dwight had begun writing for the *Dial* even before he had left the ministry, in 1840. In an article entitled "The Concerts of the Past Winter" he wrote:

> Art . . . should breathe the pervading spirit of Nature, as a whole, and not copy too carefully the things that are in it. Whoever has studied the Pastoral Symphony, or the Pastoral Sonata of Beethoven, will feel the difference between music which flows from an inward feeling of nature, from a common consciousness (as it were) with nature, and the music which only copies, from without, her single features. These pieces bring all sum-

mer sensations over you, but they do not let you identify a note or a passage as standing for a stream or a bird. (*Dial* 1 [July 1840]: 128)

Another review by Dwight of a Beethoven orchestral work suggests that Dwight had garnered enough understanding from his own chamber music experience to appreciate what was wrong in the ensemble playing of an orchestra. Thus, from a review of the first Boston performance of Beethoven's *Egmont* Overture:

We waited with trembling expectation for Beethoven's Overture to begin; so powerful a hold had it acquired upon us in a mere pianoforte arrangement, that to hear it announced for a full orchestra was like hearing that the friend had arrived whose great soul you had long owned and loved through letters. It could not be but grand, however poorly performed, to one already imbued with it. What a perfect overture! how truly Egmont, and how thoroughly Beethoven's! O! for a performance worthy of it. We were disappointed; the public, of course, were disappointed, who depended on the performance wholly for their conception of the piece. What a nightmare it gave one, to sit amid a dead, indifferent multitude, when music so intense, so deep, so grand, so crowded with the hurry and the passion of life was actually being performed! Why was it! Because the orchestra did not understand it, had not attained to anything more than a mechanical execution of it, each playing his part for himself, without feeling all the other parts; and chiefly because it was played altogether too fast. (*Harbinger,* August 9, 1845, p. 140)

The later preeminent Boston critic W. F. Apthorp commented on Dwight's level of musical literacy,

Dwight's artistic gift was of a very general sort. . . . his only native aptitude for the art consisted in what is commonly called "a fair ear" and general aesthetic sensibility. . . . his technical knowledge of the art was always slight. He could read notes and work his way through pianoforte scores on that instrument, although he never even began (or tried to begin) to master its technique. . . . he had a certain, rather superficial knowledge of the rudiments of harmony, and a somewhat more exact and extended acquaintance with the rules of musical form. His knowledge of musical terminology, however, was comprehensive, and accurate,—astonishingly so in one whose technical knowledge of the art was so incomplete. He never developed anything that could fairly be called musical facility; he never handled musical notation with the ease of a craftsman, and always found some difficulty in following performances from the score, especially when things went at a rapid tempo. His naturally musical ear never developed to more than an average pitch of delicacy; technical slips seldom disturbed him, and "rough performances" fully satisfied him, if only the right spirit was there.[11]

In any event, Beethoven's music, more than that of any other composer, embodied for Dwight the transcendentalist ideal of exalting the spirit in sound, and his published writings began to reflect that. In his address to the Harvard Musical Association in 1841, published by Hach in his own magazine, Dwight termed Beethoven's music "not formal prayer, I grant, but earnest deep unspeakable aspiration," referring further to Beethoven's music as that of "another and an unseen world which only the heart knoweth, and which the pure in heart shall enter, though they are not of the successful ones after the world's way."[12] In 1842 in Boston Dwight finally heard his first performances of Beethoven's Second, Fifth, and Sixth Symphonies, and in 1846 he attended rehearsals as well as the American premiere performance of the Ninth by the New York Philharmonic (the first performance of the Ninth in Boston did not occur until 1853).

That Beethoven had become the prime exhibit for Dwight's attempt to bring a philosophical context to the appreciation and criticism of music distinct from the music journalism that appeared in the daily press is obvious in his published comments upon hearing that premiere in 1846:

> We went away physically exhausted by the excitement of listening to so great a work, but unspeakably confirmed in all our highest faith. . . . We trust our own hearts and God's word, and the Symphony, that Light will prevail, that Society will be saved and, conforming itself at length to the Laws of the Divine Order, will become Society indeed, instead of that mere mockery of the word, that poor confused assemblage of isolated and antagonistic interests, which it is and has been. (*Harbinger,* June 13, 1846)

This is not to imply that the young J. S. Dwight's only critical tool for praising music he liked was to equate it with divine revelation, but it does reflect a flavor that, while no longer existing in musical journalism in the twentieth century, in earlier times of greater mass piety did a lot to nudge a churchgoing public toward the appreciation of the arts.

But as much as he preached the gospel of Beethoven, Dwight was equally a proselytizer for the need to promote the development of resident musical organizations throughout the United States, whether symphony orchestras, opera companies, or chamber groups. Until that time only the sacred music societies were standing organizations; orchestras and opera companies were short-term or freelance affairs. Dwight wrote of this need as early as in his *Dial* essay "Concerts of the Past Winter":

> Let a few of our most accomplished and refined musicians institute a series of cheap instrumental concerts . . . the two or three hundred, who are scattered about and really long to hear and make acquaintance with Beethoven and Haydn, could easily be brought together by such an attraction, and would form a nucleus to whatever audience might be collected, and would give a tone to the whole, and secure attention. . . . It might be a labor of love at the outset; but it would create in time the taste which would patronize and reward it.

In this proposal Dwight was following both the earlier suggestions of his mentor Theodor Hach and the model of the Classic Concerts series organized by Ignaz Moscheles in England.[13]

Though he continued to reside at Brook Farm through the 1840s, Dwight stayed active in the ferment of Boston's musical activities, remaining there even when the *Harbinger* moved to New York, where it attained a circulation of two thousand. Through his base at the Harvard Musical Association (of which from 1843 to 1845 he was vice-president) Dwight tried to boost the musical life not just of the university but of all Boston. He stumped for a new music hall for the city; he produced concerts of chamber music. He continued fraternizing with the leading literary lights of the time who were the glory of Boston in those years, among them not only the transcendentalists but also Henry Wadsworth Longfellow and Oliver Wendell Holmes Sr.

Dwight was in some ways an unlikely figure to be the leader of anything. A failed preacher, he was described by those who knew him as "unworldly, diffident, sensitive in the extreme, bashful, even, according to George Ripley, 'lacking in will.'"[14] He was a bohemian with no steady job, always living hand to mouth through the modest proceeds of his articles, occasional lectures, and

44   translations of poems by his beloved Goethe and Schiller, which he sometimes succeeded in placing in newspapers and magazines. According to Apthorp,

> What most made Dwight remarkable was his inveterate instinct for culture—as distinguished from mere learning. Perhaps it may have been in a large measure a certain unconquerable mental indolence that prompted him always to take the royal road in everything, to skip lightly over the dry rudiments of every study,—or what to men otherwise disposed would have been study,—and absorb immediately what he could of its final essence. Mentally indolent he certainly was to a high degree; he abominated work; the necessity for work seemed to him, upon the whole, a sad mistake in the scheme of the universe. And, though he did a good deal of it, first and last, in the course of his life, it was never otherwise than irksome to him; he worked, as it were, under protest. . . . Possibly the compliment paid his paper, *Dwight's Journal of Music,* that most pleased him was when Richard Grant White once wrote him that it was "not a *newsy* paper—a vile phrase for a viler thing!" He was never in a hurry, and never could understand why anyone should be.[15]

Nevertheless, it was this "indolent work-shirker" who succeeded in what no else before him had done: founding and overseeing America's first enduring magazine devoted exclusively to classical music. He was almost forty when he began publishing *Dwight's Journal of Music* as his "last desperate (not very confident) grand *coup d'état* to try to get a living."[16] Newly married at the age of thirty-eight (late for those times), Dwight had turned to his many illustrious friends for capital for his journal. As Dwight scholar Irving Sablosky puts it, "Some were doubtful that Dwight should attempt the mundane tasks even a small publishing enterprise would entail; he clearly had no head for practical matters."[17] But his friends ponied up, as did the coffers of the Harvard Musical Association, and in February 1852 Dwight was able to invite the public to subscribe to a new journal that would be, in his words, "an organ of what may be called the Musical Movement in this country, of the growing love of deep and genuine music, of the growing consciousness that music, first amid the other forms of Art, is intimately connected with Man's truest life and destiny." Eventually 1,051 issues and some eight thousand pages of *Dwight's Journal of Music* would be published, from April 10, 1852, to September 3, 1881, weekly or biweekly. Probably at no time were there more than one thousand subscribers.

In the thirty years *Dwight's Journal of Music* was published, its editor,

namesake, and chief music critic barely made a living from it; constantly on
the brink of financial ruin, he and his paper were rescued many times by his
loyal friends, but after its first six years, the *Journal*'s finances became somewhat stabler when Dwight turned its production and distribution over to
Oliver Ditson and Company. The music-publishing firm ran its own advertising in the *Journal* and added inserts of printed music, while Dwight retained
complete editorial control. But twenty years later, when Ditson pressed him to
give the *Journal* a more popular slant, Dwight indignantly declined and took
his brainchild to Houghton, Osgood, and Company, publishers of the *Atlantic
Monthly*. But once again *Dwight's Journal of Music* could not pay its own way,
and a testimonial benefit concert arranged by Dwight's friends in 1880 only
briefly deferred its inevitable demise in 1881.

In his remaining years, Dwight devoted himself to activities with the Harvard Musical Association, of which he was now president as well as librarian.
His wife, Mary, had died in 1860, and since then he had made a bachelor's
abode at the association's rooms. He turned out a brief history of Boston's music, completed the first volume of a history of the Handel and Haydn Society,
and wrote freelance pieces for newspapers and magazines to the end.

Dwight's Journal of Music was basically a compendium of critical opinion,
concert reviews from various stringers in other American cities (including
Dwight himself, who sometimes journeyed to New York to attend concerts),
and reprints of think pieces on music from comparable European music periodicals, both from England and from the Continent (translated, of course).
Taking a cue from *Hach's Musical Magazine*, the *Journal* became the American
clearinghouse for distinguished musico-literary imports from abroad: it reprinted Forkel's biography of Bach, Schumann's advice to young musicians,
Liszt's sketches of Chopin, Oulibicheff's biography of Mozart, and even some
of the controversial essays of Richard Wagner.

The reviews in *Dwight's Journal* went beyond most newspaper reviews
of the time (but set the pattern for later ones) by listing full details of concert
programs, as well as fees of teachers, salaries of orchestral musicians, and other
factual obiter dicta, thus fleshing out a documentary picture of the musical life
of America during the third quarter of the 1800s. Dwight's stable of writers at
various points in the magazine's history included Alexander Wheelock Thayer,
the illustrious biographer of Beethoven, who contributed a column "From
My Diary" to the *Journal* for many years; the aforementioned purple prose–
monger George W. Curtis, who wrote under the sobriquet of Hafiz (pseudo-
nyms à la Schumann's Florestan and Eusebius being still stylish for music crit-

46   ics); and late in the *Journal*'s run, William Foster Apthorp, who went on to
become the principal critic of the influential *Boston Evening Transcript* for a
quarter century. True to his original evangelical form, Dwight anointed himself and his other correspondents in print with the term "missionary of art"
rather than music critic, and in fact he had done much to create the editorial
pulpit function for music critics. For instance, he had campaigned hard in
print for the appointment of the American composer John Knowles Paine as
the first professor of music at Harvard; when in 1875 Paine was given the first
such faculty chair in any American university, it was thought that Dwight had
been responsible.

W. F. Apthorp wrote that Dwight disfavored the then-ultramodern composers such as Wagner because he was "essentially a Hellene and an idealist;
any too drastic and realistic presentation of the morbid side of life shocked his
finer sensibilities." However that may be, it is oversimplifying to say that
Dwight was nothing more than an old fuddy-duddy, a johnny-one-note Beethoven idolater who wallowed in quasi-mystical verbiage and doctrinairely
dismissed non-"Hellene" music. Any close inspection of his writings shows
that he thoroughly pondered both his immediate auditory perceptions and his
secondary critical reactions and then rigorously imparted them to the reader,
without prejudice or taste preconceptions, with a cogent reason for every detail. In a review of the violinist Ole Bull, for instance, Dwight carefully differ-
entiates, with musical reasons given, one kind of kitsch from another, his criticism of one kind of playing to the gallery from another kind:

> His second piece: "To the Memory of Washington" was much less to our
> taste, setting out on a false tack, which always has proved fatal to the artist
> in every department of Art,—namely, with the design of giving an imag-
> inative representation, through tones, of a historical period, of a great na-
> tional struggle,—and forced, in order to get along with it, to resort to
> mere association, by introducing hackneyed patriotic tunes, as *Yankee
> Doodle,* piped and screamed alternately with strains of "God Save the
> King," amid discordant tremolos and battle storms of the whole orches-
> tra. Really these seemed very cheap and melodramatic effects. . . . In noth-
> ing however did he give us so much unalloyed pleasure, on Saturday eve-
> ning, as in his self-accompanied playing of the "Last Rose of Summer," in
> answer to an encore. It was exquisitely, feelingly beautiful. And this is one
> of his greatest arts, which he possesses, so far as we know, beyond all other
> violinists,—this of "double-stopping" so as to give a full quartet effect; he
> makes each of the four parts firm and individual, and the middle parts

move about like the "figural harmony" in good organ music. (*Dwight's* 47
Journal of Music [hereafter *DJM*], June 12, 1852)

It may seem on first glance that Dwight has betrayed his ignorance in using the
term "double-stopping" erroneously, as no modern violinist can play *sustained*
four-part harmony on a violin, but Ole Bull played a Norwegian hardanger
fiddle with an almost flat fingerboard and bridge and a concavely curved bow
that permitted him to execute just the sort of passage Dwight is describing; in
fact, playing in this manner was part of what made Bull a "superstar," though
Dwight may well have been unaware that the reason other players couldn't do
it was that they lacked Bull's fiddle and bow.

In a review of a New York performance by Jullien's Orchestra of Rossini's
Semiramide Overture, Dwight mentions so many textural details with such evident familiarity that one can only surmise that he either had had access to a
score beforehand or had attended several rehearsals, as the leading scholarly
resource to first performances in America records no earlier performance in
the United States of the *Semiramide* Overture:[18]

> The quartet of the horns was played deliciously sweet and crisp. The
> witching little theme of the violins, starting with those light and quick it-
> erations of the first note, was given with elastic delicacy and precision by
> the broad mass of strings, and the crescendos and diminuendos and re-
> tardandos, and other points of expression were caught with sympathetic
> unity and certainty from the expressive baton and gesture of the conduc-
> tor. We never heard an overture made so brilliantly effective. . . . We rec-
> ognized the truth of what is often said of the expressive indications of Jul-
> lien's baton, it seems spontaneously to trace the outline of each melodic
> figure in the air; were it a lighted stick and moving in the dark, we might
> almost *see* the music.

But Dwight goes on in the same review to take the conductor to task for failing to maneuver his total orchestral body of tone as one voice à la Toscanini, a
high-level criticism indeed for someone who had probably never heard the
overture played before and who was reviewing probably the greatest conductor in the world at the time:

> But we cannot say that we have yet heard a genuine *pianissimo* among its
> other remarkable virtues; it can play lightly as well as play loudly, it can
> drop out voices and contract its tens to units; but we do not observe that

48   wonderfully beautiful and ideal effect of an entire tone-mass subdued to
the distinctest whisper. (*DJM,* October 15, 1853)

Again and again, we see Dwight thinking independently. Although he
wrote in praise of the operas of Donizetti, attending a Boston performance in
1858 of Verdi's *Il Trovatore,* then only a few years past its composition and first
performance, Dwight wrote many criticisms of the opera that even today are
unexceptionable:

> In the first place, its horrible baby-burning plot is disgusting and ab-
> surd—the more glaringly so when sung in English. In the next place,
> there is not a real, a natural, an interesting character in it; the persons are
> all puppets, leaving no impression beyond the action of the moment; as
> impersonations of passion they are as coarse as the dullest caricatures in
> the cheapest wood-cuts. Then again, *sentiment,* anything that can be
> called such, is utterly wanting in the opera, as a whole, with only here and
> there a maudlin reminiscence in a strain or two. The music is accordingly;
> if there is an ingenious melody, it may please, but it does not speak to you,
> sing to you, as the native and intrinsic music of a sweet soul or character,
> as does the music of Mozart's Zerlina. It is music everywhere straining for
> effect, and sometimes producing it, externally, superficially, but not in-
> ternally or deeply. It is not pathos, but a coarse imitation of its most con-
> ventional and common forms. It lacks all fine and subtle touches. It says
> more than it means or feels. It is not the music of fine natures; it is not
> refining or elevating in its tendency. . . . Its appeal is really to something
> else than heart or soul; to those who seek excitement, recklessly, for mere
> excitement's sake, and not to those who live sincerely and in earnest. . . .
> And yet the *Trovatore* is popular! (*DJM,* October 2, 1858)

Writing about new music, even late in his career, when some have accused
him of arteriosclerosis of his earlier tastes and judgments, Dwight kept his ears
open to new sounds while showing a deft awareness of how styles grow out of
their antecedents. Writing on the world premiere of Tchaikovsky's First Piano
Concerto in Boston in 1875, Dwight is not at all condemnatory of

> the extremely difficult, strange, wild, ultra-modern Russian Concerto. It
> is the composition of a young professor at the Conservatory of Moscow,
> a pupil of Rubinstein (indeed the work contained not a few suggestions

of the master). . . . it opens richly and the first Allegro is full of striking passages and brilliant, but sometimes bizarre, effects of instrumentation. One peculiarity is the frequent indulgence of the pianoforte in rhapsodical cadenza-like flights of startling execution while the orchestra waits as it were outside. This lends quite a bravura character to a movement which seemed also melodramatic rather than in the classical Concerto spirit. The second movement, opening with a gentle, pastoral commingling of reeds and flutes, seemed also of the theatre; you thought of strains by Gounod, by the author of *Mignon,* and of Meyerbeer's *Dinorah.* Yet there was a certain delicacy and flavor of originality and quaintness about it. In the finale we had the wild Cossack fire and impetus without stint. (*DJM,* November 13, 1875)

Over the years Dwight managed to arrive by his own lights, years before the writings of Sir George Grove and other European specialists arrived on these shores, at a recognition of most of our now-canonical opinions about the classical repertoire. He was prescient about late Beethoven; he refers in a review of Anton Rubinstein in 1872 to "one of the most profoundly spiritual and subtly intellectual among Beethoven's Sonatas, the last of all, Opus 111" at a time when few if any American audiences had yet heard even a partial cycle of the thirty-two Beethoven sonatas and when the late quartets were still regarded as strange.

Dwight tended to give more space to the content of the composition and to the composer than to technical virtuosity; in reviewing the 1872 Rubinstein tour (with violinist Henri Wieniawski), he said more about Beethoven than about either artist. Yet he enthusiastically praised Louis Moreau Gottschalk's pianistic brilliance even while expressing reservations about the depth of Gottschalk's music, and he praised Sigismond Thalberg's interpretations of Beethoven even while correctly judging Thalberg's own compositions as salon music. At times Dwight would disparage the "mechanical-finger school" and the tendency of virtuoso soloists to obscure an understanding of the "higher" music, yet at other times he would hail the greatest virtuosos' works "not as mere feats of execution, but as intellectual creations." Dwight was too astute not to recognize that value in music is not a matter of doctrine, not an antinomian proposition of good music versus bad music, of emotion versus intellect, or of content versus virtuosity. He reviewed the pianist Hans von Bülow with a typical appreciation for music's contradictions: "We were hearing Beethoven, as afterwards, Chopin, far more than we were hearing Bülow. And that

50 perhaps is highest praise. At the same time on reflection we feel, as so many have felt, that he plays more from the head than from the heart. The effect produced *from him* is not precisely the inspiration of genius" (*DJM,* November 13, 1875).

When he wasn't writing reviews of concerts, Dwight used the *Journal* to campaign for improvements in the organized musical life of the country. An essay advocating a permanent residency and salary base for the Theodore Thomas Orchestra—which, after the fashion of Jullien's Orchestra, had traveled around the country for years and years like a twentieth-century dance band—displays in a nutshell Dwight's way of gently exhorting the powers that be in the right direction by striking all the right chords:

> And *ought* it not be a model orchestra? It is the only orchestra in this country that can be said to have a chance. For in the first place Mr. Thomas has his pick of artists; he can offer them year-round engagements, with good, sure salaries, so that they can make this their sole and constant occupation, playing always in one orchestra, under the same superior Conductor, always "up" in all the music old and new of any high pretensions, and kept aloof from damaging associations with tasks less artistic. With that power, what can a man not do, if he have it in him? Whereas, in any given city, so small as ours for instance, a musician plays once a fortnight in a Symphony concert (for a few months only), and all the rest of the time perhaps must earn his bread and butter in a street band, or a theatre, or by playing all night for balls and parties, to come back jaded and sleepless to the next rehearsal of a Symphony. For local Symphony and Philharmonic orchestras there can be no sure hold upon the best musicians because these offer them no constant and supporting occupation, but only seek their services for six or ten concerts in a winter. . . . Besides, preparing for this endless round of concerts, they can afford to spend time and breath upon the trail of new works . . . and here again they gain a knowledge of the new effects of instrumentation, often brilliant or otherwise interesting, and in which Liszt and Berlioz and Wagner are masters . . . all this keeps up their virtuosity, as difficult *études* do with the pianist, and makes all their task more sure and easy. (*DJM,* December 14, 1872)

In a similar vein, he wrote sympathetically of a cause that outwardly seems at odds with his elitist view of art: the Gilmore Peace Jubilees—outdoor con-

certs for audiences of as many as ten thousand (the nineteenth-century equivalent of drive-in movies), where the fine points of a Beethoven symphony
could scarcely be expected to register:

> Whether the Festival, considered musically, were very good or not, it mu-
> sically *did* good. . . . It has caused hundreds of choral societies to spring
> into existence for the time being, many of which will certainly prove per-
> manent; and their first bond of union has been the practice of *good* mu-
> sic, of master-works of Handel, Haydn, Mozart, Mendelssohn, which,
> having tasted once in such deep draughts, they will not readily abandon
> for weak trash. Education must come out of it. . . . it has given to tens of
> thousands of all classes . . . who were there to hear . . . a new belief in Mu-
> sic; a new conviction of its social worth; above all, of its importance as a
> pervading, educational and fusing element in our whole democratic life;
> a heavenly influence which shall go far to correct the crudities, tone
> down, subdue and harmonize the loud, self-asserting individualities,
> relieve the glaring and forthputting egotism of our too boisterous and
> boastful. (*DJM*, June 25, 1869)

The constructively edifying tone and lack of meanness of spirit in
Dwight's attitude toward the Gilmore Peace Jubilee has to be interpreted in
light of the prevailing concert decorum of the times, which he was trying to
improve. An article from an unnamed New York journal republished by
Dwight on May 14, 1864, speaks volumes in describing the habits of American
concertgoers: old gentlemen pulling out and crinkling newspapers during the
most *pianissimo* passages; "dowagers of fashion" gossiping aloud or falling
asleep and snoring aloud; ladies knitting during the music; young people flirt-
ing, "talking, laughing, fan-gyrating . . . performing the part of wall flowers staring . . . programme crumpling, and chair-shuffling. We might almost
add lorgnetting," [19] as well as platform difficulties such as piano accompanists
drowning out the singers, performers so ready and eager to perform encores
that they repeated the entire program, and so on. In such a primitive climate
for the reception of high culture, the idealistic and high-minded Dwight per-
force had to be diplomatic and democratic in his approach if he wished to win
converts.

An excellent example of Dwight's lack of dogmatism is his attitude toward
African-American music during the heyday of Stephen Foster, white minstrelsy, and "Ethiopian" music. As a New Englander Dwight fervently opposed

52   slavery, but as a champion of European art music he was wary of African-derived music. Yet when the black Fisk Jubilee Singers became prominent entertainers after the Civil War, Dwight actually went so far as to state in print that "the American school of music has been discovered."

Still, when the end of the line finally came for *Dwight's Journal of Music,* Dwight viewed his quest as a defeated one. Despite his exertions, the American public "had not been converted en masse to classical music; its taste for popular music appeared to be undiminished, and the rising music trades were only too happy to pander to it."[20] Wrote the weary Dwight in his last issue, published September 3, 1881: "The musical papers that live and flourish financially are those . . . which abound in endless columns of insignificant three-line items of intelligence or news; the slang term 'newsy' is a description they covet. A journal which devotes itself to art for art's sake, and strives to serve the ends of culture, however earnestly and ably, gets praise and compliments, but not support."

Of course, the *Journal's* collective readership could never have been more than a few thousand, and only as a critic for a daily metropolitan newspaper could Dwight have hoped to have reached great masses of people. As Irving Sablosky notes, "He had conceived a lofty musical culture growing from a convergence of the old American singing school–convention tradition on one hand and the great German tradition of classical music on the other—a culture at once popular and pure, in which the people would have learned to prefer, spontaneously, the experience of 'the True, the *ever* Beautiful, the Divine' to anything vulgar, ephemeral, *ad captandum.*"[21] Nevertheless, Dwight's words and those of his many far-flung correspondents and the European writers that he reprinted did reach a select but influential audience of community leaders, university and literary people, and others in position to implement, sometimes directly, sometimes indirectly, many of his ideas. Dwight was the conscience of music criticism in nineteenth-century America, wreaking good works both morally and practically, promoting the higher musical consciousness of people who could form orchestras like the Boston Symphony and establish conservatories like the New England Conservatory of Music, opened during his editorship.

Dwight's Journal of Music, the first such publication in the United States to last, established the tradition in America for an enlightened, cultivated audience to seek consecration of its love of classical music between the covers of specialized magazines. *Dwight's Journal* also paved the way for general literary and cultural magazines to incorporate classical music coverage into their compass, as we shall later see.

> *America's first*
> *opera connoisseur:*   The transcendentalist gravitational field that drew so
> *Walt Whitman*   many writers and thinkers into its musical orbit was
>   not the only phenomenon responsible during those
times for literary folk taking up their pens to write and report on music. The
nineteenth century was an era that had blessedly not yet succumbed to the
modern disease of specialization, and it was then a tradition for men and
women of belles-lettres to take an interest in all the arts. Washington Irving
wrote about concerts for the New York newspapers; Henry Wadsworth Longfellow sponsored amateur musicales; Edgar Allan Poe briefly edited the *Broadway Journal,* which ran articles about music. Even a future president of the
United States left some choice words to posterity about his symphony-going
experiences: John Quincy Adams, hearing the first London performance of
Beethoven's *Wellington's Victory* on March 13, 1816, wrote, not without discernment, "Bad music, but patriotic." [22]

But one great writer of nineteenth-century American literature actually
worked as a newspaper music critic: the poet Walt Whitman. Whitman was so
influenced in his art by serious concert music (primarily opera) that he himself wrote in the *Saturday Press* of January 7, 1860, "Walt Whitman's method in
the construction of his songs is strictly the method of the Italian Opera." And
later in life he confided to his friend John Townsend Trowbridge, "But for the
opera I could never have written *Leaves of Grass.*" [23]

Whitman, born in 1819, had begun his freelance journalism career around
1840 writing for the *Brooklyn Evening Star,* about five years after he had started
to attend concerts on a regular basis, as he later recalled. [24] At first he wrote
mostly about popular music. In an article in the Poe-edited *Broadway Journal* for November 29, 1845, called "Art-Singing and Heart-Singing," Whitman
comments at length on a performance of the Cheney family, a folksinging
quartet of three boys and one girl, all children of Simeon Pease Cheney, a well-
known New Hampshire preacher, who at the time were professional rivals
to the then more famous family singers the Hutchinsons. Whitman came to
publish a reworked version of the same article, this time called "Music That
Is Music," in the *Brooklyn Daily Eagle* on December 4, 1846, a newspaper of
which he was the editor.

By then Whitman had evidently been sedulously attending concerts of
serious music by the star musicians of the day who were beginning to make
a New York tour every year, for in the article Whitman drops the names of
Ernesto Sivori, the Italian violinist and composer who had been a pupil of Pa-

54   ganini, the pianist Leopold de Meyer, and the Italian operatic contralto Rosina Pico, and with a blasé disdain also alludes to "the New York concerts with the florid Italian and French music." At this stage Whitman was on the "A" list of complimentary tickets given to music critics, along with Henry Watson, Richard Grant White, and the other critics of the Manhattan-based newspapers, and at least thirteen articles exclusively about music appeared in the *Eagle* while he was editor. On October 9, 1846, reviewing a concert of the American-born prodigy violinist Joseph Burke, Whitman referred to Burke's playing of "The Carnival of Venice" as the equal of that of Ole Bull, but whether Whitman had heard Bull or was merely fibbing à la Richard Grant White is not known.

That Whitman may have read the *Dial,* the *Harbinger,* or otherwise absorbed something of the transcendentalists' views on music is suggested by a vigorously worded editorial he wrote in the *Eagle* on September 8, 1847:

> Great is the power of music over a people! As for us of America, we have long enough followed obedient and child-like in the track of the Old World. We have received her tenors and her buffos, her operatic troupes and her vocalists, of all grades and complexions; listened to and applauded the songs made for a different state of society—made perhaps by royal genius, but made to please royal ears likewise; and it is time that such listening and receiving should cease. The subtlest spirit of a nation is expressed through its music—and the music acts reciprocally on the nation's very soul.—Its effects may not be seen in a day, or a year, and yet these effects are potent invisibly. They enter into religious feelings—they tinge the manners and morals—they are active even in the choice of legislators and magistrates. Tariff can be varied to fit circumstances— (though we don't believe it will ever be varied again in any way but a more free trade way,) bad laws obliterated and good ones formed; those enactments which relate to commerce or national policy, built up or taken away, stretched or concentrated, to suit the will of the government for the time being. But no human power can thoroughly suppress the spirit which lives in national lyrics, and sounds in the favorite melodies sung by high and low.

James Gibbons Huneker was later to write of his meeting with Whitman, "I do recall that he said . . . that music was his chief recreation—of which art he knew nothing; it seemed to him as a sounding background for his pencilled improvisations,"*[25] and, to be sure, in his concert reviews Whitman, compared with Henry Watson or J. S. Dwight, is unapologetically unlearned and impressionistic, as with his notice on the American premiere of Mendelssohn's oratorio *Elijah* by the New York Sacred Music Society on November 8, 1847:

> The music, judged by the rules of the art, is of the highest importance, but it is too elaborately scientific for the public ear. It is, besides, too heavy in its general character, and wants relief of a proper proportion of lightness and melody. There is scarcely a striking and pleasant air in it. To a mere musician, however, it would offer study and delight for years. . . . although the audience was large and sat out the performance, it was evident that no degree of pleasure was derived from it. (*Brooklyn Daily Eagle,* November 9, 1847)

Despite his nativistic tub-thumping in the *Brooklyn Daily Eagle* editorials, as the years went on Whitman became increasingly enamored with Italian opera. In March 1847, according to Robert Faner, "there is a short statement declaring the cordial treatment accorded the representative of the *Daily Eagle* by members of Palmo's opera company, about which another journal had complained. Possibly Whitman had now become known to some of the singers or managers, though there is little else from his pen to support such a belief." Then on March 23, 1847, Whitman wrote a review of Rossini's *Barber of Seville.* Adds Faner, "In it, his comments on the relative merits of members of the cast and his recommendations for substitutions show a familiarity with many of the leading operatic singers of the time which he could have gained only by having heard them sing."[26]

Whitman left the editorship of the *Eagle* in 1847 but continued freelance writing about the opera for other publications. On August 14, 1851, he published a "Letter from Paumanok" in the *New York Evening Post,* describing the pleasures of opera-going while picturing an imaginary performance of Donizetti's *La Favorita.* Whitman also writes, "After traveling through the fifteen years display in this city of musical celebrities, from Mrs. Austin up to Jenny Lind, from Ole Bull on to the conductor Benedict, with much fair enjoyment of the talent of all, none have thoroughly satisfied, overwhelmed me but Bet-

---

*Robert Faner (*Whitman,* p. 50) wrote that there existed in 1951 a manuscript fragment that shows that Whitman at one stage of his career was not even sure of the precise function of the violin in orchestral instrumentation. "The first E-flat or B-flat cornet generally leads the band," wrote the poet. "Does the first violin lead?"

56 tini." Whitman also repeatedly praised the Italian contralto Marietta Alboni. In another such long essay on opera in the November 10, 1855, issue of *Life Illustrated* Whitman discusses Verdi's *Ernani* in detail and mentions several singers prominent at the time: Marini, Steffanone, La Grange, Brignoli, and Amodio.

The four operas Whitman mentioned the most in his journalistic writings were Donizetti's *Lucrezia Borgia* and *La Favorita,* Bellini's *Norma,* and Verdi's *Ernani.* What is more interesting is that in *Leaves of Grass* he mentions the following operas: *La Sonnambula, Norma, Poliuto, Lucia di Lammermoor, Ernani, I Puritani, La Favorita, William Tell, Les Huguenots, The Prophet, Robert le Diable, Faust, Don Juan, Il Trovatore, Lucrezia Borgia,* as well as Rossini's *Stabat Mater* and Haydn's *Creation.* As well, there are 206 occurrences of musical terms in *Leaves of Grass,* of which 123 are terms relating to vocal music, and 83 of these are specifically related to the opera.[27] Perhaps only Ernest Hemingway among American writers, who as a very young man worked as correspondent in Paris for the *Toronto Star,* cannibalized as much material from his daily journalism for his literary writing.

Though relatively untutored in music, Whitman was as capable of discerning judgments as a music critic. In 1851 he heard Jenny Lind, and in an undated extract he bemusedly wrote:

> The Swedish Swan, with all her blandishments, never touched my heart in the least. I wondered at so much vocal dexterity; and indeed they were all very pretty, those leaps and double somersets. But even in the grandest religious airs, genuine masterpieces as they are, of the German composers, executed by this strangely overpraised woman in perfect scientific style, let critics say what they like, it was a failure; for there was a vacuum in the head of the performance. Beauty pervaded it no doubt, and that of a high order. It was the beauty of Adam, before God breathed into his nostrils.[28]

Whitman also told his friend Horace Traubel late in life regarding Wagner's *Ring,* "I question the wisdom of selecting Jack and the Beanstalk stories and putting them into this modern medium."[29]

∾ *Recapitulation*   As we have seen, the growth of musical journalism in the United States was paralleled almost from the beginning by a tradition of literary writers and public intellectuals taking up their pens for the cause of classical music—writing about it, appreciating it, championing it for public consumption. Whether they were poets like Whitman, moral philosophers like Emerson, statesmen like Charles Dana, or general purpose journalists like George W. Curtis, legions got into the soup. Classical music was part of the Agenda of Culture, especially literary culture. The Compleat Culture layman had to have a classical music arrow in his quiver.

Meanwhile, John Sullivan Dwight sat astride the two camps of specialized music journalism and generalized cultural exhortation. His unique style of perceiving and celebrating the idealistic content of art music had an incalculable influence on subsequent music criticism in this country as late as the 1940s, when the *New York Times*'s Olin Downes was still disclosing spiritual dimensions in the music of Sibelius to his readers. In fact, even today, the newer critical appreciations of such composers as Górecki and Arvo Pärt may have an antecedent in Dwight's approach.

Postlude: From three-part to two-part counterpoint — The traditions of daily music journalism and slower, more reflective magazine music journalism, both born in the 1830s, would survive and endure till the millennium. The tradition of writing about classical music as part of the general intellectual and public discourse would encounter a different fate, as we shall go on to see.

3

American Music Criticism's First Empire

The Long Day's Journey into Night of the "Old Guard"

The newspaper now fills the place in the musician's economy which a century ago was filled in Europe by the courts and nobility. Its support, indirect as well as direct, replaces the patronage which erstwhile came from these powerful ones.
—HENRY E. KREHBIEL, *How to Listen to Music*, 1896

[We are] knights of the inky cloak, who ride upon the high horse of aestheticism, clad in the armor of fact and armed with that small but effective lance, the pen.
—W. J. HENDERSON, *New York Times*, January 21, 1889

I t has variously been referred to as the Gilded Age; the Plush Era; the Genteel Era; the Age of the Robber Barons. Lewis Mumford dubbed the period the Brown Decades, Van Wyck Brooks the Confident Years, and the American historian Vernon Parrington even bestowed the label "The Great Barbecue." However appellated, the years from the end of Reconstruction in the United States to the First World War were years of unprecedented commitment of private wealth toward the public arts in this country, commitment on a scale theretofore, and perhaps thereafter, unmatched in constant dollars per capita. The Civil War was safely behind, and enlightened industrialists began to open their wallets not just for Mammon but for Parnassus. Museums, opera houses, symphony orchestras, and concert halls were built with the largesse of private fortunes until 1913 untaxed by the federal government. Henry Higginson in Boston financially carried the Boston Symphony Orchestra virtually single-handedly for some thirty years during this period. Later historians have borrowed the phrase "conspicuous consumption," coined by Thorstein Veblen, author of *The Theory of the Leisure Class,* to describe the behavior of Gilded Age boxholders at the opera. And concomitantly, there was an increase in the appetite and curiosity of the larger but less monied public to soak it all in, to "get Culture."

The newspapers took note, allotting far more column space to their music critics than they ever would again. The freshman class of newspaper music critics at the dawn of the Gilded Age stayed on well beyond it, from 1875 on to 1925, 1930, 1935. They stayed at their posts from gaslight and horse-and-buggy times till the era of subways, talking pictures, and airplanes, from President Garfield to FDR, veritable walking time machines. They started as cub reporters, precocious and arrogant whippersnappers, and stayed in the trenches for decades until they had become Grand Old Men, living legends whispered about in newspaper city rooms.

The marathon career critics (who numbered less than a dozen) of New York and Boston were aptly dubbed the "Old Guard" by their junior colleague Oscar Thompson. The big three of New York—W. J. Henderson, H. E. Krehbiel, and H. T. Finck—all were militant Wagner enthusiasts. They didn't make much money from music criticism. Many of the Old Guard wore extra hats as drama or book critics. Because the reviewing season was short, most of them had the time to commit energy to entire side careers, both to earn extra money and to pursue collateral paths of intellectual interest. All wrote music appreciation books and lectured to the public. Most of them were thoroughly schooled in music theory, and some were professional pedagogues at the same time as they were newspaper critics.

All of the Old Guard were opera devotees, in an era when opera was at once "by far the most important social event in the United States"[1] and, because of Wagnerism, the cynosure of the cutting edge in art. The critics of that time had about an hour and a half to turn in their copy after the concert or opera, but only at the top of the old Met was there a pressroom where the reviewer could work.

All of the Old Guard overstayed their leaves, forced to deal with new currents in the arts they couldn't understand. They started reviewing the American premieres of Brahms symphonies and endured to have to face Stravinsky, Schoenberg, and Varèse. All were more or less bitter enemies of the modernist composers that emerged on their watch: "futurists," they called them, or

60 worse. All the Old Guard were unreconstructed harmonic grammarians who judged new music according to the old rules well past Schoenberg's 1909 *Klavierstücke,* op. 11.

These men (and one woman, as we shall see) created the "first empire" in American music criticism. James Gibbons Huneker, one of their group, was different enough from the rest to be treated as a separate case. The Old Guard were the first critics to write program notes for their city's orchestras. Though they fraternized with the musicians they wrote about to a degree unheard of today, they stopped taking the graft that had been the stock in trade of their predecessors. They inherited the canonized repertoire of Beethoven, Handel, Mendelssohn, and Chopin, and added to it Bach, Berlioz, Liszt, Wagner, Tchaikovsky, Dvořák, and Brahms, among others. By the time their tours of duty had ended they had educated a new army of music lovers who made one-man philanthropies like Henry Higginson's unnecessary, music lovers who contributed their money to the support of symphony orchestras either through subscription sales or by joining the orchestra's boards. When the Old Guard critics died, their passing was attended by the press obsequies accorded other civic dignitaries. Classical music critics had never before been so important and were never again to be so influential.

The Old Guard were arguably as responsible for codifying and consolidating what we have inherited as the standardized classical repertory as were the conductors. Many now-forgotten composers were given abundant premieres by nineteenth-century American orchestras: symphonic works and operas by Hermann Gradener, Arnold Krug, Franz Lachner, Edmund Severn Jr., Gustav Strube, Robert Volkmann, Felix Draeseke, Paul Gilson, and August Lindner, to name but a few, all were reviewed by the Old Guardians at the same time that they were reviewing the premieres of now-chestnuts by Dvořák and Tchaikovsky. But when it came time to write program notes or music appreciation books or magazine essays, the Old Guard siphoned the lesser fellows out of the loop by simply not writing them up and by redoubling their focus on our now-standard repertoire items. Certainly they were wrongheaded, too, in rejecting (sometimes only temporarily) such later staples as Mahler, Strauss, Bruckner, even Brahms; but many more second-raters were justly weeded out.

In a pre-TV era when symphony and opera meant more to the community than today, whatever a music critic of the Old Guard wrote in the paper had the sort of impact that talk show hosts' ad libs can carry today. Wrote one music journalist in 1905:

In spite of our fancied independence, our musical authorities lead us pretty much where they will. . . . An amusing instance of this influence was the effect of an opinion given recently by Mr. Henderson, of the *Sun,* in one of his Sunday essays. He declared that a certain tenor's voice was going off, on account of a habit which was gaining on him of holding onto his high notes and exploding them for the benefit of his fellow-countrymen who nightly crowd the Opera House behind the rails. During the week that followed it was amazing to see how many people had discovered the sad fact of this tenor's "going off." Heads were shaken over him. "It was a pity about those high notes," "So and so isn't what he was last season," and so on, until one knew exactly what would be said should the subject of opera be introduced. They might have discovered it for themselves, but at least it was a coincidence.[2]

The daily life of a foot soldier of the Old Guard was not one of leisure; overwork and underpay was the rule. In the October 28, 1911, *Musical America,* the columnist "Mephisto" painted this picture:

Few people realize what the duties of the critic of a big metropolitan daily have become. . . . As Mr. Finck of the *Evening Post* said in your paper some time ago, "What the critics need is more sleep!" . . . Just figure for yourself for a moment the number of opera performances, orchestral performances, recitals and concerts that call for the critic's attention, and where all those personally interested expect a careful review "the morning after." The matter is indeed one that is physically impossible; some are often treated to the sight of a critic rushing away before the performance is over, that he may appear at the fag end of another performance somewhere else. . . .

I have heard Mr. Krehbiel criticized for his intimacy with a leading piano house; for his intimacy with a certain music publisher; with certain directors of orchestral concerts; with certain prime donne. . . . the business administration of our metropolitan dailies has not yet awakened to the fact that the musical activities of a New York season are wholly beyond the power of a single critic to properly chronicle [and] that the musical critic is entitled not merely to a stipend which barely enables him to live in ordinary decency, but to one that should put him not only above suspicion, but above the necessity of having to earn money by giving lectures, writing books and teaching pupils, so as to make both ends meet.

Not terribly long before the critics became so battle fatigued, conditions for the reception of music were even less propitious. Let's look back.

The state of music appreciation and criticism, 1850–1875
Notwithstanding the commitment of a few critics and the heartening advances of symphonic music for the many, by the third quarter of the nineteenth century the state of American musical letters was still primitive by certain modern standards, even in the urban centers. Henry Finck wrote in the 1920s that when Theodore Thomas began his career in New York in the 1850s he and the pianist William Mason "started a small organization for giving chamber music. They knew not how to collect an audience, so they took bundles of their programs and stood at the corners on Fourteenth Street distributing them personally to passers-by! Could anything give a more vivid idea of the 'preliminary' condition of musical affairs at that time!"[3] Twenty-five years later publicity and distribution in New York had become more professionalized but also more commercialized:

> Musical journalism in the 1880s was not, to be sure, a pretty business. Rival piano manufacturers supported the various publications and used them for advertising. When newspaper critics thumbed down artists who happened to prefer a certain make of piano, they were denounced by journals in which the manufacturer of that piano advertised. Sometimes the critics were blasted by the same journal for which, at other times, they wrote feature articles. Ugly language and libel actions were profuse.[4]

From 1850 to 1875 concert programs in the big eastern cities were gradually becoming less like vaudeville olios of arias and frontier songs and more like modern concerts, as such critics as John R. G. Hassard, writing in *Century* magazine in the 1870s, attested. When Adelina Patti returned to New York in the early 1880s with the same kind of program of popular ballads she had sung there in the early 1850s, the audiences were disgruntled that she didn't also sing the program of opera arias and lieder that she had sung in Europe. But farther west progress lagged behind, as the *Chicago Tribune* critic George Upton's review of an 1869 performance of Schubert's "Unfinished" by the Theodore Thomas Orchestra witnesses: "Did we not all think we had heard an orchestra play before? And yet this was something new! You had a crescendo! You first heard a musical ppp and, rarest of all things, you heard an orchestra play in time and tune."

Many reviews of this period, and not only from outside the Boston–New York axis, attest to frequent large-scale walkouts of the audience, even for works now considered canonical. Louis Elson reported that at the Boston premiere of Strauss's *Aus Italien,* "the auditors marched out by platoons . . . there will be no urgent demand for its speedy repetition" (*Boston Daily Advertiser,* December 22, 1888).

Despite the pioneering efforts of J. S. Dwight, Henry Watson, Walt Whitman, and William Henry Fry (whom we will meet in a later chapter), much of American newspaper music criticism by the Reconstruction was still elementary. Reviews went largely unsigned until late in the century, and Henry Finck says that even in 1880 most of the nation's newspaper critics of art and music "had only the most elementary training"; his Boston colleague W. F. Apthorp stated, "I have come across professed musical critics in this country who did not know, and showed plainly in their writings that they did not know, the real meaning of such terms as *score, instrumentation, intonation*—terms of everyday occurrence in criticism."[5] The immortal composer pantheon, and the alliterative three B's, had yet to be established; Apthorp says that before 1880 Mendelssohn, Chopin, Handel, and Schumann were accepted as canonical by Bostonians, but not Berlioz, Wagner, Liszt, Brahms, or even Bach, while the midwest critic W. S. B. Mathews reported that as late as the 1870s Schumann was considered pretty avant-garde.

Even *Dwight's Journal* sometimes ran pedicular critical prose; try stomaching this anonymous correspondent's review of an 1856 New York performance of Bach's Concerto for Three Claviers and Strings (played on pianos):

> The tyrannical exaction which this author makes of the performer in sacrificing every collateral idiosyncrasy of ornament, absolute and accurate rendering and attainment of the purposeful effect in his theme was carefully made by the different artists. . . . the leaven of blurred blockwork of the tyro instrumentalists was forgotten whilst the splendid artistic rendering of the occasion shadowed forth the truly sculpturesque effects designed by the incomparable author. . . . the crowded comprehensiveness of his works, their force and realness, their masterly vigor and their

dignified elevation and airy impress was of the full and relative value in music of what the great Rubens is in historical painting.

In his 1898 book, *What Is Good Music,* W. J. Henderson decried such "foolish and rhapsodical criticism, which pretends to see definite poetic imagery in music. A correct understanding of the true nature of musical expressiveness would at once expose the fallacy of such criticism." Harder still to swallow is the wrongheadedness of even some musically literate critics; this anonymous review of the Boston premiere by the Boston Symphony in 1882 of Brahms's easy-to-listen-to Serenade No. 1 in D is astonishing:

> The work on first hearing is generally unintelligible and not enjoyable, and in truth, if the very critical audience which listened to it on Saturday night may be considered as a competent judge, this is true as was evident from the very feeble, uncertain, and perfunctory applause which was awarded it. Musical people as a rule have not yet got "educated" by music of the future up to that point where they may enjoy passages bereft of all tonality, by meandering through doors of modulation, around corners of accidentals, and through mazes of chromatics that lead nowhere unless it be to the realm of giddiness. (*Boston Advertiser,* October 29, 1882)

How did the better music critics of the time try to raise the listening level of American audiences? One way was to write reviews so as subtly to nudge the concert producers as well as the audiences, as in this review of Schumann's oratorio *Paradise and the Peri,* a now rarely heard 1843 work given an amazing dozen performances in the United States before 1890 (oratorios were more popular and frequently programmed in the nineteenth century than in ours):

> It is a comfort to be able to record a really creditable musical enterprise for this city, for such undoubtedly was last night's performance of Schumann's lovely Cantata. Such a work necessarily falls somewhat dead on an uncultivated audience. For the great public listens to the solo voice. For this it has ears to hear. The chorus is valuable, to be sure, as a relief for the solos, and by way of contrast, but we pay our money, dear manager, to hear solos.
>
> Undoubtedly the instrumentation is too voluminous. This had the effect to minify the voices, making them sound like mannikins. It was this unspoken attitude of mind which is common to large audiences every-

where, that hindered a large part of the audience last night from putting themselves thoroughly *en rapport* with the music. (W. S. B. Mathews, *DJM*, March 7, 1874, on the Chicago performance)

Another was to pick up the gauntlet J. S. Dwight had laid down and redouble the crusade to recruit as many ears as possible to the beauties of serious music, to the joys and rewards of its appreciation that had been extolled by Emerson, as well as by Schopenhauer, Nietzsche, and Matthew Arnold. To improve the climate for appreciation and understanding of classical music, opined W. J. Henderson in an 1898 answer to a letter from a reader of the *New York Times,*

The way to elevate is to elevate. . . . First of all, abolish the music halls in which vulgar tunes set to still more vulgar words provide the musical milk upon which the young of the masses are reared. Abolish the diabolical street pianos and hand organs which disseminate these vile tunes in all directions and which reduce the musical taste of the children in the residence streets to the level of that of the Australian bushman, who thinks noise and rhythm are music. Abolish the genuine American brand of burlesque . . . and the genuine American "comic opera." . . . Abolish the theatre orchestra which plays the music hall stuff. . . . Abolish those newspapers which degrade art by filling their columns with free advertising of so-called musical performers who are of the genus freak.

In the last analysis the only real way out of this situation was for the better critics to be hired by the most influential newspapers in the cities with the largest musical activity, which is exactly what started to happen in the last quarter of the nineteenth century. W. F. Apthorp had announced to readers of the *Atlantic Monthly* in January 1875 that "culture is infectious. Where the most highly cultivated nucleus exists, there will be the highest cultivation." So the critics simply had to become better, which they did. As a group they were more musically literate, less dilettantish, and more morally committed to careers as critics than the critics of New York's penny dailies of the 1830s and 1840s, the Willises, Whites, and Saronis.

The first of the new breed (veterans like Richard Grant White and Henry C. Watson were still around in the 1870s) was John Rose Green Hassard (1836–88). College educated, he began his journalistic career in Chicago and in 1866 joined the staff of the *New York Tribune* as an editorial writer and literary and

66   music critic. Henry Krehbiel succeeded him as music critic in 1884. Henry
        Finck said in the 1920s that Hassard was considered the leading music critic in
        the 1870s. Hassard and a writer named Schwab for the *New York Times* were
        dispatched by their respective papers to cover the first Bayreuth in 1876. Has-
        sard was a sensitive, intelligent critic and a poetic but not over-rhapsodic
        writer. Had he lived longer he might well have been one of the important
        critics.

*Opening Night
with critics of the*   One way to assess the varying styles of the Boston–New
Golden Age: York critics of the Gilded Age is to make a capsule com-
A sampler   parison of their respective "first hearing" reactions to
        the same composers and works. Here are two responses
to a performance of Borodin's Symphony No. 2 in B Minor at Carnegie Hall,
February 5, 1897, by the New York Philharmonic under Anton Seidl:

> The Second Symphony is in parts picturesque, especially in the wild and
> lawless finale allegro which led a lady in the audience to remark per-
> tinently that it suggested the advance of a horde of Indians on horse-
> back bent on scalping you. The symphony was admirably interpreted.
> (Henry T. Finck, *New York Evening Post*)

> The symphony is intensely Russian in character, and modern in the com-
> plexity of its key relationships. It is energy and aggressiveness without
> power and is generally brilliant without beauty. (W. J. Henderson, *New
> York Times*)

On a performance of Borodin's *In the Steppes of Central Asia* by the Brooklyn
Philharmonic under Theodore Thomas at the Brooklyn Academy of Music,
March 23, 1886:

> It is an ingenious bit of programme music of a most obvious character
> with two melodic subjects that are introduced separately and then
> blended with original effects of harmony and instrumentation over a per-
> sistent figure, suggestive of the movement of animals, and under a sus-
> tained high note on the violins — the usual device for delineating distance
> and monotony in music. (Henry Krehbiel, *New York Tribune*)

And on the first Boston performance of the same, by Arthur Nikisch and the Boston Symphony, February 26, 1892:

> We are apt to associate the composition of the modern Russian school with alcohol and dynamite. We have been warned against evolutionary principles and we have been told that Russia's musical Nihilism included even the rejection of the modern system of tonality. But certainly this "Scene from Central Asia" is neither amorphous nor Nihilistic. On the contrary it is charming in its form, clearly written, full of an originality that attracts and does not repel. (Philip Hale, *Boston Home Journal*)

On an October 30, 1891, performance of Strauss's *Don Juan,* again by the BSO under Nikisch:

> He has out-Wagnered Wagner in the fullness of his scoring. Yet we are much mistaken if he has not overshot the mark. The single pair of trumpets in a Mozart score has more brilliancy of effect than all Strauss' seven brass instruments together. When he wishes to put an extra cut edge to his orchestra, he had nothing for it but to take to the cymbals. There is a constant strenuousness of being at 90 degrees in the shade at all times that overreaches itself. (W. F. Apthorp, *Boston Transcript,* November 2, 1891)

Whereas Henry Krehbiel found Rimsky-Korsakov's *Capriccio Italien* to be "a bit of entertainment music, a skillful toying with popular strains, an exhibition of pretty effects which can be obtained by clothing simple melodies having sharp rhythms with the brilliant hues of the modern orchestra" (*New York Tribune,* November 6, 1886), W. J. Henderson dubbed it "a sort of orchestral chow-chow with hot spicing all the way" (*New York Times,* November 6, 1886). And whereas Henry T. Finck wrote of the 1894 New York premiere of the *Pathétique* Symphony, "No other composer, not even Mozart, has written a more pathetic farewell to the world than Tchaikovsky has in this *adagio lamentoso* which in melody, harmony, and orchestration is overwhelmingly sad and lugubrious, yet of superlative musical beauty" (*New York Evening Post,* March 19, 1894), an 1886 New York premiere of Tchaikovsky's *Manfred* Overture prompted Henderson to write, "Few more pretentious and absolutely vacuous works have been made known" (*New York Times,* December 4, 1886).

Let's now meet these knights of the inky cloak, career Hall of Famers in

68   what critic and lexicographer Oscar Thompson so aptly dubbed the "Old Guard."

ॐ *W. F. Apthorp,*
    Boston's musical   Unlike New York, where musical life was already by
    Brahmin   the mid-1840s well under the influence of daily penny
                             newspaper critics such as Henry Watson and Richard
Grant White, in Boston the first music critics tended to write for small-circulation magazines such as *Dwight's Journal of Music.* The profile of music critics in Boston's daily press was slower to emerge. Cornelia Walter wrote some music reviews for the *Boston Evening Transcript* in the 1840s, but they were not discerning critiques. Perhaps the first two newspaper music critics to become name presences in Boston were George Washington Peck and Benjamin Woolf. Peck (1817–59) was, like George William Curtis and other nineteenth-century dilettante critics, a man of many seasons whom history has forgotten. Peck had chosen to study law under Richard Henry Dana, a lawyer now remembered as the author of *Two Years before the Mast.* Peck was admitted to the bar and practiced law for a while, but like Dana he was more interested in belles-lettres: he wrote and published sonnets, book reviews, and a Swiftian satire of the California Gold Rush, entitled *Aurifodina,* authored under the Ambrose Bierce–like pseudonym "Cantell A. Bigly." But Peck also was a contributor of articles on music and drama to the *Boston Post* in the 1840s. In 1845 he even founded the *Boston Musical Review,* but two years later left Boston for New York.

Benjamin Edward Woolf (1836–1901), born in London, also multifaceted, was a composer, violinist, and libretto writer who married an actress, joined the *Boston Globe* in 1870 and the following year the *Evening Gazette,* for which he wrote music and drama reviews; in the 1890s he left the *Gazette* for the *Herald.* The American organist Henry M. Dunham wrote in his memoirs of Woolf's criticism, "We disliked him extremely because of his rough and uncompromising style. He had almost no concession to offer for anyone's shortcomings, and on that very account what he had to say carried additional weight with the artist he was criticizing."[6] On the other hand, Philip Hale, Woolf's *Herald* successor, asserted that Woolf had been caustic only toward "incompetence, shams, humbugs, snobs and snobbery in art" and noted that when Woolf began to write for the *Gazette,* music criticism in Boston was mere "honey daubing" of local favorites.[7] Hale added that toward "really promising beginners" Woolf was never severe but gave personal advice and often financial aid.

But the first real "big man" in Boston newspaper music criticism was not Woolf but William Foster Apthorp (1848–1913). Apthorp was the direct descendant of officers of the British Crown; one of his ancestors had been paymaster of the British Navy during the Revolutionary War. As a boy he was taken by his parents all over Europe to be educated—France, Dresden, Berlin, Rome—and as a result was fluent in many languages. He early showed a talent for drawing and seriously considered a career as a painter; in Florence he was a fellow student with John Singer Sargent. But back at Harvard in the late 1860s he studied with John Knowles Paine and became more interested in music than in art, conducting the Pierian Sodality in his senior year. His parents had first dreamed of his becoming a great painter; now they saw him as a budding concert pianist. Apthorp himself realized he wasn't quite good enough and began a teaching career in the early 1870s; for some years he taught piano, harmony, counterpoint, fugue, and theory at New England Conservatory of Music and other Boston colleges, but retired from teaching altogether in 1886, by which time his labors as a writer on music had overtaken all else.

The Boston-Harvard literary-arts intelligentsia was a small world then, and it was William Dean Howells who recruited Apthorp when he was only twenty-four to be the music editor at the *Atlantic Monthly* in 1872, a post he held for five years; later Apthorp also contributed to *Dwight's Journal* and *Scribner's*. An early Apthorp photograph shows a young man with an upturned waxed mustache and beard and a gaunt, aesthetic mien. He began writing music criticism for the *Boston Sunday Courier* and the *Traveller* before finally settling in at the *Evening Transcript* in 1881; from 1892 to 1901 he wrote the program notes for the Boston Symphony Orchestra and was a lexicographer for *Scribner's Cyclopedia of Music and Musicians.* He also published several books and gave lectures in Boston, New York, and Baltimore on music, wrote some drama criticism (but, curiously, no art criticism), translated many books, and became an authority on Robert Franz, the German lieder composer, then celebrated, now little remembered, who had settled in Boston. Sadly, in 1903, going blind from all these toils, Apthorp retired to Switzerland.

Apthorp's powers as a musical analyst, prose style as a musical commentator, and ability to grow in harness as a critic are vividly illustrated by a comparison of his early and late reactions to Brahms's First Symphony. Upon the Boston premiere of Brahms's First on January 3, 1878, by the Harvard Musical Association conducted by Carl Zerrahn, when the symphony was only a year or so old, Apthorp found it to be "a work calculated to completely baffle the most intelligent snap-judgment" (*Boston Courier*, January 4, 1878). Two weeks later, after another performance in Boston, this time by the Theodore Thomas

Orchestra, he confessed, "After second hearing, sooth to say, it does not improve on acquaintance. To call it learned is to admit that musical science is at a low ebb today.... It was still depressing, over-laboured, unspontaneous, with more of will than of genius in it, more of enterprise and calculation than of the creative spark" (*Boston Courier*, January 18, 1878). Now compare Apthorp's program note on Brahms's First Symphony's last movement from the 1890s:

> With the thirtieth measure the tempo changes to *più andante*, and we come upon one of the most poetic episodes in all Brahms. Amid hushed, tremulous harmonies in the strings, the horn and afterward the flute pour forth an utterly original melody, the character of which ranges from passionate pleading to a sort of wild exultation, according to the instrument that plays it. The coloring is enriched by the solemn tones of the trombones, which appear for the first time in this movement. It is ticklish work trying to dive down into a composer's brain, and surmise what special outside source his inspiration may have had; but one cannot help feeling that this whole wonderful episode may have been suggested to Brahms by the tone of the Alpine horn, as it awakens the echoes from mountain after mountain on some of the high passes in the Bernese Oberland. This is certainly what the episode recalls to anyone who has ever heard those poetic tones and their echoes. A short, solemn, even ecclesiastical interruption by the trombones and bassoons is of more thematic importance. As the horn tones gradually die away, and the cloud-like harmonies in the strings sink lower and lower—like mist veiling the landscape—an impressive pause ushers in the *allegro non troppo, ma con brio* (in C major, 4-4 time). The introductory adagio has already given us mysterious hints at what is to come; and now there bursts forth in the strings the most joyous, exuberant *Volkslied* melody, a very Hymn to Joy, which in some of its phrases, as it were unconsciously and by sheer affinity of nature, flows into strains from the similar melody in the *finale* of Beethoven's Ninth Symphony. One cannot call it plagiarism: it is two men saying the same thing.

It may well be that Apthorp was thus the originator of the now hoary cliché that the fourth movement is an echo of Beethoven's "Ode to Joy."

Apthorp was not just a concert reviewer but a critical essayist and an advocate, like Dwight before him a True Believer that critics should proselytize the masses to the fold of classical music and High Culture. He wrote in the *At-*

lantic Monthly in March 1874, "Instruction cannot and must not be forced down the public throat; it must be conveyed in the most fascinating and gradual form possible. . . . It is certainly not to be done by an abrupt introduction to the higher classic music, much less by the poorer and more trashy compositions of sterling composers, such as the march from Gounod's *Queen of Sheba,* the good in which is only to be appreciated by musicians, and the bad in which is beneath the notice of anybody." He thus disapproved almost moralistically, Brahminlike, of Theodore Thomas's orchestral programs when they mixed what later came known to be "pops" with "serious" fare. "Society rapidly falls into distinct musical classes, and he who cannot keep up with the foremost must take his chance in the rear. . . . Where the most highly cultivated nucleus exists, there will be the highest general cultivation. Nothing is more fatal to general culture than that intellectual and aesthetic communism which would have the foremost wait until those who lag behind shall have caught up with him" (*Atlantic Monthly,* January 1875).

In his zeal to recruit the unwashed public into appreciation of Parnassus, Apthorp tended to be a Hellenic purist and had a blind spot not just for African-American spirituals but for *volk*-derived music of all races: upon the Boston premiere of Dvořák's *New World* Symphony he wrote in the *Evening Transcript* on January 1, 1894, "To our mind, the great bane of the present Slavic and Scandinavian school is and has been the attempt to make civilized music by civilized methods out of essentially barbaric material. The result has in general been a mere apotheosis of ugliness, distorted forms, and barbarous expression. We gladly admit exceptions; but this seems to us to be the general rule." And later in the *Transcript,* February 3, 1896, on MacDowell's *Indian* Suite, he commented, "Most barbarous tunes, of no-matter-what origin, have so much in common that it takes an expert to recognize anything very specific in their musical character." Apthorp could be puritanical at times; according to the younger Philip Hale, he once referred to even Beethoven's *Pastoral* Symphony as "obscene."

Nevertheless, characterizations of Apthorp as a hidebound conservative have been overstated. It was Apthorp who persuaded his anti-Wagnerite teacher John Knowles Paine to a sympathetic understanding of Wagner's methods. Even when his ears were most tried by new music, Apthorp was not doctrinaire: "Strauss' 'Death and Damnation'—we beg pardon—'Death and Transfiguration'—is an unholy terror. It is like a musical reflection of all the deadly and noisome diseases flesh is heir to, viewed through a magnifying glass of three thousand diameters. Such a farrago of hospital sounds vividly suggests hospital sights! The worst of it is, the man does show talent. He has something really grand and great in his mind, and moreover a certain vague inkling of how to say it grandly" (*Boston Evening Transcript*, February 8, 1897). And Apthorp, unlike Henry Krehbiel in New York, was philosophically humble about the critic's role. "The critic plays the part of fly-wheel in the art-life of the world, not that of mainspring. . . . I think that, in general, the critic can easily learn more from artists than they are likely ever to learn from him," he wrote in the *Boston Evening Transcript* in 1894. He was a genial conservative who wrote lucid, easygoing prose, less ornate in wording than Huneker's, less presumptuous of "the truth" than Krehbiel or Louis Elson.

> Dogmatic and authoritative criticism would be all very well, if the critic were possessed of one thing—OMNISCIENCE! For, without this, his field is singularly circumscribed, or else his position an exceedingly ticklish one. Just how much can a musical critic claim to "know he knows" about a composition or a performance? In my opinion, very little indeed. . . . [The critic] must remember that the progress of music, like that of the other fine arts, is essentially an evolution, and that the path this evolution has followed has been, and ever will be, hewn out by men of creative genius, and not by critics. A new genius may so comport itself as to shock the critic's most cherished convictions as to what is true, beautiful, and eternal in music; but let him think twice before trying to stem its course. It may have that in it which can scatter all his arguments to the four winds, and make all his knowledge and cultured taste ridiculous. . . . It is of no use trying to resist the onward march of a Beethoven, a Schumann, a Berlioz, or a Wagner![8]

Apthorp even predicted atonality in an "Entr'acte" he wrote in 1896 for the BSO programs. He called it "nullitonic."[9]

❧ *W. S. B. Mathews and George Upton in Chicago*

Two prominent critics early emerged in Chicago. One was William Smythe Babcock Mathews (1837–1912). Mathews, born in New Hampshire, a high school dropout from a nonmusical home, was a self-made all-around musician who taught music itinerantly around the country before settling down in Chicago after the Civil War. An organist and piano teacher, self-read in arts and philosophy, Mathews contributed articles from the midwest to *Dwight's Journal of*

Music under the nom de plume "Der Freyschutz," which alerted the New England mandarins that there actually was a musical life west of the New York–Boston axis, as he himself later wrote: "Musical effort had had its chief seat of activity in New York and Boston. Now new centres had arisen, and in the west sprang up a movement which soon put the cities of Cincinnati and Chicago upon an almost equal footing of importance in the musical sense; for the western effort, by the excellence of its direction, the high standard of its labors, gave an impulse of virility to its activity that compensated to a large extent, in a short time, for the tardiness of its approach." [10]

Mathews began also to contribute music criticism to the *Chicago Times* in 1877, the *Chicago Herald* in 1880, and the *Chicago News* from 1883, but chiefly he was a music critic for the *Chicago Tribune* from 1877 to 1886 and the editor of the magazine *Music* from 1891 to 1902. Mathews was a prodigious worker, to the end of his life contributing more than five hundred articles to the *Etude* and other musical periodicals and writing or contributing to more than thirty books, most notably penning the first comprehensive history of music in America. His myriad articles are a gold mine of documentation of audience reaction, attendance, ticket prices, performance practices, and tastes in the nineteenth-century boondocks. An excellent writer, Mathews was also forward-looking, approving of Berlioz, Wagner, and Liszt before many of his Old Guard eastern contemporaries. Free from the eastern centers, he was a fearless freethinker on musical matters; of Joachim Raff, then considered one of the great European composers, Mathews wrote he was vulgar and superficial and lacked "the inmost thing of all, the very center and motive of musical creation—an intuition of the relation of music to feeling." [11] Late twentieth-century opinion concurs.

George Putnam Upton (1834–1919), far less technically learned in music than Mathews, had a much more immediate impact on the musical life of Chicago. Born in Massachusetts, he graduated from Brown in 1854 and "went west, young man." Becoming city editor of the *Chicago Evening Journal* in 1856, he started the city's first musical column in that paper. He joined the *Chicago Tribune* in 1863 as both music critic and Civil War correspondent as well as editorial writer. Upton was a total musical amateur who did not even play an instrument, but he was a booster and activist for local performing ensembles, such as the Chicago Apollo Musical Club, which he cofounded in 1872 to help music making get going again after the Great Fire of the previous year. He was an ardent promoter of Chicago artistic life in other fields and also wrote art, book, and drama criticism.

As a music critic Upton wrote under the pseudonym "Peregrine Pickle."

74   While not a distinguished critic, neither was he a primitive, and eventually he authored many music appreciation books. His reviews disclose that audiences immediately after the Civil War in Chicago were about at the same point of evolution as New York audiences had been in the 1820s. However, twenty more years of Upton's articles and editorials created more perceptive Chicago audiences. He boomed the conductor Theodore Thomas and helped pave the way for the city fathers eventually to create the Chicago Symphony Orchestra in 1891 as a permanent ensemble for the theretofore nomadic Thomas, something New York City had never provided Thomas. Later Upton edited Thomas's autobiography.

ა *Philip Hale, the*
maestro of the
program note

Some critics are failed composers; James Huneker was a failed concert pianist. The Boston-based Philip Hale (1854–1934)—upon whom Huneker bestowed the ultimate accolade "an artist in prose"—is perhaps unique among celebrated music critics in being an organist manqué. Born in Vermont and raised in Massachusetts, Hale studied and played the organ from early boyhood. He attended Phillips Exeter Academy and graduated from Yale in 1876, where he wrote for the newspaper, sang in the Glee Club, and won composition prizes, though he majored in law and was admitted to the bar in 1880. For two years while practicing law Hale also worked as a music critic in Albany, New York, and continued playing and studying the organ. Then in 1882 he went to Europe for a five-year period of further music study, pursuing piano with Xaver Scharwenka and composition with Rheinberger and Guilmant, both primarily organ composers. When upon returning to the States he found that he could not support himself on church organ jobs alone, he took up music journalism in earnest and thus began a long and brilliant career as one of the Old Guard's panjandrums.

Settling in Boston, Hale started writing music reviews for the *Boston Post* in 1890 and the next year moved to the *Boston Journal,* where he quickly became a colorful presence, writing not only music criticism but also a daily column called "The Talk of the Town" that covered a broad human canvas. When in 1903 he moved over to the rival *Herald,* he wrote a similar column titled "As the World Wags," which retailed the exploits of such fictitious characters as Herkimer Johnson, who dithered on about writing a pie-in-the-sky endless multivolume philosophical opus, and Halliday Witherspoon, a pseudony-

mous travel correspondent. He also for a few years in the 1890s wrote for the
Musical Courier, edited the *Boston Musical Record,* and was music and drama
critic for thirty years for the *Herald* (1903–33); but he is best remembered and
most identified with the epic program notes he wrote for the Boston Symphony Orchestra.

True, W. F. Apthorp had written the program notes for the Boston Symphony in the 1890s, and Henry Krehbiel in New York wrote them for the New
York Philharmonic, but it is Philip Hale who did the most to develop orchestra
program annotator as an occupational genre for music critics ever since. In
authoritative prolixity he is the great grandfather of *Fanfare,* the book-sized
bimonthly record guide of the late twentieth century. Hale's notes, issued annually for some thirty years by the BSO in thick bound volumes that sometimes exceeded two thousand pages in length, became proverbial for exotic
erudition, literary flair, and musical encyclopedism—and also, said some
wags, for being unread. (Mencken wrote: "Philip Hale? His gigantic annotations scarcely belong to criticism at all; they are musical talmudism. Beside,
they are buried in the program books of the Boston Symphony Orchestra, and
might as well be inscribed on the temple walls of Baalbec.") [12] Eventually, a selection of them was posthumously issued in book form. The *New York Herald
Tribune* music critic Lawrence Gilman, himself no slouch as a wordsmith,
wrote of Hale and his Brobdingnagian program notes:

> He never hesitated to lighten musical instruction with diversion and with
> wit. He knew much besides music; and he was able to peptonize for the
> reader his vast and curious erudition. He could tell you about the macer-
> ation of Oriental women, and what action is described by the word "tu-
> tupomponeyer," and who invented the first chess-playing automaton,
> and how locomotive engines are classified, and what Pliny said concern-
> ing the bird called penelope. . . . [Hale's] amazing annotations, traversing
> all history and the ceaseless tragi-comedy of life, assure us that a pro-
> gramme note may sometimes, if an artist has contrived it, be more re-
> warding than the music that occasioned it. Philip Hale transformed the
> writing of programme notes from an arid and depressing form of musi-
> cal pedagogy into an exhilarating variety of literary art.

Hale did not invent the program note—he developed it and perfected it;
he was the J. S. Bach of program annotators. According to his successor annotator, John N. Burk, "From the autumn of 1901 through the spring of 1933,

76 Philip Hale contributed programme notes for everything played by the Boston Symphony Orchestra in its regular concerts—upward of a thousand works."[13]

Before Hale (and Apthorp and Krehbiel), this is what passed for a program note on Beethoven's Seventh:

> The longed-for moment is drawing near, and in blissful anticipation of the approaching consummation of their wishes, the graceful spirit-shapes move about playfully, now ascending, now descending (Bar 21 and the following, before Allegro), until at length they are loudly bidden to begin the round-dance. They hesitate, bashfully at first, as though loath to divulge their secret (the last bars before the *allegro*). Suddenly a slight tremor passes through their ranks. It is the last trepidation of joy, preceding its fullest outward manifestation which now ensues. Louder and louder the summons to the general jubilation issues forth; higher and higher still the waves of enjoyment rise; closer and ever closer their spirits join each other in the dance and unite their voices in a song of rapture. The first delirium of ecstatic joy over, the magic measure of individual tone-spirits is displayed. And alike in the sweet accents of the flute, in the loud blast of the trumpet, and in the gentle tone of the horn, the secret of every one of them becomes manifest. Then (with the organ-point upon E), the spirits again unite in loving embrace, resuming their song of joy with dithyrambic fervor.[14]

Hale's program notes, though longiloquent, were businesslike compared to this. A typical Hale note, unlike Apthorp's, would trawl in every conceivably pertinent musical or historical obiter dictum. In Hale's annotations to Mozart's "Jupiter" Symphony, he dredged up a contemporaneous anti-Mozart view that not even Slonimsky managed to locate for his *Lexicon of Musical Invective* (indeed, there is no Mozart entry at all in the *Lexicon*):

> Hans George Nägeli (1773–1836) attacked this symphony bitterly on account of its well-defined and long-lined melody, "which Mozart mingled and confounded with a free instrumental play of ideas, and his very wealth of fancy and emotional gifts led to a sort of fermentation in the whole province of art, and caused it to retrograde rather than to advance." He found fault with certain harmonic progressions which he characterized as trivial. He allowed the composer originality and a certain power of combination, but he found him without style, often shallow and confused. He ascribed these qualities to the personal qualities of the man

himself: "He was too hasty, when not too frivolous, and he wrote as he himself was." [15]

Hale codified the paradigm for all later critics writing the program note in several ways, but perhaps the most important one was to make the annotator the de facto judge and jury of the canonical repertory. When Hale wrote, "Schubert created a new lyric—the emotional song. Plod your weary way through the ballads of Zumsteeg, the songs of J. A. Hiller, Reichardt, Zelter, and the others: how cold, formal, precise they are! They are like unto the cameo brooches that adorn the simpering women in old tokens or keepsakes; as remote and out of fashion as the hair jewelry of the early 'sixties. . . . The modern song was invented by Schubert," he was effectively putting the canonical imprimatur of his profession on Schubert as the premier lieder composer. Who now knows the songs of Hiller, Reichardt, and Zelter? To be hailed by Hale into BSO annals was to be incorporated by other annotators and professional music appreciationists ever after into the composer pantheon. Tastemakers have a herd instinct.

Another thing Hale's model did was to establish standard rules of the game for the annotator. One, always give the reader/listener a section-to-section, "play by play" narrative of each piece of music. When phonograph recordings started needing jacket liners, Hale's notes were used as the model (one critic who deviated: Deems Taylor in his radio broadcasts). Two, always, *always* list the exact instrumentation from the composer's score (Hale always did but others, alas, don't always). Three, learn to distill the essence of a composer in a few descriptive phrases: "The heart of Tchaikovsky was that of a little child; the brain was that of a man weary of the world and all its vanities. And so we have the singular phenomenon of naiveté, accompanied by a superrefined skill." "He told his dreams, he wove his romantic fabric for a few sympathetic souls. . . . The hearer of Schumann's music must in turn be imaginative and a dreamer."

Four, make it the duty of the critic to separate his subjective opinions about composers, which he still can express in his daily reviews, from an objective description of the music in his program note. (In fact, sometimes Hale reviewed the very concerts he had annotated in opinions opposed to his program note views.) The twinkle-eyed Hale, of course, from time to time would violate his own precept; in his note to Beethoven's *Leonore* Overture No. 3 he digressed, "A programme composed exclusively of piano sonatas by Beethoven is an invention of the Adversary, and it deserves the attention of the police as a deliberate act against public morals," and in another on the "Emperor" Con-

78   certo he allowed as "the finale with the endless repetitions of a Kangaroo theme leads one to long for the end." Program annotators today are far more discreet. Yet his program note on Beethoven's Ninth is objective and dutifully respectful, while in an essay in the *Musical Record* (a journal that tried to support itself without advertising and folded), he iconoclastically wrote (as Slonimsky famously noted in his *Lexicon of Musical Invective*):

> We heard lately in Boston the Ninth Symphony of Beethoven. The performance was technically most admirable. But is not worship paid this Symphony mere fetishism? Is not the famous Scherzo insufferably long-winded? The Finale is to me for the most part dull and ugly. I admit the grandeur of the passage 'und der Cherub steht vor Gott' and the effect of 'Seid unschlungen Millionen!' But oh, the pages of stupid and hopelessly vulgar music! The unspeakable cheapness of the chief tune, 'Freude, freude!' Do you believe way down in the bottom of your heart that if this music had been written by Mr. John L. Tarbox, now living in Sandown, N.H., any conductor here or in Europe could be persuaded to put it in rehearsal? (*Musical Record*, Boston, June 1, 1899)

A dry understated humor was a steady weapon in Hale's armamentarium. That Mahler himself despised and disdained program notes was a fact Hale was dutiful enough to discuss at length in his own program note to the Fifth Symphony of Mahler. Of Schubert's Eighth Symphony, Hale wrote, "Let us be thankful that Schubert never finished the work. Possibly the lost arms of the Venus of Milo might disappoint if they were found and restored." Hale could be similarly droll in his daily reviews, but his acidic tendencies were feared by musicians. He was popularly known as "Philip the Great" and "Philip the Terrible"; Charles Ives referred to him as "Auntie Hale." Daniel Gregory Mason writes in his memoirs of Hale's review of his string quartet that the critic, "while admitting that the audience had 'applauded with a heartiness that approached enthusiasm,' headlined his article 'Kneisels courteously play *Quartet* by D. G. Mason,' and protested that 'the Kneisels should not so strain courtesy.' And indeed this was a fault from which Hale himself was completely free." * [16]

Hale—who, persisting in wearing a loose black silk tie on all occasions

---

* Yet Mason later paid Hale a backhanded compliment of his own by borrowing Hale's Venus de Milo/Schubert Unfinished witticism for an essay in the *Musical Quarterly* entitled "The Depreciation of Music."

into the Roaring Twenties, looked by that time like a creature from a yester era—could nevertheless be more forward-looking and unpredictable in his musical tastes than his troglodytic contemporaries. While Aldrich and even Huneker berated Berlioz, Hale wrote, "The more Berlioz is studied, the more the wonder grows at his colossal originality. . . . the music did not pass away with the outward badges of romanticism, with much of Byron's poetry, with plays and novels of the time. The emotions he expressed are still universal and elemental." Of Debussy, he said, "Debussy suffered at the hands of the ultra-orthodox and the snobs in music. The former could not find either melodic lines or the semblance of form in his orchestral and chamber works, his songs and pianoforte pieces. . . . There were some that spoke of Debussy as an ignorant fellow who, not being able to achieve greatness in the conventional manner, wrote in an eccentric way to attract attention, to make the bourgeois sit up. They forgot that Debussy had taken the chief prize at the Paris Conservatory, where harmony and counterpoint are taught rigorously." While Hale was partial to French aesthetics, he even liked Prokofiev: "Prokofieff has written superbly barbaric music. This music is something more than roaring, blaring dissonance; something more than eccentric experimentation in harmonic schemes and daring orchestration. . . . He knew what he wanted; he gained his effects. They are not episodic, spasmodic, but skillfully continuous." And he was remarkably discerning about Stravinsky's neoclassical period: "We personally prefer the Stravinsky of the *Sacre du Printemps* to the Stravinsky who of late has been attempting to compose in the manner of Bach. To begin with, we do not hear music now with the ears of the earlier centuries, and the old idiom today has no pertinence except when it has been handed down to us by a master of it, who broke through the idiom and made a universal language of it for many years to come. Stravinsky's feeble echo is simply dull, boresome. His 'Muscovism' is greatly to be preferred."

Hale also was far less moralistic and puritanical than his predecessor Apthorp or his contemporaries Krehbiel or Henderson in New York; "*Salome*, however distasteful the subject may be to some, is a stupendous work by a man of indisputable, if irregular and abnormal genius," he wrote. He could be caustic about his dislikes, such as Edward Elgar, then in vogue. Unlike Krehbiel, he was modest enough to reverse earlier negative opinions upon later hearings, as with his opinion of much of Strauss. Despite his words about Stravinsky, like Henry Finck in New York he never learned to like Brahms and is apocryphally credited with punning, when Symphony Hall was opened in Boston, that the fire exits should be marked "Exit in case of Brahms."

80   A formidable presence, oceanic in his output, Hale yet was an iconoclastic iconographer: he once airily dismissed his entire life's work in one sentence: "Mere collections of passing opinions, criticisms that prove stale in a day—whether they be signed by Reichardt in 1792, Hanslick in the Eighties or Krehbiel in 1908—those are tolerable neither to gods nor men."

ॐ *Henry E. Krehbiel,*
   the pontiff   Born in 1854 to a circuit-riding native German Meth-
   of musical wisdom   odist preacher in southern Michigan, Henry Edward
                          Krehbiel and his many siblings traveled wherever the
church sent their father. In 1864 they settled in Cincinnati, where Henry conducted his father's church choir and attended public schools. (In his book *How to Listen to Music* Krehbiel, no doubt summoning his own rural upbringing, wrote that the bassoon is "very apt to recall to those who have had a country education the squalling tone of the homely instrument which the farmer's boy fashions out of the stems of the pumpkin-vine.") Apparently Henry somehow learned a lot about music fast. The young man's intellectual precocity and cocky self-assurance, and an augury of his later pontificality, are abundantly conveyed by a letter he wrote to the *Cincinnati Gazette* when he was only sixteen. The editors published it on the front page of the December 22, 1870, issue. Young Krehbiel refers to a hometown performance by the then-celebrated American soprano Clara Louise Kellogg of Handel's *Messiah:*

> A great deal of sophomorical eloquence has been lavished on the Messiah which I am free to confess I think sadly misplaced. As a whole the Messiah is unquestionably the grandest oratorio extant. It is about 100 years old and this of itself implies that it is cast in an antiquated mold. Again, Handel never wrote much pure melody—as we in this year of grace understand the word—while the best specimens he has given us . . . are full of repetitions, and though beautiful, are not fully satisfactory to our ears, modern ears. . . .
>
> Now how much better to cut such numbers as are not absolutely necessary to the unity of the work, thus shortening the time of performance. . . . The first thing that my retrenching pen would strike the line through would be the recitative "For behold Darkness." . . . Then down goes the "Pastoral Symphony," for setting aside the normal condition of things which seems to be for reeds and strings to be at swords points

therein. . . . The air "Why do the Nations" is good as a bit of scientific writing but devoid of life, so let that drop. Then I would expunge the recitative "He that Dwelleth in Heaven."

The brilliant young man began reading law at a local law practice in 1872 but by 1874 had joined the *Cincinnati Gazette* as a general-assignment reporter. As a cub, Krehbiel reported on murders, boat races, and baseball, and as his protégé Richard Aldrich later recalled,

> he always prided himself a little on a new way of baseball scoring, which he claimed to have invented. . . . One of the stories that he sometimes told was of helping a much-distressed gentleman in tracing the body of his father, which in some unknown way had disappeared soon after his death. They went on many a mysterious and forbidding round in Cincinnati's purlieus; and the body was finally found in the dissecting room of a medical school. The distressed gentleman was Benjamin Harrison, afterwards President of the United States, and the body was that of the son of another President of the United States.[17]

Gradually, as he continued to teach himself more about music in his spare time, Krehbiel began to concentrate more on music reporting, writing both articles about outdoor Cincinnati music festivals and program notes for them. In November 1880 New York City beckoned him with the offer of editorship of the *Musical Review,* a weekly paper; he took the job and moved to New York, but only a month or so later Whitelaw Reid of the *New York Tribune* offered him the job of assistant to John Rose Greene Hassard, the *Tribune's* chief music critic. In his first years with the *Tribune* Krehbiel also interviewed nonmusical figures such as former president Ulysses Grant. Then in 1884 he succeeded the still young but ailing Hassard as chief music critic, a post Krehbiel held until his death thirty-nine years later, turning himself into the most esteemed and influential newspaper music critic America had yet seen. He also found time to teach private lessons, write New York Philharmonic program notes, lecture at the Institute for Musical Art (which after his death became the Juilliard School), author or edit some dozen books (Huneker called him a "date-hound," Mencken a "geyser of buttermilk"), supervise the three-volume revision of Thayer's *Life of Beethoven,* and advise the second edition of *Grove's Dictionary*—but these were all ancillary to his work and prestige as *Tribune* critic. The most outstanding autodidact among American music critics until

82 Deems Taylor, Krehbiel spoke fluent German and English, read French, Italian, Russian, and Latin, and became a self-trained ethnomusicologist of awesome industry, not only of indigenous European races but also of American Indians and African-Americans—all this even though, like Huneker and W. S. B. Mathews but unlike the others in the Gilded Age's critical fraternity, Ivy Leaguers all, Krehbiel never attended college.

Yet H. E. Krehbiel became the acknowledged "dean" of the profession, not only through his intellectual brilliance and hard work, but also through his self-assumption of a quasi-papal infallibility in matters musical—a paradigmatic pose of know-it-all superiority that has helped establish a lamentable cloak for subsequent critics to drape themselves in. Henry Finck, the *New York Evening Post* critic who served out virtually the same forty years as Krehbiel, said of him in his memoirs that he was

> dominating and arrogant, he would brook no opposition. Woe unto anyone who doubted that he was a musical arbiter whose word was final. He could hate like a caveman, as not a few artists found out to their cost. He never forgave a faux pas, from this point of view. And his vengeance persisted a long time. . . . His vanity was also as big as his body, and he was ludicrously jealous of his colleagues when they did anything that he thought might dim the lustre of his own fame. . . . He fiercely resented being criticized himself, even mildly—a trait shared with not a few other critics. . . . We were like two lawyers who heap mounds of abuse on one another in court and then go out and lunch together.

Krehbiel himself best described his approach to musical criticism: "The elements of criticism . . . are not matters of opinion or taste at all, but questions of fact, as exactly demonstrable as a problem in mathematics. . . . the questions of justness of intonation in a singer or instrumentalist, balance of tone in an orchestra, correctness of phrasing, and many other things, are mere determinations of fact."[18] Another writer at the time remarked, "The Germans use the word 'Maasgeband' to describe him, meaning as nearly as can be given, to measure, to give the final stamp."[19] Richard Aldrich, who served as Krehbiel's assistant at the *Tribune* before taking the top job at the *Times,* in a memorial appreciation in the *Times* seconded Henry Finck's view in remarkably similar words:

> If there was narrowness in some of Krehbiel's views as a critic, it was the outcome of his complete confidence in his own judgment and the valid-

ity of his own knowledge and opinions. He brooked, indeed, little opposition. He was apt to lay down the law; as his opponents, and the opponents of criticism in general, like to say, to "pontificate." Pontification is not a good thing in any art, and it perhaps involves a misconception of the function and the limitation of criticism. . . . A man of positive opinions, fearless in putting them forth, scorning ulterior influences that have no place in a sincere cultivation of music, he made enemies.

But Krehbiel's patriarchal mien had its charming, even lovable side, too; said his junior colleague Deems Taylor, "Most of us who saw him and talked with him night after night called him 'Pop' and thought of him as 'Pop.' 'Henry' would have been out of the question for us youngsters, and 'Mister' would have been much too cold for the affection we had for him."

Krehbiel was an imposing figure physically as well as scriptorily. "He was built like a Viking," noted Finck. "No one could fail to notice those broad shoulders, that big curly head as he walked down the aisle in Carnegie Hall or at the Metropolitan." He was tall, erect of carriage but enormously stout, of ruddy complexion, bison-mustached, with an "oddly inappropriate voice," Deems Taylor recalled. Even in his late sixties his hair was still red and just graying; one observer said he looked like a mature Lohengrin. In the popular iconography of the day Krehbiel was regarded as a ringer for President William Howard Taft. Both were of immense girth, especially seen in profile. A 1910 article in the New York Telegraph reporting a personal meeting between President Taft and Krehbiel described the pair as the "two Dreadnaughts." The "separated at birth" connection helped make Krehbiel a national celebrity: both men were natives of Cincinnati and about the same age. When President Taft spoke at the Yale commencement in 1909, where Krehbiel was given an honorary Master of Arts degree, Taft said, "I say, we know music in Cincinnati," and added that Krehbiel in his career there had "never feared to tell the people whether some of their efforts in the musical line were up to the proper standard, even if he had to flee for his life because of it."[20] According to the New York Telegram of February 17, 1912, the two men were so similar looking that patrons at the Metropolitan Opera frequently tipped their hats upon seeing Krehbiel and greeted him aloud as "The President"; Krehbiel was in the habit of dutifully returning the salutation "with characteristic good nature and a keen sense of humor."

Krehbiel was a bit of a celebrity without Taft's help. The April 1, 1914, Musical America reported in a squib: "Not long ago an electric sign was displayed on Broadway, reading: 'do you know H. E. Krehbiel is on the New York Tribune?' The glittering 'Beau Broadway' commentator in the *Morning Telegraph,* thereupon remarked: 'Yes, I have been painfully aware of the fact for thirty years.'" Henry Finck recalled, "Many music lovers also stood in awe of him, as was amusingly illustrated one day in Carnegie Chamber Music Hall [now Weill Hall] when I heard one lady say proudly, 'I came up in the same elevator with Krehbiel' and her companion answered 'How interesting!'"

As a critic Krehbiel, again according to Aldrich, "was wroth with any who attempted to tamper with the works of the great masters as they had left them; and this brought him into notable conflict with men who thought their reputations entitled them to do what they pleased." A purist, Krehbiel was antipathetic to the conductor Theodore Thomas, who interlaced his programmes of symphonies with "light" classical works in order to broaden the public for "serious" fare. He was also a detractor of Gustav Mahler's conducting of the New York Philharmonic, and some felt his bad reviews contributed to Mahler's problems with the Philharmonic Board and early demise. Krehbiel's philosophy of musical interpretation, and objections to Mahler's approach, are clear in this passage on Mahler's Beethoven's Fifth:

> The first evidence of erraticism occurred in the famous cadenza, in the first movement.
>
> This Mr. Mahler phlebotomized by giving it to two oboes and beating time for each note—not in the expressive adagio called for by Beethoven, but in a rigid andante. Thus the rhapsodic utterance contemplated by the composer was turned into a mere connecting link between two parts of the movement. Into the cadence of the second subject of the third movement, Mr. Mahler injected a bit of un-Beethovenian color by changing the horn part so that listeners familiar with their Wagner were startled by hearing something very like Hagen's call from Gotterdamerung from the instruments which in the score simply sustain a harmony voice in octaves. In the finale Mr. Mahler several times doubled voices (bassoons with cellos) and transposed the piccolo part an octave higher. Here he secured sonority which aided him in building up a thrilling climax, but did not materially disturb Beethoven's color scheme. The question of the artistic righteousness of his act may be left to the decision of musicians.[21]

In his May 21, 1911, *Tribune* article upon Mahler's untimely death, a remorseless Krehbiel actually argued that Mahler had been his own worst enemy, "wantonly . . . insult[ing] their [Americans'] intelligence and taste by such

things as multiplying the voices in a Beethoven symphony . . . by cutting down
the strings and doubling the flutes in Mozart's G Minor, by fortifying the brass
in Schubert's C Major." So outraged was the pianist and conductor Ossip
Gabrilowitsch by Krehbiel's tastelessness that he wrote an angry letter of protest to the *Tribune*.

But there is no question that Krehbiel was a prime nominator and consol-
idator of several late nineteenth-century composers into the canon: Brahms,
Wagner, Dvořák, perhaps Tchaikovsky. The *Evening Post* critic Henry Finck
wrote of Krehbiel that "he was fiercely anti-German during the war, yet in his
criticisms he was always as Teutonic as Teutonic can be. . . . he had little or no
enthusiasm for non-German geniuses like Chopin, Liszt, Grieg, Tchaikovsky,
Bizet, Gounod, Verdi; Liszt, indeed, he hated as the devil hates holy water, going so far as to intimate that he wasn't even much of a pianist!" But of the older
Viennese classics, and of both Wagner and Brahms, Krehbiel was an ardent
champion. Richard Aldrich recalled that he also praised Dvořák and Tchaikovsky, but not Debussy or Strauss; Krehbiel wrote a celebrated denunciation
of *Salome* on moralistic as well as musical grounds. "As for the 'futurists,'" remarked Henry Finck, "compared with whom Richard Strauss is a mellifluous
Bellini, [Henry and I] cordially applauded each other's pugilistic attacks." Only
a few weeks before his death, Krehbiel likened Schoenberg's music in the *Tribune*'s discreet Republican pages to "excreta."

When covering new music, Krehbiel tried to study the compositions from
the score before hearing their premieres. Hearing the 1887 New York premiere
of Berlioz's opera *Les Troyens* in a concert performance in English, he wrote on
March 12, "It is indeed a glowing score, crowded with novel and fascinating effects in instrumentation, and full of original rhythmical devices which impart
an astonishing energy to the music in the dramatic scenes." On the Saint-Saëns
Organ Symphony premiere the same year, "As music it is interesting at once
and disappointing. . . . The need which called for the few pianoforte scales and
chords in the *presto* and *maestoso* will, we fear, remain a mystery till chaos be
come again." On the Prelude to *Parsifal* performed on November 3, 1882, under Walter Damrosch, the young critic discerningly wrote: "It would be impossible to overpraise the performance of this exacting work last night. The
music is more difficult than a casual listener would suppose; the contour of the
melodic figure is often obscure and the rhythm is easily missed while the instrumental combinations require an almost phenomenal purity and softness
of intonation without which they would sometimes tend to be positively ugly."

Krehbiel was famously incorruptible. He once was offered one hundred
dollars (a large sum at the time) for merely naming a piano to be played on a

86   certain occasion without using any critical adjectives. Out of this grew an un-
written canon of the New York critics that the maker of a piano was never to
be mentioned in critics' reviews. During Krehbiel's long tenure press agents
became an ever-encroaching presence for newspapers, but he made it an iron-
clad policy to avoid knowing them socially or professionally. However, *Musical America* columnists frequently took Krehbiel to task for puffing his favorites, such as the Polish soprano Marcella Sembrich, and pillorying his
dislikes, such as Victor Herbert.

Perhaps the most surprising facet of this arch-Teuton's musical championships were his tireless efforts to record and propagate his findings of non-
European American music. At the same time that W. F. Apthorp in Boston was
decrying Edward MacDowell's *Indian* Suite, Krehbiel the ethnomusicologist
regarded Indianism as legitimate. Even more interesting, he spent years re-
searching black spirituals and published his findings in *Afro-American Folk-
songs* (1914). Though the book has been superseded by later research, and
though Krehbiel still had some problems with the more vernacular expressions of African-derived music such as ragtime, when Krehbiel died he received the following tribute from Cleveland G. Allen, a black music critic for
Musical America: "The negroes of America join with the nation in mourning
the loss of Henry E. Krehbiel, whom we regarded as one of our closest friends.
His interest in the preservation of the negro folk songs endeared him to the
negro."

In fact, when Krehbiel died in 1923, his passing was treated almost as
that of a head of state. Condolence wires and letters came from Paderewski,
Rachmaninoff, Louise Homer, Albert Spalding, Willem Mengelberg, Arthur
Judson, David Belasco, Lilli Lehmann, the young Jascha Heifetz, and many
conductors and composers. The other leading New York critics were his pall-
bearers. Krehbiel's reputation as a critic had been international. Tributes
poured in from London, Paris, and Berlin. The public attention given Krehbiel's passing was both a high-water mark and an end, not a beginning. Perhaps
never again did the community of musical artists feel so at one with the chief
nabob of the profession that makes a living by scarifying them.

∾ *W. J. Henderson,*
   singer's critic   William James Henderson (1855–1937) was the scion of
   and lord high   a theatrical family: his father was a Scotch-Irish theatri-
   executioner   cal manager and actor and his mother was an actress,

playwright, and third-generation theater professional who had come to America with her father from England in 1837. Henderson grew up in New Jersey, attending private schools and contributing to local newspapers even as a teenager; he graduated from Princeton and began to work for the *New York Tribune* in 1876 as a reporter. He had early piano and singing lessons but was, like Krehbiel, largely self-taught in music theory. In the late 1870s young Henderson briefly abandoned journalism to assist his father in the management of the Standard Theatre in New York, where the senior Henderson presented such varied bill of fare as the first American performance of *H.M.S. Pinafore, Hamlet,* and a farce entitled *Bigamy,* coauthored by Henderson's mother. In his later years Henderson confined his connection with the theater to the writing of librettos for many now-forgotten operettas (and for one forgotten opera produced in 1912 at the Metropolitan—Walter Damrosch's *Cyrano de Bergerac*). His growth into the foremost expert among the critics of his time on opera and opera singers, and his ardent early championship of Wagner and *Gesamtkunstwerk,* may in part also stem from the influences of this early theatrical background.

Henderson soon returned to journalism and joined the *New York Times* in 1883 as a general-assignment reporter, but in short order he narrowed his reportage to two subjects, concerts and yachting; music and the sea were his lifetime twin passions (though, not particularly being a Debussy fan, he failed to view *La Mer* as the ne plus ultra).* In 1887 he replaced Henry Schwab as the *Times*'s chief musical critic, and in 1902, beckoned by a much higher salary, he moved on to the *New York Sun,* where he worked as chief music critic (except for a brief management changeover to the *Herald*) almost to his death in 1937, the grand old man of New York criticism.

Among Henderson's nautical books were *Sea Yarns for Boys* (1895) and *Elements of Navigation* (1895); the latter was used by the U.S. government as a training manual for naval servicemen in World War I. His colleague Henry Finck amusingly viewed Henderson's aqueous affinities thus: "He has been writing about yachts and yachting in order to qualify himself for commenting on such nautical operas as 'The Flying Dutchman,' 'Tristan and Isolde,' and 'L'Africaine,' which shows how conscientiously he performs his duty as critic." Henderson even served in the New York naval militia from 1890 to 1899, being commissioned ensign in 1891 and lieutenant in 1898. He enlisted as lieutenant

---

*Perhaps Henderson's closest counterpart abroad in dual music and sports journalism was Britain's Neville Cardus, who was later a distinguished music critic for the *Manchester Guardian* and a prolific sportswriter on cricket.

88   in the U.S. Navy for temporary service in the Spanish-American War and, though not called for service, was put on the eligible list; he was forty-three at the time.

Henderson also wrote *Pipes and Timbrels* (1905), a volume of verse, and *The Soul of a Tenor* (1912), a Huneker-like novel. "His tales of the sea designed for juvenile readers stand in a class by themselves," avers one antediluvian reference book, but it adds, "The order of fancy reflected in his poems is so different from the cutting humor of his criticism that it is hard to reconcile them as emanating from the same individual. . . . it is unquestionably as a critic that he looms the largest in the contemporary view, and in that field, with all his wit and apparent inability to resist the opportunity to pen a bright phrase at the expense of human sympathy."[22]

Even the jolly Finck, who personally called Henderson Willie, concurred in his memoirs: "W. J. Henderson has the keenest wit of all the New York critics. . . . Much of his wit was of the cruel kind—but—tit for tat—think how cruelly *he* had suffered listening to his victims! . . . debutantes dreaded [him] as a leopard ready to tear them to pieces." Henderson's successor on the *Sun*, Oscar Thompson, agreed in an otherwise eulogizing essay, "He was little given to the gentle art of praising with faint damns," while Edward Downes euphemized, "He . . . had a passionate hatred of sham and mediocrity, and this sometimes took the form of a laconic and devastating comment."[23] Truth be told, W. J. Henderson, like H. E. Krehbiel, was a double-edged boon to American musical life. Both men, though creatures of their time unavoidably afflicted with now outdated astigmatisms of opinion, were basically shrewd, perceptive music critics and highly intelligent men. Though like Krehbiel intellectually acute and versatile, and an even better musical reporter than he, and like Krehbiel undoubtedly responsible for raising the musical consciousness of untold numbers of readers of his newspaper reviews and books on music and for bringing people to the concert hall and opera, Henderson—as with Krehbiel and his holier-than-thou posture—has also left his own negative stamp on his profession: the legacy of the art of epigrammatic cruelty. This was paradoxical in that on a personal level as a colleague, "Henderson was a kindly, warm, and considerate person."[24]

Oscar Thompson wrote in his 1937 appreciation of the "Old Guard" for the *Musical Quarterly* that Henderson had come up as a critic during an era in which the prestige of critics was founded solely on their coverage of opera and prima donnas. The Metropolitan Opera House had opened in 1883, the Wagner cult was at its height, great singers abounded, and plutocracy and Veblen's conspicuous consumption reigned. Early on in his *Times* tenure Henderson himself wrote columns advocating that the gaslights in the Met be dimmed for performances, a brave stance for a young critic in that the rich dowagers that supported the opera and held the boxes wanted to keep the gaslights up so their jewels and *toilette* could shine clearly throughout the performance. (Henderson, and the public in the cheaper seats, eventually prevailed.)

Emerging as the premier critic of singers during the premier age of opera (roughly, from the Met's opening in 1883 to the death of Caruso in 1921), at a time when opera stars were more like movie stars, Henderson came to have such prestige that some of his reviews were practically singing lessons, lectures to the divas; and they took it from him. Henderson gave Geraldine Farrar a hard time even at the height of her fame, and all but made fun of Mary Garden's singing. Despite the wild popularity of such solo artists as Paderewski in the 1890s, it was only later, after Toscanini had come to lead the Met for a few years, that critics began to make their reputations by focusing on conductors as well as singers; by that time Henderson, now in his riper years and with his prestige established, was more reserved about Toscanini than either Olin Downes or Lawrence Gilman, his junior colleagues. Recalled Thompson in 1937, "As an example of voice analysis, a review written by Henderson of Tetrazzini's first appearance at the Manhattan [Opera House] might astonish many newspaper readers of the present time; it enumerates the virtues and the blemishes of the lady's technical equipment down to the last embellishment, and is as masterly in its descriptive quality as it is precise in its wealth of critical detail. . . . [Henderson] wrote in a day when a critic could build fame on what he said about such artists."[25] By his boldness and deep knowledge of the voice, Henderson licensed all future critics to dare to meet prima donnas head on; in an 1897 review of the great Lilli Lehmann, after emitting a few florid phrases of panegyric, he almost throws away this line: "It is not faultless, for she has always fallen occasionally into bad attack, and her breathing is at times somewhat stertorous."

Indeed, Henderson's late nineteenth-century *New York Times* articles are reported with a meticulousness and a sharpness of critical acumen sometimes missing from the *Sun* pieces of his later decades. His early *Times* reviews are frequent in number per week and run on and on without paragraphing; but in his last years at the *Sun*, assistants such as young Irving Kolodin were writing most of the concert reviews. An idea of Hendersonian detail can be glimpsed in his report on the celebrated debut of the twelve-year-old piano prodigy Josef Hofmann in a November 30, 1888, *Times* article: Henderson reports that "a request was made from the stage that someone should come forward and give the little fellow a theme on which to improvise." A noted Belgian pianist came onstage and "played a theme which was somewhat severe in its demands on the boy's knowledge of harmony. Young Hofmann had it played thrice. Then he sat down and began by improvising a response, after which he returned in a musician's manner to the theme given him. Then he launched into what might be called a free fantasy, containing snatches of the original theme, but much more matter that was impromptu."

Reviewing Moriz Rosenthal playing Schumann's *Carnaval*, Henderson reported the very rubatos the pianist took in each section of the piece and the tone colors and weightings of individual chords. Such detailed music criticism can be found today only in specialized periodicals preaching to the converted, but Henderson, wrote Oscar Thompson in 1937,

> recalled the nights when he and his colleagues struggled with structural analysis as a part of their reviews, striving to communicate to the reader something intelligible about the first theme, the second theme, the development, and other details of symphonies heard for the first time. This was on the assumption that music criticism was read chiefly by musicians who "knew," or by laymen of studious and ambitious natures, who, thirsting for culture, wanted to know. More than now, newspapers of that time regarded their special departments as for the elect of particular lines; there was much less thought of music as something of a general, perhaps even of a mass appeal. If the reviewer reached the enlightened few, and in a manner that built prestige for the paper among them, he earned his salary.[26]

But then there were those barbs and skewers. Reviewing Rafael Joseffy's performance of Tchaikovsky's First Piano Concerto with the New York Philharmonic on January 14, 1888, he wrote, "There are some fluent themes in it, but they are wholly beneath the dignity of a concerto. The waltz in the second division in the work is dance music, pure and simple—especially simple." On Bruckner's *Romantic* Symphony,

> According to a note on the programme this composition is intended to give some idea of country life. Judging from the composer's expression of his ideas in this symphony, his conception of a country life is chiefly founded on green apples, colic, and thunderstorms, with recollections of the feelings of a man who mistook a hornets nest for a high white hat. Lest this be deemed too frivolous for the occasion, let us hasten to add that Bruckner's symphony is without melodious themes of any kind, is

chaotic and incomprehensible in construction, and is instrumented in an aggressively blatant style which results in confusion worse confounded. It should be put upon the top shelf of a musical curiosity shop, and kept there till the dust of ages gives it a factitious respectability which it does not now possess. (*New York Times,* March 17, 1888)

On the New York premiere of Smetana's symphonic poem *Wallenstein's Camp,* op. 14 (1858), given by the Boston Symphony Orchestra under Emil Paur at Carnegie Hall in 1897: "The concert began with fifteen minutes of trouble by the Bohemian composer Smetana . . . buzzed, banged, and spattered . . . all the ideas to be found in this symphonic poem could be written on a postage stamp and the composer's working out was, of a verity, 'much ado about nothing'" (*New York Times,* January 22, 1897).

And on Tchaikovsky's *Voyevode* premiere at Carnegie Hall, November 26, 1897, under Walter Damrosch:

The work is poor in ideas. To most of the audience yesterday it must seem to be a mere splotch of dark blue colour. During the performance most of the ladies fanned themselves, read the dentifrice advertisements in the program, and tried to look as if they had serious thoughts. But they did not. Neither did Tchaikovsky. . . . The movements were played straight through in a deadly, smooth, innocuous style that could not have stirred the emotions of an inflammable dervish. (*New York Times,* November 27, 1897)

Notwithstanding these brickbats, Henderson's sympathies were broad, at least to a point. In 1888 he called Wagner "the greatest composer that ever lived." He praised Bach and the then-new Bach revival. He wrote mixed but perceptive appreciations of Berlioz (and studied Berlioz's *Treatise on Instrumentation*) and Richard Strauss, but like his colleagues tended to dichotomize all composers into structural form builders and tone colorists. Thus, Liszt and Rubinstein were gifted colorists but not deep in their essential musical statements, and so according to Henderson the music of both was destined to disappear; but only Rubinstein's has.

Toward the later years of his career, as the "futurists" gained hold, Henderson's antimodern invectives became more virulent; even Sibelius's Fourth was too much for him. But before the gates of tonality were breached he could be sympathetic and unprejudiced to new work: of a new symphony, the fifth, by a now-forgotten British composer named Frederic Cowen, he wrote, "It

92   is not always wise to pronounce a decisive judgment on a new work at first hearing, for the hearer may be in an unsympathetic and unreceptive mood. Mr. Cowen's symphony did not make a profound impression yesterday. It is well constructed and scored with admirable smoothness and occasionally with more than ordinary effectiveness, but it seems to lack spontaneity outside of the first movement. . . . It is not impossible that this work may greatly improve on a second hearing. At present it can be set down only as a creditable but not a striking achievement" (*New York Times,* February 24, 1888).

Henderson's later opinions were sometimes tinged with a nostalgia for what he had seen in his prime, particularly for the demise of the vocal golden age. In a Sunday book review for the *Sun* from November 1923 of Luisa Tetrazzini's book *How to Sing* he said:

> No one knows better than Mme. Tetrazzini that how to sing cannot be learned from any book. . . . Singing is best taught as the old Italian masters taught it, viva voce.
>
> Now this matter of tone placing is simple enough in itself, but not at all easy to teach, and yet it is the foundation of all musical and beautiful singing. The proper placing of the tone is essential to the production of the best qualities of a voice. Every experienced observer of musical doings hears singer after singer whose voice seemed to be ever on the verge of swimming into lucent seas of beauty, but never quite succeeds in escaping some sort of grip imposed upon it by hardened throat muscles.
>
> . . . One is often aware that the message haltingly communicated to him by an impeded voice was conceived in emotion and fashioned by real imagination. Personal force, magnetism or whatever you choose to call it, frequently masters the listener. But the sensitive ear is almost invariably informed that the technical use of the instrument is defective.
>
> . . . All of which leads up to the old story that there are almost no thoroughly trained singers today. And this condition is not local. It is world wide. There are no master singers arising in Italy; none in Germany. And if you ask any of the old artists what is the matter they will tell you that the young people will not study long enough to learn their art.

Winthrop Sargeant, a junior critic for the *Brooklyn Daily Eagle* when Henderson was a Grand Old Man, recalled him as

> a dry, salty, lean old Yankee, who looked and acted more like a prosperous New England farmer than an aesthete. Henderson considered him-

self a journalist rather than a pundit, and was fond of describing himself as "just a reporter with a specialty." He lived in a hotel in the Broadway district. He was driven from his hotel to the concert halls every evening by a chauffeur in a big black limousine. He was a good reporter, a sharp, dryly objective judge of music who always went straight to the point. He would dash off his review in his hotel room in twenty minutes or a half hour, and a messenger would get it to the New York *Sun* long before midnight.[27]

Huneker died in 1921, Krehbiel in 1923, Finck in 1926, Aldrich retired, but W. J. Henderson soldiered on even past eighty; one of his last salvos was fired at the 1935 New York premiere of the suite from Berg's *Lulu* ("squalid and repulsive"). Oscar Thompson remembered the octogenarian Henderson:

In his typing he had an odd way of running off the page at the right margin and having to fill in with pencil or pen the final letters of the last word of each line. Otherwise his corrections and interlineations were reduced to a minimum. Partly as a concession to his years, he made it a point to have all "copy" finished at an unusually early hour—say 10:30 or 11 at night, instead of midnight or later, as was true of "copy" for the other afternoon papers. Gagsters remarked that whereas other departments had a "deadline," the Sun's was a "bedline." This was not, however, quite the straight of it. When the "copy" was all in hand, there was something like an hour of free-for-all chat between Henderson and his assistants, ranging from the events of the day back to the Mapleson tenor who had nothing but a high C, which he prolonged in *Di quella pira* while he walked slowly from the back of the stage to the footlights—that is, if the assistants were so lucky as to be able to divert their chief from the present to the past.[28]

Winthrop Sargeant saw it this way:

Henderson was like a gnarled oak in a forest of saplings. He had been listening to music so long and accurately that he remembered artists who were merely names in history books to other critics. . . . He remembered, apparently with complete accuracy, all the virtues and faults of singers like Adelina Patti, Jean de Reszke, Emma Calvé and Melba. Because of their enormous respect for his vast experience, other critics would often cluster around Henderson to verify their opinions in the light of his ma-

94   ture judgment. He nearly always fooled them. With a perverse, arid humor, he would air a whole set of preposterous opinions, quite the reverse
of what he actually believed, and then contradict them all in his own review which appeared the following morning.

Thompson clearly refers to the beginning of a physical impairment in
Henderson. It worsened in 1937. On June 2, 1937, Richard Aldrich—eight years
Henderson's junior, the man he had recommended to the *Times* to succeed
him in 1902—died in Rome. Hale, Parker, Elson, and Apthorp in Boston were
all now gone. Henderson was the last survivor of the Old Guard. On June 5
in his New York apartment, he opened the drawer in which he had kept his
Spanish-American War militia service pistol for forty years, placed the barrel
of the gun in his mouth, and fired. Some newspapers bowdlerized their accounts of Henderson's death.

Whether any victims of his own critical gunfire felt vindicated, history
does not record.

∾ Louis Elson and H. T. Parker

Apthorp and Hale, both of whom wrote Boston Symphony program notes, were not the only important
Boston music critics of the Old Guard. Louis Elson (1848–1920)—who holds
the dubious distinction of being the American critic with the most citations
in Slonimsky's *Lexicon of Musical Invective*—exerted, through his lecture appearances, an educative influence on an arguably broader public than either
Apthorp or Hale. A singer and composer of modest attainments, Elson was not
university trained but studied privately in Leipzig before returning to his native Boston in 1877 to begin a career of musical journalism on various magazines and newspapers. It was a high-tide juncture for Boston musical life: the
Boston Symphony Orchestra was at long last founded in 1881 by the philan-
thropist Henry Higginson. Elson settled in as the longtime chief music critic at
the *Daily Advertiser,* from 1886 until his death. At the same time that he was the
Advertiser critic Elson was also director of the theory department at the New
England Conservatory from 1882, as well as a prolific author and editor of music books and reference guides.

But Elson was probably best known to the public of his time as the premier traveling music appreciation speaker throughout New England and Can-
ada. Elson charged no admission and thus drew large, curious audiences that

were not of the diamond horseshoe crowd. Usually he would appear in modest venues—schoolrooms, municipal buildings—accompanied by homely local pickup orchestras, presumably donating their services. Elson would proceed chronologically, beginning by analyzing musical examples of Mozart and Schubert and presenting a demonstration performance of the same. He would carry the lecture through to Beethoven, opera composers, and even the then-contemporary late Romantics. In one old photograph Elson looks forbiddingly pedagogical; with his pince-nez and huge Kaiser Wilhelm mustache he is the picture of a Prussian schoolmaster about to strike you with his ferrule. But by all accounts he had a reputation as a sparklingly witty speaker, and certainly his reviews attest to his flair for the razor-edged bon mot. He called the *1812* Overture "a sweet little slumber song" (in ironic reference to its beginning) and said of Debussy's *Prélude à l'après-midi d'un faune* that the faun "must have had a terrible afternoon, for the poor beast brayed on muted horns and whinnied on flutes" and that its "suffering . . . seems to need a veterinary surgeon." He called *La Mer* "Le mal de mer."

As a teacher at the New England Conservatory, Elson instituted a rigorous syllabus based on European conservatory models of the time. His own reviews reflect a man who, while obsessed with correcting what he saw as bad musical grammar, had the discernment to report clearly what he heard, as of this first Boston performance of a work now regarded as an "easy listening" classic:

> Long deferred because of its many difficulties, the Rimsky-Korsakov Suite was performed on Saturday to the amazement of every concert-goer who had been brought up in the paths of Bach and righteousness. Yet no one dare say that the mountain brought forth a mouse; it was rather a white elephant that emerged. The Suite "Scheherezade" introduced us to a new Berlioz, a Russian Berlioz, who had been nurtured on augmented seconds, cradled in triplets, and had imbibed chromatics from his boyhood.
>
> The work is in music very much like a Turner in painting of the late period in its own domain of Art; it presents few ideas but an overwhelming glow of color; as a lesson in tone coloring of the most modern sort it is very interesting and should be given again very soon, for one cannot digest its strange effects on a first hearing. (*Boston Daily Advertiser*, April 8, 1897)

Unlike some of his contemporaries, Elson found even Debussy cacophonous. Pedantic references to theory and harmony abound in his critiques.

96   Ravel and the Sibelius Fourth Symphony were too much for him, let alone
      Schoenberg. Of *Salome* he said, "It is impossible to know whether one is play-
      ing true or false, and any misprints could not be detected by any known mu-
      sical rule." Of *Also Sprach Zarathustra* he wrote, "At the end of the work there
      is a modulation from the key of B to the key of C that is unique, for the Gor-
      dian knot is cut by the simple process of going there and going back again. If
      such modulations are possible, then the harmony books may as well be burnt
      at once." Of *Till Eulenspiegel:* "The musical dictionary of the future will cer-
      tainly give the following definitions: RHYTHM—Four or five different subdivi-
      sions of the measure which must be employed simultaneously. KEY—Any suc-
      cession of tones; but the succession which is indicated by the signature must be
      avoided, especially at the close. TUNE—The beginning of a melody; this ought
      to be sparingly employed and should never be brought to a conclusion" (*Bos-
      ton Sunday Advertiser,* November 26, 1899).

      A far more tolerant critic than Elson was Henry Taylor Parker (1867–
      1934), perhaps in part because, not even able to read music, much less parallel
      fifths, he knew not whereof Elson fulminated. Parker, a Boston native and Har-
      vard dropout, was a friend of George Santayana who pursued studies in Eu-
      rope for a few vagabond years. He eventually returned to Boston and after sev-
      eral years as a journalist in various jobs succeeded Apthorp as the music and
      drama critic for the *Boston Evening Transcript* in 1905.

      Parker, who always signed his articles "H.T.P."—facetiously deciphered
      by some as an acronym for "Hard to Please" or "Hell to Pay"—was the most
      mysterious of the long-serving critics of the Old Guard. Owlish-looking and
      bespectacled, short of stature, a lifelong bachelor, a man of polymorphous cu-
      riosity, he sometimes wrote on politics and world affairs and was also a dance
      critic and a drama critic so highly esteemed by the *New York Times*'s Brooks
      Atkinson that he described his work as "the finest chapter in newspaper drama
      criticism in America." A legendary workaholic and eccentric in journalism
      circles who avoided all social contact with actors and musicians, Parker had
      some affectations: applauding by the continental method of stamping his cane
      on the floor; cultivating an e. e. cummings–like prose style (a typical Parker
      syntax: "as the day upturns them"). What he lacked in musical booklearning
      H. T. Parker made up for in intuitive discernment and a sensitive, poetic prose
      that resembled Paul Rosenfeld's, but without Rosenfeld's sesquipedality. Of
      Mischa Elman he wrote: "He plays with the contortions of his body that have
      replaced his former 'weaving,' as though he were in mighty effort to release the

emotions surging out of him through his violin. On this score Mr. Elman sorely needs either a sense of poise or a sense of humor. . . . he seems to squeeze out his instrumental songs as though his violin were a paint tube from which in travail of spirit he was pressing them." [29]

Though musically untutored, Parker was a good enough reporter to convey important technical facts about the musicians he saw, such as the conductor Willem Mengelberg:

> With his left hand he does not signal an instrument or group of instruments, as most conductors do. He does that apparently by the concentration of his glance upon them or by inward reliance upon the players' close following of the score. Usually with his left hand he is writing the contours of the melody upon the air, flinging out emphases, catching and concentrating climaxes, like the old pictures of Jove in the classical dictionaries with a fist full of thunderbolts, or else holding the orchestra in the hollow of his palm, as it were, in a moment of transition.

His cross-training as a drama critic comes through in this remarkable description of Enrico Caruso's Canio from Leoncavallo's *I Pagliacci:*

> From year to year, he amplified it with much illuminating and defining detail. Recall, for instance, the exaggerated whimsies of a strolling player with which his matured Canio cozened the crowd at the beginning of the play; the wiping of the powder from his face as of a player resuming relievedly his own person; the intensity, brooding or ominous, that he threw into his declamation in the play while in action he was but doing the part; the fashion in which he went emotionally dead when he had struck down Nedda; how he returned a little to himself, dragged out of his throat "la commedia è finita" and huddled away, distraught, blind, blank again.
>   . . . He made tellingly but untheatrically the swift change from playful banter over the lightness of women to the amorous and vindictive words about a wife that he already suspects. [30]

There was such a local cult around Parker in Boston that when he died the *Transcript* ran articles, letters, reminiscences, and photographs of him almost daily for an entire month.

∾ *Richard Aldrich and the school of the* New York Times

By the end of the twentieth century the *New York Times* would be one of four daily New York City papers employing music critics but the only one of the four with a staff of several of them; the *Times* had become the journal of record and the last bastion of the classical music business in New York by a process of attrition. At the century's beginning, however, the *Times* was but one of fifteen metropolitan dailies, not counting Brooklyn papers. Though influential, the *Times*'s prestige was not yet greater than its own critics', and despite W. J. Henderson's years of service, a characteristic corporate *Times* critical style had not yet been defined. The critic who did create that model was one who had been Krehbiel's assistant on the *Tribune* and whom Henderson personally recommended to succeed him in 1902: Richard Aldrich.

Aldrich (1863–1937), born and educated in Providence, Rhode Island, studied the piano and at Harvard, like W. F. Apthorp and Henry T. Finck, took music courses with John Knowles Paine. He wrote music criticism for the *Harvard Crimson* but concentrated on an all-around liberal arts curriculum. Upon graduation in 1885 he became both general arts critic and a general reporter for the *Providence Journal.* He went to Leipzig for a couple of years of music study and returned to Washington, D.C., to become for a short time both an assistant to Senator Nathan Dixon of Rhode Island and a music critic for the *Washington Evening Star.* In 1891 the *New York Tribune* hired him as an assistant art, book, and music critic, in which last capacity he worked under Henry Krehbiel. He was the chief music critic at the *Times* from 1902 to 1923.

Aldrich, with a grey walrus mustache, looked more like a bookish Edwardian Londoner than a New Yorker. He became an accomplished musicologist and over the years assembled a celebrated private library of music books, eventually donated to Harvard. As a writer Aldrich was perhaps more temperate and even than any of his New York Old Guard colleagues. The young W. J. Henderson had been militant and cutting; Aldrich was mild, assiduous, scholarly, comprehensive—the archetypal boilerplate *New York Times* writer. The composer-writer Daniel Gregory Mason remembered him thus: "He was temperamentally mild and cautious, inclined to take the most kindly possible view of everything, and rather smiled at for his recurrent phrase 'There is much to be said on both sides'—especially by those who, knowing him personally, remembered how hard his stammer made it for him to say anything!"[31]

Being a *Times* critic was ample pulpit for Aldrich; unlike his colleagues, he did not issue convoys of music appreciation books. Aldrich seems to have created the Sunday think piece as an obligatory genre for all subsequent *Times* music critics. By the end of his *Times* tenure, Aldrich's Sunday articles had subtly begun to take on the tenor of self-assumed trusteeship of the institution of classical music, the subliminal air of the royal editorial "we," that has been handed down ever since to all *Times* chief music critics.

Aldrich was an excellent reporter of recitals and one of the first critics interested in music of earlier epochs. He was a sound but essentially conservative critic. Of Berlioz he wrote in his 1928 book, *Musical Discourse:* "Berlioz's musical thought is almost always superficial. His musical invention is terribly, wearisomely commonplace. How few of the themes in any of his most important compositions are expressive or beautiful, or find their way to the heart! The pomp and glitter and the wealth of color with which he sets them forth can only hide their poverty. . . . His influence has been rather through the potency of his intellectual processes than by his musical embodiment of them." How unlike Hale's, or even Krehbiel's, conception.

After leaving the chief critic post at the *Times* to Olin Downes in 1923, Aldrich continued as an adviser emeritus; tellingly, he wrote letters to the editor under the sobriquet "Sylvanus Urbanus" vehemently disagreeing with Downes on certain issues. But he maintained a gentle wit. Recounting the saga of Jenny Lind and P. T. Barnum in *Musical Discourse*, Aldrich wrote, "The Boston newspapers were in the meantime viewing critically and with disapproval all this pother in New York, as they had, and perhaps even now have, a habit of doing."

**🌿 *Henry T. Finck,
the Old Guard's
glad evangel***

Henry T. Finck (1854–1926) was by his own admission the most amiable of the Old Guard critics. Born in Missouri to German émigrés, his father a pharmacist and country physician who played many instruments and organized country bands, young Henry heard lots of music as a boy. When the Civil War loomed father Finck took the family to live in Oregon, where Henry had a Tom Sawyer boyhood and played piano and cello. He also found a local classical language tutor who taught him to read Greek and Latin so well that the boy amazed his Harvard entrance examiners. As a Harvard student Finck often played cello in the homes of Longfellow and other Cambridge arts luminaries; he once played for Rose Hawthorne, the novelist's daughter. Like W. F. Ap-

thorp, Finck studied music at Harvard with John Knowles Paine but concentrated on liberal arts; graduating in 1876, he immediately borrowed money to
travel to the first Bayreuth. In later years he recounted how, when his efforts to
crash the *Ring* rehearsals failed, he brazenly approached Wagner himself:

> I boldly walked up to him and told him I had bought tickets to all the per-
> formances, but was very anxious to attend the rehearsals, adding that I
> represented a New York and a Boston journal. At the mention of the word
> newspaper, a frown passed over his face, and he said, rather abruptly, "I
> don't care much about newspapers. I can get along without them." But,
> in a second, a smile drove away the frown and he added: "I have given or-
> ders that no one shall be admitted. However, you have come a long way—
> and as I have found it necessary to make some exceptions, I will admit
> you too." He then asked for my card and told me I would be admitted by
> mentioning my name to the doorkeeper. That he did not bear any deep
> resentment against me for unfortunately being a newspaper man, he
> showed the next day, by walking up to me and asking me if I had suc-
> ceeded in getting in.[32]

Finck briefly returned to Harvard and was awarded a fellowship that enabled him to spend three more years in Berlin, Heidelberg, Vienna, and Munich, a Rombergian "student prince" studying philosophy and psychology and
dispatching articles on music to American papers. Originally his intent was to
become a university professor of philosophy, but when he returned to the
States in 1881 his articles from abroad and letters to the editor of the *Nation*, a
New York City newspaper, persuaded someone there to hire him as a music
critic when the *Nation* merged with the *Evening Post*. In that job he stayed almost forty-three years, a tenure even longer than Krehbiel's, retiring in 1924.
(He actually was offered the *Tribune* job but declined, whereupon Krehbiel
took it.) He also lectured at the National Conservatory of Music on music history, where he was a colleague of Dvořák, Joseffy, and Huneker.

Finck described his critical credo thus: "Many critics love to dwell on flaws
in the work of the great and the greatest. I heard those flaws but ignored them,
dwelling instead on the things that raised these artists above the level of dull
mediocrity on which most musicians and other mortals dwell. . . . In looking back on my long career as a musical critic nothing strikes me as so strange
as that I should have been so often called upon to act as champion and defender of the greatest musicians against some of my colleagues." One junior

colleague, Herbert Peyser, observed that Finck was actually afraid of the effects of his negative reviews on the performer's health. Peyser once showed him a negative review of a conductor Finck favored. Finck wouldn't run it, saying that the conductor "would be so upset if he read it that he would have to go to bed at once and call a doctor. And he would never be in a condition to conduct to-morrow night." Finck himself felt that his bad reviews stung people more than other critics' because they were always expecting his usual bonhomie. Finck was generally liked by the musicians he wrote about; the composer-pianist Percy Grainger, no fan of critics, even dedicated a piece to him, *The Gumsuck-ers March.* A rare example indeed of artist gratitude; Wagner's skewering of Ed-uard Hanslick as Beckmesser in *Die Meistersinger* is more typical, though there is one European counterpart to Grainger and Finck: Ravel dedicated his *Albo-rada del Gracioso* to the critic Michel-Dimitri Calvocoressi.

Finck was an unabashed enthusiast, not a paid puffer but a booster, and he did not hesitate to write articles about his particular favorites—Paderewski, Kreisler, Novaes, Seidl, Stransky, Farrar, or composers such as Grieg and Ed-ward MacDowell—that bordered on press agentry. He cheerfully claimed that he was on intimate social terms with most of the Metropolitan's singers and that his pen had been responsible for the hire of Heinrich Conreid to replace Maurice Grau as general manager of the Met in 1903. He claimed that Maria Jeritza accepted his criticisms and that she improved her singing by acting upon them. He also says in his memoirs that he often criticized Galli-Curci for singing out of tune, but that "when I met her, first at one of Mrs. Frederick Steinway's famous dinners, and afterwards, on the steamer *Paris,* she showed not the slightest resentment at my rather violent criticisms; so we became quite chummy; our common interest in gardening supplied an inexhaustible topic of conversation." Finck then lets slip that the diva promised also to send a crate of cauliflower to his Maine summer home. "No bribe, here, if you please! She was aware that I am no longer a professional critic! (Schumann-Heink once sent me a box of oranges from her California ranch. I think I deserved more than one.)" [33]

He liked those he deemed the more lyrical, more sanguine composers: Bach, Gluck, Weber, Schumann, Schubert, Chopin, Rubinstein, Robert Franz, Wagner, Liszt, Tchaikovsky, Grieg, MacDowell, and Massenet. Mencken called him "the press-agent of Massenet." "Massenet's creations will outlive by de-cades the majority of Brahms," Finck wrote, and on another occasion, said the operas of Richard Strauss "are already moribund, whereas Massenet's are more popular than ever." His great failure of judgment was his lifelong distaste for the music of Brahms; after all, even Shaw in old age somewhat recanted his own youthful diatribes against Brahms. Finck even confessed to finding parts of Beethoven boring. Finck was less interested in sonata form than other critics, but he had definite ideas and was no fool. Some have taken Finck's good-heartedness and anti-Krehbielian preference for lyricism and miniaturism as evidence of a lack of intellectual power rather than as a committed aesthetic position.*

Looking a little bit like Theodore Roosevelt without the bully robustiousness, Finck was a German and Wagnerite who distrusted Germany. Though christened Henry Gottlob Finck, he changed his middle name officially to Theophilus years before World War I, before it was politically correct to be anti-German, in order to sound less Teutonic. He claimed that Wagner hated Prussia, too. "There were days during the war when, if I could have done so, I would have eagerly touched a button that would have exterminated every man in the German Empire," he wrote in his memoirs.

Finck published eighteen books, including volumes on Wagner, Chopin, Anton Seidl, Grieg, Massenet, and Strauss, as well as an autobiography, indispensable to historians of the period, that discloses an unusually humane and kindly temperament for a critic. He also maintained a lively interest in other subjects, some of them eccentric. He wrote travel books about Spain, Morocco, the Pacific Coast, and Japan. One of his first books, *Romantic Love and Personal Beauty* (1887), advanced the argument that romantic love was a concept unknown and unpracticed by ancient Greek, Roman, and Hebrew peoples; he expanded the thesis in a second volume to monumental lengths, *Primitive Love and Love Stories* (1900), to a mixed critical reception. Another nonmusical Finck book was *Gardening with Brains:* "Klingsor with all his magic never went in for horticulture more thoroughly," said one colleague;[34] indeed, Finck socialized with Luther Burbank. Finck was also a gastronome and in his book *Food and Flavor* nurtured a pet theory that the sense of smell was a neglected psychological phenomenon; he made into a corollary of this theory the notion that people could inhibit their appetites and lose weight if they practiced his unique method of reinhaling the odors of their food, a crackpot idea retailed into a best-selling 1920s diet book entitled *Girth Control.*

Not surprisingly, Finck was a health faddist who enthusiastically attended

---

*Richard Franko Goldman, in his scholarly article about American music critics in the June 1955 issue of *The Score,* thought Finck execrable for such comments as describing Tchaikovsky's Fourth Symphony as "adorable" and Mozart as "dull and trivial as music can be."

W. H. Kellogg's Battle Creek, Michigan, health farm. Yet he could not resist gormandizing and in his later years began suffering arteriosclerosis and strokes, despite his career-long practice of retiring early for a good night's sleep and refusing to stay up late after concerts to write his reviews; the *Evening Post* allowed him to send his copy to the composing room as late as noon the next day. Finck could never have been a critic on a morning paper. Recalled Herbert Peyser, a *Times* critic who was a one-time protégé of Finck, "He had such a belief in the hygienic value of sleep before midnight that not even if the celestial choir had given a concert at special prices with the archangels as soloists would he have remained after ten o'clock. . . . He would have retired from the profession rather than have done his writing at night, and he could not expend enough pity (seasoned with dark warnings) on those of his colleagues who had to cudgel their brains directly after an evening performance."[35] Moreover, Finck, who summered in Bethel, Maine, raised flowers, and was exquisitely olfactory, refused to abide ill-ventilated auditoriums and recital halls. According to Peyser, "He once walked out of a recital he wanted especially to hear because 'the temperature was more suitable for raising palms and pineapples than for listening to music.' He carried an assortment of phials and tubes (whose prophylactic virtues he never tired of retailing) and a menthol inhaler of high visibility was his inseparable companion wherever he went."

Perhaps the most interesting facet of this interesting man is that much of Henry Finck was not written by Henry Finck at all but by Abbie Cushman Finck, his wife from 1890 on. When Mrs. Finck died in 1940, Herbert Peyser told *Musical America* readers,

> It would be splitting hairs to argue that Mrs. Finck did not hold an official position as a New York music critic; actually, she was one of the most industrious of the lot for a period of decades. . . . Early in her married life Mrs. Finck had learned to write so amazingly like her husband that, as time passed, it became almost impossible to tell their styles apart. And not only were their writings as such almost indistinguishable; their musical tastes were practically identical. Time after time they collaborated in reviews, he writing one part, she another. When these articles appeared in print it often took an expert to tell which portion was by which. . . . The couple had developed this critical teamwork almost to the point of a fine art. . . . In the concert hall or the opera house one could often see her writing with great industry in the little black leather note-book (and

when she was so engaged one knew that the performance she was hearing bored her).[36]

Finck's critical colleague Albert Steinberg of the *New York Herald* called Mrs. Finck "Mrs. Boswell." Percy Grainger, the aforementioned dedicator, kept a photograph of Henry Finck in his piano studio that was signed "From Abbie's Henry." Abbie was the Edith Galt (Mrs. Woodrow) Wilson of American musical letters.

Finck retired in May 1924 to pen his memoirs. In one photograph, the desk at his home on Manhattan Avenue in Harlem in the 1920s appears shockingly cluttered with papers. In the final proofs revision for his publisher, he penned these valedictory words on September 30, 1926:

> I became a musical editor almost at the beginning of the cult of highbrow music and remained so to the end of the Golden Age and beyond. . . . There will never be another age like it. The radio is making terrible havoc in the activities and earnings of professional musicians (ask them!) while the cacophonists, sarcastically dubbed "futurists," are doing their level best, with their insane cult of dissonances, to assassinate whatever interest is left in the divine art. They are greater enemies of music than the jazz bands. "Paradise Lost" might be an appropriate sub-title for my reminiscences of The Golden Age of Music.[37]

Eerily, but with a poetic justice that speaks for all the Old Guard, Finck passed away the very next day, October 1.

And with his comrade-in-arms and last Old Guard survivor W. J. Henderson's suicide eleven years later, *sic transit gloria mundi.*

Gilded Age Gadfly

James Gibbons Huneker,
Garrulous Steeplejack of the Arts

*Almost singlehanded, he brought the new currents of European
art and thought to America and made them fashionable.*
—ALFRED KAZIN

*My first visit to Lüchow's Restaurant was inspired by the fact that
I had read somewhere that Huneker went there. I asked the head
waiter if my hero was around, allowing him to believe that I was
an important figure in Huneker's world, and when I was told he
was not, I went out to Fourteenth Street.*
—S. N. BEHRMAN, playwright and humorist

With the passage of time, perhaps the only music critic of the Gilded Age to have achieved a truly legendary eminence is James Gibbons Huneker (1857–1921), who, in foresightedness of judgment, broad artistic culture, and sheer literary stylishness, single-handedly eclipses the entire lot of Krehbiel, Finck, Henderson, Aldrich, Apthorp, Hale, and all the other incumbents of daily newspapers at the turn of the century. He is the only nineteenth-century American newspaper music critic who can be spoken of in the same breath with the great nineteenth-century European critics: Taine, Sainte-Beuve, Gautier, Shaw, Ruskin, Pater.

Huneker was a geyser of prose who effluviated critical writing about all the arts—not just music but literature, painting, and the drama—in voluminous gouts in magazines, newspapers, and books from the 1870s to the beginning of Prohibition, an event he detested but mercifully did not live to endure. Jack of all seven lively arts he was, although music was his *primus inter pares*. The term Huneker preferred to describe his polymorphous artistic interests was "steeplejack of the arts"; he entitled his autobiography *Steeplejack*. His mighty

106   pen was his scepter as America's arts czar sans portfolio, before ever there was a WPA or an NEA.

Huneker was doubtless the most influential and most widely read by other writers and intellectuals of all the music critics in our history. The critic and playwright Channing Pollock called Huneker "the greatest figure in criticism in this country." The eminent Danish critic Georg Brandes told the American critic George Sylvester Viereck that Huneker was "strangely brilliant for an American." The playwright Ben Hecht wrote, "In the years that I read him, 1914 to 1921, I regarded [Huneker] as my alma mater." H. L. Mencken, Huneker's friend and disciple, who had scourged America's south as the "sewer of the bozart," cribbed from himself to dub Huneker a "bolshevik of the bozart." Added the Sage of Baltimore, "If a merciful Providence had not sent James Gibbons Huneker into the world we Americans would still be shipping union suits to the heathen, reading Emerson, sweating at Chautauquas, and applauding the plays of Bronson Howard."[1]

Even in the late nineteenth century—when religious belief still was commonly taken as the yardstick to measure the worth of art and such worldly writers as Dostoyevsky and Tolstoy still couched their skepticism within the frame of organized faith—Huneker's God was Art. The wife of one friend found him kneeling in front of a bust of Beethoven in the late 1870s praying, "O Divine Creator of the Ninth," and Huneker, himself Catholic but iconoclastic, retailed the saga of the dying pianist who, when asked by a priest if he was Catholic or Protestant, replied, "Father, I am a pianist."[2]

Huneker was "the man who listened to Oscar Wilde's conversation, joined forces with pranksters to play an elaborate joke on Oscar Hammerstein I, knocked on Whitman's door in Camden, saw Flaubert, shook hands with Browning, met Swinburne, Victor Hugo, and Shaw, and was a familiar of Havelock Ellis, Arthur Symonds, Victor Herbert, and Maxwell Perkins."[3] He went to Europe some twenty times and seemingly met every art dignitary of the time both there and in America. A character out of fiction himself, his real-life encounters with the famous might otherwise seem the wishful confabulation of some historical novelist. In 1903 he met Strauss and Debussy. He saw Oscar Wilde speak in Philadelphia in 1882 and also heard Matthew Arnold give a lecture there. In his 1912 voyage he met Henri Bergson, Matisse, and Conrad. In 1913 he met Chesterton and H. G. Wells in England. In New York he attended parties given by the critic W. J. Henderson and met Marcella Sembrich, Josef Hofmann, and the de Reszke brothers. The list is endless. Like some Edwardian Zelig, he was ubiquitous, present at every event poetic justice would

put him, from hearing Boito's *Mefistofele* at the Metropolitan Opera during the
Met's maiden season of 1883 to meeting Shaw at Bayreuth in 1896.

∾ *Early years:*
Scenes from a   Huneker was born in Philadelphia in 1857, though all
Philadelphian   his life he publicly claimed the date was 1860. His father
vie de bohème   was a housepainter of Magyar descent, his mother of
                       Irish ancestry. But Huneker's grandfather had been a
professional musician: a church organist and a charter member of the Musical
Fund Society of Philadelphia, America's oldest musical organization after Boston's Handel and Haydn Society; and his father became friendly with bohemian types, mixed with prominent music patrons in the city, and even managed to become personally acquainted with both Edwin Booth and Edgar Allan Poe. John Huneker also amassed a collection of paintings for his home, while his wife, Mary, published a book on engraving in 1872. Engravers, etchers, and illustrators were frequent guests *chez* Huneker. Young Jim began piano lessons at age eight. He learned more about music at the Broad Street Academy, the Christian classical school where he attended secondary school; he also went to concerts and operas with his father and attended musicales in the private homes of music lovers. Later, he avidly attended the theater in Philadelphia.

Despite these arts-friendly influences, Huneker's mother wanted him to become a priest or, failing that, a church organist, while his father didn't want him to become a musician and hang out with bohemians, though Jim was serious about his piano lessons and practiced a lot. According to Huneker's autobiography, *Steeplejack,* upon discovering books by Whitman, Baudelaire, Gautier, and Flaubert on his table, Mrs. Huneker said to her son, "What can you expect in the future if you turn your mind into a sewer for all those vile poets and infidels?"

Huneker went to work for a while at fifteen in a machine tool shop and in 1873 began apprenticing to a lawyer. Like Mencken, he never attended college, but all the while he was reading on his own omnivorously. While continuing to study law, Huneker took up music criticism for the *Philadelphia Evening Bulletin.* At the Philadelphia Centennial Exposition in 1876, Huneker met and heard the great Hungarian pianist and Liszt pupil Rafael Joseffy. Joseffy took a fraternal interest in the young Philadelphian and suggested he try for admission to the Paris Conservatoire as a piano student.

Two years later, Huneker, now a married man, took up Joseffy's proposition. In 1878 (not long after Huneker had visited the aging Walt Whitman in Camden, New Jersey, an event he was later to chronicle in his book *Ivory Apes and Peacocks*), Huneker and his wife, Elizabeth, sailed for Paris. There for nine months they lived—on a small allowance from home—the life of Murger's *Scènes de la vie de bohème*. Huneker failed his audition for the piano class at the Conservatoire, but found his way to a private teacher of both piano and harmony. More importantly, he began sending travel dispatches back to the *Philadelphia Evening Bulletin*. He was paid five dollars for each—a princely sum for one living in a Paris garret—and thence began his lifelong practice of supporting his perennial European peregrinations through the proceeds of contemporaneous freelance assignments for American newspapers.

In his wanderings about Paris, the young Huneker managed to encounter Manet, Degas, Victor Hugo, Turgenev, de Maupassant, Mallarmé, Zola, Daudet, and Flaubert. He attended the Paris exposition of painters of 1878. He attended many operas and heard Nicolai Rubinstein and Camille Saint-Saëns play the piano (in the United States in 1873 he had heard Anton Rubinstein, but was never to hear Liszt in Europe). By now he spoke French and German passably and could read both languages fluently.

Later, back in Philadelphia, Huneker gave piano lessons while studying with other teachers himself; while continuing his nascent reviewing career he still aspired to a career as a concert pianist. He spent time with, if not took actual lessons from, the Hungarian violinist Eduard Reményi in the early 1880s when Reményi visited Philadelphia and evidently learned a good deal from him. In 1883 Huneker met Theodore Presser, the music publisher, who had just started the *Etude* magazine. Within two years Huneker was a regular contributor.

Though Huneker was married and had an infant daughter (an earlier infant daughter had died a few months after birth), he could barely support himself. Then the Hunekers' second baby daughter died on November 12, 1883; Elizabeth bore no further children. By 1886, almost thirty, Huneker was still unable to support himself by sporadically teaching piano (which earnings he liquidated by paying for his own piano study with them), occasionally clerking at a piano manufacturer, and writing for the *Etude*. His wife had to work at dressmaking to support both of them, and his father was still helping them financially.

In February of that year Huneker separated from his wife and departed for New York City without her. He found lodgings at Morton House, overlooking

Union Square near Lienau's Cafe, a watering hole where such great pianists   109
from Europe as Joseffy and Moriz Rosenthal were known to give impromptu
concerts in a back room. He also began a lifetime of Lüchow's-going. Living
the hand-to-mouth existence embodying the classic Manhattan down-and-
outer in the archetypal O. Henry tale (oddly, Huneker later disdained O.
Henry's writing), Huneker moved from boardinghouse to boardinghouse,
usually places inhabited by artists and bohemians. He also frequented fringe
areas such as the Bowery and the Lower East Side (Huneker knew some Yid-
dish and evinced such an enthusiasm for Jewish artists in his writings that
some readers mistook him for Jewish).

Some years later Huneker's *Sun* colleague Edward Mitchell was to observe
that even the mature and successful Huneker was "childlike in his conception
of pecuniary relations"; even with allegedly the highest salary paid an American newspaper critic at the time, said Mitchell, he had trouble holding on to
cash. Toward the end of his life, when reviewing for the *New York Times* and
New York World, the ailing Huneker declined an offer from the millionaire
banker Otto Kahn to put a liveried cab at his disposal after concerts to chauffeur him home. Ever the bohemian, the diabetic sexagenarian still insisted on
navigating the stairs of the subway with his ever-present cane.

Huneker's

journalistic career   Already contributing to the *Etude,* in July 1887 the
                                           freshman Manhattanite began contributing to the
other leading musical magazine, the *Musical Courier.* His unsigned review in
the *Courier* of the Liszt-Wagner correspondence became a sensation in 1888
and thereafter his work was bylined. Huneker's column in the *Musical Courier*
was called "The Raconteur," while in the *Etude* he authored irreverent squibs
under the nom de plume "Old Fogy." In 1891 Huneker also became music critic
of the short-lived (till 1896) *New York Recorder.* By 1893 the dean of American
music critics, W. S. B. Mathews, was referring to the thirty-six-year-old Huneker as "a brilliant and versatile writer of wide journalistic experience." Huneker also began writing drama criticism in the 1890s.

In 1895 Huneker and his friend Vance Thompson, a polymath reviewer
like himself who covered drama, music, and literature for the *New York Commercial Advertiser,* started *Mlle New York,* an irreverent arts magazine for the
"smart set." At about the same time the *London Musical Courier* ran Huneker's
Musical Courier articles, establishing his reputation abroad as a leading Ameri-

110   can critic, and Huneker left the *Recorder* to become music and drama critic of the *Morning Advertiser,* the morning edition of the *Commercial Advertiser.* In October 1897 he became music critic for a weekly magazine named *Town Topics,* in which Huneker wrote a column called "Crotchets and Quivers" and signed it "The Melomaniac."

In the fall of 1900 Huneker became the music critic of the *New York Sun,* for which he also wrote drama criticism. By 1902 his weekly earnings were around one hundred dollars, a very good income for the time. But he was official music critic at the *Sun* for only two years, though continuing to serve as drama critic till 1904, later as art critic, still later as freelance correspondent. Huneker inveterately freelanced both during and after salaried employment; he wrote freelance for *Harper's Bazaar, Scribner's, Lamp, Success Magazine, Theatre, Smart Set,* and the *New York Times.* By 1904 he was turning out five thousand words a day as a freelancer; in one six-week period he made $2,000, whereas on the *Sun* payroll he had never made more than $125 a week.

In 1899 Scribner's published *Mezzotints in Modern Music,* the first of his more than twenty books, many of which were reworkings of his previously published articles from magazines and newspapers. Some dealt exclusively with music; some focused on other arts (*Iconoclasts* on the drama, *Promenades of an Impressionist* on painting); still others were olios of criticism of painting, music, and literature interspersed with his own short stories. And then there were the two biographies, of Chopin and Liszt. After about 1902 drama, literature, and painting criticism represented an increasing portion of Huneker's daily journalism output, so the reworked cogitations published in his books represent how his musical thought matured years after the original reviews.

In need of the money from his freelance work to the end of his life, Huneker continued at an unabated pace. In 1914 he joined the staff of *Puck,* writing a column called "The Seven Arts." When Huneker was hired to be music critic for the *Philadelphia Press* in 1917 (to which he commuted by train), he had not been a regular music critic since leaving that capacity at the *Sun* and the *Musical Courier* in 1902. Huneker became a music critic for the *New York Times* in 1917, and in 1919 Herbert Bayard Swope brought him to the *New York World* as music critic for an op-ed page that soon included the writings of such future Algonquin luminaries as Franklin P. Adams and Alexander Woollcott.

It was not until America declared war on Germany in 1917—some forty years after his cub reporter days, thirty after his first regular bylines—that James Huneker for the first time in his life signed his columns James *Gibbons*

Huneker; such Anglo underlining was what the anti-German hysteria in the nation at the time demanded (we were at war with the "Hun"). Oddly, this three-barreled moniker, which he seldom used, has settled into posterity's embrace.

Pianist manqué,
pianophile
nonpareil

Despite his profligate output of words, criticism did not become Huneker's exclusive métier until fairly late in life. Huneker persisted in trying to be a concert pianist until Joseffy, with whom he studied, finally told him he didn't quite have what it took. (Also, Huneker had had the notorious operation to sever the tendon connecting the fourth finger from the fifth of his left hand, and the results of the surgery evidently impaired rather than improved his technique.) Even so, the composer Arthur Farwell remembered being ravished by hearing Huneker play passages of Chopin and Liszt through the walls adjoining his friend's apartment. Though he was still practicing up to two hours a day as late as 1905, Huneker wore the pose of the disappointed would-be performer, even as he sublimated that energy into becoming the leading literary pianologist of the turn of the century.

The great pianist and pedagogue Isidore Philipp declared that Huneker "knew more about the literature of piano than many great pianists." The pianist Arthur Friedheim, the personal secretary and disciple of Liszt who became good friends with Huneker after converting him to the Liszt banner after his initial anti-Liszt attitude, claimed that it was Huneker who coined the now-proverbial phrase "the grand manner" to describe the romantic style of the schools of Liszt, Rubinstein, and Leschetitzky. (In his initial hearing of Rachmaninoff, Huneker felt the composer-pianist lacked the "grand manner"!) Friedheim also wrote in his memoirs that Huneker was so discerning a piano connoisseur that he "went so far as to say publicly that he was unable to express an opinion of the abilities of a certain pianist owing to the fact that he did not use a Steinway piano in his American concerts and that, since the piano he used was an unfamiliar one, the critic could not distinguish what was lacking in the artist." [4]

Huneker reviewed for the *Musical Courier* the two-volume *Life of Chopin* by Frederick Niecks published in New York and London in 1888 by Novello, Ewer and Company, but he wrote in his review, "The real Chopin life has yet

112   to be written, a life that shall embrace his moral and physical natures, that will not shirk his marked abnormalities of vision, of conduct, and will not bow down before that agreeable fetish of sawdust and molasses called 'Frederic Chopin.'" In other words, Niecks was too pedantic for Huneker; herein he gives his whole critical summa. Huneker's *Chopin: The Man and His Music* (1900), which includes florid but accurate commentary on every note of Chopin's music, is still in print. His 1911 biography of Liszt is somewhat less successful but still in the "grand manner." Huneker edited Chopin's music for publication by Oliver Ditson, and also edited and fingered volumes of other piano music and lieder. In 1888 he became a member of a six-man piano teaching faculty at the National Conservatory of Music in New York, where he taught side-by-side with Antonín Dvořák. While on the faculty Huneker acted as facilitator between the German-speaking Dvořák and the librettist of a planned cantata on Longfellow's *Hiawatha*. When the project was abandoned, Dvořák incorporated into his *New World* Symphony some of the sketches originally intended for the cantata.

Huneker's friend H. L. Mencken—not himself a piano or Chopin buff— shrewdly noted that Huneker's true affinity was with piano music, not symphony or opera. Even in writing about chamber music he tended to favor combinations with piano. "One often feels," said Mencken, "in his discussions of orchestral music, that he only thinks orchestrally, like Schumann, with an effort—that all music, in his mind, gets itself translated into terms of piano music."[5] And in Huneker's long essay on Brahms in his book *Overtones,* he devotes far more space to the D Minor Piano Concerto—commonly regarded as a symphony with piano obbligato—than to any of the four symphonies.

ॐ *Huneker as*
fiction writer   Frustrated as a pianist, Huneker was also a frustrated, if persistent, creator of fiction. Throughout the 1890s he still entertained hopes of leaving criticism as a profession for full-time fiction writing. But deep down he knew his talent was second-rate; he was too good a critic not to know. He said of himself in his autobiography *Steeplejack:* "Life has been the Barmecide's feast to me . . . no sooner did I covet a rare dish than fate whisked it out of reach. I love painting and sculpture: I may only look, but never own either pictures or marbles. I would fain be a pianist, a composer of music: I am neither. Nor a poet. Nor a novelist, actor, playwright. I have writ-

ten of many things from architecture to zoology without grasping their inner substance. I am Jack of the Seven Arts, master of none."

In all his fiction Huneker depicted the lifestyle, dilemmas, and psychology of performing and creative artists, the milieu he knew so well from outside and in. His short stories first appeared in the *Musical Courier* and were first gathered in book form in *Melomaniacs* (1902), later in *Visionaries* (1905). In one of them, "The Corridor of Time," he depicts a man who aspires to be a great writer of fiction but lacks the talent. "I swear that the most miserable men are those who have caught a glimpse of the eternal beauty of art, who pursue her ideal face, who have the vision but not the voice." A later and somewhat racier book, the novel *Painted Veils* (1920), said to depict in cryptic form the sexual incidents from Huneker's own life he could not include in *Steeplejack*, sold well for some years after his death.

A rake's progress—
and a tosspot's   The lurid elements in Huneker's short fiction stemmed from a personal life that was baroque for a newspaper critic. While living in New York as an estranged married man, Huneker lived in the same building as Josephine Ahrensdorf Laski, a painter of miniatures who was unhappily married to Maksymilian J. Laski, a Polish-born merchant who committed suicide in 1890. Josephine became Huneker's lover, eventually claiming to be his common-law wife (she lived until 1950). In the meantime, Huneker had become friendly with Howard Hinton, a journalist and contributor to the *New York Home Journal,* an upscale arts and politics weekly to which Huneker also began to contribute. Hinton's wife, Lucy, was a sculptor, and two of their children had taken up art. Huneker—still married to Elizabeth and shacked up with Josephine—fell in love with their daughter Clio, a talented sculptor born in 1869.

By 1891 Huneker wanted to marry Clio, but his Catholic mother disapproved of his wish to divorce Elizabeth. His mother was terminally ill with tuberculosis, however, and at length Elizabeth served Huneker with divorce papers, his mother dying before the divorce became final. Eventually Clio and Lizzie even met in Philadelphia, and Lizzie lived on until 1916.

In 1892 Huneker married Clio and soon moved into Maison Félix, a brownstone on West Twenty-fifth Street near Sixth Avenue in Manhattan that was home to the usual omnium-gatherum of artists that Huneker favored, in-

114   cluding the clerical-collared theatrical producer David Belasco, whom Huneker befriended. Clio and Huneker separated only a few years later, however; after the birth of their son, Erik, Clio went to Paris to study sculpture further.
Then Josephine reemerged. *O tempora! o mores!*

In 1896 Huneker made his first pilgrimage to Bayreuth and saw the
Swedish-American Wagnerian soprano Olive Fremstad perform there. Huneker became infatuated with Fremstad, gave her great notices, met and developed an ongoing friendship with her, and may well have had an affair with her.
Interestingly, Fremstad was the real-life model for Thea Kronberg, the opera-
singer-from-the-prairie heroine of Willa Cather's 1915 novel, *The Song of the
Lark.* In *The Song of the Lark,* Thea Kronberg is pursued by a number of men
and finally gets married to one of them "offstage" in the novel's epilogue. In
real life, Cather interviewed Fremstad for *McClure's Magazine* and later got
to know her as a friend, after the diva had been divorced and had her alleged
fling with Huneker. One wonders whether Fremstad told Cather about Huneker, and whether Huneker was a model for any of the characters in *The Song of
the Lark.* In any event, Huneker did have an affair with the opera singer Geor-
giana Carhart, and he divorced Clio in 1899. Most of the rest of his years were
spent with Josephine Laski, whom he ultimately married in a civil ceremony.

It may seem as inconceivable today for a performer to sleep with a critic as
a psychiatrist with a patient, but the canons of journalistic ethics in those times
were more relaxed. According to Huneker's biographer Arnold Schwab, "The
better known he became as a critic, the more frequently female singers and pianists, not averse to furthering their careers by what Huneker called 'approved
horizontal methods,' sent him flowers, gifts, and invitations difficult to decline, no matter how hard he tried not to get involved with those he had to criticize."[6] Toward the end of his life, when Huneker wrote especially ecstatic ap-
praisals of the soprano Mary Garden for the *New York Times,* it was widely
assumed that he was romantically involved with her, but this doesn't appear to
have been so. But other rumored involvements with opera singers probably
had some truth to them, and Huneker may have chronicled his secret love life
in *Painted Veils.*

Sex wasn't Huneker's only vice: was Huneker ever sober when he wrote his
logorrheic criticism? As a freelancer Huneker was paid by the word and thus
had to produce, produce, produce just to survive. In later years he claimed to
have maintained a weekly rate of ten thousand words for years—all the more
remarkable in that he wrote in longhand all his life, never learning either to
type or to dictate. But he did have a secret weapon to help release the torrents

of his prose: he claimed he drank twelve to fifteen bottles of beer a day to help put the "buzz" into his pen.[7]

Huneker once allegedly bested an ex-prizefighter in a drinking contest by downing twenty-two seidels of beer. The critic Benjamin De Casseres recalled being regaled with hours of Huneker's own Chopin playing, "cases of Pilsner and Chianti conveniently placed under the piano." According to George Jean Nathan, Huneker amazed even seasoned pilsner lovers by being able to identify "every known brand of beer by the slightest taste."[8] Not surprisingly, Huneker by late middle age had chronic kidney, bladder, and liver problems, and incipient diabetes. Photographs show that his face took on a W. C. Fieldsian appearance in his last years. Nevertheless, he never seriously attempted to dry out; for Huneker, the joyous refrain wasn't *Wein, Weib und Gesang* so much as *Bier, Weib und Gesang*.

The Lucullan raconteur

His conversation, indeed, made his books seem almost funereal.
—H. L. MENCKEN

Unleashed by liquor, Huneker was a Vesuvius of conversation, a filibusterer of the seven lively arts. Perhaps in only this way did he miss his era: he would have been a natural guest or host for the culturally upscale talk show of today. Henry Finck recalled that "his conversation was as brilliant as his writings. During intermissions at opera or concert he usually had a sort of reception around his seat."[9] A young friend of Huneker's during the 1890s, Charles J. Rosebault, a *Sun* reporter, recalled Huneker in midflight to the *New York Times* in a 1921 memorial article: "Imagine the Encyclopedia Brittanica suddenly becoming vocal and giving tongue with all its potential eloquence; skipping from A to L and thence to G and on to Z, selecting topics helter-skelter, so that the pattern on the whole, if reduced to design and color, would be very like a crazy quilt of many hues. Have the speed of speech equal to that of the motor of a twin-six at an exhibition tryout. Lend to it the fire and enthusiasm of a young Sicilian at the climax of his first love avowal."

Walter Damrosch wrote of Huneker's "torrents of seething aphorisms and witticisms" and Benjamin De Casseres wrote of his first meeting with Huneker at two hours past midnight on a Sunday morning in 1908 or 1909 at a restaurant, looking like "a fat Anarch Cherub straight from a conference with Lucifer or Bacchus. . . . What a night. I had met the most extraordinary talker America has ever produced. Seidel after seidel. The dawn peeped in through the win-

116   dow. Huneker had abolished time. He raced on: Chopin, Spencer, Roosevelt, Brillat-Savarin, Howells, Goya, Ireland, Cellini, Rembrandt, Lincoln, Culmbacher, Paracelsus, George Ehret, Poe, Harry Thaw, Renoir, William Penn. . . ."

The arena for these nuclear detonations was Lüchow's or its equivalent: says Schwab, "Almost every day, at any rate, he would encounter Krehbiel, Steinberg, and the rest of what he liked to call the 'critical chain gang,' exchange intermission pleasantries with them, and, after they had all turned in their copy, join them at Lienau's, Mould's, or any one of a dozen cafes, where they would talk far into the night, drinking beer and eating the free lunches that helped sustain Huneker." [10] Mencken describes the scene best:

> Down went a Seidel of Pilsner—and out came the authentic last words of Whitman, gasped into poor Horace Traubel's solicitous ear, and too horrible, almost, to be remembered in a Christian land. Down went another—and out came a precise and meticulous description of Liszt's vast flotilla of warts and wens: the purple ones and the pale ones, the big ones and the little ones. Down went a third—and the theme was the virtuous love affairs of Gounod, or Wagner's encounter with the lascivious Swedish baroness, or the true story of Zola's asphyxiation, or the details of the affair between Duse and D'Annunzio, or Shaw's heroic but vain efforts to throw off the Thirty-Nine Articles, or the secret causes of Tchaikovsky's suicide, or the early lives of the de Reszke brothers in their Polish home, or the varying talents and idiosyncrasies of Lillian Russell's first four husbands. Down went a fourth—and there was coruscating, confidential discourse upon the defects in the Boehm system, the merits of German bathrooms, the difficulties of Brahms' capriccio in B minor, the proper tuning of the viol da gamba, the metaphysical errors of the Gnostics . . . the bad red wines at Wiesbaden, the worse red wines at Capri, the Pilsner at Carlsbad, the Pilsner at Vienna, the Pilsner at Prague, the Pilsner at Pilsen. . . .
>
> He was full of strange and fantastic information, much of it plainly apocryphal, but all of it immensely amusing. His musical anecdotes went back to the days of Johann Georg Albrechtsberger and embraced the latest conductor in Broadway. Raphael Joseffy was his authority in all things pianistic—with Pachmann as a sort of court of appeals. Joseffy told him this; Pachmann assured him of that. He knew how much Rubinstein could drink, and why d'Albert left his second, third and fourth wives. . . . I have heard them all, but he was the best. [11]

As late as 1961, two surviving former waiters from Lüchow's still remembered Huneker: his dignified carriage, his favorite dishes, his typical evening's
tosh: ten to fifteen glasses of beer, which according to surviving eyewitnesses
hardly affected him at all. He often ordered in German, and sometimes even
talked philosophy and poetry with the help.[12]

Came the Great War in 1914, and, said Huneker, "As to the war, it's a bore;
besides, as Stendhal says, it interrupts conversation."[13]

ꙮ Huneker's
prose style

Huneker's literary style naturally reflects his extem-
pore style. His every paragraph runs on forever before
the reader can come up for air. He sweeps great brushstrokes of garish verbal
color, spatulates impastos of ingenious metaphor, jungle thickets of extramusical poetic evocations—of which he is the unparagoned master among music
critics—to describe the psychological states engendered by a particular music
in the listener, to which painted canvas he subsumes an ordered reasoned
argument.

Huneker was so gifted a writer that he could burlesque the early nineteenth-century critics' style of lexiphanic nonsense and at the same time secretly aim a legitimate point with it. Here he is as the unenlightened-but-not-
so-dumb "Old Fogy" on Brahms:

> And yet Brahms dreams of pure white staircases that scale the infinite. A
> dazzling, dry light floods his mind at times, and you hear the rustling of
> wings,—wings of great, terrifying monsters, hippogriffs of horrid mien;
> hieroglyphic faces, faces with stony stare, menace your imagination. He
> can bring down within the compass of the octave moods that are outside
> the pale of mortals. He is a magician, often spectral; yet his songs have the
> homely lyric fervor and concision of Robert Burns.

Writing again on Brahms, but now signed as "James Huneker," he uses language still rich but not quite so steroidal; the logical progress of the metaphors
is more focused:

> Brahms is an inexorable form-maker . . . he is not a great colorist . . .
> simple, flat tints, primary and cool, are superimposed upon an enormous
> rhythmic versatility and a strenuousness of ideation. Ideas—noble, pro-

118 fundity-embracing ideas—he has. They are not in the smart, epigrammatic, flashy style of your little man. He disdains racial allusions. He is a planetary Teuton. You seek in vain for the geographical hints that chain Grieg to the map of Norway. Brahms's melodies are world typical, not cabined and confined to his native soil. This largeness of utterance, lack of polish, and a disregard for the politeness of his art do not endear him to the unthinking. Yet, what a master miniaturist he is in his little piano pieces, his intermezzi.

Using sobriquets like "Old Fogy" and "The Raconteur" in alternation with his real persona, Huneker, whether consciously or unconsciously, was adopting Robert Schumann's strategy of creating a cast of critical alter egos (Schumann's Florestan, Eusebius, and Master Raro) to carry on a debate about how to analyze, describe, and hear the music, affording the undecided critic an entertaining and jolly way to hedge his bets and defer any definitive judgments.*

Huneker, like most great wordsmiths, was a great punster. Lillian Russell's favorite composer was "Divorceshack"; standees at the opera were "railbirds"; Tchaikovsky was "shriek-hoarsely" to Old Fogy. But Huneker was more usually a sly fox as a humorist, and, as with his Lüchow's conversation, his writings fairly wink at the reader with apocrypha; musical talmudists could spend years trying to sort out the documentary from the fictive in Huneker's collected works. For instance, he not only retails the story that the Jewish actor Ludwig Geyer was Wagner's real father (now discredited by most scholars but then accepted by Ernest Newman and other Wagnerites), but embellishes the flourish that Cosima's maternal grandparents were Jewish. Is Huneker having us on, or does he really not know?

The contemporary musicologist and Chopin biographer Herbert Weinstock writes of Huneker's book on Chopin, "If contrasted with Niecks's patient labors among primary sources and his biographical formality, Huneker's book is disorderly, impressionistic, and amateurish. . . . Huneker the biographer and the handler of factual data must be approached warily; as enthusiast and textual critic, however—and allowing for the lapses inevitable in the heedless haste with which he wrote—he nearly always was right and always was vivid." [14]

---

*We can safely infer that Huneker had read Schumann's criticism, because toward the end of his life he wrote, reversing the proverbial Schumann phrase about the young Chopin, "How often have we felt like crying aloud, 'Hats on, gentlemen, this is not a genius!'"

Huneker's tastes, methods, and quirks as music critic

Though his criticism has sometimes been likened to Shaw's, there is a more apposite, Continental model for Huneker: the French poet, novelist, and sometime painter Théophile Gautier (1811–72), whom Huneker clearly had read. Gautier is perhaps best remembered as the literary critic who invented the "art for art's sake" doctrine. Gautier helped establish the idea that the highest service a critic could perform was to exhort for and enhance appreciation of art, rather than to function as a mere judge or fault-finder (i.e., the H. E. Krehbiel modus operandi). And certainly the body of Huneker's newspaper and magazine writings constitutes a campaign to bring the larger metacritical dimensions of a Gautier-like approach to those precincts where it had least existed before in America: the columns of the daily newspaper.

This is not at all to say that Huneker was wishy-washy or limitlessly eclectic. To the contrary, he was highly and assertively opinionated both about specific composers and general precepts, but he was overarchingly occupied with beating the drum for the general cause of Great Art rather than with stumping for any good art in particular. He also was incurably charming in person and in his writing, and that always takes the edge off controversy and polemic.

His reviewing career poised at the cusp of modernism in music, Huneker was both open and cogently cautious:

One thing is certain. . . . The old tonal order has changed forever; there are plenty of signs in the musical firmament to prove this. Moussourgsky preceded Debussy in his use of whole-tone harmonies, and a contemporary of Debussy, and an equally gifted musician, Martin Loeffler, was experimenting before Debussy himself in a dark but delectable harmonic region. . . . Every stronghold is being assailed, from the "divine" rights of property to the common chord of C major. With Schoenberg, freedom in modulation is not only permissible, but is an iron rule. . . . They tell me that Schoenberg once wrote freely in the normal manner, but finding that he could not attract attention he deliberately set himself to make abnormal music. I don't know how true this may be; the same sort of thing was said of Mallarmé and Paul Cézanne and Richard Strauss, and was absolutely without foundation. . . .

120

> I feel that "progress" as usually understood is a glittering "general idea" that blinds us to the truth. Reform in art is not like reform in politics; you can't reform the St. Matthew Passion or the Fifth Symphony. . . . This talk of reform is only confusing the historic with the aesthetic. . . . I consider it a pathetic fallacy . . . in criticism to be over-shadowed by the fear that, because some of our critical predecessors misjudged Wagner or Manet or Ibsen, we should be too merciful in criticizing our contemporaries. (*Ivory Apes and Peacocks*, p. 63)

Later, in the same essay:

> Probably Stravinsky and his musical fireworks will be called Futurist, whatever that pretentious title may mean. However, Tchaikovsky, Rimsky-Korsakov, Rachmaninoff and the others are no longer revolutionary but may be considered as evolutionary. Again the theory of transitional types comes into play, but I notice this theory has been applied only to minor matters, never to creators. We don't call Bach or Handel or Mozart or Beethoven intermediate types. Perhaps someday Wagner will seem as original to posterity as Beethoven does to our generation. Wasn't it George Saintsbury who once remarked that all discussion of contemporaries is conversation, not criticism?

Of the great composers, Huneker loved Chopin most, but expressed no militant chauvinism for him, as Dwight had, and Mencken would, for Beethoven. His personal pantheon for the nineteenth century is a little quirky from a twentieth-century perspective. He thought Berlioz a brilliant and innovative orchestrator who gussied up vacuous ideas, "a small fry, indeed, yet not without interest"; Tchaikovsky and Dvořák ranked only slightly higher in his estimation (he judged Smetana Dvořák's superior, even though Huneker had taught beside Dvořák at the National Conservatory). He felt that Meyerbeer was a far greater melodist than Wagner. "Humperdinck is a mediocrity, even more so than Puccini," Huneker wrote, perhaps getting it half right. "And what of the banalities of Bruckner?" Huneker could be unpredictable. He didn't like Prokofiev's music, but neither did he like Rachmaninoff's. He was unabashedly Euro-worshiping, yet he also wrote articles praising or encouraging performances of American composers such as MacDowell, Loeffler, Chadwick, Horatio Parker, and the short-lived Griffes.

As always with Huneker, one has to consult several opinions by his different critical personae to sift out self-contradictions. Huneker at one point says he regards a single Beethoven string quartet superior to the entire works of Wagner—he generally prefers concerted music to opera—and then adds that he feels that symphonic excerpts from the Wagner operas ("The Ride of Valkyries," for instance) simply do not stand on their own as absolute music in the concert hall. Yet elsewhere he goes on at great length on how Liszt's tone poems lead to Wagner's magnificent symphonic counterpoint and thence to Strauss's tone poems, which he prefers to Strauss operas, not observing any inconsistency in his musical analysis. He may have been only partly funning by having Old Fogy call Mozart the greatest of all composers because Bach was too studied and pedantic by comparison, and Beethoven too unbeautiful and guilty of starting the whole Romantic business of having the composer look into the ugliness of his own soul. As for the post-Berlioz and post-Gounod French, Old Fogy says of Debussy, Ravel, Florent Schmitt, Dukas, Déodat de Sévérac, Roger-Ducasse, D'Indy, and Roussel (he does not mention Fauré), "they are all makers of anxious mosaics; never do they carve the block; exquisite miniaturists, yet lack the big brush work and epical sweep of the preceding generation. Above all, the entire school is minus virility; its music is of the distaff, and has not the masculine ring of crossed swords." Yet elsewhere he writes that Debussy was onto something genuinely new and unique.

Whenever Huneker found new music hard to understand, he tended to fall back on saying it had been "decomposed," as in, "Strauss composes by decomposing his themes."

> Take this *Pelléas* music, for example. It is a perfect specimen of decomposition. The musical phrases dislocated, the rhythms are decomposed, the harmonic structure is pulled to pieces, melts before our eyes—or ears; is resolved into its constituent parts. And his themes are often developed in opposition to all laws of musical syntax. In Debussy's peculiar idiom there seems to be no normal sequence—I say seems because our ears are simply not accustomed to the novel progressions and apparent forced conjunctions of harmonies and thematic fragments. Tonalities are vague, even violently unnatural. (*Overtones*, p. 315)

This passage is a good example of Huneker's sometime method of impressionistic rather than structural analysis. In point of fact, standard sequence structure, even direct repetitions, are evident in many of Debussy's larger works, such as the orchestral *Nocturnes*, but Huneker's ear was thrown off, as were others' at the time. For that matter, there are some pretty abrupt and remote modulations in Beethoven and Schubert; is that decomposition, too? Yet

122   Huneker, when he's not playing the duffer Old Fogy, can suddenly turn around and apply the same "decomposition" idea with eminent analytical precision:

> Strauss has experimented in the *disassociation* of harmonies, and, in company with his contemporary, the master-impressionist Claude Monet, has divided his tones—set up, instead of the sober classic lines or the gorgeous color masses of the romantic painters, an entirely new scheme of orchestration, the basic principle of which is individualism of instruments, the pure anarchy—self-government—of the entire orchestral apparatus. (*Overtones*, p. 1)

In December 1912 in Berlin Huneker heard his first performance of any music by Schoenberg: *Pierrot Lunaire.* His prose reactions to it record the seismic tremor of one aesthetic tectonic plate scraping up against another: the sacheted Chopinesque "grand manner" sensibility meeting the atonal expressionist revolution head on. He did not have a score to follow, but in recording his reactions he wrote an expanded treatise on his views on musical "decomposition":

> It is a decomposition of the art, I thought, as I held myself in my seat. . . . What did I hear? At first, the sound of delicate china shivering into a thousand luminous fragments. . . . The very ecstasy of the hideous! . . . The borderland between pain and pleasure is a territory hitherto unexplored by musical composers . . . Schoenberg not only arouses the image of anguish, but he brings it home to his auditory in the most subjective way. You suffer the anguish with the fictitious character in the poem. Your nerves . . . are literally pinched and scraped. (*Ivory Apes and Peacocks,* p. 60)

Huneker displays an astonishingly acute and retentive ear for someone encountering a brand new idiom for the first time, an idiom

> without themes, yet every acorn of a phrase contrapuntally developed by an adept . . . rhythms that are so persistently varied as to become monotonous. . . . There is no melodic or harmonic line, only a series of points, dots, dashes, or phrases that sob and scream, despair, explode, exalt, blaspheme. . . .
>
> And the ear, like the eye, soon "accommodates" itself to new perspectives and unrelated harmonies. . . . If such music-making is ever to

become accepted, then I long for Death the Releaser. More shocking still would be the suspicion that in time I might be persuaded to like this music, to embrace, after abhorring it.

Finally, he courageously tries to make aesthetic sense of the new experience, even while rebuffing it. No other critic of the day—certainly not Huneker's comrades-in-arms W. J. Henderson, Henry T. Finck, or Henry Krehbiel— took such a high-road approach:

> Of Schoenberg, I confess I do not understand at one hearing the curious dislocated harmonies, splintered themes (melodies they are not) in the *Pierrot Lunaire*. I have been informed that the ear should play a secondary role in this new "music"; no longer through the porches of the ear must filter plangent tones. . . . It is now the "inner ear," which is symbolic of a higher type of musical art. A complete dissociation of ideas, harmonies, rhythmic life, architectonic is demanded. . . . The entire man in you must be made over before you can divine Schoenberg's heart. Perhaps his aesthetik [*sic*] embraces what the metaphysicians call the Langley-James hypothesis; fear, anxiety, pain are the "content," and his hearers actually suffer as are supposed to suffer his characters or moods or ideas.

Huneker's memory, ear, and eye for score were estimable; even more so was his confidence in his own faculties of memory, ear, and eye. It took a lot of that confidence to go out on a limb and write that Wagner had cribbed themes whole from Liszt; but according to Huneker in *Overtones,* Liszt's *Orpheus* and *Faust* Symphony were to be found in *Tristan und Isolde,* the *Faust* Symphony in *Die Walküre,* the *Bénédiction de Dieu dans la Solitude* in Isolde's "Liebestod," and "one of the principal themes of the Faust symphony appears note for note as the Blick motive in Tristan und Isolde, the Gretchen motive in A Faust Overture is also derived from Liszt, and the opening theme of the Parsifal Prelude closely follows the earlier written Excelsior of Liszt."

Being a writer-musician himself, Huneker was acutely sensitive to inadequacies he perceived in the musicalization of opera librettos. He thought Boito was more poet than composer in *Mefistofele* and was not impressed with the work. "Of rich red musical blood, of vital figures, we are offered but little. This composition is a product for the closet. . . . To give the world a Faust in tone, one must be a musical Goethe. Neither Gounod nor Boito was strong enough to cope with the grandeur and beauty of Goethe's masterpiece among master-

124 pieces. Gounod was a musical sensualist lacking lofty imagination; Boito fails in the sensuous temperament and is ever cerebral."

The surest way to get the sense of Huneker's superiority to his contemporary critical colleagues is to compare his statements with theirs on then "new" composers. In the *New York Sun* in 1901 Huneker described Strauss as the greatest living musician and the greatest orchestrator in the history of music, at a time when his most distinguished colleagues in the profession were routinely penning dismissals such as this of Strauss: "The work is labored, verbose, and incoherent. It is weak in invention. . . . It is 'made' music, the rhetorical contrivings of a man that has really little to say" (Philip Hale, *Boston Home Journal,* reviewing the Boston Symphony premiere of Strauss's *Don Juan* conducted by Arthur Nikisch, November 6, 1889). Edward MacDowell wrote Huneker that his comments on Richard Strauss could not "fail to have a great effect on the art of criticism, and must set a standard that will help the whole country. It's enough to make the direst pessimist have faith in America's musical future." [15]

Huneker's defenses of Brahms—who at the turn of the century was still not fully accepted into the Western canon by critics—were similarly rendered *vox clamantis in deserto.* Mencken observed that while Huneker was singing Brahms's praises, Brahms was "then still under attack by Henry T. Finck of the *[New York] Evening Post* (the press-agent of Massenet: ye gods, what Harvard can do, even to a Würtemberger!)."

❧ *Huneker's literary, art, and dramatic criticism*

> *I had a high opinion of him as a taster, and a taster who wanted to tell others what and how to taste. That is the foundation and essence of criticism in all fields of art— literature not least, and painting most.*
> —BERNARD BERENSON, art connoisseur

Huneker was as much an advance scout ahead of the critical wagon train in his drama, art, and literary criticism as he was in his music criticism. While the reigning monarch of drama criticism, William Winter of the *New York Tribune,* was calling *Hedda Gabler* "a long-winded, colloquial exposition of disease" and Ibsen "slimy mush," Huneker was singing Ibsen's praises. When Huneker's Nietzschean book of portraits of the avant-garde of the time, *Egoists: A Book of Supermen,* was published in 1909, even such enlightened people as the Harvard psychologist William James tended to view the book as a study of bizarre personalities (Baudelaire, Ibsen, Stendhal) rather than as a guide to canonical artists. But to Huneker, his egoists were merely cases of what he admiringly would call "anarchs of art." Wrote Mencken in his long essay on Huneker from his *Book of Prefaces:* "He was, I believe, the first American . . . to write about Ibsen with any understanding of the artist behind the prophet's mask; he was the first to see the rising star of Nietzsche . . . he was beating a drum for Shaw the critic before ever Shaw the dramatist and mob philosopher was born . . . he was writing about Hauptmann and Maeterlinck before they had got well set on their legs in their own countries . . . he did a lot of valiant pioneering of Strindberg" (p. 162).

Huneker disdained the potboiler comedies on Broadway at the time by such playwrights as Clyde Fitch. But he also thought Oscar Wilde a minor and superficial figure. Huneker thought Shaw's plays were more sermons than dramatic constructions, more vehicles for preachment of Shaw's phantasmagoric olio of various doctrines than live drama, although he wrote favorable reviews of Shaw plays. In literature, Henry James was his favorite American novelist. He judged Kipling's then world-renowned verse as mere "banjo-strumming" and regarded both Meredith and Hardy as Kipling's superiors. He wrote discerningly about all the French novelists, German playwrights, and Russian writers, though he preferred Turgenev to Tolstoy. And in 1916 in the *New York Sun* he was the first American critic to write favorably of Joyce's *Portrait of the Artist as a Young Man.*

Huneker was ahead of almost all other American art critics in his praise of Cézanne, Manet, and Matisse, of the photographers Edward Steichen and Alfred Stieglitz, and of the American painters John Sloan and Rockwell Kent. Sloan wrote of Huneker's art criticism, "He's different from the average critic in that they usually think they are sent by God to shield mankind from what they don't care for themselves." [16] Of Picasso's first American exhibition in 1911, Huneker, in the manner of his criticism of Schoenberg's *Pierrot Lunaire,* wrote of the "appalling ugliness" but also of "searching after the expressive in the heart of ugliness." Most of the other American critics of the time dismissed Picasso out of hand.

Huneker's influence on other critics

The greatest of American critics . . . Huneker's books are our foremost university. The man himself was our foremost cultural force. . . . He did more to free America from its slavery than any Lincoln.
—GEORGE JEAN NATHAN, drama critic

126 Huneker's own favorite critics among his contemporaries were the British Arthur Symonds, the essayist and sometime sexologist Havelock Ellis, the Dane Georg Brandes, and the Frenchman Rémy de Gourmont. He seems not to have had any idols among his American contemporaries and New York colleagues. Henry E. Krehbiel of the *Tribune* he jibed as "a datehound." He had Old Fogy act as mouthpiece for his sarcastic views of other writers on music:

> I don't mind telling you that the majority of books on music bore me to death, particularly books containing apocryphal stories of the lives of great composers or executive musicians. Pshaw! Why I can reel off yarns by the dozen if I'm put to it. Besides the more one reads of the private lives of great musicians the more one's idea . . . of things is shocked . . . after years of reading I've reached the conclusion the average musical Boswell is a fraud, a snare, a pitfall and a delusion. The way to go about being one is simple. First acquaint yourself with a few facts in the lives of great musicians. Then, on a slim framework, plaster with fiction till the structure fairly trembles. Never fear. The publishers will print it, the public will devour it, especially if it be anecdotage. (*Old Fogy*)

Irving Kolodin asserted that Krehbiel, Henry Finck, William J. Henderson, and the slightly later Lawrence Gilman and Richard Aldrich all regarded Huneker as their "universal choice as elder statesman . . . not only for erudition and wit, but also for the racy fluency of his writings."[17] Edmund Wilson admired him, and his biographer Arnold Schwab nominates as Huneker's chief American disciples Mencken, George Jean Nathan, Benjamin De Casseres, Carl Van Vechten, Lawrence Gilman, and Paul Rosenfeld. The ultimate testimonial may be Sigmund Spaeth's. As a young man Spaeth—the popular radio broadcaster of the "music appreciation racket" Virgil Thomson later famously berated—worked under Huneker at the *New York Times*. In 1950 Spaeth wrote, "He was the best music critic I ever met—which includes Henderson, Krehbiel, Gilman, H. T. Parker, and all the current crop. He had the broadest outlook, the greatest tolerance, and the most human reactions."[18]

Huneker was unique in being a critic of all the arts, and he had a direct influence for a time in inspiring other critical polymaths. In particular, Carl Van Vechten (1880–1964), the Iowa-born music and drama critic, novelist, photographer, and enthusiast of Harlem, known for his "cutting edge" sympathies and racy interest in the demimonde, was the outstanding immediate successor to the Huneker type. The two men met occasionally and were mutual admirers if not close friends. Later, such critics as Claudia Cassidy in Chicago and Alfred Frankenstein in San Francisco covered both music and the other arts, but as the century wore on and the Age of Specialization became entrenched, no one ever quite followed in Huneker's shoes as a critic accepted as equally authoritative in all areas. Not long after Huneker's death, the critic Fanny Butcher wrote in the *Chicago Tribune* (October 29, 1922) that Huneker was the only man in America who knew enough about art, music, literature, and the drama to criticize all of them without sounding ridiculous.

On the other hand, literary critics after Huneker have not always adopted him as enthusiastically as music critics have. The young T. S. Eliot wrote a review of Huneker's *Egoists* in the 1909 *Harvard Advocate:*

> Mr. Huneker's style may impress us as unpardonably hasty, crammed, staccato. . . . But (among American writers, still further distinction) a style it decidedly is, and shares with that of Mr. Henry James . . . a conversational quality; not conversational in admitting the slipshod and maladroit, or a meagre vocabulary, but by a certain informality, abandoning all the ordinary rhetorical hoaxes for securing attention. In the matter of English style, by the way, his criticism of the later Henry James is illuminating. . . . Mr. Huneker's book titles are a little noisy, and in this case vague and unsatisfactory.

In later life, however, Eliot wrote: "Later it came to seem to me that the actual value of his criticism was slight, and the parade of names . . . rather tiresome. But I think his work may have performed a useful service for others as well as myself, in bringing to their attention the names of distinguished contemporaries and men of the previous generation, in the various arts."[19]

The literary critic Granville Hicks in 1930 in the *Nation* praised "his brilliance, his independence" but added, "his work is seen to be— O damning phrase!— of merely historical importance." However, the same could be said of such "dated" nineteenth-century critics as the Shakespearean A. C. Bradley. Anyone who obtains a copy of *Ivory Apes and Peacocks* today and imbibes the chapter on Joseph Conrad, to take but one example, will have an enormously enriched appreciation of Conrad's subtle verbal art.

Later, in the pages of *Modern Music,* Minna Lederman disparaged what she viewed as Huneker's insufficiently analytic impressionistic style. She found some aspects of Huneker's work already old-fashioned in the 1930s, though even she was enthusiastic about the unique electricity of his writing.

128

⚘ *Huneker as morals*
  Bolshevik among   Huneker wore many hats as critic, and yet another of
  the Comstocks   them was as protector of freedom of artistic expression
                          and adversary of the efforts of the notorious Anthony
Comstock (1844–1915), the self-appointed morals crusader and head of the
New York Society for the Suppression of Vice, an organization that actually
burned books and destroyed paintings. Amazing as it may seem today, Huneker had to protest in print repeatedly about public efforts to drape nude stat-
ues. He called Comstock and his followers "morality yowlers." He also in print
defended actors as a class from the pious social view of them as immoral, a bigotry that then prevailed among the Comstock element of American society.

Huneker vigorously defended Nietzsche when Nietzsche was considered
the apostle of degeneracy. He was ahead of any of his newspaper critic colleagues in freely admitting Whitman's homosexuality and suggesting that
Tchaikovsky's death was a suicide. He praised the Irish novelist George Moore
for never calling a leg a limb, for not being afraid to remind us that the "facts
of sex, of birth, of death, are gross." Huneker was appalled by Tolstoy's apos-
tasy into half-mad pseudo-religioso reformer, and by the Russian author's
wholesale rejection of art for art's sake in his book *What Is Art?* In his own second volume of short fiction, *Visionaries,* Huneker concocted a tale in which
"a Roman Catholic priest wonders whether the entire account of Christ's life
was not a work of art, a great drama . . . based only on a 'slight foundation' of
fact." [20]

In one chapter of his final effort at fiction, *Painted Veils,* Huneker enu-
merated several epigrams that place his philosophy of human behavior on a
more sardonic rung than his estimate of exalted art. Two of them: "Food, shel-
ter, fornication, the fight for daily existence—these are the prime levers; not
sentiment," and "The twin pillars of all religions have been, still are and ever
shall be, superstition and fornication."

⚘ *The real*
  "Old Fogy"   The most enlightened critic of his time nevertheless
                          was not quite yet ready to sprint off into futurism (the
term then used to denote what only later came to be known as modernism). In
1915 he wrote: "'Abstract Art,' as they call it nowadays, is not art at all; it is an
abstraction, and art is concrete or it is nothing. . . . Music alone can express the

inexpressible, but the arts of painting and sculpture must represent" (*Puck*,   129
November 13, 1915). Huneker apparently did read some Freud but was dismis-
sive of Freudianism, especially of what he perceived as Freud's inclination to
see artists as wish-fulfillment-fantasy neurotics. And he had his limits when it
came to the sexually explicit: describing an exhibit of modern art in Munich,
he wrote, "The modeling was both grotesque and indecent. The human figure
as an arabesque is well within the comprehension of the average observer, but
obscenity is not art—great art is never obscene." Still, he hedges the call:

> The tricksy god of irony has decreed that if you last long enough, every
> anarch will end a conservative. . . . I might add that beauty and ugliness
> . . . are relative terms. The truth is, the normal never happens in art or life,
> so whenever you hear . . . [a] professor of aesthetics preaching the gospel
> of health in art, you will know [he] is preaching pro domo. The kingdom
> of art has many mansions, and even in the greatest art may be found the
> morbid, the feverish, the sick, and the mad. Beauty . . . is a shibboleth of
> the mediocre . . . in a word, of the academy. (*Ivory Apes and Peacocks*,
> pp. 151–52)

The great critic of the seven arts, interestingly, could not make way for an
eighth: the art of the moving picture. He detested silent movies and described
his reactions in the *New York Times* of October 4, 1914:

> A monstrous olla-podrida of incidents, a jumble of movements, all with-
> out sense or relevance, nevertheless so filled with action that the eye is
> raped by the sheer velocity of the film. No story can ever be definitely re-
> lated, for the essence of photography is the arrest of motion, and despite
> the ingenious mimicry of movement there is no narrative, only poses.
> The very faults of photography are exaggerated; the figures in the fore-
> ground are giant-like, in the middle distance or distance perspective they
> are those of pygmies. . . . The truth is that the moving pictures are a re-
> markable mechanical device, but never for a moment can be considered
> in the category of art. . . . They demand a minimum of thought from their
> spectators . . . and give to the eye the maximum of sensation. . . . You
> watch untouched by emotion the most "thrilling" spectacles and hair-
> breadth escapes. . . . This shadowland is never dramatic, never poetically
> suggestive, never human. The absence of the human voice . . . is depress-
> ing. . . . The substitute, usually vulgar, noisy music, is an impertinence. A

diversion for children, an aid to science, anything you will, but not an art for intelligent people.

∾ *Huneker as seer?*   Apart from a higher-than-average batting average in predicting the ultimate received wisdom of posterity on various composers, Huneker now and again let out an uncanny nugget of prescience. In 1914 he wrote in *Puck* that Shaw's *Pygmalion* was a latent comic opera libretto "fairly begging for a musical setting"—some forty years before *My Fair Lady* was written. In *Old Fogy* he looked into his crystal ball to the "music of 1955" and prognosticated not only the jukeboxes of the 1950s but the digital synthesizers of the 1980s and beyond: "In the turbulent times to come music will have lost its personal flavor. Instead of interpretive artists there will be gigantic machinery capable of maniacal displays of virtuosity; merely dropping a small coin in the slot will sound the most abstruse chords of Richard Strauss."

Writing in *Puck* on October 28, 1916, he even predicted television, music videos, and the Internet. Entire cycles of dramas in the future, wrote Huneker, would be condensed into free "Luminovelocious Shows"—"vivid flashes of luminosity in a key higher than the violet rays of science." In this teleported brave new world, "there were no longer books and newspapers; the news was announced free of cost by monster photographs." When such a time came to pass, even writers like the venerable George Bernard Shaw, he added, would be writing for the "Lumies."

∾ *A critic who was the darling of the artists he reviewed*

What mental agility! What a flexible liveliness of style! And, of course, he is very far from being shallow—very far; but the light of his intelligence has such wonderful surface play that one is dazzled at first.
—JOSEPH CONRAD

Because his critical style was yea-saying rather than the opposite, Huneker attracted an affection from the artists he reviewed perhaps unique in the annals of newspaper reviewers in this country. When he wrote glowingly of Caruso, Caruso repaid the compliment by writing Huneker a letter in which he called him by his first name. Rosa Ponselle, whose Met debut in 1918 as Leonora in *La*

Forza del Destino Huneker raved about in the *New York Times,* wrote thirty-five years later, "What singer would not remember with gratitude such a critic!"[21] Huneker also praised Mary Garden lavishly in the *Times,* and much later in the 1950s she described him to Schwab as "the greatest music critic this country ever had."

Huneker even won over through charm artists he initially alienated. Arthur Friedheim recalled that Huneker's review of his American debut at Carnegie Hall in 1891 was so scathing as to do his career damage, yet later the two men became friends and Friedheim converted Huneker to a Liszt enthusiast. Later, Friedheim cited Huneker's *Musical Courier* review of his March 31, 1912, Carnegie Hall recital as the most discerning appreciation of his art he ever received from a member of the press in his entire career. Huneker originally had a notorious feud with the antic pianist Vladimir de Pachmann (whom Huneker dubbed—in a triple entendre—the Chopinzee). When in 1890 the pianist had a fight with his manager, asked to make up with a kiss, and gave his manager a bite in the neck instead, Huneker reported to the world that "his Bach was worse than his bite." But later the feud ended and Huneker became socially friendly with de Pachmann.

Finale   The thoroughly unmechanical Huneker not only disliked the movies and the typewriter but also deplored the phonograph, the telephone, and the automobile, judging them all to be "sinister agents in the decivilization of mankind." As the war years ran on and ended and his own health began to decline, he began to feel himself a creature out of water, a living embodiment of a culture of gentility and cultivation that was already on the way out. The *New York Sun* put him out to pasture for the final time in 1918, and upon the occasion he penned a few lines of self-obituary for the *Philadelphia Press* (September 9, 1918): "Newspapers have lost their personal flavor. Huge syndicates have taken the color and character and quality from daily journalism. I am quite sure that if ever a comprehensive history of the Sun is written my name will be absent simply because I would be considered myth, a figment of a fantastic imagination." (A terrible irony it is that this assertion became yet another accurate Huneker prophecy: in two book-length histories of the *Sun* papers, published in 1928 and 1933, his name was indeed not even mentioned.)

As usual, Huneker himself said it best: he did then, and does now, seem "a figment of a fantastic imagination"—the great connoisseur among American

132   music critics, the only one of them who could be called the Bernard Berenson
of music criticism; the greatest press agent for the Religion of Art that art criticism in this country has ever had; the only person who could legitimately, and
not pejoratively, be dubbed the Great Impressionist among all critics of distinction; and perhaps the prime nominator to the Western canon of what he
called the "anarchs" of art—all this wrapped in the package of a fantastic character Dickens or Balzac would have been tested to create.

When Huneker died on February 9, 1921, of a pneumonia that was the result of the diabetes and kidney and liver problems inevitably brought on by his
chronic bacchanal, hundreds of actors, producers, pianists, conductors,
singers, painters, poets, and other foot soldiers in the ranks of High Bohemia
came to his funeral service. That probably had never happened before at the
funeral of any critic, and probably never will again.

Perhaps Huneker was, in a word, the greatest artist among our critics.

To have dared the impossible, to have tried to fly to the sun, to have
wooed the moon, to have burned your boats behind you and resolutely entered the trackless region of art where the soul must be its own
compass, its own rudder, its own captain, is to have done something. . . .
Better a million times to have failed than the success of the sleek, smug
philistine who counts his coupons and his steps. (*Musical Courier*,
May 27, 1896)

Thumbing His Nose at the Old Guard

H. L. Mencken, Maestro of the Bozart

I'd rather have written any symphony of Brahms's than any play of Ibsen's. I'd rather have written the first movement of Beethoven's Eroica than the Song of Solomon; it is not only far more beautiful, it is also far more profound. . . . In music a man can let himself go. In words he always remains a bit stiff and unconvincing.
—from a letter to Fanny Butcher, literary critic of the *Chicago Tribune*, February 20, 1921

I believe that "Die Meistersinger" is the greatest single work of art ever produced by man. It took more skill to plan and write it than it took to plan and write the whole canon of Shakespeare.
—from a letter to Isaac Goldberg, May 6, 1925

He was the most venerated lexicographer in English-speaking culture since Samuel Johnson, though he himself dismissed the comparison, calling Dr. Johnson the "first Rotarian." He was called "America's first satirist," a twentieth-century Voltaire, of whom Walter Lippmann wrote in 1926 that he was "the most powerful influence on this whole generation of educated people." He was Henry Louis Mencken— Baltimore reporter, newspaper editor, book critic, magazine editor of the trend-setting *Smart Set* and the *American Mercury,* philologist author of the incomparable study of American speech idioms, *The American Language,* champion of Theodore Dreiser, Sherwood Anderson, Eugene O'Neill, and other struggling literary artists on the side of the angels, scourge of Babbittry and Comstockery and the petit bourgeois in American life.

And this same Henry Louis Mencken, one of our literature's great un-

134   pigeonholable polymaths, was not only America's greatest amateur musician among its great writers, but also America's most outspoken but unappreciated, unsung, and unheralded music critic. It is Mencken—not Deems Taylor, Virgil Thomson, W. J. Henderson, Olin Downes, or Lawrence Gilman—who was James Gibbons Huneker's heir apparent. Mencken, who died in 1956, was the last great generalist of American letters to write extensive music criticism, the last of the proud line that had started with the transcendentalists and continued with poets such as Whitman and Sidney Lanier. Both the eighteenth-century American tradition of men of letters' playing music (Franklin, Jefferson) and the nineteenth-century American tradition of literary men to write about music had their last gasp, lamentably, with Mencken.

Although neither a freelance reviewer nor a salaried journeyman, Mencken throughout his prime years as journalist and book critic wrote concert reviews, orchestra program notes, and, most importantly, extensive critical essays on music for newspapers, magazines, and books. One biographer avers that he probably penned more musical terms throughout his vast oeuvre of prose than any other nonmusical scribe of literary distinction ever did—far more than Whitman—and he arguably performed more music with other musicians, and with more passionate devotion, than any other great American writer who was not a professional full-time music critic—and he did so continuously every Saturday night for forty-four years, longer by far than most marriages or careers last. Because of his unique national prestige via his articles in the *Smart Set* and the *American Mercury,* as well as the large Maryland–District of Columbia readership of the *Baltimore Sun* papers, it is possible that he reached and influenced as many classical music fans as any *New York Times* critic ever has. Mencken was certainly the only national institution ever to write symphony program notes in our history.

True to his sardonic stance toward the world's "boobs," Mencken mercilessly lambasted audiences for serious music in this country, yet did so in a way that enhanced their appreciation of the beauty and depth of great music. He praised the top-drawer composers with uncommon insight, yet was respectful and supportive toward composers he regarded of the "second table," in contrast to the Dantean hell rings he consigned to writers he regarded of the second rank. He made such a distinction because he regarded music as a superior art form to literature, and stated so expressly and repeatedly in his writings.

Revering the creative act of musical composition, he saved his venom for the music critic establishment, going after them like no other prestigious writer either before or after him. Even Virgil Thomson, in his notorious diatribes against the "music appreciation racket," or B. H. Haggin, in his unabashed sniping at his colleagues' opinions, did not go so far as Mencken in excoriating so many practitioners of the profession of music critic.

Mencken mounted a life mask of Beethoven in a wall of his backyard garden at his home on Hollins Street off Baltimore's Union Square, a unique honor he did not bestow upon any of the writers—Goethe, Nietzsche, Conrad—he similarly revered. Of all H. L. Mencken's many seasons, his intensive involvement with the art of music is the one least documented. It is an uncharted and unaccountably neglected chapter in American musical letters and in American letters in general.

꙰ *H. L. Mencken's literary and journalistic career* Born in Baltimore in 1880, Mencken was educated at private schools there. His father had him join the family cigar factory business, but young Harry was a reluctant tobacconist, remaindering from the experience only a lifelong penchant for his ubiquitous stogie. He dropped out of the cigar business to work in odd jobs. Curiously, Mencken never attended college, but as a teenager, already one of history's great autodidacts and omnivorous readers, he devoured whole shelves of the local Enoch Pratt Library, reading virtually all the great literature of the world. Also as a child and adolescent Mencken tried various creative experiments: poetry, story writing, playwriting, chemistry, drawing, watercolors, as well as piano lessons.

Reading everything he could about journalism and trying mightily to land a job in the field, he finally began his illustrious career as a cub reporter on the *Baltimore Morning Herald* shortly after his father's death in 1899 and commenced the worldly education in cynicism such as can come only to an underpaid city desk man who works twelve-hour days six days a week and sees everything in the human comedy from murders to political shenanigans. From there he worked his way up the ladder meteorically, becoming drama critic of the *Herald* in September 1901, editor of the *Sunday Herald* in October 1901, city editor of the *Morning Herald* in October 1903, and eventually managing editor of the paper in 1905. When the *Herald* folded the following year, Mencken went on to become editor of the *Baltimore Evening News,* and only a few months after that became editor of the *Baltimore Sunday Sun.* In 1904 he

136 had already covered the first of his many quadrennial presidential conventions; his last as a presidential convention newspaper correspondent would be in 1948, shortly before a devastating stroke destroyed his ability to read or write. (Mencken lived on with this ironic disability until he died in his sleep in January 1956 at his lifelong Hollins Street home in Baltimore.)

At the same time that his boy-wonder newspaper editor career was blossoming, Mencken was also beginning to publish books—the first, *Ventures into Verse*, in 1903, with volumes on Nietzsche, Shaw, and social and literary criticism to follow at a steamroller rate—and in 1908 he became book editor for the magazine *Smart Set*, in which position he eventually reviewed, by his own count, two thousand books, becoming America's foremost literary critic. Among the writers who publicly kowtowed and salaamed at being reviewed by Mencken were Sherwood Anderson, Theodore Dreiser, James Branch Cabell, Eugene O'Neill, Sinclair Lewis (who wrote him that "I'm more interested in your review than in that of anyone else"), Aldous Huxley, and F. Scott Fitzgerald, who wrote Mencken *after* Mencken had given a mixed notice to *The Great Gatsby*, "as you know I'd rather have you like a book of mine than anyone in America"; Mencken had dismissed the book as "no more than a glorified anecdote, and not too probable at that."

Mencken became editor of the *Baltimore Evening Sun* in 1910 and there began writing the daily "Freelance" column in which he unleashed his most outrageous iconoclasms. He became coeditor with the drama critic George Jean Nathan of *Smart Set* in 1914. He was a war correspondent in 1917, began contributing writing for newspapers in New York and Chicago at about the same time, and published the first edition of his epic lexicographical tome *The American Language* in 1919. Mencken and Nathan both relinquished editorship of *Smart Set* in December 1923 to found the similarly highbrow *American Mercury* the following month. In 1925 Mencken filed a famous dispatch from the Tennessee Scopes trial.

Smart Set, labeled "The Aristocrat among Magazines" by Mencken and Nathan, published fiction by James Branch Cabell, Sherwood Anderson, Sinclair Lewis, Willa Cather, Waldo Frank, Ben Hecht, Theodore Dreiser, and F. Scott Fitzgerald; poetry by Ezra Pound, Edgar Lee Masters, Sara Teasdale, Stephen Vincent Benét, Elinor Wylie, and Louis Untermeyer; plays by Eugene O'Neill (although, as Mencken professed not to like the legitimate stage, Nathan was more responsible for the championship of O'Neill); and essays by Joseph Wood Krutch, Lewis Mumford, and James Gibbons Huneker. It was in *Smart Set* articles as well as in freelance newspaper columns that Mencken took his now-famous potshots at his Victorian bêtes noires: middlebrow literati like William Dean Howells, potboiler novelists like Richard Harding Davis and Mary Roberts Rinehart, poetasters like John Greenleaf Whittier, public moralizers like Anthony Comstock, and novelistic apotheoses of cultural rotarianism like *Rebecca of Sunnybrook Farm, The Trail of the Lonesome Pine,* and *Pollyanna.* Mencken became the chief crusader against what he lamented as the "respectable mediocrity . . . timorous flaccidity . . . [and] amiable hollowness" of America's then accredited literature. This was a literature that subserved "Puritanism as a Literary Force," as Mencken entitled one of his chapters in *A Book of Prefaces.* "Suspicious of beauty of any kind," as one Mencken scholar describes it, such puritanism "took a particularly dim view of the beautiful in art. Both implicitly and explicitly it held that the purpose of fiction was to edify and improve and that that of criticism was to uphold the principles of the moral law, and the notion that the artist might live only to create beauty was anathema to it. The result was that it sternly put down anything that did not conform to its own aesthetic and encouraged the production of work in which artistry was very definitely secondary to purity of content."[1]

Leaping into the breach as the knight-errant against puritanism both literary and social, Mencken, during the years from 1908 to the beginning of the Great Depression, was arguably the most influential general critic in America, even though *Smart Set* had a limited circulation, *American Mercury* was often near bankruptcy, and none of his books sold more than fifteen thousand copies.

But all through his life Mencken had another antipuritan crusade parallel to his literary and social concerns: that for the beauty of great music.

The young Mencken as music enthusiast

Mencken started piano lessons at the age of eight. From the age of twelve he wrote small genre or salon piano pieces, including marches and waltzes. At fifteen he wrote the book and music for a musical comedy produced at Baltimore Polytechnic Institute, was the pit band pianist as well, and made notes for a comic opera libretto based on Bluebeard. It is interesting to speculate on how Mencken acquired his abundant knowledge of the works of the masters. Recordings were still primitive in his childhood and early adult years; the Baltimore Symphony Orchestra was not founded until 1915; and by his own account he never became much of a pianist and was thus perhaps somewhat

138   impeded in playing four-hand orchestral reductions, the route to hearing orchestral scores that had permitted J. S. Dwight and others in the nineteenth century to learn the symphonic repertoire: "I know very little about piano music, and seldom play the piano alone. Piano music, in the main, seems to me to lack dignity. Even the Beethoven Sonatas fall below old Ludwig's usual level. But maybe I underestimate them because most of them are beyond my technique. That may also explain my feeling that Chopin is a sugar-teat."[2]

Louis Cheslock, a friend and fellow chamber music player of Mencken's who was a distinguished professional musician—a violinist in and sometime guest conductor of the Baltimore Symphony and a teacher of theory and composition at the Peabody Institute—closely observed Mencken's pianism and wrote of Mencken's piano playing at a Saturday Night Club concert: "The program opened with the Cesar Franck symphony. From the first notes it was obvious that Mencken knew his music. With each new shift in tempo and tonality he was the soul of the ensemble. Sudden pianissimo—and he hushed the bass and horn. He signaled each entry."[3] Mencken's inveterate reading was apparently the source of his musical knowledge. Cheslock says Mencken's main musical education, after mediocre early piano teachers, came from collecting and reading books about orchestration and harmony and pocket orchestral scores. Mencken picked up enough to be able to make an arrangement of Beethoven's First Symphony for violin, cello, and piano.

When Mencken joined the *Herald,* what he lost in free time to pursue this reading of scores was made up for by his acquaintance with newspaper colleagues who knew about music. Several colleagues on the paper played various musical instruments. For two years a young man from Cincinnati named Robert Carter was managing editor of the *Herald.* Carter, a Harvard alumnus with a red goatee and a gimpy leg, looked the part of the aesthete. He befriended Mencken and became a kind of artistic mentor, acquainting him not only with Schubert and Schumann but also exchanging ideas about Ibsen and Shaw. He appointed Mencken Sunday editor of the *Herald* in 1901 and the next year left to become managing editor of the *New York Herald. Herald* copywriter Joseph Callahan played the violin (and wrote the music to the song "The End of It All" [1904], lyric by Mencken); night editor Isidor Goodman played the flute; even the assistant sports editor, Emanuel David, played the violin. According to Cheslock, Mencken also learned more of music theory and harmony from the *Herald*'s Kiplingesque music critic, Wilberforce G. Owst—although the Teutonophile Mencken later disowned Owst for making pro-British statements at the onset of World War I.

The frustrated composer

Mencken's score study took him far enough to glimpse the top of Parnassus but not quite over the cusp. For all of his life this verbal genius saw himself as a would-be composer without enough brains to master the craft. He wrote in his book *Happy Days* (1940), "My lack of sound musical instruction was really the great deprivation of my life. When I think of anything properly describable as a beautiful idea, it is always in the form of music. I have written and printed probably 10,000,000 words in English, and continue to this day to pour out more and more. But all the same I shall die an inarticulate man, for my best ideas beset me in a language I know only vaguely and speak only like a child."

There are repeated references throughout his writings to the technical difficulties of the craft of music composition, invidious comparisons of it with the art of literature, and an almost rueful envy of those gifted human beings who have succeeded in mastering the difficult tools of the composer, as in this commentary on Schubert in the *Sun,* November 19, 1928: "All morning he would work at his desk, as steadily and busily as a bookkeeper. When he finished one composition he would start another, sometimes on the same page. Most men, completing so formidable a thing as a string quartette, are exhausted, and have to resort to drink, travel, politics or religion for recuperation. But not Schubert. He simply began an opera or a mass." As Mencken summed it up in the *Sun,* August 2, 1926: "More than any other art, perhaps, music demands brains. It is full of technical complexities. It calls for a capacity to do a dozen things at once." He had developed this premise at greater length in an article for *Smart Set,* June 1922:

> Music is enormously handicapped as an art by the fact that its technique is so frightfully difficult. I do not refer, of course, to the technique of the musical executant, but to that of the composer. Any literate man can master the technique of poetry or the novel in ten days, and that of the drama—despite all the solemn hocus-pocus of the professors who presume to teach it—in three weeks, but not even the greatest genius could do a sound fugue without long and painful preparation. To write even a string quartet is not merely an act of creation, like writing a sonnet; it is also an act of applied science, like cutting out a set of tonsils. I know of no other art that demands so elaborate a professional training. . . . Perhaps the art which comes nearest to music in technical difficulties is archi-

140   tecture—that is, modern architecture . . . the modern architect, with his complex mathematical and mechanical problems, must be an engineer before he is an artist, and the sort of engineering that he must master bristles with technical snares and conundrums. The serious musician is an even worse case. Before he may write at all he must take in and coordinate a body of technical knowledge that is about as great as the outfit of an astronomer.

Frustrated or arrested composer he may have been, but what Mencken couldn't himself express in musical notation he fairly bled into his prose. One of his early books—a collection of aphorisms—is entitled *A Little Book in C Major,* and to some others he actually gave opus numbers. Many of the "Monday Articles" bear musical titles, such as "Overture in C Major" (February 28, 1921), "Da Capo" (September 28, 1925), "Variations upon a Popular Tune" (July 5, 1926), "Götzendämmerung" (March 4, 1935). It was not at all unusual for him to use musical terminology in his literary criticism; as far back as the Nietzsche volume, in describing the philosopher's *Der Antichrist,* he said: "Beginning *allegro,* it proceeds from *forte,* by an uninterrupted *crescendo* to *allegro con moltissimo molto fortissimo.*" He spoke of Dreiser's "dreadful cacophony," and called Cabell's novel *Jurgen* "a devil's sonata, an infernal *Kindersymphonie.*" Of Conrad's *Heart of Darkness* he wrote that it is "as thoroughly *durch componiert* as a fugue," and of a speech by William Jennings Bryan at the Democratic National Convention of 1904 he later said that "it swept up on wave after wave of sound like the finale of the first movement of Beethoven's Eroica."

ᑫ *The Saturday*
    Night Club   Throughout his life, Mencken attended concerts—he accompanied Alfred Knopf to the annual Bach Festivals in Bethlehem, Pennsylvania, every year well into the 1940s—but from 1904 to 1948 Mencken's most personal involvement with music came from playing virtually the whole standard repertoire in chamber music arrangements with an informal association of musician friends called the Saturday Night Club. "His loyalty to it probably surpassed his loyalty to any other person, institution, or custom, with the possible exception of the *Sun* papers. In those forty-four years he hardly ever missed a meeting if he was in town; it is said that the only time he ever let something else take precedence was when he attended the wedding of his biographer William Manchester. He arranged the programs. He was principally responsible for building up the library."[4] There

is no parallel or precedent for Mencken's long-term committed music making   141
among famous writers, particularly journalists, with the possible exception of
William F. Buckley's harpsichord playing; it's as if James Reston, Walter Lippmann, and Alfred Kazin rolled into one spent all their leisure time for fifty
years playing chamber music.

Manchester himself has etched a verbal tintype of a Saturday Night Club
evening:

> Saturday evenings were always spent with the club, over Hildebrand's
> violin shop on Fayette Street, bang[ing] out two-handed [*sic*] piano parts
> with Max Broedel amid a shambles of cigar butts, ashes, and music
> scores. The meetings began at 8 o'clock: at 8 sharp Mencken, always the
> first arrival, sat at the piano and demanded, "What are we going to play?"
> A terrific argument inevitably followed, with Hildebrand, perhaps, sug-
> gesting a Brahms sextet; Broedel, Beethoven; and Buchholz, Mozart. The
> arguments often grew heated, but they were part of the club; without
> them the members would have missed part of their Saturday nights. Once
> a new member, thinking to clear up an obstacle to harmony, suggested
> the program be settled each week in advance. There was a shocked si-
> lence; later he learned there was dark talk of heaving him out for heresy.
> In the end, Mencken always settled matters through compromise. They
> would play a *new* symphony, he informed them, made up of the first
> movement of the Eroica, the second movement of the Haydn Surprise,
> etc. At the stroke of 10, all playing stopped and they headed for the Ren-
> nert [Hotel], there to drink beer and eat sandwiches until midnight.[5]

Newspaper colleagues, Johns Hopkins physicians, and friends or friends
of friends who played instruments, as well as Baltimore Symphony and Peabody musicians and nonmusician kibitzers who liked music, were all eligible
provided each had been voted in unanimously by the membership. The
proficiency of the players thus ranged widely. The charter 1904 members were
Mencken at the piano, Joseph Callahan and Samuel Hamburger, both violin-
ists, and cellist Albert Hildebrandt. Later, Heinrich Buchholz, the *Baltimore
Herald*'s financial editor, joined as librarian. They first met in the homes of
members, later in Hildebrandt's violin shop, still later in the Rennert Hotel.
Max Brödel, an anatomical artist, joined Mencken as pianist *primo,* Mencken
secundo. Other early members included Paul Patterson, who was business
manager of the *Sun* papers, Willard Huntington Wright, who was author of
the Philo Vance mystery stories published under the pseudonym S. S. Van

142 Dyne, and William W. Woollcott, brother of the more famous Alexander. And there were occasions, in the almost fifty years Mencken participated, when Dreiser, or George Jean Nathan, or Alfred Knopf would sit in as a guest.

The club repertoire contained some five hundred works, including almost all the standard symphonies, the chamber music repertoire, opera and operetta selections, original works written by members, even arrangements of waltzes and popular songs like "Ol' Man River." The German-born Theodore Hemberger, a violinist and conductor, made many of the arrangements of works for the club, including a piano version of Brahms's Second Symphony, but there were other cooks stirring the broth, probably including Mencken himself, as well as published arrangements. Most of the scores for club musicales were contributed by Mencken. Said William Manchester, "His happiest moments in New York, indeed, were spent shopping for Saturday Night Club scores—full parts for five Haydn symphonies, or four-hand piano parts for the gay waltzes."[6] The group met every Saturday night of the year except when Christmas fell on Saturday.

As the decades went by, many of the members of the club inevitably died. During World War II, Manchester recalls, "Mencken was the last charter member alive, and the newer members were somewhat awed by the tangle of legends which had grown up around him. But the relaxation of music was still priceless. He never missed a meeting, was always the first to arrive, and threatened, indeed, to get out writs against those who were tardy. When a member's birthday rolled around, it was Mencken who remembered and struck up 'Happy Birthday to You'; when the old piano became dilapidated, he it was who arranged for a new one—after solemnly proposing that the money be raised through a series of bingo games."[7] After Mencken's stroke of November 23, 1948, took him hors de combat, the Saturday Night Club—unbroken in continuity since 1904 through two world wars and a depression—survived only another two years. Mencken had been the lifeblood of the group.

ꞵ *Mencken as journeyman reviewer and musicologist* From 1916 to 1918 Mencken wrote the program notes for the newly formed Baltimore Symphony Orchestra, notes he would then cannibalize in his column in the *Sun*. A typical passage from the *Sun*, April 13, 1916, on Schumann's *Spring* Symphony: "His Symphony in B Flat was thus his initial essay in writing for the whole band, and naturally enough he did not master the difficult technique of that enterprise at one stroke. When the work was first played the opening measures, being ineptly scored for the horns, sounded so badly that the audience laughed, and Schumann at once raised the whole passage a third, in which form it appears now." Mencken then proceeds to do a program note analysis of the symphony that would be regarded as competent and scholarly even by standards of the *New York Times*. Like many of his essays on writers he admired, his musical criticisms were at once exegeses and celebrations of the work at hand.

Mencken heard and reviewed several performances of Bach's B Minor Mass by the Moravian Bach Choir at the annual Bethlehem, Pennsylvania, Bach Festival. After one such concert, he wrote of the choir, "Its attack shows an almost mathematical precision, and its divagations from pitch are so rare and inconsiderable as to be unnoticeable. When it tackles a diminuendo the fall in sound is beautifully clear and smooth, and when it has the chance to roar it makes the whole Lehigh Valley ring" (*Baltimore Evening Sun*, May 20, 1929). Two years later, Mencken wrote: "This year's performance, in some ways, was better than usual, and in other ways it was worse. The chorus, it seemed to me, showed a certain weakness, especially in the tenor and alto sections. I suppose the tenor voice is not natural to Pennsylvania Germans; at all events, they do much better as basses. As for the altos, they suffer by the fact that, in general, they seem to be somewhat older than the sopranos; thus the singing of the latter shows more freshness, always an important element in female warbling" (*Baltimore Evening Sun*, May 25, 1931). But Menckenian mischief is never far from the fore. In the same review he adds:

Unluckily, the English words used in the cantatas are completely idiotic . . . :

> *Sergeant! Hell-horror!*
> *Dost not feel terror?*

The music to this drivel is magnificent, but the words will not down. . . . The lady soloists have even worse to sing . . . :

> *I'd fain earthward instant fly.*
> *Idle Mammon, hence from me!*

Alas, the German original is almost as bad!*

---

*Mencken advocated performances of opera in English, somewhat naïvely ignoring the fact that even English, when sung, can be hard to understand.

144   In his reviews and program notes Mencken wrote with informed authority about music history as far back as Palestrina. In one program note–cum–article in the *Sun* on November 23, 1916, he pedantically refuted claims that Haydn had had to eat with the servants at Esterhazy's: "The text of his contract with Prince Paul Anton, published in J. Cuthbert Haddon's life, shows plainly that he was not ranked as a servant at all, but that it was provided that he should be considered and treated as a member of the household." But at other times when it served him, he would take poetic license and sound as though he was retailing old apocrypha, as in this about Schubert: "He sold some of his songs to [his publishers] for as little as 20 cents" and that Schubert was "handy with the girls" (both from the *Sun,* November 19, 1928).

〰 *Mencken as philosopher music critic: On the immortals*   The bulk of Mencken's published expressions on music appears not in reviews of transient occasions but in essays he contributed to the *Smart Set,* the *American Mercury,* the *Baltimore Sun* papers, and his books. These writings disclose an independent thinker, no honorer of received wisdom, with an instinct for understanding the structure of musical materials almost unique in a non-music-specializing literary man. George Bernard Shaw is Mencken's only competitor as a music critic whose primary allegiance was to nonmusical media, but the analogy is imperfect inasmuch as Shaw was a full-time professional music reviewer (before he became a playwright). And Mencken was shrewd enough to call Shaw to the carpet on Shaw's more fatuous judgments, as in the sly allusion to Shaw in this excerpt on Brahms:

> It seems an astounding thing that there was once a war over him, and that certain competent musicians, otherwise sane, argued that he was dull. As well imagine a war over Beauvais Cathedral or the Hundred-and-Third Psalm. The contention of these foolish fellows, if I recall it aright, was that Brahms was dull in his development sections—that he flogged his tunes to death. I can think of nothing more magnificently idiotic. Turn to the sextet that I have mentioned, written in the early 60s of the last century, when the composer was barely thirty. The development section of the first movement is not only fluent and workmanlike: it is a downright masterpiece. There is a magnificent battle of moods in it, from the fiercest to the tenderest, and it ends with a coda that is sheer perfection. True

enough, Brahms had to learn—and it is in the handling of the thematic material, not in its invention, that learning counts. When he wrote his first piano trio, at twenty-five or thereabout, he started off, as I have said, with one of the most entrancing tunes ever put on paper, but when he came to develop it his inexperience threw him, and the result was such that years later he rewrote the whole work. (*Baltimore Evening Sun,* August 2, 1926)

The only bias that occasionally mars Mencken's musical judgment is the German chauvinism that was so much a part of his temperament. He actually wrote to Isaac Goldberg, "There are, indeed, only two kinds of music: German music and bad music." Throughout his writings he repeatedly invokes the first movement of Beethoven's *Eroica* as the greatest piece in music, sloughing off even the Funeral March from the same symphony as not top drawer.

Structural genius was the paramount criterion for artistic excellence in music for Mencken, and in this aspect Beethoven was Mencken's ne plus ultra (he claimed to be insufficiently versed in the music of Bach to accord him that honor). Comparing Haydn with Beethoven, he notes of Haydn, "his far readier inventiveness, his capacity for making better tunes." But, Mencken explains,

The feelings that Haydn put into tones were the feelings of a country pastor, a rather civilized stockbroker, a viola player gently mellowed by Kulmbacher. When he wept it was the tears of a woman who has discovered another wrinkle; when he rejoiced it was with the joy of a child on Christmas morning. But the feelings that Beethoven put into his music were the feelings of a god. It is almost a literal fact that there is no trace of cheapness in the whole body of his music. He is never sweet and romantic; he never sheds conventional tears; he never strikes orthodox attitudes. . . . He concerns himself, not with the transient agonies of romantic love, but with the eternal tragedy of man.

Later in the same essay, he uses this same logic airily to write off some of music's immortals: "What ails the music of all the Tschaikowskys, Mendelssohns—and Chopins? It is often, in its way, lovely. It bristles with charming musical ideas. It is infinitely ingenious and workmanlike. But it is hollow, at bottom, as a bull by an archbishop. It is music of second-rate men." Then he recapitulates his first argument to buttress his iconoclasm: "It would be hard to think of a composer, even of the fourth rate, who worked with thematic material of less intrinsic merit. He [Beethoven] borrowed tunes wherever he found them; he made them up out of snatches of country jigs; when he lacked one altogether he contented himself with a simple phrase, a few banal notes. All such things he viewed simply as raw materials; his interest was concentrated upon their use. To that use of them he brought the appalling powers of his unrivalled genius."[8] In the *Baltimore Evening Sun* of August 2, 1926, he amplifies: "But in music emotion is only half the story. Mendelssohn had it, and yet he belongs to the second table. Nor is it a matter of mere beauty—that is, of mere sensuous loveliness. If it were, then Dvořák would be greater than Beethoven, whose tunes are seldom inspired, and who not infrequently does without them altogether. What makes great music is simply the thing I have mentioned: brains."

In writing paeans to Schubert's incomparable gift of melody, Mencken appeared to contradict his argument for Beethoven's architectonic superiority; but a foolish consistency is the proverbial Emersonian hobgoblin, and in praising such works as the neglected Schubert piano sonatas back in the 1920s Mencken was ahead of his time in presaging the Schubert revival. In the *Sun* on November 19, 1928, he wrote of Schubert's harmony in the piano sonatas, "Not infrequently one finds anticipations in it—even of Wagner! . . . Schubert's harmonies were unlike the harmonies of any composer who had gone before him. They were not only different; they were better." He tried further to support his pro-Schubert logic-by-architecture by claiming that the notion that Schubert had no counterpoint was a canard:

> There is the legend that, in his last days, he thought of taking lessons in counterpoint from Simon Sechter. The story has always appealed pleasantly to the musical biographers; mainly ninth-rate men, they delight in discovering imbecilities in artists. . . . What Sechter had to teach him was precisely what a Hugh Walpole might have taught Joseph Conrad, no less and no more. . . . In all the history of music there has never been another man of such stupendous natural talents. It would be difficult, indeed, to match him in any of the other fine arts. . . . No composer of the first rank has failed to surpass him in this way or that, but he stands above all of them as a contriver of sheer beauty, as maker of music in the purest sense. There is no more smell of the lamp in his work than there is in the lyrics of Shakespeare. It is infinitely artless and spontaneous. (*American Mercury*, November 1928)

Earlier, in the *Sun,* October 19, 1916, Mencken had also given a waiver to another composer of lyrical inspiration—Dvořák: "His natural bent was toward a gigantic and somewhat disorderly piling up of ideas, as in his Dumky trio, his string quartets and the scherzo of the [*New World*] symphony. So many melodies buzzed in his head that it was hard for him to settle down to the laborious development of two or three; new ones were always pressing to be heard."

One relative blind spot for Mencken was the opera, where his tendencies to *épater le bourgeois* would sometimes get the better of him. He wrote Isaac Goldberg: "I seldom go to the opera; it is to music what a bawdy house is to a cathedral. The spectacle of fat women sweating, with their mouths wide open, is very offensive." He also opined, in the *Sun,* November 19, 1928, "A successful opera composer is half musician and half clown; sometimes the clown part of him is two-thirds, or even nine-tenths." In fairness it should be recalled that Mencken had developed an aversion to theatergoing from early in his career as a second-string *Baltimore Herald* drama critic reviewing vaudeville and burlesque, and that his celebrated falling-out with the drama critic George Jean Nathan had much to do with his increasing intolerance for drama onstage; Mencken preferred reading an Ibsen play to seeing a production of it.

Nevertheless, despite his Germanism Mencken could be peculiarly ambivalent about Wagner. The author of the celebrated book *In Defense of Women* misogynistically opined that both of Wagner's wives, Minna and Cosima, impaired his ability to write more and greater operas; asserted that Cosima secretly thought her father, Liszt, the better composer (although Cosima's diaries, published years after Mencken's death, refute this interpretation); and even claimed that Cosima's ugliness was "damaging to the creative faculty" (*Smart Set,* July 1922):

That he had a king for a backer and was seduced by Liszt's daughter— these facts, and not the fact of his stupendous talent, are the foundation stones of his fame in the opera house. Greater men, lacking his touch of the quack, have failed where he succeeded—Beethoven, Schubert, Schumann, Brahms, Bach, Haydn. Not one of them produced a genuinely successful opera; most of them didn't even try. Imagine Brahms writing for the diamond horseshoe! . . . Schubert wrote more actual music every morning between 10 o'clock and lunch time than the average opera composer produces in 250 years, yet he always came a cropper in the opera house.

148

∾ *On the musical booboisie: The sewer rats of the bozart*

Mencken was an unabashed elitist who hated snobbery. Unlike John Sullivan Dwight, he had no illusions about the convertibility en masse of the great unwashed to the purposes of higher culture, in music or anything else. As his friend William Manchester wrote of him, "His position, which is of course controversial, is that the vast majority of humanity resents being asked to think, resorts to mindless clichés if pressed, and is best described as functionally illiterate. Best-selling books are usually pap; even so, the most popular of them had been bought by some 200,000 customers—less than a tenth of one percent of the American population." [9]

He reserved his highest contempt for the musical venue where the artistic philistine and the social plutocrat converge—the opera house:

> The sort of person who actually delights in such spectacles is the sort of person who delights in gas-pipe furniture. Such half-wits are in a majority in every opera house west of the Rhine. They go to the opera, not to hear music, not even to hear bad music, but merely to see a more or less obscene circus. A few, perhaps, have a further purpose; they desire to assist in that circus, to show themselves in the capacity of fashionables, to enchant the yokelry with their splendor. But the majority must be content with the more modest aim. What they get for the outrageous prices they pay for seats is a chance to feast their eyes upon glittering members of the superior *demi-monde,* and to abase their groveling souls before magnificoes on their own side of the footlights. . . . A soprano who can gargle her way up to F sharp *in alt* is more to such simple souls than a whole drove of Johann Sebastian Bachs. (*New York Evening Mail,* February 22, 1918)

His definitive statement on the role, and limits, of music appreciation and nineteenth-century-style transcendentalist cultural evangelism—almost a direct rebuttal of the transcendentalist ideal—appeared in *Smart Set,* December 1919, and deserves to be reproduced at length:

> Of all the forms of the uplift, perhaps the most futile is that which addresses itself to educating the proletariat in music. The theory behind it is that a taste for music is an elevating passion, and that if the great masses of the plain people could only be inoculated with it they would cease to

herd into the moving-picture parlors, or to listen to demagogues, or to beat their wives and children. The defect in this theory lies in the fact that such a taste, granting it to be elevating—which, pointing to professional musicians, I certainly deny—simply cannot be implanted. Either it is born in a man or it is not born in him. If it is, then he will get gratification from it at whatever cost—he will hear music if Hell freezes over. But if it isn't, then no amount of education will ever change him—he will remain indifferent until the last sad scene on the gallows.

No child who has this congenital taste ever has to be urged or tempted or taught to love music. It takes to tone inevitably and irresistibly; nothing can restrain it. What is more, it always tries to make music, for the delight in sounds is invariably accompanied by a great desire to produce them. All genuine music-lovers try to make music. They may do it badly, and even absurdly, but nevertheless they do it. Any man who pretends to cherish the tone-art and yet has never learned the scale of C major—any and every such man is a fraud. The opera-houses of the world are crowded with such liars. You will even find hundreds of them in the concert-halls, though here the suffering they have to undergo to keep up their pretense is almost too much for them to bear. Many of them, true enough, deceive themselves. They are honest in the sense that they credit their own buncombe. But it is buncombe none the less.

In the United States the number of genuine music-lovers is probably very low. There are whole States, e.g., Alabama, Arkansas and Idaho, in which it would be difficult to muster a hundred. In New York, I venture, not more than one person in every thousand of the population deserves to be counted. The rest are, to all intents and purposes, tone deaf. They cannot only sit through the infernal din made by the current jazz-bands; they actually like it. This is precisely as if they preferred the works of the Duchess to those of Thomas Hardy, or the paintings of the men who make covers for the magazines to those of El Greco. Such persons inhabit the sewers of the bozart. No conceivable education could rid them of their native infirmity. They are born incurable.

∾ *On the critical booboisie: Debunking musical Comstocks*

What they deal with, ordinarily, is merely the thing that is before them; what they have to say of it is without background, without relevancy, without roots. The conductor, it appears, took the first movement of the Eroica too fast. The Hexentanz *of the new genius, Sascha Ganovski, is by Eric Satie out of "Roll, Jordan, Roll." The new*

tenor sang flat, i.e. the Prohibition agent took a bribe, the movie wench said she loved her art, the dog had fleas. What is most music criticism? A banal and nonsensical discussion of performers, i.e., of mountebanks, musical scullions, nonmusicians, enemies of music. The critic, exposed incessantly to their monkeyshines, takes on their character. He becomes a virtuoso. He gives his show—at the expense of music.
—*American Mercury,* December 1925

As a book reviewer, Mencken had unstintingly flayed the pettifogging moralists and Calvinist criticasters of his professional class, the now forgotten but once influential panjandrums such as Paul Elmer More, Stuart Sherman, and Irving Babbitt who were his era's leading literary scholars. And true to form, as scathingly candid as his characterizations of the American concert and opera audiences were, Mencken saved his most withering remarks for the music critics. He saw the problem with American music critics in generic terms that applied equally to criticism and appreciation of the other arts.

> The body of native criticism remains as I have described it; an endless piling up of platitudes, an homeric mass of false assumptions and jejune conclusions, an insane madness to reduce beauty to terms of a petty and pornographic morality. One might throw a thousand bricks in any American city without striking a single man who could give an intelligible account of either Hauptmann or Cezanne, or of the reason for holding Schumann to have been a better composer than Mendelssohn. The boys in our colleges are still taught that Whittier was a great poet and Fenimore Cooper a great novelist. Nine-tenths of our people—perhaps ninety-nine hundredths of our native-born—have yet to see their first good picture, or to hear their first symphony. Our Chamberses and Richard Harding Davises are national figures; our Norrises and Dreisers are scarcely tolerated. . . . Criticism, as the average American "intellectual" understands it, is what a Frenchman, a German or a Russian would call donkeyism.[10]

Nevertheless, Mencken added, American music criticism, as distinct and apart from criticism of the other arts, had its own singular, special donkeyisms. "In general the critical writing done in the United States has been of a low order,"[11] he wrote:

> Musical criticism in America confines itself chiefly to transient reviewing, and so the number of books by American critics is pitifully small. James

Huneker has printed two or three good ones and W. J. Henderson and Henry Krehbiel* have contributed a few punditic volumes, but after these the tale is soon told. . . . Philip Hale's copious pedantries scarcely belong to criticism at all; besides, they are buried in the program books of the Boston Symphony Orchestra. As for Upton and other such fellows, they are mere agents of *Ladies' Home Journal* Kultur, and their tedious maunderings have little more value than the literary criticism of such empty sophomoralists as Hamilton Wright Mabie and Paul Elmer More. It is astonishing that Henderson has not been encouraged to reprint more of his New York Sun articles. They are not only full of novel ideas, but extremely well written—and good writing is quite as rare in musical criticism, both at home and abroad, as good writing in music. Henderson's books, however, have the air of being written down to a low level of stupidity. They are not aimed at musicians, but at singers, phonographists and the women's clubs. Only Huneker has reached out for the sophisticated. He never explains the difference between a first violin and a second violin; he doesn't rehearse the plots of the Wagner music dramas.[12]

Mencken retooled and expanded these ad hominems and named other mugs in his critics' rogues' gallery in his *Book of Prefaces:*

[Henry Krehbiel's] most respectable volume, that on negro folksong, impresses one principally by its incompleteness. It may be praised as a sketch, but surely not as a book. The trouble with Krehbiel, of course, is that he mistakes a newspaper morgue for Parnassus. He has all of the third-rate German's capacity for unearthing facts, but he doesn't know how either to think or to write, and so his criticism is mere pretense and pishposh. . . .

Lawrence Gilman? A sound musician but one who of late years has often neglected music for the other arts. Philip H. Goepp? His three volumes on the symphonic repertoire leave twice as much to be said as they say. Carl Van Vechten? A very promising novice, but not yet at full growth. . . . As for Upton and other such fellows, they are merely musical chautauquans, and their tedious commentaries have little more value than the literary criticisms in the religious weeklies. One of them, a Harvard *maestro,* has published a book on the orchestra in which, on sepa-

---

*On another occasion, breaking with a landsman, Mencken referred to Krehbiel as "a German pedant of the dullest type" (*Chicago Sunday Tribune,* November 15, 1925).

rate pages, the reader is solemnly presented with pictures of first and second violins![13]

For Mencken, the essence of the problem was the social act of being part
of a professional trade—that of newspaper music critic.

> Mere reviewing, however conscientiously and competently it is done, is
> plainly a much inferior business. Like writing poetry, it is chiefly a func-
> tion of intellectual immaturity. The young literatus just out of the uni-
> versity, having as yet no capacity for grappling with the fundamental
> mysteries of existence, is put to writing reviews of books, or plays, or mu-
> sic, or painting. Very often he does it extremely well; it is, in fact, not hard
> to do well, for even decayed pedagogues often do it, as such graves of the
> intellect as the New York *Times* bear witness. But if he continues to do it,
> whether well or ill, it is a sign to all the world that his growth ceased when
> they made him *Artium Baccalaureus.* Gradually he becomes, whether in
> or out of the academic grove, a professor, which is to say, a man devoted
> to diluting and retailing the ideas of his superiors—not an artist, not
> even a bad artist, but almost the antithesis of an artist. He is learned, he
> is sober, he is painstaking and accurate—but he is as hollow as a jug.
> (*Prejudices: Third Series* [1922], pp. 88–89)

Ironically, for this lifelong cigar-chewing newspaperman, the only serious
art criticism possible was that unconstrained by the strictures of deadlines and
column space, unfettered by newsmongering and the need to apply some hidden "ratings scale" to its subject:

> The motive of the critic who is really worth reading—the only critic of
> whom, indeed, it may be said truthfully that it is at all possible to read
> him, save as an act of mental discipline—is something quite different.
> That motive is not the motive of the pedagogue, but the motive of the
> artist. It is no more and no less than the simple desire to function freely
> and beautifully, to give outward and objective form to ideas that bubble
> inwardly and have a fascinating lure in them, to get rid of them dramati-
> cally and make an articulate noise in the world. It was for this reason that
> Plato wrote the *Republic,* and for this reason that Beethoven wrote the
> Ninth Symphony, and it is for this reason, to drop a million miles, that

I am writing the present essay. Everything else is afterthought, mock-modesty, messianic delusion—in brief, affectation and folly.[14]

Sainte-Beuve, Hazlitt, Macaulay, Carlyle, Matthew Arnold: each had achieved real greatness as critic, according to Mencken in this same essay, because each had precisely this "motive of the artist":

> Every critic who is worth reading falls inevitably into the same habit. He cannot stick to his task: what is before him is always infinitely less interesting to him than what is within him. If he is genuinely first-rate—if what is within him stands the test of type, and wins an audience, and produces the reactions that every artist craves—then he usually ends by abandoning the criticism of specific works of art altogether, and setting up shop as a merchant in general ideas, i.e., as an artist working in the materials of life itself.[15]

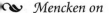

Mencken on
African-American
and popular music
In one way only was Mencken like J. S. Dwight: he saw himself as a literary musical missionary beating the drum for the symphonic canon. He was a true-blue believer in the Platonic idea of the beauty of art. But he was also an instinctual newshound who by lifelong habit was sniffingly curious about all new phenomena. And by prowling the beat in the early twentieth century he could hardly avoid confronting musical elements that were not part of his beloved canon: popular music, jazz, and avant-garde music.

Despite his distaste for the legitimate theater, Mencken liked Gilbert and Sullivan; what he disliked was contemporary American musical comedy. He looked upon ragtime and Tin Pan Alley with contempt. "The jazz-band fetches only vulgarians, barbarians, idiots, pigs," he wrote in an article extolling the Viennese waltz. "But there is a mystical something in 'Wiener Blut' or 'Kunsterleben' that fetches even philosophers."[16] His distaste for jazz stemmed not at all from anything puritanical: "I venture to say that the compositions of Johann Strauss have lured more fair young creatures to complaisance than all the movie actors and white slave scouts since the fall of the Western Empire."[17] He wrote to Isaac Goldberg, "Some day a composer of genuine talent will put a jazz scherzo into a symphony. A hundred years hence that is all that will be

154   remembered of jazz"—this after George Gershwin's *Rhapsody in Blue* had already been given its Carnegie Hall premiere by Paul Whiteman's orchestra
(though Mencken probably was not in New York to hear the premiere).

Yet Mencken was also capable of nostalgia and at times could extol melody
in popular and folk song as worshipfully as he had melody in Schubert. In 1909
he wrote in the *Sun* what may have been the earliest published lament that
"they don't write 'em like they used to":

> What has become of "In the Gloaming"? Who sings it today? . . . The old
> songs had a certain unblushing sincerity about them that the songs of to-
> day seem to lack. "Love Me, and the World is Mine," for example, is too
> pretentious and strenuous to be convincing. In singing it the vocalist gets
> out of breath. No man, actually in love, ever wooed his inamorata with
> such studied magnificence. The phrases are rococo; they require the sup-
> port of arduous piano thumping. The song drips with perspiration and
> midnight oil. One finds no such tortuous elaboration in "Wait Till The
> Clouds Roll By." Here the words of love are as simple as the words of
> Francis Bacon, and the music is as frankly sentimental as a waltz by
> Chopin. Such songs please the girls and make for happy homes. If they
> were sung today, instead of the artificial, anarchistic compositions of the
> ragtime kings, there would be fewer divorces, less scandals in the news-
> papers and less sorrow at the domestic hearth.

Generally speaking Mencken disapproved of jazz (as did many classical
music commentators of those times) and was prone to use now-offensive adjectives in describing music of African-American influence. In an article in the
Sun, October 19, 1916, he used the word "niggerish"* several times in describing the American influences in Dvořák's *New World* Symphony. Yet in the same
essay he praised the symphonic music of the black British composer Samuel
Coleridge-Taylor, who had died in 1912.

A notion of Mencken's ambivalence and open-mindedness about African-
American musical elements can be gleaned from this review of James Weldon
Johnson's *Book of American Negro Spirituals,* which appeared in the *Chicago
Sunday Tribune,* November 15, 1925. It also demonstrates Mencken's own gift
of ear and his knowledge of harmony:

---

* Recent scholarship has disclosed Mencken's use of racial and ethnic epithets in his private letters
and diaries, but these usages could be at total odds with Mencken's socially liberal public stances.

Mr. Johnson, himself a colored man, has gathered all his materials from original sources. He grew up in the south, he was interested in music from his earliest years, and with his brother, J. Rosamond Johnson, he was mainly responsible for the rise of what has since come to be known as jazz. But the Johnsons are by no means mere jazzhounds. On the contrary, they are both educated musicians. Thus their book is one of solid dignity and value. . . .

The purely Negro contribution to [spirituals]—good rhythm—was the more important part, and by far. To this day Methodist hymns seem banal to musicians because they lack variety of rhythm; nine-tenths of them bang along in the same depressing sing-song. But the spirituals are full of rhythms of the utmost delicacy, and when they are sung properly—not by white frauds or by high toned dephlogisticated Negroes from Boston, but by black singers from the real south—they give immense pleasure to lovers of music. Beethoven would have delighted in them, and Brahms, had he ever heard them, would have borrowed them for his uses—as, indeed, Dvořák did after him.

The Negroes, having started with Methodist hymns and improved them by joining them to decent rhythms, went a couple of steps farther. First, they improved them as mere melodies. That is, they displaced their obvious cadences with cadences of greater piquancy and relieved their monotony with bold modulations. Some of these modulations . . . went back to Africa. Savages knew nothing of the modes—or keys—that white men use. They see nothing wrong about inserting a glaring B flat or C sharp into the key of C major. They did this in many of the spirituals, and sometimes the effect was extraordinarily brilliant and thrilling.

Second, they improved the harmonies of the hymns, and for much the same reason. That is, they wandered into "errors" because they knew no better—and the errors turned out to be lush and lovely. The history of civilized music during the last two generations, indeed, has been largely a history of the discovery and adoption of such errors. When white musicians began to put them into music there were bitter protests from all the pedants, but now many of them have become quite orthodox, and music that is bare of them begins to seem bald and insipid. The Negroes were using some of them all the while. They were satisfactory to the African ear long before the Caucasian ear learned to tolerate them.

As Mr. Johnson shows the Negro is a harmonist far more than he is a melodist. He doesn't care much for tunes; the things that interest him

156   are harmonies and rhythms. Let a crowd of colored fellows begin to sing
any current song, however banal, and they will presently give it a new
interest and dignity by introducing strange and often entrancing harmonies into it. They seem to have a natural talent for that sort of thing. A
gang of white boys, attempting song together, will usually sing in unison,
or stick to a few safe harmonies of the barber shop variety, but darkies almost always plunge out into deeper waters, and not infrequently, in the
midst of harsh discords, they produce effects of extraordinary beauty.

∾ *Mencken on the*
futurists and   Mencken's record of expression on the avant-garde is
"modern" music   similar to that of his expatiations on jazz and spirituals:
somewhat prejudiced and hidebound, and yet open-
eared and intelligent enough to admit the presence of elements of artistic superiority. It must be remembered that for all his iconoclasm and foresight in
championing daring writers in the first two decades of the century, Mencken
by the mid-1920s had become too fixed to keep up with the then-new currents
in literature. For instance, Mencken judged Joyce's *Ulysses* "pornographic
hooey" and "deliberately mystifying" (a judgment not too different from
Shaw's opinion) and said that "no one would pay any attention" to either
Ulysses or *Lady Chatterly's Lover* "if it were not for the frequent obscenities."
T. S. Eliot, he told Edgar Lee Masters, represented "the very worst type of literary quack." Nor did he have any appreciation for Faulkner's works, and this
great appreciator of Poe, Twain, Whitman, and Conrad was strangely unaf-
fected by a late-in-life reading of Melville's *Moby Dick*.[18]

Thus, while Mencken encouraged American composers to be more daring
and less beholden to received Germanic forms (an implicit criticism of such
composers as Horatio Parker and George Chadwick), he also drew a line where
he thought a certain level of experimentation had exceeded felt musical value:

The so-called moderns interest me very much, for I am fond of experiments in the arts. But I'd rather read their music than hear it. It always
fails to come off: it is *Augenmusik*. . . . So far as I can make out, Stravinsky never had a musical idea in his life—that is, in the sense that Schubert and Mozart had them. . . . The neglected genius turns out to be an
utter myth. He simply does not exist. There is no record in musical his-

tory of a man of the first talent who languished for recognition, or even lacked fame. . . . But what of the Schoenbergs, the Stravinskys, the Ornsteins, the Saties? Such fowl have always existed, world without end—and every generation has promptly forgotten those of the generation before. (*American Mercury*, December 1925)

Mencken could thus be said to have been an early example of a neoconservative music critic—a critic open to modernity and new concepts but who wished not to throw the baby out with the bathwater:

No melodramatic rejection of all harmony is needed to work a reform. The business, indeed, is already gloriously under way. The dullest conservatory pupil has learned how to pull the noses of the old-time schoolmasters. No one cares a hoot any more about the ancient laws of preparation and resolution. . . . But out of this chaos new laws will inevitably arise, and though they will not be as rigid as the old ones, they will still be coherent and logical and intelligible. . . . And when the boiling in the pot dies down, the truly great musicians will be found to be, not those who have been the most daring, but those who have been the most discreet and intelligent—those who have most skillfully engrafted what is good in the new upon what was sound in the old. Such a discreet fellow is Richard Strauss. His music is modern enough—but not too much. One is thrilled by its experiments and novelties, but at the same time one can enjoy it as music.[19]

Mencken was careful to demonstrate that he was musically au courant enough to understand what changes had been wrought in commonly practiced harmony and to subscribe to their worth: "A new wedding march is sorely needed. The march from 'Lohengrin' is as archaic as populism, and the Mendelssohn march is a doddering antique. Time was when this last composition, by reason of the harmonic handsprings of its first measure, fell upon the ear with a pleasant tickle. But now such felonious modulations are common, and first-year students at the Peabody master them before passing on to greater difficulties of the C Major triad" (*Baltimore Sun*, June 14, 1908).

In his reviews of music both modern and old, then, Mencken tended to underline his idea of a rapprochement between daring and coherence, with a

158   subtle hint that much of modern music's cacophony was due to too much of a careen on the former:

> Their very simplicity, in fact, is what makes [Haydn symphonies] hard to play properly; the slightest error in tone or dynamics sticks out like a sore thumb. Modern music, by its bewildering complexity, gives tone artists hedges to hide behind. Once in Munich, hearing "Elektra" from the front row of the orchestra, I observed several of the first violins lose their places. A kindly brother in art hauled them up by stabbing them in the ribs with his fiddle bow. But though they had been playing fortissimo, it made not the slightest difference to the audience, and even the conductor was unaware of their mishap. . . . Imagine this sort of things in Haydn! The very ushers would scream! (*Baltimore Sun*, November 23, 1916)

Mencken was far from unaware of cutting-edge developments in classical music. In a review of Carl Van Vechten's book *Music after the Great War*, he noted that Van Vechten was arguing that the next great direction would come from Stravinsky and his rhythmic innovations. In his *Book of Prefaces* in 1920 he mentions having urged James Gibbons Huneker to write about Puccini, Stravinsky, Schoenberg, Korngold, and Elgar. In an essay in the first issue of the *American Mercury*, January 1924, Mencken had the musicological smarts to say that the innovations of both Debussy and Schoenberg had come out of Mussorgsky. And in a review of Ezra Pound's eccentric *Treatise on Harmony*, he inadvertently issued a proleptic critique of John Cage's notorious 1954 piece for piano, *Four Minutes and Thirty-Three Seconds*, in which the player simply sits at the piano for that duration of time without playing a note:

> For a poet, and especially an American poet, to have acquaintance with music at all is surely sufficiently unusual: perhaps it would not be going too far to put the prodigy beside Lindbergh's flight. Most of our native minnesingers, like most of our native artists in prose, seem to labor under the delusion that jazz is music, and some of them even appear to think that it is better than the music written by Beethoven. . . . Nor is there any visible sense in Pound's notion that his hero, Antheil, has contributed something to music by talking idiotically of "silences twenty minutes long, *in the form.*" This is pure bilge. A form with a hole in it that large would simply be no form at all; as well talk of a circle with a broken perimeter. (*American Mercury*, August 1928)

~ Finale   Mencken's closest personal friend who was a professional musician, Louis Cheslock, perhaps gave Mencken the musical epitaph that would have most tickled him:

> In the same sense that Beethoven was aware of the language of sound, Mencken was aware of the sound of language. In the same way that Beethoven would not and could not conform to the threadbare conventions of his art, neither could Mencken countenance the continuance of Victorianism in any of its forms. Both were disturbers of complacency. They were bold, forthright, and strong personalities. Both gave battle— stormy, vigorous, and even brutal. Neither cared whether what he had to say was liked or not. . . . There was no attempt to plush-cover the hammer-head.[20]

And Mencken himself wrote a perfect envoi of his credo of music criticism in his review of Rimsky-Korsakov's autobiography in the first issue of the *American Mercury:*

> Is there a lesson in the chronicle, say for American composers? I half suspect that there is. What ails these worthy men and makes their music, in general, so dreary is not that they are incompetent technicians, as is often alleged, but that they are far too competent. They are, in other words, so magnificently trained in the standard tricks, both orthodox and heterodox, that they can no longer leap and prance as true artists should. The stuff they write is correct, respectable, highly learned—but most of it remains *Kapellmeistermusik,* nay, only too often mere *Augenmusik.* Let them give hard study to this history of the five untutored Slavs who wrote full-length symphonies without ever having heard, as Rimsky-Korsakoff says, that the seventh tends to progress downward. Let them throw away their harmony-books, loose their collars, and proceed to write music.

In his last years, after the stroke, when he could no longer read or write, Mencken, oddly enough, was still able to listen to and appreciate music. In the 1950s a violinist from the old Saturday Night Club came to visit Mencken at 1524 Hollins Street, bringing him a long-playing record of Liberace playing the classics. Liberace was then at the height of his fame, appearing on his own television program.

160   Meanwhile, it so happened that Mencken in his post-stroke years was in the habit of walking around the neighborhood, scavenging strange objects, and bringing them home to put in the backyard garden he and his brother had cultivated for decades. He one day had brought home, for no apparent reason, the seat to an old commode.

With a fire crackling in the dining room hearth, Mencken listened carefully to the Liberace recording. The violinist then asked him what he thought of it. Mencken thereupon went out to the backyard, picked up with one hand the old toilet seat he had found, came back into the house, picked up the vinyl Liberace LP with the other hand, and threw them both on the fire.[21]

6 The American Composer-Critic Tradition

From Pierian Spring to Self-Promotion

Art is degraded to the level of soap and cheese, and there is never a word of cheer or a thousand dollars of assistance for the young composer—though pictures good, bad and indifferent are freely bought of American artists—generally with the same spirit that money is laid out for furniture or horses.
—WILLIAM HENRY FRY JR., *New York Tribune*,
    October 10, 1864

It is odd and a little unfair that Europe gets all the credit for the composer-as-critic tradition. True, with critics such as Berlioz, Weber, Schumann, Debussy, and Hugo Wolf—not to mention cameo appearances by Wagner, Liszt, Smetana, and Tchaikovsky—nineteenth-century Europe embodied a unitary cultural life, less of a grand divide between opposing camps of creator and critic, wherein a Théophile Gautier and a Claude Debussy could naturally cross over into each other's territory. But then, America had that, too, a century or so ago with Huneker and his novels and short stories, and with the novels of music critic Carl Van Vechten a little later. Nor are we bereft of our own tradition of composer-critics. And like Europe's, many of our own composer-critics have been part-time or full-time opera or theater men.

Though Virgil Thomson may arguably be chief deity of the pantheon, among American composers who have served as music critics there are other Olympians. As with their European counterparts, any gallery of American composer-critics is a gallery of self-promoters. Though all critics beat the drum for their pet likes and dislikes, composer-critics are fundamentally not disinterested persons. They are at all times working on their creations and

162 thinking about and acting out ways to enable the performance of their works. An element of opportunism must always exist in a creator-critic, but a high-minded, rather than crass, opportunism: the evidence shows that composer-critics in this country seldom if ever took the graft that earlier journalistic critics indulged. Composer-critics, too, have generally been more forward-looking and open-minded than other critics, and their writings have generally been free of johnny-one-note advocacies such as that of Eduard Hanslick for Brahms or Olin Downes for Sibelius, for the simple reason that composer-critics are ulteriorly advocating for their own music, not someone else's.

ꙮ William Henry Fry: The Virgil Thomson of the mid-1800s

One hundred years before Virgil Thomson wrote for the *New York Herald Tribune,* a kindred spirit and sharer of similar hats—like Thomson, an opera composer, fearlessly outspoken critic, and proselytizer for new and American music—wrote for the predecessor *New York Tribune:* William Henry Fry Jr. Fry was the precocious, multitalented son of the newspaper publisher William Henry Fry Sr., the leading printer of books in early nineteenth-century Philadelphia, a mover and shaker who helped establish the city's public schools and went on to found the daily *National Gazette* there in 1820. Not surprisingly, several of William Henry Fry Jr.'s brothers, while not musical, became playwrights and librettists. The *National Gazette* reflected Fry Sr.'s artistically enlightened culture, passed on to all his sons, by printing music and drama reviews in a greater abundance than the other Philadelphia papers of the time. Unsigned, these pre-1836 reviews are ascribed by scholars to one Robert Walsh.

Some music historians give Fry pride of place as America's first serious native-born orchestral composer. Others deem him, and not J. S. Dwight or Henry Watson, the first important critic, "the first musical critic upon a daily newspaper in America to gain the ear of the public, and to employ his position for the purpose of bringing his readers as far as possible upon his own high plane."[1] Born in Philadelphia in 1813, William Henry Fry Jr. did show musical aptitude as a child, but the degree of precocity of his achievements, while real, seems to have been slightly exaggerated; some sources have him completing an orchestral overture at age fourteen as a student at Mount St. Mary's School in

Emmitsburg, Maryland, while others claim he had finished three such pieces by age ten.[2] He did see much opera in Philadelphia as a youth, and as a teenager became the prize pupil in theory and composition of the city's then-reigning European émigré pedagogue, Leopold Meignen; Meignen in fact conducted public performances of early orchestral works by his protégé when William was still in his early twenties.

When an increasingly aging and deaf Robert Walsh had to leave the *National Gazette* in 1836, the twenty-three-year-old son of the publisher stepped into the breach to become its music critic for the ensuing five years, during which time the paper's publication gradually tapered from daily to semiweekly to weekly. By this youthful age Fry was already a trained and performed composer, a seasoned concertgoer with a taste for Italian bel canto, and, by the evidence of his prose, a mature and polished writer. After the *National Gazette* folded, Fry served as a Paris-based correspondent covering music for the *New York Tribune* and the *Philadelphia Public Ledger* from 1846 to 1852, when he returned to New York to become chief music critic for the *Tribune* until his early death in 1864 from tuberculosis. During his years as *Tribune* correspondent, Fry, a relentlessly inquisitive and polymathic intellect, wrote extensively for the paper on politics, including the revolutionary movements in Europe.

Fry as composer Fry pursued large-scale composing projects concurrently with his newspaper reviewing, but neither his contemporaries nor (especially) posterity have been kind to his music. He wrote in all forms—symphonies, operas, overtures, choral works, chamber music, and songs—but most of his works, as befits a literary-minded composer, are tone poems, with sometimes risible descriptive titles. Jullien, the leading conductor of the 1850s, perhaps sincerely, perhaps dutifully politic to Fry's status as the leading New York music critic, performed four of Fry's symphonies in New York: *Childe Harold, A Day in the Country, The Breaking Heart,* and *Santa Claus: Christmas Symphony.* The New York critic Richard Storrs Willis described *Santa Claus* as "a kind of extravaganza which moves the audience to laughter, entertaining them seasonably with imitated snowstorms, trotting horses, sleighbells, cracking whips, etc."[3] However, none other than that dour Beethovenian, J. S. Dwight, reviewed the *Santa Claus* Symphony respectfully and with good cheer.[4] Willis also wrote some good reviews of Fry's music, but he tempered his praise severely in a letter to Fry: "Your com-

164 positions lack sequence, connectedness, logical arrangement, musical coherence. . . . I admire your genius but it is genius astray. A splendid frigate at sea without a helm."[5]

It is interesting to compare composer Fry's poetical programs and gargantuan tendencies with those of his Continental counterpart, Hector Berlioz (whom he probably met in Paris). The piano-vocal score of Fry's opera *Notre Dame of Paris* carries the notation "first performed by 350 executants" on its title page, and the *Santa Claus* Symphony has a program note by the composer of epic length and illustrative detail that seems to aspire to Longfellow. Ironically, in 1850 Fry wrote of "the celebrated critic Berlioz—and composer too, but in the latter capacity he has acquired more fame than admiration,"[6] a characterization that may have been accurate at the time but invites a fatal invidious comparison in retrospect.

Bitten by the opera bug upon seeing Bellini and Donizetti performed in Philadelphia in his teenage years, Fry seems not only to have apishly copied their musical style but even to have emulated Donizetti's manic rapidity of composition; Fry's last opera, the four-act *Notre Dame of Paris* (based on Victor Hugo's novel), was written in thirty days! As a young man Fry made several false starts at operas, finishing his first complete one, *Aurelia the Vestal,* to a libretto in Italian by his brother Joseph, in 1841, and thereupon dispatching the singer Giubilei to England with the score to interest some London impresario in producing it (none was). His second opera, however, *Leonora,* to an English libretto by his brother Joseph, was performed in Philadelphia by the Seguin Troupe in 1845. He offered to pay out of his own pocket to have a staged reading of *Leonora* in Paris, but no one there, either, would let him do it. His third opera, *Notre Dame of Paris,* was produced in 1864 in Philadelphia, conducted by Theodore Thomas, who also performed Fry's symphonies years after the composer's death. A second production of *Leonora,* this time in Italian, was staged in New York in 1858 but was poorly received, and a 1929 New York City mounting of this work also did not persuade music lovers that Fry was a revivable composer (although the Bel Canto Opera Company performed *Leonora* in New York City in 1987).

The most remarkable fact about William Henry Fry's career as a composer—about all of his careers—is that he had inherited wealth and could have been a gentleman of leisure. Yet not only did he pursue a hyperactive schedule of journalism and lecturing (in the early 1850s in New York he gave the first noteworthy adult education lectures on music appreciation in America), but he footed the bill for the premieres of all his operas, an out-of-pocket expense then as now only for the very rich. Perhaps the need to do this is what drove him to his jeremiads about the lack of support for musical art in America.

Yet if he could afford to hire an opera production, why would he take valuable composing time away from himself by slaving as a print journalist and political columnist? This curious aspect of Fry's multifarious life, in which his music composition seems like a monstrous hobby, was noted some twenty years after his death by Frédéric Ritter in his survey volume *Music in America*, in which Ritter also expressed a more charitable view of Fry's pros and cons as a composer:

> All these musical labors would seem to have been sufficient for the strength of one man. In Mr. Fry's case they were only the fruits of leisure hours. He was a professional journalist, taking an active part in the absorbing political life of his country. He wrote numerous political, economical articles for the press, made political campaign speeches, and was musical critic of "The Tribune." His musical imagination was a rich one, and he was well equipped as a practical composer. Lack of time and repose sufficient for the full working out of his original ideas, and absence of frequent opportunities of having his efforts brought out, were the reasons that prevented a ripe development of his fine natural powers.[7]

As a fellow composer-writer, Ritter knew better than most whence he spoke. The double life has its occupational hazards.

Fry as music critic   Fry's principal contribution as a composer-critic was less that of a musical mandarin initiating the untutored into the "inside" mysteries of music—the Virgil Thomson style of composer-critic—than that of relentless booster and polemicist in his newspaper reviews for the cause of American art music. His contemporaneous critics saw the latter as merely a thin veil for self-promotion of Fry the composer; but his posthumous critics may well express puzzlement why this strident tub-thumper for Americana chose to couch his own musical compositions in such shamelessly derivative echoes of Europeanisms, Italian and German. Nevertheless, in his stumping for the performance of contemporary music, at a time when Dwight, Henry Watson, and others were simply trying to get Americans to listen to Beethoven, Fry was unquestionably the Virgil Thomson of his era.

166   Thomson himself would have written the following had he lived in the 1860s: "It is the chief business of Philharmonic Societies to play living pieces or compositions by men alive; by that means Art is advanced. If they are not played Art dies; for Art cannot be sustained by studying the works of the dead almost exclusively. The age must be heroic to itself or it deserves to be covered by ignominy and stricken from human annals" (*New York Tribune*, May 11, 1863). Likewise, "There is no taste for, or appreciation of true Art in this country. The public, as a public know nothing about Art. . . . it is time we had a Declaration of Independence in Art, and laid the foundation of an American School of Painting, Sculpture, and Music. . . . The American composer should not allow the name of Beethoven, or Handel or Mozart to prove an eternal bugbear to him, nor should he pay them reverence; he should only reverence his Art, and strike out manfully and independently into untrodden realms."[8]

But the exhortatory Fry could also wax pedantic, shaking a schoolmasterish finger at the very landsmen he meant to encourage:

> We receive a good deal of sheet music which is grammatically, as regards harmony, and so forth, inaccurate. We cannot undertake to make a list of grammatical errors, either in literature or in music. It ought to be understood that at least the elements of composition be studied for some years devotedly before a man rushes into print. It would be well for the music publishers to combine and employ one contrapuntist to correct such wretched blunders. They have no parallel in literature. No one writing books or for the journals would say "them is"—but a "them is" in music is as common as good musical syntax. (*New York Tribune*, October 6, 1862)

As a critic of the European masters of the time, Fry is uneven: sometimes brilliantly ahead of his time in distilling the *gestalt* of a composer, other times striving for some effect of technical analysis that lapses into incoherence. Unlike the case with Virgil Thomson, his equipment as a trained composer does not invariably translate into insights unavailable to noncomposer critics. Nevertheless, the following appreciation of Beethoven in a review of *Fidelio* is impressive indeed, coming from the pen of a twenty-six-year-old American who had never been to Europe, especially as the recently deceased Beethoven then was a "modern" composer not yet adjudged immortal:

The cast of Beethoven's mind was essentially sentimental and sombre, and his playfulness, with a rare exception, is allied to eccentric wildness, a quality kindred in its way with its expression of sadness and misanthropy. Such a preference for instrumental combinations and effects, together with a seriousness and mystery of feeling, is not calculated to render the conception and style of an opera popular, where in the performance the chief interest should be attracted to the singers, and the audience expects to be regaled with delightful melodies . . . which stand out in relief from everything else, sink deep into the heart. . . .

This work, however it may delight the sentient or enquiring amateur, is not destined to become popular here. . . . Its chief interest is essentially allied to the expression and detail of the orchestra and unless that embraces some fifty or sixty instruments, justice is not done to its massive ideas and contrasts of force and softness. Many, however, are strongly impressed with the music as given here, with its sobriety, darkness, and grandeur. . . . The music is of such a kind that its interest increases generally by repeated hearings, and is a subject for intelligent and critical attention. (*Philadelphia National Gazette*, October 23, 1839)

Fry had written a week earlier that "a fault of Rossini's music is a multiplicity of volatile notes which prevents the auditor from hearing well sustained impressive passages—therefore the less extra ornament the better." But applying this "note multiplicity" idea to a review of *The Magic Flute* in February 1841, he gets too clever by half:

The overture was well performed. It is with the exception of the short Adagio, a kind of mystical, musical outworking of the fugue class. It makes no appeal to one's sensibilities beyond the pleasure it can produce by measured and precise rapidity. Its solution is therefore for the head, not the heart. As a piece of musical mathematics, a graceful and ingenious problem, it may never be surpassed. It is lively but not impulsive, elevated though not sublime, and may from its performance produce a learned and national, but not a popular and universal, ecstasy of delight.

Fry was proud of his ability to read orchestral scores and worked sedulously at procuring the scores of works he was reviewing before the event—too sedulously, according to one fellow music journalist who criticized Fry for re-

168   viewing the score more than the aural evidence of the actual concert.[9] Though
he had to rein in a tendency to relate all merit in musical theater to a reductive
criterion of catchy melody, Fry was at his best as a critic when reviewing vocal
music:

> [Gluck] simplified the theory always,—though not always in practice—
> of [reducing] vocalization to the recitative method, of making each syl-
> lable answer to a single note of music—sometimes two notes offering
> an exception; instead of many notes to the syllable, constituting the florid
> or effeminate or false style. This and constructing the relations of the
> melodic sequences, the harmonic combinations, and the orchestral de-
> tails, all originally according to the varied character of the sentiment of
> the poetry and the nature of the situation, constituted his new and true
> scheme. (review of Gluck's *Orpheus, New York Tribune,* May 26, 1863)

His evaluation of fellow polemicist–music dramatist Richard Wagner not only
turns a tin ear to Wagner's melodies but also, like his critique of Berlioz, is a
case of the pot calling the kettle black:

> Mr. Richard Wagner, the writer of the words and music of the opera
> Tannhauser, played last night at the Academy by Mr. Anschutz's German
> Opera Company, sets himself up as a great musical reformer, both of
> words and music for opera. He has issued, besides, a volume detailing his
> theory. . . . we consider it a beggarly mode for a composer to seek to in-
> terest the public by so describing his musical ideas and notions regarding
> the music and words for operas. If the musical ideas and words have the
> true ring of genius, they speak for themselves. . . . Mr. Wagner's theory
> and practice [ignore] most of the established laws of musical beauty . . .
> and set up in their place sheer ugliness and melodies so-called which even
> the most acute and attentive ear finds nearly impossible to apprehend or
> retain. (*New York Tribune,* January 19, 1864)

William Henry Fry may have had an unrequited love affair with the operatic stage, but posterity can thank him for paving the way for a series of verbally gifted composers who enriched America's newspapers and magazines
with intelligent music criticism for at least a hundred years more, until changes
in the late twentieth century made the newspaper-based American composer-
critic go the way of the dodo.

Mid-nineteenth-century composer-critics   By 1850 Fry, Watson, and others had paved the way for the professionalization of the newspaper music critic, but not yet the institutionalization of the post as that of a full-time specialist. For the rest of the nineteenth century, it was not uncommon for newspaper music critics to be concurrently practicing musicians. It was only with the advent of the Krehbiels, Fincks, Hendersons, and Hunekers at the century's end that newspaper critics gradually began to retreat from teaching, performing, and other musical activities to concentrate solely on criticism. But before 1900, for every George Upton (the first prominent Chicago music critic, but an amateur as a musician), there was a William Smythe Babcock Mathews, who, while writing for the *Chicago Times, Herald,* and *News,* as well as *Dwight's Journal of Music* and the *Etude,* was concurrently a church organist, piano teacher, and music history professor at the Chicago Musical College. While Upton had come to music as a branching-out generalist, Mathews wrote on music with a pedagogue's understanding of technicalities.

Mathews's learnedness was not an exception, and Fry was but the first of a line. A surprising number of America's nineteenth-century critics were composers of various levels of attainment. The myth of the ignorant newspaper garden editor moonlighting as music critic, so cherished by disgruntled musicians, could not derive from this era, a time when the critic pool drew both from musically cultivated European émigrés and from Americans aspiring to European high culture and often educated there.

Of the Europeans there was, for example, Emil Liebling, the German pianist, Liszt pupil, and composer (mostly of salon works) who settled in Chicago and became a noted critic and reviewer there. Another was J. O. Von Prochaska, the prolific Russian-born and Vienna-trained composer who became editor of the *Keynote,* a monthly New York–based magazine that Sir Arthur Sullivan praised as the best critical journal in America. The German-born and -educated composer Karl Merz emigrated to America shortly before the Civil War and later taught at various American colleges, wrote copious musical journalism, and published several best-selling music appreciation books, precursors of those of Daniel Gregory Mason and Deems Taylor. Not all the émigrés were Continental; we have already mentioned England's Benjamin Woolf in chapter 3.

The American-born composer-critics range from Albert Emerick, a critic for *Dwight's Journal* who wrote both hymns and popular songs, to the sym-

170   phonist Frédéric Ritter, who wrote both books and journal articles. Other critics, if not composers themselves, appear to have taught composition, as did the
Boston Herald's Louis Elson at the New England Conservatory of Music. Of
the native-born Americans, the most accomplished composer-critic after Fry
seems to have been Frederic Grant Gleason (1848–1903). Gleason studied
composition with the American composer Dudley Buck and in Europe at
Leipzig and Berlin and wrote everything from chamber music to opera. He became the critic of the *Chicago Daily Tribune* in 1876.

ᗯ *Reginald De Koven*   A leaf in the annals of American composer-critics belongs to Reginald De Koven (1859–1920), probably the
richest composer theretofore in the history of the country. In his book *American Music since 1910,* Virgil Thomson makes room for De Koven among his list
of 106 notable post-1910 American composers, remarking, "as a composer of
operettas he was the most melodious of them all, more soaring even than Victor Herbert." However, *pace* Thomson, the operettas not only of American
composers Herbert, Rudolf Friml, and Sigmund Romberg but of Gilbert and
Sullivan, Noel Coward, and the Viennese Lehár and Oscar Straus all have survived, while those of Reginald De Koven have not. Posterity little remembers
the composer of the erstwhile wedding perennial "O Promise Me" who married a senator's daughter, lived like a king in a Park Avenue manse, summered
in an Italian villa, and hobnobbed with presidents and the *haut monde* of Europe. Rarely, if ever, have his stage works been recorded or revived (though in
the spring of 1997 the Little Orchestra Society in New York City included selections from De Koven's *Robin Hood* on a concert program of early American
operetta).

The mystery is, why did De Koven, who was in his youth handsome as a
movie star, at the height of his fame, wealth, and activity as a light opera composer, even bother to write journeyman music criticism for newspapers and
magazines? Almost all composers who become critics do so because they need
the money (another well-known American exception is William Henry Fry).
Perhaps for De Koven it was Oxonian noblesse oblige: writing to educate
the unwashed classes of America was simply what a cultivated gentleman did.
Born in Middletown, Connecticut, two years earlier than he claimed for most
of his life, De Koven was the son of a minister who followed the Henry James
model by taking his young son to Europe to be educated when he was only
thirteen. De Koven thus finished a degree at Oxford in England in 1879 and be-

fore returning to the United States in 1882 had managed to study with many Continental teachers. Reference works until recently credited von Suppé in Vienna and Delibes in Paris as among his teachers, but the De Koven scholar Orly Krasner has disproven that.[10]

De Koven was by all accounts a natural melodist and a facile, if uninnovative, composer; eventually his output embraced some twenty operettas, two operas, some four hundred songs, orchestral music, a piano sonata, and ballets. He hit the jackpot early on with his third operetta, *Robin Hood,* produced in 1889 in Chicago; the "Broadway musical" did not yet exist, and before 1900 most of De Koven's operettas were premiered in Chicago, Boston, and other cities outside New York. Huneker regarded *Robin Hood* as pretty fluffy stuff, though he wrote more respectfully about De Koven's later operetta *Rob Roy;*[11] W. J. Henderson remarked of De Koven's operetta *The Begum* that it was of the type to tickle the ear of the public who didn't care about its traces of reminiscences of other composers. Elsewhere De Koven's style has been variously described as Rossini amalgamated with American folk song or Gilbert and Sullivan Americanized. Certainly the hit song "Brown October Ale" from *Robin Hood* owes more to Gilbert and Sullivan than to von Suppé or Offenbach.

Robin Hood, with more than three thousand performances in its first run and then constantly revived, was the *My Fair Lady* of its time. De Koven continued producing operettas in a steady stream of about one a year for two decades, although toward the 1910s—with the advent of the George M. Cohan–style musical comedy and the Broadwayized operetta of Victor Herbert, Sigmund Romberg, Rudolf Friml, and the young Jerome Kern—his later efforts began to be seen as passé and self-derivative by the public. He then turned to pseudo-Verdian "grand opera": *The Canterbury Pilgrims* was produced at the Metropolitan Opera in 1917, *Rip van Winkle* at the Chicago Grand Opera in 1920, but they were not as successful as his lighter works. De Koven even died theatrically; at a banquet in his honor on the night of the third sold-out performance of *Rip van Winkle* in 1920, he collapsed. He died within minutes of a stroke.

De Koven married Anna Farwell (1860–1953), the talented daughter of a senator from Illinois, in 1884. Mrs. De Koven, an intelligent woman who was a novelist, translator, and scholar in her own right, as well as world-class social hostess, wrote a memoir not long after her husband's death marvelously redolent of the damasked settings in which monied artists mingled with the international elite of the Vanderbilt–J. P. Morgan era. The De Kovens were welcome guests at the McKinley and Roosevelt White Houses; they were

172   jet-setters before there were jets. According to Mrs. De Koven, their fortune was totally earned by her husband's music. According to several other sources, though, De Koven had initially undertaken a business career in Chicago upon his return from Europe; it was the marriage to the wealthy Miss Farwell that enabled him to concentrate on the composing that led to fame and fortune. Mrs. De Koven wrote in her memoir that editors began courting De Koven to write for them after he became a successful operetta composer. Why? "His literary style, developed by his Oxford studies, was clear and balanced and sometimes eloquent."[12] The timing of their pursuit of him, however, may suggest other motives. Nevertheless, Reginald De Koven—the only millionaire known to have persisted in the daily drudgery of journeyman reviewing—may simply have enjoyed the *jeu d'esprit* of exercising his writing abilities on a subject he knew well. The amusing upshot was that the Old Guard critics tended to knock his critical opinions, not his operettas, as if out of sour grapes.[13] And apparently, De Koven could dish it but he couldn't take it. The "easy" critic Henry Finck says he wrote a bad review of De Koven's *Canterbury Pilgrims*, which he says De Koven thought the best opera since *Carmen*. De Koven sent "a long telegram to the Editor of the Post in which he said I didn't even know the difference between major and minor! Poor Reggie!"[14]

By late in his career, De Koven's Sunday pieces in the *New York World* concentrated on opera, with mere mentions rather than reviews of the appearances during the week of instrumental recitals and orchestra concerts. The following excerpt by De Koven from a review of Franz Lehár's *Merry Widow* appeared in the same edition of the *World* in which a massive Prince Valiant–style cartoon appeared illustrating the latest cast changes in the long run of De Koven's own *Robin Hood*. For 1990s readers, that's as if Andrew Lloyd Webber were the regular Sunday drama critic of the *New York Times* and reviewed the

De Koven wrote criticism for the *Chicago Evening Post* and the *New York World, Herald,* and *Journal* at different times; the dates given by the *New Grove, Baker's,* and Mrs. De Koven for these and other jobs are all at odds, and some are not borne out by archival searches. She writes, "During these years from 1892 to 1897 my husband was critic of the *World,* and never ceasing composing, long and trying rehearsals, and our habit of dining out almost continually, his energy and health and really astonishing productivity were put to severe tests."[15] She also notes, "His criticisms were considered authoritative by all the singers." Considered authoritative indeed: perhaps because they wanted to be cast in his next show. How much critical detachment could De Koven have mustered?

latest show by the creators of *Les Misérables*. De Koven at first dishes some rueful insider talk: "Mr. Lehar was fortunate in being allowed to have his piece produced as he wrote it, without any interference from all-wise managers and bumptious stage managers, whose idea of a musical effect is generally limited to the possibilities of kicks from the chorus which it may suggest. Many a good opera has been spoiled by being messed about and fussed with in rehearsal. For it needs almost divine prescience to discover what will or will not be a success before it is tried before an audience." Here may lie one key to why De Koven became a reviewer: to crack the whip over the producers so they would be less likely to maul his own stagework. But next he tips his hand to his own somewhat shallow aesthetic position:

> The durability and permanence of a work of art may be predicted in direct ratio to its truth to nature, and more especially human nature. Those human emotions which are the most readily recognizable and appreciated by the general public, whether in literature or on the stage, are those which they most enjoy and are most swayed by. . . . it is this theme [love] which is the basis of every great opera and every great play that has ever been written. Those that lack it, however great intellectually or from a purely dramatic standpoint, sooner or later fall by the wayside, while the pure love interest, which may almost be said to be the characteristic of all great dramas, remains and endures. Operas like *Faust* and *Carmen* will be played and enjoyed when the dramas of the *Ring* are forgotten. (*New York World*, October 27, 1907)

As though the *Ring* was not about love! But of course, Wagner was a modern in those days. In a later Sunday piece, in which he raves about the plethora of artists who are European imports in New York and the presence of not one but two opera companies, De Koven unwittingly betrays his own oxymoronic outlook: a nouveau riche toiling in the vineyards of peasants:

> American music per se was never at a lower ebb. The prevalence of the one-fingered composer—and be it noted that this gentleman is representative of the musical taste and the extent of musical culture of his time—has brought American music to be synonymous with ragtime, coon songs, and Tenderloin ditties. In the musical atmosphere thus created, which is the first essential to a genuine popular love of music and the consequent expression of a national feeling therein, even the one-

fingered composer may in time be spurred on to endanger his gift of melody by a little serious study. (*New York World,* November 3, 1907)

Here De Koven was being a poor prognosticator even of his own business, the commercial theater. The time of Victor Herbert, of the European-trained musical comedy composers who wrote their own orchestrations, was fading out, and the one-fingered composers were to hold the boards for the next half-century and more.

Melodious composer or no, as a music critic De Koven was resolutely Edwardian and derrière-garde to the end. No Huneker he: "Mr. Prokofiev strikes me as a somewhat ribald and Bolshevist innovator and musical agitator. . . . The human ear may in time become accustomed to anything, however weird and terrible. . . . We are faced by the inevitable conclusion that music must in time recur to primal conditions—barbaric noise and rhythm without melody—which is unthinkable" (*New York Herald,* November 24, 1918).

Deems Taylor, the great communicator

If one judges a critic's influence by the sheer numbers of people he reached, the greatest figure among American composer-critics—vastly more influential than Virgil Thomson, more comparable to Leonard Bernstein—was the native New Yorker Deems Taylor (1885–1966). In fact, it is likely that Taylor, in his best-known role as radio commentator for the Metropolitan Opera and the New York Philharmonic in the 1930s, reached a larger, more diverse audience than any other music critic in our history before or since. Taylor's radio intermission commentaries on the Metropolitan Opera and New York Philharmonic broadcasts, in their friendly, informative, but unpatronizing (unlike Walter Damrosch) tone, were probably classical music's closest counterpart to FDR's fireside chats.

Taylor's biography illustrates every Algeresque archetype of the self-made man. Originally born Joseph Deems Taylor, he dropped his unpicturesque first name early on. A self-taught composer who somehow perfected his craft while making a living for years as a hack writer and general-purpose journalist, he made his way unassisted and unsponsored into the highest echelons of his profession: he became a top New York music critic, his works were performed immediately by the top international conductors, and he still holds the record for the most performances of an American composer by the Metropolitan Opera—an amazing total of thirty-nine for both house and tour performances of *The King's Henchman* and *Peter Ibbetson* (Virgil Thomson had to wait until 1972 to get even a mini-Met performance of his *Four Saints in Three Acts*). He even made it into the movies with Mickey Mouse, as narrator for the 1940 Walt Disney film animation of classical music, *Fantasia.* He also had time for an ornate personal life; he married three times, his third wife a twenty-year-old costume designer whom he wed when he was sixty. Professionally, until about the start of World War II, the timing of every event in Taylor's careers as both composer and writer seems to have been charmed.

Posterity, alas, has not favored Deems Taylor the composer as fortune and men's ears did during his lifetime; even in the current revival of American neoclassic and neoromantic composers, his not exiguous catalogue of compositions has almost vanished. But his career as music critic, in newspapers, magazines, but especially on the radio, is undoubtedly one of the most important in American history, because Taylor succeeded in what previous critics as diverse as J. S. Dwight, Sidney Lanier, and W. S. B. Mathews could only dreamily aspire to: he introduced the great masses to classical music, and it stuck.

Taylor as autodidact

Though Taylor may not have been a great composer, he by all evidence was endowed with a prodigy-level capacity for learning on his own. He taught himself foreign languages well enough to be a translator; mastered the basics of photography, cabinetmaking, and landscape painting; and built his own country house in Stamford, Connecticut (though he was fond of claiming he did his composing in his apartment at the corner of Fifth Avenue and Sixtieth Street in Manhattan). As a young man of many talents and potentials, he toyed with various career ideas, among them writing, architecture, and the stage (and briefly appeared in a vaudeville act after college). As a child he only briefly took piano lessons, and it appears that he never learned to play any instrument well. But composing music, one of his many early directions, took firmer shape when one college musical he wrote, *The Echo,* was optioned by the theatrical producer Charles Dillingham and actually produced on Broadway in 1909, while another, *The Oracle,* was heard by Victor Herbert in 1907, who advised the young man forthwith to afford himself the benefit of further serious music study. (Per-

176   haps Herbert, who orchestrated his own Broadway scores without help, concurred with De Koven in the need for one-fingered composers to study more seriously.)

By this time Taylor had graduated from New York University and was making a living as a writer for encyclopedias, which may explain his later facility as a digester of musical information for a general audience. A magisterial self-tutor, Taylor the 1907 neophyte was by 1919 already giving paid public lectures in music history. Taylor's one music teacher for harmony, counterpoint, and instrumentation was an unknown but musically expert ex-bandsman from upstate New York named Oscar Coon, who at seventy-five was still working as a copyist and arranger for music libraries in Manhattan when Taylor somehow found him. The young man worked with Coon off and on from 1908 to 1911, but that was the extent of his formal training; thereafter Taylor's knowledge of orchestration and theory was obtained entirely from his own study of scores and textbooks, and his subsequent compositional efforts were entirely self-guided. To acquire the skill in coloristic orchestration evinced by Taylor's symphonic works through this kind of self-study alone, without exposure to musicians, apparently without the experience of playing in an orchestra or conducting one, is a remarkable, even baffling achievement, seldom equaled even by the great composers. Even Rimsky-Korsakov, the naval officer turned composer, taught himself while teaching and working among professional musicians at St. Petersburg Conservatory. Is there an undisclosed secret to Taylor's masterful musical self-education? Did the journalist in him interview musicians and chat shop talk with them off the record? Did he have secret help? By the time of his 1930s radio talks, Taylor seems to have assimilated the orchestral player's platform perspective to an extent that would have done Cecil Forsyth proud:

> A singer, or an instrumental soloist can, at a pinch, find his place in an ensemble by ear; either he is playing or singing the tune, or can take his cue from someone else who is playing it. But . . . the orchestra player cannot guess. Before him, on his desk, is a sheet of paper containing one part: his own. The notes he must play may be buried somewhere in the middle of a harmonic mass so complicated that his ear is of no avail at all. . . . His ability to play virtually anything at sight is taken for granted. If he is a brass player, half of his time is spent in playing notes that aren't there. For he is playing all sorts of imaginary instruments that existed when the older scores were written, and whose parts still remain unchanged. . . .

These parts must all be transposed at sight, so as to sound right on the modern instrument he happens to be playing.[16]

In 1913 Taylor won a National Federation of Music Clubs contest with his first orchestral work, *The Siren Song,* which was not performed until 1923 (but then by Damrosch and the New York Symphony), and went on to compose many songs and choral pieces, two large cantatas for voice and orchestra, and the earlier chamber orchestra version of his most famous piece, *Through the Looking Glass,* based on the book by Lewis Carroll. (A pleasant, charming enough work when listened to today, it sounds bland when compared with composer David Del Tredici's more recent tonal but spiky "Alice in Wonderland" pieces for huge Straussian orchestra.) Taylor accomplished all this during a period in which he continued to pursue a livelihood as a journalist, first for an industrial house organ; then for the *New York Tribune,* first as an assistant editor and then as a correspondent from France during World War I; then for *Colliers' Weekly*—a double life seldom essayed by apprentice composers, requiring an awesome self-discipline. He said later, "I tried teaching and found it an intolerable bore. No one would dream of hiring me as a conductor, and I am a dreadful pianist. So I hit on a fourth choice: I subsidized. I, the composer, would be supported by me, doing other things."[17]

Unfortunately, this strategy may also have cost him some intensity of focus on the creative act. By his own account he tried mightily to compose a work inspired by the horrors he had witnessed in World War I as a correspondent, only to recoil and revert to the decorative whimsy of Lewis Carroll. Several of his other musical works are also based on children's stories or fairy tale–like adult romances. One may speculate whether, had Taylor been able to apply his musical palette to the expression of deeper emotions, his compositions might have survived longer; nonetheless, his idiom of light tonal impressionism was a respectable one practiced at the time by a whole school of estimable American composers, including John Alden Carpenter, Charles-Martin Loeffler, Charles Tomlinson Griffes, and Edward Burlingame Hill.

∾ *Taylor the news-*
paper music critic   For a man whose name today adorns music criticism's most prestigious award (the ASCAP–Deems Taylor Prize, established the year after his death), Taylor had a surprisingly brief career as full-time daily music critic: only six seasons. In 1921, shortly af-

178   ter the death of Huneker, Taylor was hired as principal music critic for the *New York World;* some at the time already viewed him as Huneker's natural successor.[18] He remained there until 1925, when, upon receiving the Metropolitan Opera's commission for an opera, he resigned to work full-time on what was to become *The King's Henchman.* He became editor of *Musical America* in August 1927 and resigned that, too, in 1929 to work on his second opera, *Peter Ibbetson.* In 1931 and 1932 he again wrote for a daily newspaper, Hearst's *New York American,* but this time around he contributed only Sunday pieces, leaving the daily reviewing to Grena Bennett. After 1932 he concentrated on working as a radio commentator, writing books, and composing; never again was he a newspaper reviewer. (He also became a director of ASCAP from 1933 to his death, and in the 1940s served as the organization's president.)

At the time Taylor was hired by the publisher Herbert Bayard Swope to join the *New York World,* the paper's cultural prestige rivaled if not exceeded that of the *New York Times* and *Herald Tribune.* It was the first daily to feature an op-ed page, in the early 1920s. Walter Lippmann ran its editorial page. Heywood Broun, Franklin P. Adams, and Alexander Woollcott were regular columnists. It was perhaps *the* New York paper for the "smart set." Taylor joined the *World* as an already name-brand journalist and an up-and-coming name composer, and his articles from the beginning were given a columnist's banner byline instead of a journeyman's initials at the end of the article. It was still a golden age for daily newspapers in New York City; there were thirteen in 1921, and little radio (and no television, of course) to compete for the reader's attention. Taylor wrote two or three articles during the week reviewing one to three concerts in each article, and then a big Sunday think piece.

His *World* daily reviews display a witty if mordant sense of humor and a stout and stalwart refusal to be conned. In a later era with fewer reviewers and more power accorded to the few, Deems Taylor's waspishness would have been more noticeable to and grating on the behind-the-scenes musical community: "The reviewer coming away from the average debut recital generally feels like a public hangman, and once in a while like Balboa. Last night lay somewhere between the two extremes. There were two debuts to hear, and after they were over one felt rather like a journeyman astronomer, or whoever it is that discovers if not the full-sized stars at least an asteroid or two" (*New York World,* October 17, 1922). On hearing Glazunov's Fifth Symphony played by the New York Symphony under Stransky, Taylor wrote: "if the other four are not heard oftener it must be because of the difficulty of keeping them from blowing off the players' desks. Someone has called Glazonouv the Mendelssohn of Russian music. The Bartlett of Russian music would be an apter term, for a readier hand at familiar quotations it would be hard to find. Indeed, his borrowings are so utterly without guile that they rather discount one's detective work in finding them" (*New York World,* November 4, 1922).

In his Sunday *World* pieces one can discern the beginnings of the "great communicator" style of his later radio commentaries. In an early example, October 23, 1921, he discusses the then-controversial platform placement of the violins in Leopold Stokowski's Philadelphia Orchestra. The article is illustrated with two detailed diagrams of the configurations of the orchestra—the standard one and Stokowski's—and the text carries the educated reader seamlessly into the "inside" world of the orchestra professional.

Like Virgil Thomson, Deems Taylor continued to compose throughout his tenure as *World* critic and, as Thomson later did, found that his newspaper notoriety seemed to help him get performances. When his 1913 prize-winning work, *The Siren Song,* was finally performed for the first time, it was reviewed favorably not only by Henry Finck of the *New York Post* but also by Taylor himself in a tongue-in-cheek piece in the *World.* As Thomson did, Taylor also earned income as a composer while he was working as a journalist: he was commissioned, for instance, by Walter Damrosch to compose *Jurgen,* a tone poem for orchestra based on the popular James Branch Cabell novel. Most of Taylor's critic colleagues praised his compositions when they had occasion to review him; of *Through the Looking Glass* Lawrence Gilman wrote in the *Tribune,* "an admirable piece of music—distinguished in invention, ingenious in facture, and expertly scored." *Through the Looking Glass,* rescored by the composer for large orchestra, was also performed in London and Paris while Taylor was *World* critic. In a London review, even the formidable dean of British critics Ernest Newman wrote favorably of Taylor's music.

As was the case with Reginald De Koven, composing for the legitimate stage beckoned Taylor even while he worked at the newspaper. Taylor's major commissions during his *World* days were for incidental music for nine Broadway plays, a genre that once kept many American composers of symphonic music (Thomson, Marc Blitzstein, Paul Bowles) out of hock but now scarcely exists (except occasionally in regional theater). According to one observer, Taylor at the time was embroiled in a "whirl of activity attendant upon daily reviews of musical performances for his paper with his work often interrupted by conferences with producers, scenario writers, playwrights, actors, managers and others, to say nothing of the supervision of rehearsals." [19]

During this busy period Taylor also was coeditor, with the music and

180 drama critic Gilbert W. Gabriel, of the short-lived *Music: Illustrated Monthly Review,* a "smart" classical music magazine that appeared and disappeared in 1924, styled as a cross between Mencken's *American Mercury* and Frank Crowninshield's *Vanity Fair.* The first issue featured not only articles by Taylor, W. J. Henderson, Albert Spalding, and Pitts Sanborn but also a Fischer Brothers advertisement for Taylor's current published catalog of compositions. Taylor's article "All Dressed Up and Nowhere to Go" presented—in the course of a review of the legendary Paul Whiteman Band concert of February 12, 1924, at which Gershwin's *Rhapsody in Blue* was first played—an extended appreciation and analysis of jazz equally as perceptive as the young Virgil Thomson's article about jazz that appeared at about the same time in the *American Mercury.* After a brilliant anatomizing of the Whiteman Band's multiple doubling instrumentation, Taylor writes: "It is, of course, an orchestra without a diapason. It is all color and high-lights, lacking the smooth, silken tone that comes only from a large body of strings and that forms the 'norm' of sound for the symphony orchestra. There is no way, for example, of approximating in a jazz orchestra the sound of the double-bass recitatives in the last movement of the Ninth Symphony, or the drowsy murmur of the 'Waldweben' scene in 'Siegfried.'" But, he added, the nonsymphonic jazz combo could do other things the symphony orchestra could not do: "The clarinet might stop the tune (but not the rhythm) at any moment to interpolate an al fresco cadenza of squeals and gurgles, the trombone would furnish an obligato of portamento runs—'smears' is the technical term—the cornet, tiring of the pedestrian labor of melody-playing, would emit a few brass barks or, using the palm of his hand as an intermittent mute, give an imitation of a talking doll. . . . Both brass and woodwind now produce hyena-like laughs that are uncannily realistic."

Practicing what he preached, Taylor went on to compose his own jazz suite, *Circus Day,* op. 18, scored for jazz orchestra by the same Ferde Grofé who had orchestrated Gershwin's *Rhapsody,* while Taylor arranged his own symphonic version later, in 1933.

In his Sunday *World* pieces Taylor, like most other critics at that time writing Sunday pieces, focused on opera. He felt the answer to the lack of American appreciation of opera was to perform all opera in English translations written by acclaimed playwrights like Maxwell Anderson, so that "two-thirds" of the libretto would be understandable to the man and woman in the galleries. Taylor stumped for these ideas and for an "American" opera so repeatedly that it makes one wonder whether he was in fact lobbying for the commission the Met eventually did issue to him in 1925. Of the premiere on February 17, 1927,

of *The King's Henchman,* with a libretto by Edna St. Vincent Millay based on a
medieval legend, the *Post* declared that "never in the history of the Metropolitan Opera House had a native offering been attended by such advance interest
and such good omens of success as *The King's Henchman.*" Only two days later,
the board of the Metropolitan Opera threw caution to the winds and commissioned Taylor to write a second opera.

Peter Ibbetson was based on a George du Maurier novel that in its dramati-
zation by Constance Collier had been a stage vehicle for John and Lionel Barry-
more on Broadway in 1917; Taylor at first undertook to do the libretto himself
but then enlisted Collier's help. The opera premiered on February 7, 1931, to
less resounding critical notices than *The King's Henchman;* still, it remained in
the Met repertory for four seasons, a record for any American opera there, and
in 1932 was one of the first operas to be broadcast from the stage of the Met.
From 1934 to 1937 Taylor wrote a third opera, *Ramuntcho,* to his own libretto
based on a novel by Pierre Loti, which was premiered in Philadelphia in 1942.
Late in life, when his composing was slowed by arthritis, he completed a one-
act chamber opera to his own libretto, *The Dragon,* which was premiered in
New York in 1958. The Met has never revived either of his two early operas.

∾ *The composer-critic*
  as radio celebrity   In 1927 the Columbia Broadcasting System was
                           founded. In one of its inaugural coast-to-coast trans-
missions—marred by technical problems such as thunderstorm static—one
hour of *The King's Henchman* was broadcast from a Newark, New Jersey, studio with Howard Barlow conducting principals from the Met production.
Deems Taylor himself explained the libretto over the air.

It was the beginning of yet another career for Taylor. In 1931 he broadcast
a series of music appreciation talks on the opera over the National Broadcasting Network and later appeared as a commentator on Metropolitan Opera
broadcasts. From 1938 to 1943 he was intermission commentator for the broadcasts of the New York Philharmonic. He didn't stop there; Taylor also emceed
a number of nonmusical radio programs and appeared as a guest on the popular radio quiz show "Information Please!" He had quickly become an early
prototype of that small club of intellectual and cultural luminaries who are accepted on radio and television as popularizing, mediagenic explicators to the
layman of serious subjects. The late scientist Carl Sagan is a good recent example in television; in the 1930s and 1940s, Clifton Fadiman, John Erskine,

182   Hendrick Willem van Loon (author of *The Story of Mankind*), and Stuart Chase (author of *The Tyranny of Words*) were other examples of the phenomenon in radio, in their cases literary intellectuals who became, in effect, entertainment's thinking men. They, also, were "Information Please!" panelists.

In the field of classical music broadcast commentary, Deems Taylor took over the precedent begun with the conductor Walter Damrosch's "Music Appreciation Hour" for children and considerably upscaled the genre into commentary for the intelligent general adult audience. Not until Leonard Bernstein made his first "Omnibus" television broadcast in the mid-1950s was any comparably high-level conversation about classical music transmitted to so vast an audience.

By his own estimation eight million people typically heard him on one New York Philharmonic broadcast, more than the sum total of all those who had attended every Philharmonic concert live since its founding in 1842, as Taylor marveled in his first book-length collection of his radio talks, *Of Men and Music.* The talks were usually reworkings of earlier Sunday pieces from the *World* or the *New York American,* or of articles he had written for *Ladies' Home Journal,* the *Saturday Evening Post,* or the *New Yorker.* In fact, a comparison of the actual newspaper pieces and the essays in the published books shows that, from newspaper to radio to book, Taylor often quoted himself verbatim.* Taylor's three books of his collective radio talks were best-sellers, staying in print for years. He had found the goose that laid the golden egg. It's no wonder he told one interviewer, "I'll stay in radio until I'm thrown out, and I'll keep on writing music because I can't help it." There was another side to the fame: all newspaper music critics are inundated by mail, but as a radio commentator, Taylor by his own account each season "received about seventy shipments of manuscript music, ranging from single sheets to bundles of orchestral scores. Their composers wanted me to tell them, first, what I thought of their music; second, how to get it published." [20]

❧ *Taylor-made*
opinions   Taylor's music criticism is everywhere characterized by
                              three strains: an intuitive sense of judging the merit of
music by evaluating "how it sounds" and whether it "goes" without regard to

---

*Both James Gibbons Huneker and H. L. Mencken also quoted themselves verbatim when reworking their newspaper and magazine pieces into books, sometimes artfully altering their material to avoid copyright conflicts with their papers by deftly replacing a few words in the original with syn-

propaganda about the music either old or new; a constant, ongoing attempt to synthesize and synopsize technical and historical lore for his reader at every turn; and an ever-present dry sense of humor.

All critics in all eras are, in the last analysis, operating by ear and by feel in judging whether a performance or a composition is really "musical." But Deems Taylor was probably the last prestigious American composer-critic to maintain a healthy disrespect for composition by system before serialism and its cousins became established practice; Virgil Thomson, who himself wrote in a mostly diatonic idiom, was far more dutifully respectful to schools of modernity than Taylor. "The test of music is not the mathematics behind it, but how it sounds. Too many modern composers are trying to make technical innovations take the place of musical ideas," declared Taylor. In another passage, he wrote, "There's one thing to listen for. It is hard to define. The easiest way of expressing it is by asking the question: does the music seem to run under its own power? In other words, does it give the impression of possessing some spark of life of its own, something that makes it go without your being conscious of the composer constantly trying to push it along?"[21] Taylor formulated a kind of mission statement of his stance on modern music in an article about Rimsky-Korsakov's autobiography; the book may have had a particular resonance for him because the Russian composer was also an autodidact. Notice, though, how Taylor deftly hedges his bets at the end of the extract:

> Inspiration doesn't depend on theory, and doesn't wait upon it. I think you will find that in the career of any real creative artist, his ideas have sprouted, so to speak, well in advance of his technical ability to handle them. . . . Technique and form are, in the last analysis, more or less intuitive. Almost any artist is born knowing, or discovers for himself, most of what is between the covers of his text-books. . . . if a man has the character to be a great artist, he generally has enough application and intelligence to educate himself. . . .
>
> The history of music has always been, that the theorists of one generation collect examples, and make rules out of them, from the works produced by the preceding generation, which didn't know that it was making rules. I've often thought that if there is any one thing wrong with modern music, it is that it is not unconscious enough; in a sense it is too

---

onyms. It appears that many journalistic critics of the time routinely recycled their works in this manner so they—rather than their newspapers—could receive their books' royalties.

well schooled. I can't help distrusting artists who are too conscious of being path-breakers. . . . Ernest Newman once said that most of the great technical discoveries and innovations in music have been made by composers without talent; because the geniuses were too busy creating masterpieces out of familiar materials to have time to experiment with new ones.

Yesterday, a musician wrote music; then came the professors to explain how he did it and what he meant by it. Today, too often, the musician first writes a treatise on harmony and then composes music to conform to the rules that he has just made up. He may be right. What sounds to me so pedantic, so colorless and arbitrary about the conscientious bleakness of some contemporary music may sound profound and beautiful to another generation. Just the same, there is something to be said for Rimsky-Korsakov's method of writing it first and finding out later how it was done.[22]

Thus, though Taylor probably would have regarded the Second Viennese School apologist Theodor Adorno with bemused contempt, he liked Alban Berg, who sounds and feels like the least "mathematical" of the Second Viennese School, even though *Wozzeck* is as formally designed as a building by an architect. Taylor criticized *Wozzeck,* a work he greatly admired, in eminently sensible, practical musical terms:

The least successful element in the work seems to me to be the vocal writing. Berg's idea, presumably, is to get away from the idiom of traditional operatic singing, to make the musical speech of the singers approximate the rise and fall and intonation of the spoken speech of actors. Much of the time he directs them to use a tone that preserves the relations of the written notes to one another, without trying for exact intonation (a procedure that is almost imposed by the impossibility of singing true notes against an atonal orchestra). This is an excellent idea, but in carrying it out he elects to write the vocal parts in a register that would be comfortable only for a contralto. Wozzeck must be prepared to negotiate a low E natural in the bass clef, yet sings most of his lines in a fairly high tenor register. Berg, who would not dream of asking a French horn to spend half the evening screaming away on its top C, does not hesitate to demand that Marie do just that. As a result, the actors neither speak nor sing. They just holler. On the rare occasions when they do manage to sing-speak as Berg demands, their vocal loops and nose-dives are so abrupt and far-reaching that they sound like bad actors ranting.[23]

Thus would Taylor argue every case on the aural merits, not on the party platform of the ideology. He had an equivocal affinity with jazz; admiring Whiteman and Gershwin and even attempting to write in a jazz style himself, he still was unconvinced. "The trouble with jazz, to this observer at least, is twofold. First, it is, so far, extremely limited in its emotional range. The best jazz appeals, as Gilbert Seldes once put it, exclusively to the feet. It stimulates, it stirs, it cheers—even inebriates; but it opens no doors to the unseen and the inexpressible. It neither inspires nor consoles. When it does essay the tragic mood, as in the much-admired 'blues,' it is merely mawkish."[24]

Taylor's sense of humor often found expression in some rueful, oblique dig at the lot of composers. Noting that Mozart was born into domestic service in the household of the archbishop of Salzburg, he quipped, "Such was the social standing of nearly all composers in his day. Things have improved since then, of course. Formerly, we paid them to compose, and made them eat with the help. Now, we let them eat with the family, and don't pay them anything."[25]

It is evident from reading any of Taylor's anthologies that he had read and thoroughly assimilated a vast bookshelf of musical history and biography, but occasionally an inaccuracy creeps in. The New York Philharmonic was founded in 1842, not 1845. Percy Grainger was Australian-born, not British-born. And sometimes he would embroider at greater length to prove a point: his chapter on how bad orchestral playing must have been in the old days reads more like intelligent speculation than musicology, and his account of the relationship between Frederick Delius and his American teacher Thomas F. Ward is true in its essentials but confabulated into docu-fiction by Taylor.[26]

Taylor was neither so surgical nor so audacious as Virgil Thomson in going after sacred cows: where Thomson criticized Heifetz's violin technique as though Thomson himself were Leopold Auer, Taylor wrote of Fritz Kreisler, "An industrious analyst, whose interest in violin-playing somewhat transcended his interest in music, could, I fancy, discuss any Kreisler recital at voluminous length. I cannot. I don't know enough about violin-playing in the first place, and I don't care enough in the second." On careful inspection, though, what sounds like a carefree rhapsody to Kreisler is actually an astute analysis:

186   Kreisler is at his finest, emerges at his full stature, in unaccompanied passages, in the Bach Saraband and Gigue that he played the other night, or the cadenza of the Mozart G Major Concerto. Unaccompanied violin music can be, and usually is, unbearably dull. For in such music everything is up to the player's sense of line and structure. The harmony is necessarily meagre, there is no orchestra to lend deceptive color to his tone or cover up his slips in intonation, no helpful piano to accentuate the rhythm that he may not feel. He must wrestle with his musical angel alone and in the open. For Kreisler the victory is complete. Without accompaniment, the eloquence of his tone and the subtlety of its coloring, the flexibility and clarity of his rhythms, are more than ever apparent.[27]

Certainly he had his share of crotchets and opinions that don't hold up to posterity's judgment. He thought Strauss's *Don Juan, Till Eulenspiegel,* and *Death and Transfiguration* made musical sense without their program notes, while *Zarathustra, Don Quixote,* and *Ein Heldenleben,* "despite many pages of beauty and eloquence, involve a fearful amount of required reading to make them completely understandable. . . . Eventually, all program notes run out of print. The programs are forgotten, and the brilliant descriptive bits lose their salience. Only the music—if any—survives." (But so it has.) Bruckner, Taylor opined, was "a reversed Mahler. In the latter's music one senses a great musical intellect crippled by a defective talent. Bruckner has the talent, but not the mind to control it. . . . Mahler's tragedy was personal; with all his eloquence, he could not think of what to say." But both Bruckner and Mahler are secure in the repertory today.

Unlike some other smug critics (including many of the critical fraternity of his era), however, Taylor seems to have given thought to the possibility of his own false prophecy. In one Sunday essay early in his *New York World* career, Taylor threw down the gauntlet to posterity's judgment on him. It is eerie to read seventy-five years later. After calling the reader's attention to a withering critical account of the premiere of Saint-Saëns's opera *Samson et Dalila* forty-seven years earlier, Taylor muses: "What will our own opinions about contemporary music read like half a century hence . . . ? Are our remarks about Casella and Malipiero going to sound as silly as Mr. Cohen's critique of Saint-Saëns? Probably. . . . About 1970 we will be remembered either as the idiot who considered Schoenberg's 'Fuenf Orchesterstuecke' an evil noise or as the intrepid pioneer who, way back in 1921, called Szymanowski's Second Symphony a masterpiece" (*New York World,* October 22, 1922).

Critics fiddle while composers starve

While Deems Taylor was basking in the limelight of newspapers, radio, and the Metropolitan Opera, other young, now famous but then unknown composers such as Aaron Copland were banging on the doors of Taylor and his fellows merely to get them to attend their concerts and review them. "Futurism" in music was still anathema to many critics on newspapers, while the magazines *Musical America, Etude,* and *Musical Courier* were also conservative in their outlook on modern music. Most of the printer's ink spilled at the time was allotted to the great soloists from Europe, to the opera, to the standard symphonic repertoire. The only contemporary American composers who got coverage, if at all, through the standard channels of publicity were those who were still writing in the idioms of the nineteenth century. The composer, writer, and librarian John Tasker Howard (1890–1964), for example, wrote a series of monographs for the music publisher Fischer Brothers about the composers on their roster. Deems Taylor was among them, but most of the others are forgotten today: Eastwood Lane, Emerson Whithorne, Alexander Russell, James P. Dunn, A. Walter Kramer, Bainbridge Crist, Charles Sanford Skilton, Cecil Burleigh.

In such an Old World climate, young modernist composers had to produce concerts themselves in order to get their music performed and wield any influence. The International Composers' Guild was the first such organization, lasting from 1922 to 1927, lead by the radical French "noise" experimenter (as he was then regarded) Edgard Varèse and the avant-garde harpist-composer Carlos Salzedo. But only a year after the guild's founding, its secretary—a well-heeled, artistically forward-looking young woman named Claire Reis (1888–1978), who had received a musical education in prewar Berlin—bolted with others to form the League of Composers in 1923, of which Reis became the nominal chairman and Copland the de facto boss.

For either the guild or the league, it was nearly impossible to get mainstream critics to attend member concerts, and when the critics did come, their reviews of the new music played were invariably scathing.* When the guild first started giving concerts in the 1920s, Henry T. Finck of the *New York Post*, for example, called Schoenberg's *Pierrot Lunaire* "musical tomfoolery." [28] Reis says in her memoirs that "critics loomed very large in the life of the League; to

---

*One of the few exceptions to this among the older critics, according to Reis, was Pitts Sanborn (1879–1941), music critic of the *New York Evening Mail* and later the *New York World-Telegram.*

188 a certain extent our very continuance depended on them."[29] She also recounts a conversation many years later with Olin Downes of the *New York Times* in his West Fifty-seventh Street apartment in which she thanked him for the many Sunday pieces in the *Times* about the League of Composers' activities on behalf of contemporary music that Downes eventually did write. She quotes the following exchange:

> DOWNES: I must tell you now, I swore many a time after those early concerts that I'd never come to hear another such program of . . . I think what I called it was unmitigated tonal asperity!

> REIS: Admit it now, though, Olin, in the 'twenties you and a few other critics practically competed with each other to see who could write the most disparagingly humorous review for Monday's paper about those Sunday concerts at the Klaw Theater! All of you threw the word "cacophony" about. . . .

> DOWNES: Remember my using the phrase "sonorous acerbities"— or was it "acerbic sonorities"?[30]

According to Reis, a large part of the new music coverage problem was that the newspaper critics simply would not travel below midtown to hear the music in its native venues. In the early 1920s the International Composers' Guild had presented concerts in Greenwich Village but then decided to move to the Klaw Theater on West Forty-fifth Street "in the hope of overcoming the apathy of critics who were reluctant to take time to travel below Times Square."[31]

∾ *Enter* Modern Music: *House organ of young Turks*

But composers at the league got no more press attention than composers at the guild. The time had come for some dramatic, innovative move. Claire Reis decided that the answer was for the league to publish a magazine about new music after the model of small European magazines such as the then recently founded *Revue musicale*. For this project she enlisted Minna Lederman (1896–1995), a Barnard graduate who had studied piano at Juilliard, worked as a culture reporter on the *New York Evening Mail*, and was, like herself, from a well-to-do family. The first issue of the magazine—then called *The League of Composers' Review,* and illustrated with Picasso drawings of De Falla, Satie, and Stravinsky—appeared in February 1924, *mensis mirabilis* of the Whiteman Band Gershwin concert. The following year the name was changed to *Modern Music* because, as Lederman told the *New York Times* in 1983, "I didn't want it viewed as a house organ."[32]

With *Modern Music,* finally there was an American answer to the *Gazette musicale de Paris,* the French magazine of the 1830s that had been founded as a vehicle for the music criticism of the then-advanced modern composers: Berlioz, Liszt, and Wagner. But it actually shared more characteristics with *Dwight's Journal of Music:* both were chronically underfunded and subsidy-searching (Charles Ives and Nelson Rockefeller contributed funds to *Modern Music*); too expensive (*Modern Music* cost seventy-five cents at a time when newspapers and subways cost a nickel); passed around their respective reader constituencies like a football rather than widely purchased; and subscribed to by only a few thousand. Nevertheless, *Modern Music,* an almost homemade quarterly for which the writers were paid a penny a word and the editors received no pay, lasted till 1946.

Despite Lederman's disingenuous disclaimer about the house organ, one of *Modern Music's* cardinal functions was to serve as a de facto flacksheet on avant-garde composers. "We sent most of the copies to the press. The press was our real target and the press fell in love with the magazine," Lederman recalled in a 1983 newspaper interview.[33] In her 1983 book, *The Life and Death of a Small Magazine,* Lederman defined the target audience as the "mandarin" press of the New York and Boston papers, with their "ambivalent" attitude toward new music: "The concerts of contemporary works which they attended were legitimate prey for the ridicule they felt was acceptable to their daily readers. But literature about this music appearing in the pages of an apparently exotic magazine was instantly recognized as a source for spectacular quotation. Advance copies were soon in great demand, and both *The New York Times* and *The New York Herald Tribune* began to compete for first go at our page proofs." And indeed, Lederman told *Musical Quarterly* editor Joan Peyser in 1983 that she believed the magazine had succeeded in "eroding" the critics' hostility to contemporary music; Peyser went one further by writing that "Lederman probably shaped pre–World War II American music more than any single composer did."[34]

Copland, Roger Sessions, and Virgil Thomson were the big three among the composer contributors, but the pages of *Modern Music* also saw essays by Henry Cowell, Paul Bowles, Colin McPhee, Lou Harrison, John Cage, David

190   Diamond, and Conlon Nancarrow, all of whom are more entrenched in the repertory in the late 1990s than the Fischer Brothers gallery of Deems Taylor and company, worthy though the latter may be. Such was the prestige of the journal that composers from abroad such as Alban Berg, Béla Bartók, and Darius Milhaud also contributed, as did critics such as Alfred Frankenstein and Irving Kolodin, who were then young Turks themselves, only later senior eminences.

The pages of *Modern Music* ironically also saw perhaps the last gasp of the unbridled invective of nineteenth-century journalism. The contributing composer-critics removed their gloves and civilly punched not just at the New York and Boston critics but at their own colleagues. Here's Aaron Copland reviewing the work of George Antheil in 1925: "Although Antheil has a considerable list of works to his credit, few of them withstand close examination. The Symphony for Five Wind Instruments has no backbone, no structural significance, the Sonata for Violin and Piano lacks a sense of climax, the Jazz Sonata is simply a poor re-statement of Stravinsky's Piano-Rag Music. And if Antheil's music did not make us suspect his lack of natural feeling for form, the articles he has written on musical subjects would."

Of course, Antheil wrote a scathing letter in rejoinder that Lederman published. Such epistolary counterthrusts between composers were among the glories of *Modern Music*. In "The Composer and His Critics," in 1932, Copland also hurled his lance at the Boston and New York press: "If the critic of the daily press is unwilling or unable to criticize in this real sense, let him not obfuscate matters by setting up first impressions and half-baked opinions as standards by which a man's work can be judged."* As Virgil Thomson later put it, Lederman saw to it that the "unknown bright young [were] given their right to speak up" among "distinguished world figures of creation and criticism, [and were] trained to do so without stammering and without fear." It may be fairly assumed that *Modern Music* had a powerful effect on forcing the daily critical chain gang to look and listen more closely to the moderns. Would Lawrence Gilman of the *New York Herald Tribune* have called Ives's *Concord* Sonata "extremely great music" in 1939 without the subliminal influence of *Modern Music*?

Virgil Thomson dubbed *Modern Music* "the most vigorous forum of its kind in the world; it is the indispensable journal of our tonal times." When

---

*Copland even berated George Jean Nathan in *Modern Music*, although Nathan was strictly a drama critic and had commented only in passing on contemporary composers.

it folded not long after the war, Irving Kolodin wrote, "Where now are we to   191
turn for the latest information on what composer thinks of composer? Minna
Lederman succeeded in creating and maintaining for nearly a quarter of a century . . . the only first class journal of musical opinion in this country." In fifty
years, no comparable periodical has ever stepped in to take its place.*

Decrescendo of the American composer-critic tradition

When Virgil Thomson took over at the *Herald Tribune,*
he made a policy of hiring other composers as assistant critics whenever possible. Several of them, in fact,
were *Modern Music* alumni: Paul Bowles, Lou Harri-
son, John Cage. Bowles, like De Koven and Deems Taylor before him, also contributed music to theatrical productions during his critic tenure. Even after
Thomson left in 1954, to be replaced by the musicologist Paul Henry Lang, the
Trib continued to hire composers as music critics. Peggy Glanville-Hicks continued to contribute reviews until 1958; William Flanagan, best known as an art
song composer, was a contributor from 1957 to 1960.

Perhaps the best postwar example of a composer-critic who, like William
Henry Fry and Deems Taylor, was a mover and shaker above and beyond the
print galleys, was Eric Salzman, a New Yorker who trained with Roger Sessions,
Milton Babbitt, and the electronic composers Otto Luening and Vladimir Us-
sachevsky, and who as a composer is best known as one of the early practitioners of multimedia music theater. Salzman wrote both for the *Herald Tribune* and the *New York Times* into the early 1960s and authored a widely used
textbook, *Twentieth-Century Music: An Introduction.* Virgil Thomson in 1971
called him "the best critic in America for contemporary and far-out music"
but added, "his own work, as can happen to critics, is in danger of neglect."[35]

As a critic writing for years prolifically in various newspaper and magazine
articles (and on record liner notes), Salzman could be said to have matched
pen strokes with the earlier Taylor and Fry, for he like them stumped for an
Americanized opera; but Salzman differed from his predecessors in advocating
for a uniquely American fusion form of musical theater, comparable to the
"third stream" in American jazz espoused by the composer Gunther Schuller.
In 1983 he got his chance to implement his ideas: Salzman cofounded and be-

---

*In the 1990s grass-roots newsletters with reviews written by composers about concerts of new
music began to spring up, the outstanding examples perhaps being New York City's *New Music Connoisseur* and California's *Twentieth Century Music.*

192   came artistic director of the American Music Theater Festival in Philadelphia, a seven-figure-budget, not-for-profit theater that produces contemporary, cutting-edge, post-Menottian music theater and opera. Though he left the festival a decade later, Salzman as composer-critic-turned-impresario left his imprint on the redefinition of American opera theater through the works he either produced, coproduced, or encouraged from his Philadelphia theater base, from the operas of Philip Glass and John Adams to the musicals of William Bolcom.

Outside New York and Boston the composer-critic tradition persisted a little longer. The composer Herbert Elwell (1898–1974) during the 1930s simultaneously headed the composition department at the Cleveland Institute of Music, wrote the program notes for the Cleveland Orchestra, *and* was chief music critic for the *Cleveland Plain Dealer.* After the war he confined himself to composition and criticism for the *Plain Dealer.* The last prominent American orchestral composer to work for a newspaper as a critic was probably Lester Trimble (1920–86), who studied with Lopatnikoff, Milhaud, Copland, Boulanger, and Honegger, and whose works were performed and recorded. Trimble began writing criticism for the *Pittsburgh Post-Gazette* shortly after the war, then wrote for the *New York Herald Tribune* from 1952 to 1962 and for the *Nation* from 1957 to 1962. While teaching composition at the University of Maryland from 1963 to 1968 he was also critic for the *Washington Evening Star;* he was composer-in-residence for one season during this period, not for the Baltimore or National Symphonies but for the New York Philharmonic, which kept him out of that conflict-of-interest dilemma composer-critics always have. After 1971 he taught at the Juilliard School. As newspapers grew fewer in number in the 1960s, both Trimble and Salzman (along with fellow *Trib* composer-critic William Flanagan) joined the growing numbers of critics writing reviews of recordings for such specialty magazines as *HiFi/Stereo Review, High Fidelity, Ovation, Opus,* and others.

Eric Salzman was also the last actively practicing composer the *New York Times* hired as a music critic. The *Herald Tribune,* for so many years the culturally upmarket foil to the *Times* in New York City, folded in 1966, and with it went its enlightened policy of hiring composer-critics, the last on any prominent American newspaper. Since then the *Times* has refused as a matter of policy to hire composers as music critics, and most other large American newspapers have observed a similar policy de facto or de jure, as the profession of music critic became ever more specialized by the newspaper industry, and its labor pool more and more insularized. By the 1980s composers who were also

critics had either to choose the one métier over the other or to find outlets for   193
their criticism outside the loop of the big urban market newspapers. But the
record review magazines—the only real such outside outlet—not only didn't
offer salaried jobs to reviewers but paid little or nothing for the reviews and articles written for them.

℘ Recapitulation and finale

Many other names could be added to the roster: Roy
Harris, Carl Ruggles, Irving Fine, Lawrence Powell, Ar-
thur Farwell. These, and still others such as Goddard Lieberson, Paul Bowles,
Carman Moore, and Arthur Berger, mentioned elsewhere in this book, were
all seriously committed composers who devoted time to writing music criticism for newspapers and magazines of general circulation. Though the common thread among them seems their prodigious industriousness, some devil's
advocate might argue that their only common denominator was their self-
interested desire to use their critical pulpits in whatever way bolstered and
promoted their own composing careers.

Composers must, and do, self-promote, self-promote, self-promote; they
have done so since Mozart and Beethoven threw themselves on the mercy of
the marketplace, and they always will. An opposing view might counter with a
musical version of trickle-down theory, that is, that composer-critics function
for good and for ill like nineteenth-century robber barons—the Rockefellers
and Carnegies who, in the pre-union era, while exploiting workers, also were
responsible for vast improvements to the commonweal, and who also, ultimately, contributed monetarily to the arts. Composers, who as Virgil Thomson perhaps egoistically put it, tend to know more about music than any other
personnel on the musical scene, may also, while exploiting the situation for
their own purposes, be natural resources for improving public perception and
appreciation of the art of music. But they are going untapped in the postmodern era because of an increased corporate self-consciousness about conflict of
interest. Yet in the olden days—certainly in the cases of men of means such as
Fry and De Koven who were unsusceptible to the blandishments of black-
mail—even self-interested critics wrote their reviews and essays largely if not
entirely from the altruistic motive of public betterment. This was not the case
in Europe, where composer-critics, like other critics there, have, at least on the
Continent, often been intensely partisan and propagandistic, if not outright
corrupt.

194   Composer-critics, with their unparalleled command of the inner game of music, can only elevate the critical profession even as they, naturally, occasionally bend it to their own purposes. Is it too daring to suggest that one reason for the diminished vitality of classical music in the United States could be the exile of practicing composers from the daily newspaper critic profession?

∾ *Coda*   By century's end the American composer-critic—whose pedigree is as impeccable as that of the better-known European line of Berlioz, Schumann, Debussy, César Cui, Reynaldo Hahn, Philip Heseltine, Constant Lambert, and Sorabji—had gone the way of the American buffalo. There are no composers today who wield an influence over musical life through their pens the way William Henry Fry, Deems Taylor, or Virgil Thomson once splendidly did. And even though our leading novelists routinely review books by their peers in the pages of the *New York Times Book Review* and the *New York Review of Books,* no more is there a composer commissariat fighting the good fight under a Minna Lederman and tossing a *Modern Music* into the laps of newspaper critics like a Molotov cocktail. Nor would any contemporary newspaper hire a successful Broadway composer to take up a pen and write reviews praising symphony concerts and operas and urging readers to attend.

One can hardly not conclude that our national cultural life is the poorer for it.

Richard Grant White, originally a music critic, became better known as a Shakespeare expert. His son was the architect Stanford White, murdered by Evelyn Nesbit's husband, Harry K. Thaw, in 1906. © *Collection of The New-York Historical Society.*

John Sullivan Dwight, who despite "abominating work" became the founding father of American musical magazines.

At a 1905 Delmonico's dinner honoring Mark Twain's seventieth birthday, honored guests included William Dean Howells (second from left) and Rupert Hughes (second from right), both music critics. © *Museum of the City of New York / The Byron Collection.*

James Gibbons Huneker, many-hatted
critic, avant-garde champion, and
explorer of the risqué, 1906. *Photo by
Pirie MacDonald. © Collection of The
New-York Historical Society.*

Reginald De Koven (right), an operetta-composing millionaire who deigned to work for a pit-
tance as a critic, with his *Canterbury Pilgrims* librettist Percy Mackaye, 1916. *Music Division,
The New York Public Library for the Performing Arts, Astor, Lenox and Tilden Foundations.*

W. J. Henderson reviewed the Met premieres of Wagner's Ring operas in the 1880s and endured to pan Berg's *Lulu* at its New York premiere in 1935. *Music Division, The New York Public Library for the Performing Arts, Astor, Lenox and Tilden Foundations.*

H. E. Krehbiel, on the right, with two unidentified gentlemen. *Music Division, The New York Public Library for the Performing Arts, Astor, Lenox and Tilden Foundations.*

Henry T. Finck, *New York Evening Post* critic for more than forty years. Note the signature, "From Abbie's Henry," referring to Finck's wife, who secretly wrote much of the prose that appeared under his name. *Courtesy of the International Percy Grainger Society.*

H. L. Mencken playing the piano in the parlor of his Baltimore home on Hollins Street, 1928. *Courtesy of the Enoch Pratt Free Library Mencken Collection. Reproduced by permission of the Enoch Pratt Free Library in accordance with the terms of the will of H. L. Mencken.*

So esteemed and influential was the critic Henry Krehbiel that the tenor Enrico Caruso, famous for his caricatures of opera singers and other dignitaries, paid him the ultimate honor in 1909. *Music Division, The New York Public Library for the Performing Arts, Astor, Lenox and Tilden Foundations.*

Deems Taylor (left) with Sigmund Romberg and Alexander Woollcott at NBC's Radio City studios, New York, for a broadcast of "Swift Studio Party," October 29, 1935. *Courtesy of Thomas A. DeLong and McFarland & Company, publishers of* Radio Stars.

Olin Downes, second from left, with the conductor Serge Koussevitsky, center, and others at Tanglewood. *Reproduced courtesy of the Hargrett Rare Book and Manuscript Library, University of Georgia Libraries.*

Henry C. Watson late in life as the editor of the *American Art Journal,* circa 1870. *Music Division, The New York Public Library for the Performing Arts, Astor, Lenox and Tilden Foundations.*

At the 1947 music criticism symposium at Harvard: George Garner III of the black-owned *Los Angeles Sentinel;* Olga Samaroff; Virgil Thomson; and Hilmar Grondahl of the *Portland Oregonian. Virgil Thomson Papers, Yale University Music Library. Used by permission.*

Paul Rosenfeld, verbal pyrotechnician and heir to Huneker, 1920. *Alfred Stieglitz,* Paul Rosenfeld, *Alfred Stieglitz Collection, National Gallery of Art, Washington. Photograph © Board of Trustees, National Gallery of Art, Washington.*

Carl Van Vechten, perhaps the first classical music critic to embrace the vernacular arts and other cultures on an equal footing, May 1, 1935. *Photo by George Hoyningen-Huene. Courtesy of The Beinecke Rare Book and Manuscript Library, Yale University.*

Minna Lederman, 1937, firing away another salvo for the cause of *Modern Music*, which she co-founded and edited. *Courtesy of the Estate of Minna Lederman Daniel.*

7

Highbrow, Lowbrow, Middlebrow

The Music Appreciation Racket, or Flacking for Parnassus

I have been told that there are many people who read the news-papers on the day after they have attended a concert or operatic representation for the purpose of finding out whether or not the performance gave them proper or sufficient enjoyment.
—HENRY E. KREHBIEL, 1896

usic appreciation, a commonplace the modern music lover takes for granted, became a secular American institution only with the advent of journalistic music critics in the mid-nineteenth century. According to W. S. B. Mathews, the prolific hymnodist and educator Lowell Mason (1792–1872), paterfamilias of a musical dynasty we shall meet a little later in this chapter, was the first influential American musician to educate Americans how to separate the emotion behind church music from its liturgical purpose. But Lowell Mason's lesson was still a work in progress by the nineteenth century's end. As late as 1902, *Musical Pastels,* a music appreciation book by George P. Upton of Chicago, included an essay, "Music and Religion," in which Upton, arguing for the artistic value of great music to churchgoing readers not used to concert halls, tried to show that Bach, Handel, Haydn, Mozart, and Beethoven were devout believers in God, thus echoing the earlier nineteenth-century idea of music as the nearest thing to godliness. Even so, Upton loused up his argument by not only quoting Ignaz Moscheles's inscription on his piano arrangement of *Fidelio*—"Finished with heaven's help"— but by including Beethoven's verbal graffito on same ("Man, help thyself").

For all the efforts of Theodore Thomas and his itinerant orchestra and of

196 Ureli Coreli Hill and the New York Philharmonic, for all the blandishments of
J. S. Dwight and his *Journal* contributors and of Henry C. Watson, Richard
Grant White, and other early music critics, by the 1870s American society still
was without a centralized, universally subscribed ethos of culture appreciation. Presently the Old Guard critics of the Gilded Age would do much to establish that ethos through the newspapers, but more yet needed to be done to
implant in the American social conscience the intrinsic platonic good of high
art, of fine music. In time, other channels than newspapers would be brought
to bear by the culture proselytizers (who were often enough our same newspaper critics moonlighting): channels such as music appreciation books, magazines, and later, radio.

∾ *Matthew Arnold's*
High Culture as   The first influential thinker to wave the flag of High
a model for music   Culture, of poetry as the modern world's handmaiden
appreciation   to old-time religion, was the great British poet, essayist,
                         and critic Matthew Arnold (1822–88). Though he was
not American, Arnold's book *Culture and Anarchy* (1869) was probably read
by such 1870s American intellectuals as the music critics W. F. Apthorp and
J. R. G. Hassard, and Arnold came to the United States to expound his ideas in
person on lecture tours in the early 1880s and thus entered America's public
cultural debate.

By "culture" Arnold meant "high culture," artistic culture, or as Arnold
put it, "the knowledge of the best that has been thought and said in the world."
Conversely, Arnold's "anarchy" referred to the centrifugal tendencies of the
new European democracies and their lack of cultural standards for appreciation of the classical canon of literature and art going back to the ancient Greeks
and Romans; Arnold supported democracy, but a culturally and ethically aristocratic democracy. The term by which Arnold designated the best in art and
literature—"high seriousness"—has become a touchstone ever after for criticism of all the arts. For Arnold, appreciation of works of "high seriousness"
was essential to achieve high culture in a society.

But British Victorian society, according to Arnold, was divisible not just
into the conventional class system but into three echelons of art depreciators.
On top were what he called the "barbarians": the monied, propertied, noble
class, economically overprivileged but largely indifferent to high art. On the

bottom were the "populace," uncultured low-class louts who cared for little but "beer, gin, and fun"—the same element H. L. Mencken later referred to as "inhabitants of the sewers of the bozart" in America. Sandwiched in between the barbarians and the populace was the only group for which Arnold held hope that its art depreciators could be converted into art appreciators: the financially ambitious but culturally uncultivated middle class, which he dubbed, somewhat inexactly, the "philistines." (Were not all three of Arnold's divisions effectively philistines?)

In the half-century after Matthew Arnold, both American music and cultural critics superseded his "barbarians," "populace," and "philistines" with three counterpart Americanized words—"highbrow," "lowbrow," and "middlebrow"—with the one difference in meaning coming from the change of "barbarian" to "highbrow," now denoting what Arnold had denoted by "high seriousness" and "high culture." As we'll see in this chapter, the history of the music appreciation movement in America, and indeed the declining place of classical music criticism amid cultural criticism in general in this country, has had much to do with the subsequent permutations of the three "brows" and their various critical exponents.

Eat your classical music, it's good for you   Prior to the spread of the Matthew Arnold gospel, and notwithstanding the transcendentalism of J. S. Dwight, Richard Grant White could still tell early 1870s readers of the *Atlantic Monthly* that "a fine appreciation of even the noblest music is not an indication of mental elevation, or of moral purity, or of delicacy of feeling, or even (except in music) of refinement of taste." But during the ensuing Gilded Age, notions expressed by critics on the subject began to change to the endorsement of classical music as a kind of self-help nostrum or panacea needed by Americans of all elements in its society. Wrote the *New York Post*'s Henry T. Finck,

> Music can impart only good impulses; whereas, we hear every day of boys and men who, after reading a dime novel or the police column in a newspaper, were prompted to commit the crimes and indulge in the vices they had read about. Hence, if people could be weaned from the vulgar pleasure of reading about crimes and scandals, and taught instead to love in-

198   nocent music, can any one doubt that they would be morally the better for it? . . . a love of demoralizing and degrading amusements can best be eradicated by educating the poetic and musical sensibilities of the masses.

A little further on he added,

> In America, more than anywhere else, is music needed as a tonic, to cure the infectious and ridiculous business fever which is responsible for so many cases of premature collapse. Nowhere else is so much time wasted in making money, which is then spent in a way that contributes to no one's happiness—least of all the owner's.[1]

The *New York Tribune*'s Henry Krehbiel seconded Finck's motion, adding as fillip a self-advertisement about the redoubled need for the musical critic:

> We, in America, are a new people, a vast hotchpotch of varied and contradictory elements. We are engaged in conquering a continent; employed in a mad scramble for material things; we give feverish hours to win the comfort for our bodies that we take only seconds to enjoy; the moments which we steal from our labors we give grudgingly to relaxation, and that this relaxation may come quickly we ask that the agents which produce it shall appeal violently to the faculties which are most easily reached. Under these circumstances whence are to come the intellectual poise, the refined taste, the quick and sure power of analysis which must precede a correct estimate of the value of a composition or its performance?[2]

To which voices the *New York Times*'s W. J. Henderson descanted that when the great American "populace," in the Matthew Arnold sense, received such guidance from knights of the inky cloak such as himself, Finck, and Krehbiel, the results would be automatic: "People who have been brought up on dance music, variety-stage songs, and music-hall ditties have to be educated up to Beethoven and Wagner. So do people who have never been in the presence of any art at all, musical or pictorial. But even these people very speedily learn to perceive the superiority of Beethoven's melodic ideas to those of David Braham."[3]

∾ *Sidney Lanier,*
musical Matthew
Arnold of the
Confederacy

One of the most remarkable case histories in this coming of age of American culture is that of the writer and musician Sidney Lanier (1842–81). The short-lived, tuberculosis-afflicted Lanier, best known to posterity as a poet, was also a flutist, a composer, a novelist, a literary theorist, a sometime journalistic music critic, and perhaps our first important music appreciation writer. Born and raised in Macon, Georgia, son of a local lawyer, Lanier believed he was the direct descendant of the family of Nicholas Lanier, court musicians for the Crown of England in the Elizabethan, Jacobean, and Caroline eras; Nicholas Lanier had composed music for the masques of Ben Jonson and Thomas Campion. This genealogy has been disputed by some, but not all, modern scholars.

Sidney Lanier was raised in a strictly Calvinistic Presbyterian family and attended Oglethorpe University, a local college of religious affiliation, but even as a youth he fashioned flutelike instruments out of reeds and gravitated to literary pursuits. The religiously pious Southern antebellum environment he knew as a child was completely inimical to bohemian or artistic endeavors, and he later described his college education as "farcical." Nevertheless, he fought willingly, even enthusiastically as a soldier for the Confederacy during the Civil War and was a prisoner of war for several months, during which time he managed to play the flute and write poetry. He married shortly after the war and fathered four sons, but life on the material level for him was an unending struggle of hotel clerking, drudgery in his father's law office, and fighting off with rest cures the tuberculosis that eventually took his life.

Despite all of this and having to support a family, Lanier not only wrote poetry and novels but in 1873 decided to abandon all further nonintellectual work and become a full-time professional musician and poet. Apparently he was a good enough flutist to play first flute in the newly formed orchestra of the Peabody Institute in Baltimore, where he had settled, and he also tried his hand at musical composition, both for flute and for orchestra. A manuscript for "Wind-Song," an 1874 solo for flute, shows a technically florid part, and also an A# below middle C, not a note on the Boehm flute, but apparently Lanier was trying to build a "long flute" that went down to the G below middle C (evidently he was unaware of the alto flute just then being developed on the Continent). Lanier made numerous trips to New York City in the late

200   1860s and early 1870s to hear Theodore Thomas and his orchestra; he even took some music lessons from Leopold Damrosch there. Meanwhile, having already written a novel, he was also writing ambitious poems, the first of which achieved national publication in *Lippincott's Magazine* in 1875. His best-known poem today is probably "The Marshes of Glynn."

By the mid-1870s Lanier's reputation as a writer-musician had traveled far enough that the U.S. Centennial Commission hired him to write the libretto for the *Centennial Meditation of Columbia,* a cantata to be set to music by Dudley Buck and performed at the inaugural ceremonies of the centennial celebration at Philadelphia, May 10, 1876. Lanier's libretto was even printed in newspapers before the actual musical performance, to derisive comments from editorialists too uncultured to understand that opera librettos are not meant to be read like independent poems. Hassard of the *New York Tribune* commented, however, that the music was "simple and clear in expression, while Mr. Lanier's language is sometimes obscure," and W. F. Apthorp, reviewing for the July 1876 *Atlantic Monthly,* wrote that "Mr. Buck has been unfortunate in the text to which he was written music." Apthorp also commented unfavorably on the explanations of his theories of music that Lanier had expressed in a letter to the *New York Tribune:* "Mr. Lanier says that he saturated his mind with a theory and then waited for the poem to come. He would have done better to keep his mind clear from theories, and to have gone ardently and without prejudice in search of his poem."

Such experiences did not deter Lanier from further theorizing about literature and music, nor from proselytizing for their support and respect as public weals. Along with J. S. Dwight, he was perhaps the nation's first public advocate for establishing endowed chairs of music in universities. In "From Bacon to Beethoven," published posthumously in *Lippincott's Magazine,* he asserted that the time had come "when the musician will become quite as substantial a figure in every-day life as the politician"; in "Mazzini and Music," published in the *Independent* in 1878, Lanier suggested, writes biographer Aubrey Starke, that "art and thought reveal not complementary but the same characteristics. In an age of science music will not fail to reveal the influence of scientific thought." [4] Lanier's essay "The Orchestra of Today," which appeared in *Scribner's* in April 1880, is one of the first music appreciation texts by an American writer describing the orchestra for nonmusicians. Only later would W. J. Henderson and H. E. Krehbiel devote chapters of their best-selling music appreciation books to the same orchestra-for-the-layman explication.

Lanier also contributed articles to local Baltimore newspapers on music: in May 1878 the *Baltimore Sun* published his reviews of the Maryland Music Festival, in January 1880 his reviews of some orchestral concerts.

Toward the end of his life Lanier was appointed to a lectureship in English literature at the then newly formed Johns Hopkins University; he also found time, when not engaged at Hopkins or in writing children's novels as potboilers, to publish his lectures on Shakespeare and the English novel and to author a scholarly treatise, *The Science of English Verse,* which attempted, somewhat crankily, to apply musical notation not just to iambic scansion of verse but to a complete system of prosody. (H. L. Mencken praised this book, though he disdained Lanier's poetry.)

In retrospect Lanier, who has received a surprising amount of scholarly attention in the last century, might be viewed by some as merely a gifted dilettante: more distinguished by the tragic circumstances of his life, and by the striking fact that such a would-be polymath would even exist at that time and place of our history, than by the intrinsic merit of his writings and music. He was not a great poet, not a Poe, Whitman, or Emily Dickinson, nor even a great popular versifier like Longfellow; both his verse and his prose theorizing show excessive preciosity. He composed, but undoubtedly more amateurishly than William Henry Fry; his efforts both at composing and at theorizing about the connections between poetry and music are much closer to those of the British Jesuit priest who was almost his exact contemporary, Gerard Manley Hopkins (1844–89), a much greater poet than Lanier, but a similarly amateur, and probably less competent, musician. Even so, upon the Lanier centenary in 1942, Louis Biancolli, music critic for the *New York World-Telegram,* wrote a celebratory article on Lanier lamenting what music he might have written had he lived longer, and Bernard Herrmann actually conducted a performance of Lanier's "Dance of the Mosquitoes."

However one sizes up his eminence as a poet, Sidney Lanier's importance as a missing link in our cultural history, particularly the history of our literary musical culture, lies not only in that he continued the tradition of Emerson, Whitman, Longfellow, and Poe as an American literary man evangelizing for classical music appreciation, but also in that his own life was a parable of Matthew Arnold's philosophy of converting the "philistines" to high culture and high seriousness. Although Lanier, because of his Southern religious upbringing, couldn't entirely escape the moralistic antibohemianism that had been bred into him, he was antitrade and anticommerce in the best way he knew

202 how: Lanier tried valiantly, desperately, to be a bourgeois while being at once musician, artist-philosopher, belles-lettrist, and freelancer, no less than did Tolstoy before his anabaptism. Lanier delivered over his working hours wholly to the life of the mind and the pursuit of art, behavior that ran radically against the grain of his time and upbringing: it was not easy being a twentieth-century Greenwich Village bohemian in the time and place of Scarlett O'Hara. Lanier was the American Southern continuator of the grand New England transcendentalist tradition of Emersonian ideas about the art of music. He died at thirty-nine, a quirky footnote of our history whose life cries out for an intelligent, sensitive film biography.

If anyone doubts that Sidney Lanier had an influence on appreciation of classical music in this country, consider the career of Esther Singleton (1865–1930). Born in Baltimore to a distinguished family and educated in private schools and by private tutors, she went to New York in 1887 to commit herself to the study of music and a career as a violinist. Though a good fiddler, she wasn't sufficiently confident in her ability to make her living that way, and she turned to writing. Among her books were *A Guide to the Opera* (1899), *A Guide to Modern Opera* (1909), and *The Orchestra and Its Instruments* (1917)—the first widely distributed music appreciation books in America not penned by a music critic or composer (she also contributed articles to the *Musical Courier*). A culture popularizer as committed to spreading the gospel of fine art as to music, Singleton also authored books about travel, architecture, art appreciation, historical furniture, and antiquities.

And as it so happens, Esther Singleton was a student and disciple of Sidney Lanier, who had been a friend of her parents in Baltimore.

ᴄᴡ *Gilded Age literary magazines and the cult of music: The vanished tradition of enlightened dilettantism*

During the last quarter of the nineteenth century there was an unprecedented explosion in articles about music appearing in the genteel literary magazines such as the *Atlantic Monthly, Harper's, Century Illustrated,* and *Scribner's. Harper's* had been founded in 1850, the *Atlantic Monthly* in 1857, *Century Illustrated Monthly* (which folded in 1930) in 1870, and *Scribner's* in 1887 (it folded in 1939). All of them published short fiction, poems, and articles on art, music, politics, and social criticism. The average annual subscriber base ranged from one hundred thousand to two hundred thousand, though at peak (circa 1887) each had about half a million subscribers and enjoyed a total readership of some three million, which was about 5 percent of the total U.S. population at the time. By any measure, then, the articles about music that appeared in these magazines enjoyed a far larger readership than did *Dwight's Journal of Music* at any time.

These magazines were subscribed to by the same middle-class strivers dubbed the philistines by Matthew Arnold, people who had some discretionary spending money and typically owned a piano in the parlor. In the words of the historian Joseph Mussulman, "The integration of the art of music with life in America was the principal musical ambition of the class of individuals that composed the audience of the quality monthly literary magazines."[5]

In fact, there was a shared community of interest between the readership and the writers of these magazines in this same "integration of music with life in America." The magazines promoted an enlightened dilettantism among literary men about classical music never seen again in subsequent epochs of American letters. "The Easy Chair" in the early years of *Harper's* was frequently occupied with writings about classical music, with subjects including Jenny Lind, the conductor Jullien, Paganini, Rossini, Ole Bull, and Thalberg; hardly ever in the twentieth century did "Easy Chair" writers similarly editorialize about the star classical musicians of the day. At the *Atlantic Monthly*, Howard Malcolm Ticknor, an assistant editor under James Russell Lowell, the poet and critic who was the *Atlantic's* first editor, doubled as a music critic for three different Boston newspapers.

William Dean Howells, the novelist (*The Rise of Silas Lapham*) and critic who was editor of the *Atlantic Monthly* from 1872 until 1881 (he also wrote *Harper's* "Easy Chair" from 1900 till his death in 1920), instituted a regular music department in the magazine from January 1872 to July 1877 by hiring the young W. F. Apthorp, just out of Harvard, to write for it. Howells liked vocal music and was friendly with the popular American songwriter Francis Boott, whose songs he would share with such literary friends as Samuel Clemens. Howells tried "to encourage American composers by commissioning a series of songs for publication in the Atlantic in 1877."[6] In the early 1880s Howells even wrote the libretto for a comic opera, *A Sea Change,* to music by the Boston composer George Henschel. Howells occasionally also reviewed books about music or concerts and opera performances. Other *Atlantic Monthly* contributors of articles about music before 1900 included Howells, Alexander

204   Wheelock Thayer, Louis Gottschalk, J. S. Dwight, Amy Fay, Henry T. Finck, John Knowles Paine, Richard Grant White, and even the Western novelist Owen Wister (*The Virginian*), who had originally gone to Europe after Harvard intending to study music composition for two years.

At *Century* magazine, Richard Watson Gilder, who, like Lowell, Howells, Longfellow, and other Boston literati, liked music, became editor in 1881. The New York–based Gilder and his wife held a Friday evening arts salon for years at their East Fourteenth Street home, known to writers, actors, musicians, and other artists as "The Studio." Henry Finck in his memoirs recounts one musicale at "The Studio" with Samuel Clemens present. Noted musical performers there included the singer Clara Louise Kellogg and the pianists Adele aus der Ohe and Ignace Paderewski. In the late 1880s and early 1890s *Century* ran a series of articles on "great composers and virtuosos," including a piece on the then-superstar Paderewski authored by Gilder himself.

At *Harper's*, writers contributing articles on music included George W. Curtis, George P. Upton, and Antonín Dvořák, who was teaching at the National Conservatory in New York at the time. Curtis, whom we last encountered in chapter 2, wrote both for *Harper's* "Easy Chair" and independent music reviews. At *Scribner's* magazine, editor Edward L. Burlingame from its inception in 1887 until 1914 commissioned many articles about music from Apthorp and Krehbiel. Richard Grant White, who was actually better known at the time as a Shakespearean scholar than as a music critic (though he was a competent cellist), contributed articles on music to both the *Atlantic* and to *Century*. According to Mussulman, most of the music article writers for *Century* and *Scribner's* were "professional performers, teachers, composers, or critics," while most of those for *Atlantic* and *Harper's* were "merely knowledgeable dilettantes."[7]

At no subsequent time in our history did *Harper's* and *Atlantic* run so many articles, and so high a proportion of their articles, about classical music. The notion that appreciation of classical music was construed as a part of the mainstream of high culture, a culture that embraced literature, fine art, and music equally, seems to have been a notion that reached its apogee with the Gilded Age. As music appreciation writing after 1900 devolved into highbrow, lowbrow, and middlebrow audiences of readership that did not interact with one another, the ideal of classical music as a common denominator of aspiration for all people of culture in America got attenuated and ultimately, toward the late twentieth century, eliminated.

ꙮ *Typical music appreciation book thinking, circa 1898: The critics wax philosophical*   The leading critics of the time who wrote music appreciation books tended to lace these books with references to German idealistic philosophy or Arnoldian artistic moralism that would seem foreign (even quasi-religioso) today in books about music addressed to the general reader; but then, the general reader of that time was conditioned to aspire to "high seriousness." In his appropriately titled *What Is Good Music? Suggestions to Persons Desiring to Cultivate a Taste in Musical Art,* when W. J. Henderson tells his readers that his view of musical aesthetics is similar to Immanuel Kant's, it tells us how educated those readers must have been:

> [Kant] holds that "the Beautiful is that which, through the harmony of its form with the faculty of human knowledge, awakens a disinterested, universal, and necessary satisfaction." By disinterestedness in relation to beauty, Kant means freedom from gratification of sensual appetite or preconceived conceptions. The Beautiful gives pleasure, not because it satisfies any physical appetite or corresponds to any extant idea, but because in and through itself it imprints its own Ideal upon the soul, which, by its faculty of knowledge, is capable of receiving it.[8]

Similarly, Henry Krehbiel in his equally popular volume *How to Listen to Music* tells the reader, "The vile, the ugly, the painful are not fit subjects for music; music renounces, contravenes, negatives itself when it attempts their delineation."

> If I were to attempt a definition it would be this: Classical composers are those of the first rank (to this extent we yield to the ancient Roman conception) who have developed music to the highest pitch of perfection on its formal side and, in obedience to generally accepted laws, preferring aesthetic beauty, pure and simple, over emotional content, or, at any rate, refusing to sacrifice form to characteristic expression. Romantic composers are those who have sought their ideals in other regions and striven to give expression to them irrespective of the restrictions and limitations of form and the conventions of law—composers with whom, in brief, content outweighs matter. This definition presents Classicism as the reg-

ulative and conservative principle in the history of the art, and Romanticism as the progressive, regenerative, and creative principle. It is easy to
see how the notion of contest between them grew up, and the only harm
which can come from such a notion will ensue only if we shut our eyes to
the fact that it is a contest between two elements whose very opposition
stimulates life, and whose union, perfect, peaceful, mutually supplemen-
tal, is found in every really great art-work.[9]

For his part, Henderson expatiates about the sensuous, the emotional, and
the intellectual as the three attributes governing artistic merit. One must recall
that there was great interest in the second half of the nineteenth century in aesthetic theories, not just Matthew Arnold's but Schopenhauer's, Tolstoy's (viz.,
his book *What Is Art?*), Walter Pater's and John Ruskin's, and in thus writing
Henderson was simply trying to bring his American readers up to speed. Henderson, like Krehbiel, tended to equate the "sensuous" with the uncultivated
listener. "He does not wish to understand music. He wishes only to hear it. . . .
He refuses to trouble his mind sufficiently to detect evidences of design in the
work. He reduces music to the level of confectionery." The true masters of tone
color were the masters of form and structure, he told his "philistine" readers:
"The noble artistic reticence of Beethoven, whose tonal schemes are full of the
solid yet subdued glory of Corot's landscapes, is seldom found in new orchestral works, many of which seek to cover up barren melodic subjects, feeble
development, and insincere emotion with Turneresque outpours of gorgeous
color."[10]

These books, however, consisted of more than just highfalutin philosophical rehashes and moralistic I-tell-you-so's. Krehbiel wrote in his own work,
How to Listen to Music, "This book being for the untrained, the question might
be put thus: With how little knowledge of the science can an intelligent listener
get along? We are concerned only with his enjoyment of music, or, better, with
an effort to increase it without asking him to become a musician," and went
on in a clear and accessible manner to teach the rudiments of theory: chords,
cadences, phrases, motives, periods, and so on, as does Henderson's book; both
then also go into a description of the instruments of the orchestra, the instruments' physical arrangement on the platform in the concert hall, and so forth.
It cannot be doubted that thousands of Americans at the turn of the century
learned the rudiments of music and how to listen to concerts not from private
teachers or schools but from these two books of Krehbiel's and Henderson's, if

one can judge from the perennial reprints of both well into the first decades of the new century.

Soon enough the other New York and Boston critics, such as Henry T. Finck and W. F. Apthorp, got out their own books, but more often than not these were anthologies of their previous newspaper and magazine essays, rather than systematic how-to-understand-music primers like Henderson's and Krehbiel's. As for the now familiar genre of book-length repertoire survey, the most ambitious early attempt was the three-volume *Symphonies and Their Meaning* (1897–1913) by the organist and sometime composer Philip H. Goepp (1864–1936). An American-born, German-educated Harvard graduate who studied with Paine, Goepp was also a lawyer, which may account for his long-winded musical exegeses. Or the Germanic schooling may have accounted for the vein of philosophic idealism that runs through his writing. He spent most of his adult life in Philadelphia, where he wrote Halean program notes for the Philadelphia Orchestra but did not serve as a newspaper critic.

Another by-product of the passion for classical music culture characteristic of turn-of-the-century America was the weekly classical music magazine, several of which started up, ironically, just as *Dwight's Journal* was folding for good. Two such periodicals that were addressed primarily to music educators were the *Etude,* published by Theodore Presser in Philadelphia, lasting until 1957, and the *Musician,* which ran from 1896 to 1948. Even longer lasting were the *Musical Courier* (established in 1880) and *Musical America* (from 1898). If aspects of the books of Henderson and Goepp had been highbrow, these weeklies were usually more middlebrow in their treatment of music. In fact, Nicolas Slonimsky, describing certain features of the weeklies with tongue in cheek, paints them as decidedly lower than middlebrow:

> They published weekly issues that featured dispatches by specially assigned European correspondents and reproduced excellent photographs of the current celebrities who bought advertising space. For a modest fee even for those times, these publications carried cover portraits of exotic-looking mustachioed tenors and ample-bosomed prima donnas, and occasionally even an American face. The ads informed on the activities of music teachers ("Mr. X has returned from Europe and will accept a limited number of exceptionally talented pupils"), voice teachers with Italian surnames ("Guarantee bel canto within six months by inhaling bottled compressed air from Naples"), "Miss Y triumphs in Muleshoe,

Texas," and so on. . . . *The Etude* purveyed information to music lovers and amateurs; it published sentimental biographies of contemporary musicians, as well as simplified selections of some digestible compositions.[11]

With the advent of these populist musical weeklies, the step downward from the rarefied precincts of the *Atlantic Monthly* to music appreciation in the *Ladies' Home Journal* seemed inevitable. Sure enough, the *Ladies' Home Journal,* the monthly magazine of the Curtis Publishing Company run by Edward and Mary Bok in Philadelphia, did step into the breach. "Bok induced many of the best-known writers, artists, scientists, musicians and public figures of the day to contribute to the *Journal's* pages. . . . The articles were designed to emphasize the *Journal's* commitment to culture, practicality and self-improvement," noted pianologist Gregor Benko.[12] In 1901 the Boks began running a regular feature in the magazine in which readers put questions about playing the piano to the great pianist Josef Hofmann. The patrician and intellectually brilliant Hofmann, to his credit, answered the questions for thirteen years in anything but a dumbed-down manner. But the way was paved for later, less careful efforts and the twentieth-century version of lowbrow, mass music appreciation.

ᔕ *Episode: Rupert Hughes, the genteel age's missing link*   Of all the careers embodying the Gilded Age's beau ideal of the musical gentleman *culturatus,* the most spectacular was that of Rupert Hughes (1872–1956), the only classical music critic to become a millionaire and Hollywood celebrity. Hughes started out in life much like Krehbiel, Henderson, and company, that is, as a quiet journeyman classical music critic and appreciation book writer. He ended up the author of fifty books of fiction and nonfiction (one of which helped influence the creation of the observance of Mother's Day); prolific screenwriter; silent movie director whose films are even today generating a cult among cinephiles; soldier under Pershing in the 1916 Mexican expedition to catch Pancho Villa; radio commentator; controversial George Washington biographer; publicly declared agnostic; and Hollywood chum of the stars. He was also the uncle of the billionaire Howard Hughes, but Uncle Rupert earned his own fortune, thank you.

Hughes was born and raised in Missouri. His parents (his father was a rail-

road president) encouraged study of the arts. He studied music in college in
Ohio and later privately with the composer (and sometime critic) Edgar Still-
man Kelley, while his brother and sister trained as serious musicians in Europe. Hard of hearing from youth, Rupert gradually grew deaf as he grew
older; by the 1930s he had to learn to read lips. Hughes moved to New York
City in the 1890s, befriended James Huneker, and became music critic of the
Criterion, a vanguard weekly of the late 1890s and early 1900s that was a kind
of precursor of Mencken's *American Mercury*. He also wrote articles about music for *Godey's*, *Century*, and *Criterion* in the 1890s, collecting his magazine essays in the 1900 book *Contemporary American Composers*. In the 1910s he wrote
for magazines such as *Smith's*, *Ainslie's*, *Century*, and Theodore Dreiser's *De-
lineator*, but also started writing novels, one of which sold to the movies. By
the 1920s he had relocated to Hollywood and became a screenwriter and director there.

In all his writings on music Hughes was unusually progressive: he championed homegrown American composers; he was way ahead of other critics in
recognizing the validity of African-American vernaculars, writing "A Eulogy of
Ragtime" in the April 1, 1899, issue of the *Musical Record* and later, in 1920,
writing in the *Etude*, "Jazz . . . is Ragtime raised to the nth degree." So far ahead
of his time was he that he even included a chapter on "Women Composers" in
his 1900 book on composers; Hughes was a staunch advocate of women's rights
in those suffragist days. In 1921 Hughes endorsed the Golden Hour, "a plan to
present daily cultural programs in schools" that anticipated Walter Damrosch's radio "Music Appreciation Hour" by several years.[13]

Even after he started to earn big money in Hollywood, Hughes wrote and
published songs (both lieder and pop songs). He even composed an extended
monodrama, *Cain*, which no less esteemed a musicologist than John Tasker
Howard referred to as late as the 1950s as "modernist, showing an investigation
of dissonance." But his big music book was *The Musical Guide*, first published
in 1903 and later reissued as *The Music Lovers' Cyclopedia*. After selling some
one hundred thousand copies over the years, the book was completely revised
in the late 1930s by Deems Taylor and Russell Kerr. It was reprinted as late as
1971. Taylor wrote in a preface, "Mr. Hughes, who is chiefly known to the world
as a novelist, is a musical amateur in the finest sense of the word, a music-lover
who has studied and practiced the art of music all his life, purely for the fun of
it. To realize that profound scholarship can be coexistent with an amateur
standing, you have only to read his [introductory] chapter."

Later, Hughes wrote a three-volume biography of George Washington that

210 generated a cause célèbre for its depiction of Washington using profanity and lusting after his friends' wives. Yet Hughes was a superpatriot who testified against alleged Communists in the entertainment industry at the House Un-American Activities Committee in the late 1940s.

Rupert Hughes, a magnificently paradoxical figure, Whitmanesque in his multitudes: a women's rights advocate two of whose three wives committed suicide; a deaf composer; an iconoclastic, irreverent biographer of George Washington who was a superpatriotic anticommunist; a mainline religionist who ended up rejecting belief. And a writer who continued to promote the cause of classical music throughout all his gaudy activities via the reissues and reworkings of *The Music Lovers' Cyclopedia*. Why did he bother? Because of an ingrained ethos that doesn't exist in American life any more.

‿ The highbrow apostasy

By World War I, a new crowd of critical Young Turks were shaking the foundations of American arts and letters. The Old Guard music critics were still around (though Huneker was starting to fade), and the Victorian holdover literary critics H. L. Mencken loved to hate, such as Hamilton Mabie and Irving Babbitt, still held court. But critic-editors like William Dean Howells and Richard Watson Gilder, literary men who liked classical music and had provided regular coverage of it in their magazines, were dying and were being replaced by a new breed of journalistic cultural critics who felt no such allegiance to Euterpe. Only Carl Van Vechten, and Mencken in the *American Mercury,* survived to bear the standard of Walt Whitman and Sidney Lanier of the literary man's crossover into the art of "high serious" music. The new critics—Gilbert Seldes, Lewis Mumford, Waldo Frank, Kenneth Burke, Van Wyck Brooks, Edmund Wilson, Randolph Bourne, and others—wrote for a group of new "smart" magazines, such as the *Dial, Seven Arts, Esquire, Vanity Fair,* the *New Republic,* the *Nation,* and the *New Yorker,* that stole the limelight from *Century, Scribner's,* and the other venerable cultural magazines of nineteenth-century origin still publishing. In fact, freelance American arts critics never had it so good before or after the 1910s and 1920s, when a unique profusion of journals provided them with many different paying outlets for their writing.

It was this group of critics, sometimes questioning the received wisdom of the Matthew Arnold philosophy of high culture, sometimes attacking the opera house–tier stratification of American culture, that opened a Pandora's box that ultimately defeated literary appreciation of classical music. Van Wyck

Brooks's antiaristocrat 1915 book, *America's Coming of Age,* and a series of articles he published from 1914 to 1918 widely popularized the words (and notions behind) *highbrow* and *lowbrow,* while the promising Randolph Bourne (he died of influenza in the 1918 epidemic at thirty-two), indifferent to Matthew Arnold's definition of philistine, wrote of rejecting both highbrow and lowbrow in favor of a middle ground: the middlebrow.

The trouble was, none of these new critics much cared for or knew about classical music; none of them was a Huneker who could be a "steeplejack" of all the arts. As Van Wyck Brooks wrote to the composer-writer Daniel Gregory Mason in 1933, "My knowledge of music is not much, but after all, the arts are all closely connected, and I am growing not to care very much for any criticism that is not based on a fairly generous understanding of art in general, though I still suspect the kind of criticism that professes to deal with more than one of the arts." [14] A *Dial* and *Seven Arts* critic like Paul Rosenfeld got compartmentalized into music without being allowed to unleash his intellect on the other arts, but the Brookses and Mumfords were in effect permitted to exercise influence over the discourse about music by default, by dint of their very ignorance steering them away from commentary on it.

Gilbert Seldes and the challenge to "high seriousness"

Carl Van Vechten was the last all-around critic in the Huneker mold to embrace both "high seriousness" in music and middlebrow and lowbrow music (we look at him in detail in chapter 10). Shortly, both he and Huneker were supplanted by the first highbrow pop culture critic (an oxymoron?): Gilbert Seldes. Seldes (1893–1970) had briefly been classical music critic for the *Philadelphia Evening Ledger* in 1914–15. That was the end of his coverage of classical music. The rest of his illustrious career as a critic was devoted to his enthusiastic exponency of what he at first dubbed the minor or popular arts, that is, movies, comic strips, vaudeville, musical comedy, and other expressions of what we now call pop culture. Seldes's book *The Seven Lively Arts* (1924, rev. 1957), a manifesto supporting not just the coexistence of popular art with high art but its sometime superiority to it, must in retrospect be regarded one of the seminal books in twentieth-century American art criticism. It was surely not thought of in that way at the time: too lightweight for Arnoldian mandarins.

Seldes was a highly intelligent critic who with astounding prescience anticipated by decades almost every development that eventually occurred in the entertainment mass media. He was not an advocate for mass mediocrity; he

212 apparently liked Picasso and Stravinsky and read *Ulysses* with understanding; in later years he deplored the dumbing-down trends already evident in television, especially in his book *The Great Audience,* a look at how the lively arts had devolved into the mass media with a resultant "degradation of taste and the emergence of cultural mediocrity on an unprecedented scale." [15]

But Seldes not only personally preferred musical comedy and jazz to opera; not only did he, with Henry Pleasants, prefer Gershwin's musical comedy songs to *Porgy and Bess;* but he actually posited in *The Seven Lively Arts* the artistic superiority of good "lively art"—say, a Ziegfeld Follies or Jerome Kern musical—to what he viewed as second-rate "high art," what he called "bogus art," a label he applied, for instance, to opera he didn't like (Puccini, evidently). Seldes simplistically referred to stuff he viewed as pretentiously highbrow as "faux bon." One cannot but feel that Seldes, for all his gifts, simply didn't have an ear for "highbrow" music. He just didn't understand or appreciate opera! That's pardonable; but to generalize an artistic theory from one's crotchet of personal taste is to create the potential for intellectual mischief.

Seldes wrote in *The Seven Lively Arts* of the distinctions between highbrow, lowbrow, and middlebrow: "The lively arts are created and admired chiefly by the class known as lowbrows, are patronized and, to an extent enjoyed, by the highbrows, and are treated as impostors and as contemptible vulgarisms by the middle class, those who invariably are ill at ease in the presence of great art until it has been approved by authority." In a 1932 article in the *New York Evening Journal,* he only slightly amended his thinking: "It is long since I have had a propagandist's enthusiasm for what I carelessly called 'the lively arts.' I can take them or leave them alone. Yet I still find more pleasure in a good farce than in a bad tragedy, more in a good piece of jazz than in a pretentious opera, more in a good comic strip than in an imitation of Picasso by a talentless painter." What Seldes really meant, in the opinion of the historian Michael Kammen, was that "there is no necessary opposition or conflict between the great and the lesser arts. Because they complement one another, a person really isn't culturally alive who fails to appreciate both. . . . His 'discovery' . . . was that the popular arts were worthy of 'intelligent criticism.'" [16] In other words, *pace* Clement Greenberg, not all popular art was necessarily synonymous with kitsch; to like some popular culture was not to wish to paint a mustache on the Mona Lisa.

But at moments, Seldes would go so far as to imply that Irving Berlin was superior to Puccini, or Gershwin to Mozart. In his later years, he tried to recouch his earlier statements: "I wasn't against the fine arts, I was only against 'high-class-trash' as, indeed, I was against low-class trash," he said in February 1968. Seldes also rebutted the idea that mass reproduction of fine art, as with photographic reproductions of paintings or phonograph records of classical music, would harm appreciation of the original. He had said privately in 1967,

> Before the coming of [the] highspeed press and what is called "universal literacy," the popular arts were oral—the singer, the minstrel show, the theatre, the evangelist, the Chautauqua lecturer, and so on, and the intellectual's attitude was indifference to the point that one wonders whether he knew what was going on; and at the other extreme, the entertainments which began with the dime novel and the comic strip, and then movies and broadcasting, transforming the popular arts into the mass media, have created a sort of panic among the intellectuals, fearful that the arts they cherish will somehow not survive.[17]

Practicing what he preached, Seldes wrote not only for highbrow journals like the *Dial* and middlebrow ones like the *Saturday Evening Post*, but also for lowbrow ones like *TV Guide*; he also appeared on numerous middlebrow radio talk programs in the 1930s and 1940s. Seldes's address of highbrow encomiums to Tin Pan Alley was a sea change from the sentiments expressed by such nineteenth-century critics as Richard Grant White and W. F. Apthorp; even Henry Krehbiel, in his 1914 book on African-American folk song, did not approve early jazz and ragtime.

Daniel Gregory Mason: Music appreciation's nineteenth-century man in the twentieth

Just because a young whippersnapper like Seldes had come along to say you could prefer Gershwin to Mozart and still be—well, at least middlebrow— didn't mean that the Matthew Arnold tradition had gone belly up everywhere. Perhaps the most persistent reactionary among music appreciation writers, a walking anachronism who carried the musical ethos of the Gilded Age into the 1940s, was the composer and writer Daniel Gregory Mason (1873–1953). Born into what one could call America's first musical dynasty (an even earlier dynasty than the Steinways or Damrosches), he was the nephew of the pianist William Mason (1829–1908) and the grandson of Lowell Mason (1792–1872),

214   one of the unheralded founding fathers of American music. Lowell Mason
(himself the descendant of the first known family musician, Barachias Mason
[1723–83]) was a prolific composer of hymns, an anthologizer of church music, the man responsible for the addition of music education to the Boston
public school curriculum, a choirmaster, and the founder of one of the nation's
earliest conservatories, the Boston Academy of Music (1832). Lowell and his
son Henry founded Mason & Hamlin pianos with Emmons Hamlin. Henry's
brother William was a distinguished concert pianist who studied with Liszt
and left a remarkable volume of memoirs, replete with firsthand anecdotes
about Liszt, Brahms, Schumann, Wagner, and other immortals, which reads as
though it had been written yesterday.

Daniel Gregory Mason was the son of Lowell's son Henry. He played piano and composed as a child, although one of his arms was partially paralyzed
(a disability he largely overcame). Like every musician who went to Harvard at
the time, he studied with John Knowles Paine there, and also with Chadwick
and Goetschius in Boston; Mason also had a late "finishing" period of study
with Vincent d'Indy in Paris when he was about forty. He moved to New York
City around 1900, where he immediately started giving adult education lectures and began a teaching career, first at Princeton, then at Columbia, where
he was based from 1905 to 1942; throughout his life he also continued giving
public lectures. Mason left a substantial body of works composed for orchestra, as well as much chamber and vocal music; though now largely forgotten,
his symphonic works were given performances in his lifetime by top conductors: Stokowski, Stransky, Walter, Reiner, Gabrilowitsch, and Barbirolli. His
best-known piece is probably the *Chanticleer* Overture. Unlike several other
American writer-composer-critics, he seems to have steered clear of opera and
the stage.

In addition to his teaching, lecturing, and composing—and composing
was a trial for him, as he was a frequent reviser—Mason produced a stream of
eighteen music appreciation books that brought him accolades as the most
widely read American author of his time of books about music and composers.
His earlier books include *From Grieg to Brahms* (1902), *Beethoven and His Forerunners* (1904), *The Romantic Composers* (1906), *The Appreciation of Music*
(1907), *The Orchestral Instruments* (1908), and *A Guide to Music* (1909). His
later volumes, such as *Artistic Ideals, Tune In, America,* and *The Dilemma of
American Music,* are more in the form of polemical commentary on musical
issues of the 1920s and 1930s. Mason also published articles in *American Mercury, Harper's, Musical America,* the *Nation,* and *Musical Quarterly,* but unlike

such fellow composers as William Henry Fry, Reginald De Koven, Deems Taylor, and Virgil Thomson, he never once worked as a newspaper music critic (holding a faculty position at Columbia undoubtedly rendered his earning a critic's salary unnecessary).

But as an intelligent illuminator of the "inner game" of composers and music, Mason, at least in his early books, ranks with Deems Taylor and Virgil Thomson as a peerless musical guide, quite free of the gaseousness that sometimes afflicts Henderson and Krehbiel. Like Thomson, Mason anatomizes the music he describes as a composer looking out from inside, not as an explicator looking in from outside. He'll explicitly define in musical terms what it is about Chopin's piano figuration that creates the illusion of sustention of tone, or demonstrate exactly why Berlioz's melodies are conceived for each instrument they are written for. For all his powers of analytical insight, though, Mason had a retro bias. Mason freely owned that he was an unreconstructed conservative, even a little priggish; in his 1948 memoirs he gives vent to the following reactionary sentiments:

> [My] deep convictions . . . by the turn of the century had formed themselves clearly in my mind, and . . . since then have never essentially changed. . . . one of my deepest convictions has always been a sense of the supreme value in art of balance, restraint, proportion—in a word, of classic beauty. Hence my lifelong adoration of men like Bach, Mozart, Schubert, Beethoven, Brahms, in whom this ideal is supremely realized. Contrariwise I have always felt an instinctive antipathy toward excess, unbalance, romantic exaggeration, sensationalism, typified for me in such composers, great artists though they be, as Wagner, Tchaikovsky, Liszt, Strauss. . . . On Thanksgiving Eve of my first New York autumn, for instance, I was repelled, exasperated, and bored (as, if I am to be honest, I must confess I have been on all subsequent occasions) by a performance of *Tristan und Isolde*.[18]

Where indeed would this kind of thinking leave Debussy, Stravinsky, and Schoenberg? According to the musicologist H. Earle Johnson, a former student once said, "Professor Mason never quite made it into the twentieth century."

Once modernism got under way in earnest, Mason's books joined the fray about highbrow and lowbrow; only, he added his own wrinkles to the debate about high, low, and middle. In *The Dilemma of American Music and Other Es-*

216   *says,* which consisted largely of reprints of his magazine articles of the 1920s, Mason referred to the monied culturati, those who sat on the boards of and bought the subscriptions to the opera and symphony, as "moronic conservatives," philistines who paid a conspicuous consumer homage to the umpteenth performances of orchestral warhorses by preapproved celebrity conductors: "Our national timidity in artistic matters, our fear of making fools of ourselves by individual activity before the herd, our superstitious reverence for great names and reputations, and above all for great prices, have cheated us." But he stingingly added that "certainly their [the moronic conservatives'] menace to our musical health is far less than that of 'moronic radicals,' with their unintelligent clamor for ceaseless novelty, reverberated by box office and press."[19] (In less fulminant moments, Mason tended to characterize the moderns merely as "pseudo-original.") As for the lowbrows, as Mason (and many other musicians of the time) saw it, they were those who listened to ragtime and jazz, danced to foxtrots, and attended musical comedy. Such a mind-set would have put Gilbert Seldes squarely in the lowbrow camp.

To his great credit Mason argued in the 1920s what composers and critics were still arguing in the 1990s, that American orchestras should necessarily serve a dual function of both museum and laboratory—one, to present the established classics to the general audience, the other to advance the art by premiering new work—and he suggested that American orchestras had been launched onto the free market of gate revenue too soon, that the philanthropists should dig deeper into their pockets to subsidize the orchestras to help support that laboratory function. "Selling commodities for profit is static, time-serving, and safe, a matter of adjustment of supply with demand. Art is dynamic, creative, experimental, innovating: hence strenuous, venturesome, full of risk, succeeding only through failure, and demanding alert activity of all who participate in it."[20]

This was an enlightened point of view, marred only by the disingenuousness of Mason's intending that only composers of his conservative ilk should get the "laboratory" premieres, not the Edgard Varèses or Leo Ornsteins. For Mason, even Ravel could be "pseudo-original": "The quasi-mechanical repetitions of short phrases in Ravel's String Quartet, for example, beginning at the very start, soon grow almost intolerable to the sensitive listener. Ernest Newman has commented on the 'short breath' and in general the melodic insignificance of Ravel, truly pointing out that if you scratch his surface you find Chaminade underneath."[21] Mason's ultimate dismissal of modernism was that it was "boring": Milhaud's polytonality, Cowell's tone clusters, almost all of

Stravinsky, and even some of Debussy, all were "boring," because their novelty wears off quickly. (He also felt exaggerations of emphasis in playing and conducting, that is, excessive interpretation, were boring for similar reasons.) Even this hidebound reactionary, however, occasionally hedged his bets: "There is of course no reason why the most complex harmonies, the most ferocious dissonances, should not be used, provided the thought calls for them; it is the valuing of the medium above the thought that is decadent. . . . many phrases of Debussy, built on the far-famed 'whole-tone scale,' achieve a distinction obtainable in no other way; some of Stravinsky's dissonances are equally happy." [22]

Some of Mason's commentaries on techniques of musical modernism ham-handedly anticipate arguments in Constant Lambert's later *Music Ho!* For the most part, Lambert's anti-modern analyses are more ingenious and less biased than Mason's. But the jeremiads of Mason that have held up the best are those that argued that mass-produced machines for the democratic dissemination of art and music to the "common man" were destined merely to produce an explosion of "moronic conservatives."

What are the effects upon us, good and bad, of mechanical inventions such as phonograph, movietone, and radio? Do their dissuasion from piano-playing and from amateur participation in music-making generally, and their invitation to passivity and inattention even in listeners, seem to be compensated by their initiation of a new public, their wholesome subordination of the virtuoso as star to the music as art, and other advantages?

. . . As for the extraordinary development of mechanical instruments that marked the second decade of our century, and of radio, which began in the third, its first incidence was undeniably to aggravate the bad influence of the thoughtless and vulgar segment of the public, by increasing access to rubbish and inattentiveness to everything. Quantity production in the pianola, the phonograph, and the radio at first cheapened taste in music just as, in newspapers and magazines, it had earlier cheapened taste in literature. [23]

The irony here is that Gilbert Seldes, in his later years increasingly alarmed by the cultural passivity induced by the ease and convenience of listening to and watching radio and television, brought his arguments in his books *The Great Audience* and *The Public Arts* more closely in line with Daniel Gregory

218 Mason's earlier critique. The substitution of corporation-produced, bottom line–managed orchestras and mechanical media for active participation in making music was what was gnawing at Daniel Gregory Mason in the early twentieth century (he quoted Arthur Whiting's characterization of the player piano, or pianola, as a "musical Ford" or "horseless pianoforte"); the ever-aggrandizing media conglomerates' monopolistically taking over the role of culture provider and thereby rendering Americans passive and undiscriminating of mediocrity was what was gnawing at Seldes late in life. Both critics, however dissimilar in artistic sympathies, saw with some chagrin the potential brow-lowering effects of the mass industrialization of culture (now sometimes called "masscult"), a phenomenon also addressed by such nonmusical culture critics as Dwight Macdonald.

ᥩ *Music appreciation goes lowbrow: Tune detectives & radio quiz shows*   Some twenty-five years after Josef Hofmann began his column in the *Ladies' Home Journal,* a greater Rubicon was crossed when the aging conductor Walter Damrosch actually retired from the podium to become the host of an early morning radio program entitled "The Music Appreciation Hour" (with a hidden homage to Longfellow's "The Children's Hour"?). "Good morning, my dear children," intoned the grandfatherly Damrosch (1862–1950) every Friday morning from 1928 to 1942 on NBC, and five million American schoolchildren listened, some of them sitting before loudspeakers at school, as "Papa" Damrosch, the vocal incarnation of the stock type of the kindly German professor, taught the classics by singing mnemonic verse along with recordings: for instance, to the tune of Schubert's Eighth, "This is the sym-pho-ny/that Schu-bert wrote and ne-ver fi-nished." Damrosch had himself established children's concerts at the old New York Symphony back in 1903. For many American children "The Music Appreciation Hour" was required listening in school: it was said that American schoolchildren knew Damrosch's voice better than Mickey Mouse's.

Damrosch's children's hour was only part of what got Daniel Gregory Mason's goat: there was also Sigmund Spaeth, the "tune detective." Spaeth (1885–1965), the son of a German Lutheran minister, had a remarkable, if chaotically diverse, musical life; he was a kind of highbrow-middlebrow-lowbrow all in one. Trained as a pianist, violinist, and singer, he taught music and English and even coached football at various times in his career; he became the preeminent

American authority on barbershop quartet singing and wrote books about popular songs. Yet he also held a musicological doctorate from Princeton on the subject of John Milton's knowledge of music, and he served on the faculty of Princeton as a teacher of German while Woodrow Wilson was still the college's president. Spaeth was also a newspaper music critic, first at the *New York Evening Mail* in the early 1910s, then toward 1920 apprenticing briefly to Huneker at the *Times* and New York stringing for the *Boston Transcript*'s H. T. Parker. Later he was a magazine music critic for *McCall's* and *Esquire.* But his lasting fame came from the 1931–40 radio program "The Tune Detective," in which he popularized classical music by discovering for his listeners the antecedents of a pop song in a classical composition: "Yes, We Have No Bananas" in Handel's "Hallelujah Chorus" from *Messiah,* or "I'm Always Chasing Rainbows" in Chopin's *Fantasie-Impromptu.* Spaeth even served as an expert witness in court at plagiarism suits involving hit songs of the day, and he appeared as a vaudeville act, "The Tune Detective," at Radio City Music Hall. He also was a radio pioneer of media interactivity, broadcasting piano lessons to listeners who followed them on their pianos at home using predesigned instruction sheets.

The truth is, radio, with its national broadcasts of the New York Philharmonic and the Metropolitan Opera (and later, the NBC Symphony), had recruited a hugely populous new audience for classical music, and some highbrows thought that these classical music greenhorns needed some middlebrow, or lowbrow, orientation. There was, for instance, Alec Templeton (1910–63), the Welsh-born blind ex-prodigy pianist and composer, whose radio shows "You Shall Have Music" (1935–36), "Universal Rhythm" (1937), and "Alec Templeton Time" (1939–41, 1946–47) took a cue from Spaeth and invented "crossover" music: Templeton composed the popular "Bach Goes to Town" as well as a "St. Louis Blues" in a Chopinesque style and "Stompin' at the Savoy" done as a Bachian fugue. Templeton had been a pianistic wunderkind at twelve, appearing on the BBC in Britain, and he also composed many serious, "longhair" symphonic pieces, but his classical pastiches heard by millions of radio listeners may have been the grandfathers of all the pop-classic crossovers to come.

Damrosch, Spaeth, and Templeton were lowbrowing it, as did the Yale English professor William Lyon Phelps in broadcasts with the operetta composer Sigmund Romberg. Others middlebrowed it. Deems Taylor was the most ubiquitous music commentator; he started as intermission speaker for the Metropolitan Opera broadcasts in 1931 and went on to a weekly series of his

220 own, "Deems Taylor Commentaries," in which he talked in a serious way about contemporary music, interviewing classical musicians. But his appearances soon devolved into guest host turns on lowbrow entertainment programs such as "Kraft Music Hall," "The Prudential Family Hour," "Chesterfield Presents," "Studio Party at Sigmund Romberg's," "The RCA Victor Show," and "Chamber Music Society of Lower Basin Street."

Taylor did, though, appear on the middlebrow quiz program "Information Please!"; this popular weekday evening half-hour show ran on various radio networks from 1938 to 1952. With Clifton Fadiman moderating, the panelists would field a series of intellectual "stumper" questions sent in by listeners; if none could answer them, a cash register rang, and the listener would be awarded a set of the *Encyclopedia Britannica* and cash prizes. Knowledge of classical music figured into the questions, and though Taylor appeared some forty times as a guest panelist, joining such regulars as the pianist Oscar Levant, John Kieran of the *New York Times,* Franklin P. Adams of the Algonquin set, Hendrick Van Loon, and Stuart Chase, the most regular guest from the "longhair" classical music establishment was John Erskine, who was perhaps America's last surviving example of the nineteenth-century genteel tradition of the literary writer who also cultivated musicianship.

Erskine (1879–1951) was raised in Manhattan and Hoboken, New Jersey, in a "Life with Father" setting complete with governesses. A serious piano student who aspired to a concert career from childhood, he attended Columbia, studying music there with Edward MacDowell and literature with Brander Mathews, but getting his doctorate in English poetry. Initially teaching at Amherst, he returned to Columbia in 1909, where he initiated a "great books" program for Columbia undergrads after World War I; one of his students was Clifton Fadiman, later the "Information Please!" emcee; another was Mortimer Adler, who took Erskine's Great Books idea to the University of Chicago curriculum and, later, to a mass-marketed series of popularizing books. Erskine, however, something of a kindred spirit of Daniel Gregory Mason (though less prissy and dogmatic), disapproved of Adler's adaptation of his Great Books idea to the masscult. Even so, he deigned to appear on Fadiman's radio program, and with Spaeth on the NBC radio program "Keys to Happiness." Erskine continued to teach literature at Columbia until 1937 and also authored *The Private Life of Helen of Troy,* a best-selling novel of 1925 that was a portrait of racy jazz age mores. He also published several music appreciation books.

The most arresting fact about Erskine's life was that he not only took up the piano again in middle age after twenty years of little practice but achieved a modest but real concert career (a slap in the face to jazz age laureate F. Scott Fitzgerald's dictum "There are no second acts in American lives"). Erskine went on leave from Columbia in the early 1920s to resume practicing and playing chamber music privately, then in 1924 began intensive piano studies with Ernest Hutcheson; soon thereafter he was performing piano concertos in public with the New York Symphony. He was also an important arts administrator, helping to reorganize the Institute of Musical Art into the Juilliard School, of which he became president from 1928 to 1937 (he was succeeded in that post by Hutcheson). He also served as head of the Juilliard Foundation and as a board member of the Metropolitan Opera and, as many music critics had done (Erskine was a music appreciation writer, not a critic), wrote opera librettos. He continued playing the piano till the end of his life, despite a serious automobile accident in the 1930s that fractured his skull and cost him part of a little finger.

With regard to the question of how far to tilt classical music toward the new lowbrow hordes entering the appreciation arena, Erskine toed a middle line. In his book *The Memory of Certain Persons* Erskine writes of how his philosophy of music education differed from Josef Hofmann's at Curtis:

> I made a point of asking Josef Hofmann, then directing the Curtis School, to join us in enterprises which affected the country as a whole. . . . But Mr. Hofmann replied that the business of a music school, as he understood it, is to train performing artists, not to worry about the needs of the general public. Our points of view were diametrically opposed. I too wanted to train artists, but not to send them out to starve; I thought the school that trains artists has some responsibility to prepare an audience for them; and audiences as well as performers need training.[24]

Yet on the other hand, he also wrote, in *My Life in Music,* with dyed-in-the-wool Genteel Age sentiments, "Democracy is a generous social ideal, but in art it may carry with it the threat of commonness, of vulgarity—at times, of meanness. The democratic artist is too often content to express his fellow men as they are. The artist in the grand style, on the other hand, the aristocratic artist, dedicates himself as a kind of high priest to speak for human nature at its best."

Overall, radio's pull toward popularization, toward masscult, was inexorable. Olin Downes of the *New York Times* and Lawrence Gilman of the *Herald Tribune* both were early radio intermission commentators for the

222 New York Philharmonic broadcasts, along with their erstwhile press colleague Deems Taylor. And the mass market magazines followed suit: George Marek, who was a radio panelist on the Metropolitan Opera Quiz, started a music appreciation column in *Good Housekeeping* in 1941, itself the proverbial "seal of approval" on anything wholesomely American. And other writers continued to make careers out of music appreciation volumes. The most prolific in America was undoubtedly David Ewen (1907–85), who had worked only briefly as a critic but as a freelance authored eighty-odd books on music appreciation both longhair and popular, many of them translated into a dozen or more languages.

Ironically, after World War II, with the inception of a new bandwidth for classical music reproduction in FM radio, there was a recrudescence of highbrow music appreciation, as music critics became both concert and opera intermission commentators and "first hearing" reviewers on FM radio panel shows. But paradoxically, this very segmentation of listening audiences (nonclassical music listeners simply tuned in to AM stations) helped ensure the drift of classical music away from the American mainstream and the balkanization of highbrow, lowbrow and middlebrow. The ears of mainstream America were never again as saturated with classical music and its explicators as they had been during the brief "golden years" of AM radio before television.

ॐ *Recapitulation*   Before World War II, the leading American periodicals for highbrow writing on classical music were *Modern Music* and *Musical Quarterly,* the former a journal written by contemporary composers, the latter a journal written by the leading musicologists. *Modern Music* folded in 1946, and nothing similar took its place immediately. In the postwar years, the only highbrow journals consistently publishing articles about classical music were *Musical Quarterly, Perspectives of New Music,* and the *Hudson Review* (mostly by Joseph Kerman); the *New York Review of Books* occasionally ran articles and reviews by Virgil Thomson, the conductor and Stravinsky amanuensis Robert Craft, and the pianist-intellectual Charles Rosen. A few nominally highbrow small-circulation periodicals continued with regular music critics, such as B. H. Haggin and David Hamilton for the *Nation.*

But the regular classical music features of the big-circulation monthly magazines (with the possible exception of the nonfiction book author Martin Mayer's music column in *Esquire*) were all but gone. And in a telling 1967 as-

sessment that appeared in *Perspectives of New Music,* the critic Richard Kostelanetz, nephew of pops conductor André, then a young man at the beginning
of a prolific career as one of the few old-type music-and-cultural critics at century's end, wrote:

> In . . . quality magazines, the coverage of music, particularly modern mu-
> sic, is . . . bleak. . . . As for *Ramparts, Commonweal, The Progressive, Con-*
> *gress Bi-Weekly,* and *Christianity in Crisis,* their conception of cultural
> coverage simply does not extend to music. . . . One might expect to find
> more serious concern about music in those intellectual quarterlies sup-
> posedly committed to a general understanding of all significant tenden-
> cies in contemporary art and thought; but few of them publish music
> criticism regularly and most print it not at all.

Kostelanetz singled out the neglectfulness of the *Partisan Review,* the *Nation,*
the *Kenyon Review,* the *Sewanee Review,* and the *American Scholar* along these
lines. Why the *Nation,* too? Didn't Haggin hold the fort? No, because Haggin's
"equivalent as a theater critic, say, would scoff at nearly all plays written after
1900, emphasize the efforts of actors and directors, regularly pounce upon
newspaper critics and never approach such questions as the influence of scholarly or critical ideas upon contemporary performance of classic works and the
criteria for evaluating one playwright as better than another." Reiterating the
notorious oft-quoted pronouncement of composer Aaron Copland (himself a
best-selling music appreciation book writer) that "if a literary man puts two
words together to characterize a musical experience, one of them is almost certain to be wrong," Kostelanetz ended his diatribe by saying, "Although I have
read much of [Irving] Howe, and, for that matter, Dwight Macdonald, I cannot remember either of them remarking on music (aside from Howe's passing
1954 complaint against Olin Downes) or using a musical reference with any
intelligence. . . . I have not been able to find any work written by a cultural historian that treats music in an intelligent way." [25]

Unfortunately, Kostelanetz's 1967 words were just as applicable in 1997.
American cultural critics by century's end had all but abandoned commentary
on classical music. Serious intellectual horsepower, however, and column
space, were devoted to coverage of popular music forms of all types, notably
rock. What coverage of classical music remained was bountiful but relegated
to niches of readerships, not extended to a broad mainstream readership. Relatively few people, for instance, have read the late Samuel Lipman's probing es-

224 says on music in *Commentary,* or even know that the cultural critic John Simon, well known in mass-circulation magazines for his theater and film reviews, has also contributed a number of essays about music and opera to the *New Criterion* and other small journals, or have read the music criticism of the Columbia foreign policy specialist Edward Said.

Paradoxically, at no time in our history have so many knowledgeable writers on music written so many critical reviews as those for recording review magazines: first *American Record Guide,* then *HiFi/Stereo Review* and *High Fidelity* in the 1950s and 1960s, then later such publications as *Ovation, Opus, Keynote,* and *Fanfare.* Some have folded, others have stayed the course. These publications, replete with information for the specialist, speak largely to the converted. Gone are the days of the Genteel Era when a critic's duty and function was both to explicate and to convert.

❧ Postmodern perspectives on high culture and "browism"

The subject of the admission of vernacular musics into the art canons of American music criticism in the twentieth century is too large to inject here; we take it up more fully in chapter 10. But by century's end it was becoming clear that the terms of battle as known to Gilbert Seldes and Daniel Gregory Mason, and the locus of the Arnoldian highcult versus the low- and middlebrows, were being redrawn. One eloquent spokesman for the new order is a current classical music critic for New York's weekly *Village Voice,* Kyle Gann, himself a composer of what is labeled by some as experimental or "downtown" music ("downtown" embraces avant-garde, world, and vernacular musics, as opposed to "uptown," referring to music and art of Eurocentric biases, so-called). According to Gann, even for the new, now artistically respectable downtown musics, the old editorial philosophy, born in the nineteenth century, of a critic's responsibility to bring the audience up to appreciation speed, is ignored and discouraged by management. Gann tellingly writes,

> There is currently no editorial consideration given to the idea of what used to be called educating the audience, or more accurately arousing their interest in something they hadn't heard of before. The mass assumption among literary people seems to be that people only want to read things they already know. This is a new development, a result of the corporatization of the publishing business. Introducing a new idea into

the marketplace has become a capital crime. I was hired ostensibly with the old-fashioned aim of ferreting out new talent, but if I wrote a piece on Michael Jackson, the editors would dance in my honor.

As for highbrow, lowbrow, and middlebrow, they are reconfigured in the post-modern dispensation, says Gann:

> Nothing like *Modern Music* exists any more. . . . the culture is divided at present between the old white farts who are upholding the bastions of European music (mostly 12-tone and derivatives) and the populists who feel that only the latest vernacular—rap, hip-hop, techno—have sufficient validity, validity being equated with numerical superiority. I don't believe in 12-tone music or the continuation of sonata form, and so the academic journals are de facto closed to me. . . . Nor am I interested in rap, multiculturalism, deconstructionism, DJs, or any of the latest pop trends. I am devoted to what used to be called culture, and which is now a void similar to the air occupying the Grand Canyon, around which armies are arraigned whose ignorance makes them worthy of each other.[26]

☙ *Postlude*   In the current Age of the Lowbrow, perhaps some hope can be gleaned from the fact that *Time* magazine occasionally runs classical music "picks" alongside those for movies, videos, and rock music. But one wonders what would happen if Kyle Gann and other music critics appeared on a television program, not like that of the movie critics Gene Siskel and Roger Ebert, but more like William F. Buckley's "Firing Line" or Bill Moyers's "Journal." Or if John Simon, instead of the eminently able Peter G. Davis, wrote a few classical music reviews for *New York* magazine. Would not that be a better way of "educating the audience," in Gann's phrase? The general audience?

It did happen once—in the olden days of Matthew Arnold, Sidney Lanier, Rupert Hughes, and John Erskine on radio. Perhaps with a little more thinking—and daring—on the part of those of influence in culture and media, it could happen again.

Virgil Thomson

Sacred Cow Sharpshooter

I never got into feuds with artists or composers. I get into feuds with management. I'm an artist. I defend the artist.
—VIRGIL THOMSON

American newspaper and magazine music critics of distinction have generally not been composers. They have usually been either part-time musicians eking out their livings with supplementary music journalism or retired musicians who segue into full-time professional journalism, thereby to wield an influence they could not from marketing themselves as musicians. (A third very real category, gross amateurs and incompetents, we have tried to steer clear of throughout this book, except for the earliest historical period.) The fact remains that truly distinguished creative artists have rarely doubled as professional critics of the arts in America. In the drama, the only recent examples of creator-critics on large newspapers or magazines are Walter Kerr of the *New York Herald Tribune,* who as a playwright was occasionally produced on Broadway, and director Harold Clurman, who managed to write criticism for the *Nation* throughout his active directorial career. Among famous American novelists, perhaps only John Updike has been a long-term, continuing book reviewer of fiction, for the *New Yorker.*

In music, of the pre-1875 American critics, William Henry Fry is the only example of a prominent composer-critic, yet at this same time Berlioz and Schumann in Europe were earning a substantial part of their livings from professional journalism. Of the Old Guard era of American music criticism, Upton, Krehbiel, Henderson, Apthorp, Parker, Aldrich, Finck, Elson, Hale, Huneker, Mencken—whatever their gifts, these men were not composers. De Koven and Deems Taylor came along, but again, in Europe at this time, great composers such as Debussy and Hugo Wolf were matching penstrokes as music critics with noncomposers such as George Bernard Shaw, Ernest Newman, and Eduard Hanslick.

In his autobiography, the composer and critic Virgil Thomson (1896–1989) expresses his own view of the relative importance of these dual careers by devoting merely one chapter out of thirty-five to his experiences as chief music critic for the *New York Herald Tribune* from October 1940 to October 1954, despite the opinion of his distinguished composer-writer colleague Ned Rorem that "he probably (has already) become history no less as a reporter of the years 1940 to 1955 than as a musician." [1] Thomson appears never to have alluded to Shaw as music critic in his published writings,* and he once devoted an entire article to expressing his contempt for the great Eduard Hanslick ("second-rate clean through").

He rarely talked in his writing of his critic colleagues, except when specifically answering readers' letters or scholarly inquiries; when he spoke of critics as a group, it was to dispatch them en masse as a de facto accessory of the management apparatus he loved to hate, a characterization that appears in his wickedly polemic book *The State of Music,* the book that, ironically, got him hired as critic at the *Herald Tribune.* In one epistolary reproof to the music critic of the *Hartford Times,* the usually courtly Thomson tongue-lashed the man with an almost truculently self-assured reference to the "dominant role that composers have always played in European musical criticism," which was "an ascertainable fact." [†]

There actually have been many composer-critics in the annals of American journalism, including one with an influence equal to Thomson's (Deems Taylor). But Thomson is probably first choice for the greatest American music critic on more ballots (there are, to be sure, demurrers) than any other. His concert reviews written under deadline pressure are unique in being infinitely rereadable fifty years after the fact. They resurrect the actual sounds heard at Carnegie and Town Hall with amazing specificity, as in the following description of Marian Anderson, whom he describes as "a lovely icicle" who needs to become "a flame": "Rarely does she attack a note frankly; she hums her way into them nearly all. Almost never does she end one, either, without tapering

---

* At a marathon performance of the complete Virgil Thomson Portraits for piano in New York City on November 9, 1996, the author and broadcaster David Dubal recalled for the audience that he had once suggested to Thomson in a radio interview, "You'll be remembered with James Huneker," to which Thomson replied without missing a beat, "I'll be remembered with Shaw."

† One surprising example of Thomson's dictum, little known even to music connoisseurs, is that the tragically short-lived Romanian composer and pianist Dinu Lipatti (1917–50) was for a time a newspaper critic in Europe. There exists a remarkable Lipatti review of a Vladimir Horowitz recital from 1939.

228   it off. This constant crescendo and decrescendo, though most tastefully encrusted upon every phrase, gives to the whole articulation of a song or aria, as well as to its phrases, a carved-in-mahogany quality that is more genteel . . . than wholly frank" (*New York Herald Tribune* [hereafter NYHT], November 4, 1943).

He is the one critic whom composers as well as amateurs can profitably read and learn about music from, instead of hearing recycling of the usual classical "hit parade" pap (which platitudes he sarcastically referred to as "music appreciation"). Virgil Thomson doesn't paint a layman's picture of the haze of sound so much as, like a great music teacher, tell specifically why, for example, though the string chords in Koussevitsky are better balanced, those in Ormandy are lusher. His superior trained composer's ear was a unique palette from which he drew his word pictures. What other American newspaper music critic could lay out "the sonic results of every physical combination of instruments" in a single orchestration lesson for a student composer?[2] What other critic would have described Vladimir Horowitz's clangorous piano tone as more resembling the trombone than the trumpet?

Unlike other critics, even other composer-critics, with Thomson one learns how conductors make orchestras sound; how different nuances of both left-hand fingering and right-hand bowing technique make for differences in string tone; how to set English to music (he was the best opera and lieder critic we ever had). One learns the basics of twelve-tone writing more succinctly from reading a paragraph or two of Thomson than from any textbook or encyclopedia definition, because his prose is pellucid and his musical understanding rock-solid and laser-clear. Reading Thomson's collected reviews and Sunday think pieces is like attending a high-level academy of music without needing to do homework or practicing.

The contemporary critic Tim Page says, "He was the first important American newspaper music critic after James Gibbons Huneker to place a strong emphasis on contemporary works."[3] True, but Thomson went beyond Huneker or anyone else in American journalism by becoming the only critic with both the equipment and the nerve to blue-pencil other composers' handiwork. He'll opine, for example, that Shostakovitch treads water during transitional passages by writing two-part counterpoint so neutral and colorless that it's tantamount to underscoring a film section where you're not supposed to notice the music. And what other critic would have the temerity to question why Wagner had excluded strictly accompanimental textures from his operas' orchestras? Most other critics would think only in terms of uncritically ac-

cepting Wagner's method and result, and then explicating it to the hoi polloi. 229
Thomson went above and beyond this to first causes.

Thomson said from the beginning that he "assumes that a musician's account of a musical event has legitimate interest for readers."[4] To the lay public of classical music lovers—even to some non-theoretically oriented musicians—some of the things he said might have seemed gnomic or recondite. But he was merely expressing his own thoughts as a composer without "dumbing down" for the reader. Deems Taylor was more the explicator for the layman and music novice. All his life, Virgil Thomson was two personalities: as composer, he is deftly artless, a Gertrude Steinian automatic writer by design, a master of composition "sans arrière-pensée," as Aaron Copland so well put it.[5] But as critic, his every sentence is imbued with and motivated by structured thinking about the sound he is hearing. His "inner baseball"-of-music logic is unimpeachable even when the taste in a given instance is cranky or eccentric. As simple and nostalgically tintypal as is much of Virgil Thomson's music, rather is his music criticism, while unpretentious in prose style, viselike in its intellectual grip, even monumental.

~ Formative years:
The Parisian-
Bostonian-
Missourian

Virgil Thomson's forebears were not musicians (though his older sister Ruby became an accomplished china enamel painter). His father was, so he writes, tone-deaf; his ancestors fought for the Confederacy. Born in Kansas City, Missouri, in 1896, he grew up a churchgoing Baptist in a picture-postcard setting, studying piano and organ and from age twelve giving recitals on both instruments in local churches and schools and accompanying professional singers. He attended public schools and a local junior college, where he founded a literary society. According to one biographer, "Outside his circle, Thomson was regarded as a young man with a destiny, but was thought to be conceited, eccentric, and even foppish. . . . He had not yet decided whether to pursue music as a vocation and keep writing for a hobby or to reverse the two, but he was convinced that he could achieve success in either field."[6]

Thomson enlisted during World War I and spent part of his tour of duty training as an airplane radio operator at Columbia University, where in off hours he took in his first New York concerts. Back in Missouri after the war he persuaded a local clergyman to tender him the loan that made Harvard af-

230 fordable in the fall of 1919. He was already twenty-three, beyond the age most students are when they graduate college, and in fact his first surviving piece of music dates from 1920, his twenty-fourth year. But like Walter Piston, another late-starting composer, Harvard classmate, and Nadia Boulanger pupil-to-be, Thomson more than made up the time in the ensuing years.*

Young Virgil took a broad liberal arts curriculum at Harvard. He also signed up for organ lessons with the organist of the Boston Symphony Orchestra, joined the Harvard Glee Club, and took orchestration with the composer Edward Burlingame Hill. In 1921 he won the John Knowles Paine Traveling Fellowship for study in Paris and traveled to Europe with the Harvard Glee Club. Once there, he settled in Paris and sought out Nadia Boulanger for lessons in composition, organ, counterpoint, harmony, and orchestration. After a year his fellowship ran out and he returned to Harvard for further work with Hill, assistant teaching, and local Boston employment as an organist and choir director; he graduated from Harvard in 1923. Another fellowship took him to New York for a year where he studied composition with Rosario Scalero (unhappily) and orchestral conducting with Chalmers Clifton, and also took cello lessons (many consider Thomson's 1950 cello concerto among his best pieces). In 1925 he returned to Paris to work with Boulanger for another year. He would make Paris his primary residence for the next fifteen.

Despite Thomson's reputation as devotee to Boulanger's teaching (affirmed by him in later life), in a letter to fellow Boulanger pupil Aaron Copland describing his second tour of lessons with Boulanger in 1926, five years after his first, he expresses the fearless irreverence toward sacred cows and refusal to be conned by hype that would later mark his musical journalism:

> The guidance wasn't worth a damn. . . . Once the habit of composition was established, she used every art of sympathy and generosity to make it grow into her pet channels. I refused and stopped my lessons and she has never forgiven me. . . . She rooks any work in progress she can get her hands on. . . . She lives in a temple of adulation and knee-bending that is disgusting and her aged parent scents any heresy a mile off and begins putting the screws on to make you feel ashamed of eating her cakes and

---

*In a conversation with the author on February 19, 1977, Thomson said he felt that for late-starting composers like himself, by age twenty-six one's brain has already begun to lose the flexibility and elasticity needed to absorb the maximum from such studies as species counterpoint and canon. Yet his own intensive work in counterpoint with Nadia Boulanger took place when he was twenty-five, and he went back to her in 1925–26 to do further work in fugue at the "advanced" age of twenty-nine.

tea while you are secretly questioning the divine oracle. It's all very debasing. (Letter of November 26, 1931)

Staying on in France because he found French life congenial to his composing muse, Thomson began to live a charmed bohemian life there. He managed to meet and fraternize with most of the artistic legends of interbellum Paris, from Joyce to Picasso.* By late 1927 he was ensconced in a flat on the Quai Voltaire, which he retained for some fifty years, subletting it most of the year, and he had begun to acquire a string of patrons who helped support him. Typical guests at a Friday night musicale at Thomson's Left Bank apartment were Gide, Cocteau, Hemingway, Scott Fitzgerald, Christian Dior, and, of course, Gertrude Stein, with whom he collaborated on the work that made him famous, the opera *Four Saints in Three Acts.* Thomson set Stein's libretto in 1928, but the work was not produced until 1934 in America, at first in Hartford, Connecticut, and later, briefly, on Broadway.

After the succès d'estime of *Four Saints in Three Acts,* John Houseman, who had directed it and who was on the cusp of a distinguished career producing adventurous theater, commissioned Thomson to write incidental music for Orson Welles's *Macbeth,* which led to other commissions for incidental theater music and eventually to commissions for the ballet *Filling Station* and for film scores to the Pare Lorentz documentaries *The Plow That Broke the Plains* and *The River.* Despite these forays back to the United States and the echt-American folk idiom he composed in during these years, Thomson returned every time to his adopted home, Paris, where in the 1930s he concentrated on composing music for stringed instruments and commenced his lifelong series of piano "portraits"—short piano pieces he would improvisationally sketch of friends and acquaintances who would "pose" for him as would a sitter for a portrait painter.

Thomson's pre-Herald Tribune journalism — On his 1921 Harvard Glee Club trip to Paris Thomson was traveling with a letter of introduction from the distinguished music critic of the *Boston Evening Transcript,* H. T. Parker, which brought him press passes to almost any concert

---

* Though Thomson in the early 1920s was introduced to his idol Erik Satie, apparently he was too young and daunted at the time to attempt a friendship with him.

232   or opera he wished to attend. And so as a kind of Paris apprentice stringer
to Parker did Thomson imperceptibly slip into what was to mushroom into
a full-blown side career almost twenty years later. Articles that the twenty-
something composer sent back to Boston praising a conductor little known in
America named Serge Koussevitsky led directly to the trustees of the Boston
Symphony hiring Koussevitsky to replace Pierre Monteux as music director of
the orchestra in 1924.

Then, remarkably, H. L. Mencken (though not a Francophile, a kindred
spirit in many ways) commissioned Thomson, in New York at the time, to
write an article explaining jazz, which was published in Mencken's *American
Mercury* in August 1924. "It was H. L. Mencken who got me started. Feeling a
little bit the urge to write (and to be paid for it), I had gone to see him and
asked for advice, suggestions. 'Write me an article,' he said, 'answering the
question, "What is jazz?" Everybody talks about it; nobody defines it.' So I did
just that; and he published it in The American Mercury, the first attempt, I believe, to describe jazz in technical terms."[7]

Shortly thereafter, back in Boston with a teaching job at Harvard, Thomson began contributing articles to *Vanity Fair* at the rate of one per month,
farming out to the *New Republic* one piece that *Vanity Fair* editor Frank
Crowninshield killed. In September 1925, having turned down jobs teaching at
the University of South Carolina and playing organ at a Kansas City church, he
left for Paris thinking *Vanity Fair* would help support him. Once there, however, though he received further solicitations for freelance journalism from the
New Republic, the *American Mercury,* and *La Revue Européenne,* he brushed
them off, rejecting further immersion in professional criticism in order to give
himself maximum time and space for creating his own music. Writes one biographer, "His essays on the contemporary music scene were so sound in
judgment that many of his colleagues advised him to adopt criticism as his life
work. Then, as now, however, composing was for him the paramount concern.
As he expressed it, 'My business is making music, not talking about it.'"[8] Instead, he gave piano lessons, composed a lot, and was poor. Aaron Copland did
manage to persuade Thomson to contribute articles to *Modern Music,* but
these were analytical essays, not musical reviews.

By the late 1930s, with the success in America of the Thomson-Stein *Four
Saints in Three Acts* and Thomson's theater and film scores, plus the cachet of
his articles in *Modern Music,* Virgil Thomson was beginning to become something of a thinking man's celebrity, and several publishers took note by offering him book contracts. It was William Morrow and Company who reeled him

in. Thomson described his book-in-progress to Morrow president Thayer Hobson in a letter as "a complete account of the present-day music world. . . . Not an encyclopedia, of course. Just my opinions about that world. . . . the meat of the book . . . is my economico-esthetic theory."

To this day *The State of Music* (slightly revised and reprinted in 1962 by Random House) is a book-about-music unlike any other, a kind of musical de Tocqueville's sociological textbook on the composing profession—on how composers, those most otherworldly of creators (except for the poets, Thomson says), make their way around barrier reefs such as the monied philistines who manipulate the strings of public arts institutions, and through Catch-22 situations such as a lack of pay commensurate with their work efforts. In one chapter Thomson enumerates "How Composers Eat" with the dispassion of a taxonomist. In another, with tongue only partly in cheek, Thomson purports how the nature of a composer's income source determines the very sound and sense of the music he writes. Mussorgsky and Ives, being "naifs" who derived their livings from jobs outside music, thus were liberated to be the trailblazing primitives they were. Conversely, "when a composer who has been living for some years on patronage and gifts starts earning money," Thomson writes, "his musical style becomes less emphatic and a good deal easier to follow. He eventually stops over-writing the brass in his orchestral scores."[9] Neither Aaron Copland's nor Deems Taylor's books nearly so well lay out the situation of the composer in the ecostructure of modern industrial society. In all but a few details, the book is as timely at the end of the century as it was in 1939.

Coincidentally with publication of *The State of Music*, the longtime music critic of the *New York Herald Tribune*, Lawrence Gilman, died in September 1939, just after the invasion of Poland by Germany. Geoffrey Parsons, then chief editorial writer of the *Herald Tribune*, read Thomson's book and felt that he had found the replacement for Gilman, even though the *Trib* already had Gilman's assistant, Francis Perkins, on staff. Ogden Reid, the paper's editor, agreed. But it was almost a year before they could get him; Thomson, a confirmed Parisian, stayed until the bitter end, until even after Hitler had occupied the city. At the Connecticut summer home of the conductor Alexander Smallens late in August 1940, Parsons finally got his chance to beard a repatriating and illiquid Thomson and tender him the offer. As Thomson cannily saw it, "the general standard of music reviewing in New York had sunk so far that almost any change might bring improvement. Also I thought perhaps my presence in a post so prominent might stimulate performance of my works."[10] He had some misgivings, though, as his biographer Anthony Tommasini writes:

234   At first Thomson demurred. His friend Theodore Chanler's experience
        during a brief tenure in 1934 as music critic for the *Boston Herald* had
        warned him off newspaper criticism as a profession. As Thomson re-
        called it, Chanler had dared to write of the Boston Symphony Orchestra
        "as if it were a human organization possibly capable of error," and had
        written "daily-press criticism as composers would like to see it written."
        Through representatives, Koussevitsky complained bitterly; Chanler was
        fired. Mrs. Olga Koussevitsky was affronted that Chanler's dismissal was
        slowed down at all by professional protocol. "In Europe," she confided
        to Thomson some time afterward, "we handled these situations more
        efficiently."[11]

        Furthermore, as the earlier Thomson biographer Kathleen Hoover put
        it, how "could he, as a composer with clear allegiances to certain styles and
        schools, consider himself fitted for reviewing music in the daily press. To his
        friends it seemed that his competence in the practicalities of life had failed
        him."[12] But Virgil took the bit, even as his friend Janet Flanner, the Paris cor-
        respondent of the *New Yorker,* recommended Thomson to her editor, Harold
        Ross. Ross blinked, though, and the result was "the greatest loss in the non-
        capture of a born columnist and consummate critic we have ever suffered."[13]
        The next year, Thomson declined an offer from the *New Yorker* to double his
        Trib salary.

ᐁ *The* Trib's *ageless
    enfant terrible*   By the time Virgil Thomson took over the reins at the
                              Trib he was a middle-aged man who had a successful
        career as a composer already behind him, but as a daily music reviewer Virgil
        was virginal. Although he had written and published articles about music for
        a variety of publications since the early 1920s, he had never worked a regular
        beat as a music critic, unlike any of his New York metropolitan daily colleagues
        who had had to climb the job ladder and toil in what Huneker used to call
        the daily "critical chain gang." On his transatlantic voyage away from Hitler,
        Thomson took five trunkfuls of his life's work—his compositions—but no
        copies of his articles from *Vanity Fair* or *Modern Music.* Clearly he viewed him-
        self as a composer of music, not a professional critic. His elevation to Gilman's
        empty chair was by far the most unorthodox appointment to such a post on a
        major American newspaper before or since—a kind of musical journalism

wildcard to counterpart the nomination of political tyro Wendell Willkie for president that year.

But Parsons and Reid had hit upon an inspired heresy. Thomson's plain speaking and utter refusal to be cowed or conned by any hype or cant was a salutary physic to the sacerdotal pieties of journalistic criticism, to the master-piece syndrome and music appreciation religion that had been entrenched and institutionalized since the late 1800s. Virgil Thomson took nothing for granted as received wisdom. Wagner, the unassailable cult figure of Shaw and Ernest Newman? "Mozart and Bizet remain greater composers and more expert men of the theater." In his very first review, of the New York Philharmonic under John Barbirolli, he wrote:

> Twenty years' residence on the European continent has largely spared me Sibelius. Last night's Second Symphony was my first in quite some years. I found it vulgar, self-indulgent, and provincial beyond all description. I realize that there are sincere Sibelius-lovers in the world, though I must say I have never met one among educated professional musicians. . . . The concert as a whole, in fact, both as to program and as to playing, was any-thing but a memorable experience. The music itself was soggy, the play-ing dull and brutal.* (NYHT, October 11, 1940)

Yet what did his chief comrade-in-influence, the New York Times's Olin Downes, who was also the Western world's chief Sibelius booster, write to Virgil?

> I'm simply forced to write you a letter of homage. Your review this morn-ing hits off to utter perfection the exact character of the performance and of the music. I've read it half a dozen times and realize that in spite of the ease with which it was evidently thrown off, one wouldn't change a word or add or subtract a sentence. . . . What a blessing that you have come to town! The whole bumbling business of music criticism as it is written to-day has been perked by your arrival. Life is the better for it, less stupid, less logy, less bumptious. You will do everybody in our line a world of good, provided none of us is fool enough to try to imitate you.[14]

---

* Thomson also found fault aplenty with Barbirolli's conducting, on this and other occasions, and was credited by some with driving Barbirolli out of his job. Barbirolli, who had replaced Toscanini in 1937, was replaced by Artur Rodzinski in 1943, but he went on to a long and distinguished career con-ducting the Hallé Orchestra of Manchester, England.

236 Much later Thomson wrote:

> I did observe standards of description and analysis more penetrating and
> of coverage more comprehensive than those then current in the press. I
> was aware of this; the music world was aware of it; my colleagues on the
> paper were immediately aware of the fact that my work had presence. . . .
> The method of my examination and my precepts for progress turned out
> to be those laid down exactly one year earlier in *The State of Music*. These
> principles, as I understood them, engaged me to expose the philanthropic
> persons in control of our musical institutions for the amateurs they are,
> to reveal the manipulators of our musical distribution for the culturally
> retarded profit makers that indeed they are, and to support with all the
> power of my praise every artist, composer, group, or impresario whose
> relation to music was straightforward, by which I mean based only on
> music and the sound it makes. The businessmen and the amateurs, see-
> ing what I was up to, became enemies right off.[15]

Though acknowledging these adversaries, he was also aware that this same
class was buttering his bread at the *Trib*. Thomson had been given wide lati-
tude to review what he wanted, and that included not only the mainline attractions at the Met and the Philharmonic but fringe events, university concerts, and concerts in New York's bedroom communities. The only occasions
Parsons and the Reids gave him any editorial admonitions not to offend were
when he had to review some mediocre suburban orchestra concert: the dowagers in the audience were thought to be *Trib* subscribers.

> The *Herald Tribune* represented in politics the liberal right, a position
> usually favorable to the arts. The know-nothing right and the Catholic
> right, as well as the Marxist left, are in all such matters, as we know, un-
> duly rigid. And papers of the moderate left tend, in art, to be skimpy
> of space, the sheets of massive circulation even more so. But papers that
> are privately owned and individually operated make their address to the
> educated middle class. The *New York Times* has regularly in its critical
> columns followed a little belatedly the tastes of this group; the *Herald
> Tribune* under Ogden Reid aspired to lead them. . . . My quality as a re-
> viewer came from my ability to identify with the makers of music; and
> when I spoke both as an insider to music and warmly, my writing,
> whether favorable or not, was communicative. But I simply could not
> identify with organizers and promoters, however noble their motives.[16]

Thomson quickly became known for slaying sacred cows of classical music celebrity, but in so doing he had no motive of *épater le bourgeois*. He simply hadn't heard many of these artists before, and with open ears, *sans parti pris*, he was telling it "like it is," at least for Virgil. In addition to being less than dutifully reverential toward such different personages as Sibelius, Marian Anderson, and Wagner, he freely owned that he preferred Fritz Reiner to Toscanini. Of Rachmaninoff, then living and immensely popular, he wrote answering a reader's letter, "It is really extraordinary, after all, that a composer so famous should have enjoyed so little the esteem of his fellow composers." He wrote several famously caustic reviews of Vladimir Horowitz ("It [Liszt's music] is the only kind that he approaches without fidgeting, and last night it was the only kind the audience didn't cough through") that nevertheless dutifully rendered credit to Horowitz's "wowing technique." * Thomson, who had studied stringed instrument technique just as intensively as he had studied the voice, surely must be the only writer who ever has criticized Heifetz in print in this way:

The faults . . . have to do with irregularities in the application of right-arm weight. His bow-stroke is likely to be so emphatic that it produces, even on an up-bow in a soft passage, accents that are no proper part of the music's line. He makes crescendos, too, in the middle of notes that have no rhetorical importance. . . . As a result, his melodic line, for all its perfection of pitch and sweetness of sound, has no continuing emotional tension and makes no sustained musical sense. . . . this teasing way of treating musical sounds . . . led me long ago to consider Mr. Heifetz as essentially a frivolous artist, in spite of his incomparable mastery of violinistic operations. (*nyht*, November 22 , 1951)

He expressed his thoughts with the disarming and guileless brutality of a child, yet at the same time did so with infinite civility and charm. Irate letters deluged the *Trib*, especially during Thomson's first few years, some asking for Thomson's scalp. A typical example of Virgil's senatorial-courtesy-style response to a letter from a disgruntled reader:

The Editor has passed me your charmingly indignant letter. It would have been a little more courteous, I must say, if you had written directly to me

---

* Many years later, according to *Evenings with Horowitz* by David Dubal, when Virgil Thomson's name was mentioned to Vladimir Horowitz in a private conversation, the pianist replied, "I want for him to die. I look every day in the obituary page."

your disagreements with the ideas expressed in my review of Eugene Onegin, since those ideas are my ideas and not the Editor's. I am afraid also that you misread my review. It carefully avoids, I think, assuming that my opinion as to the practical nature of this work by Pushkin and Tchaikovsky proves either of those classic writers to be inferior workmen or Eugene Onegin to be an inferior work. I consider it to be a great work but not, at least for Anglo-Saxon or Latin audiences, a completely successful one; and I think I am entitled to express this opinion, even though I may be incorrect. You are wrong, of course, in thinking I have a limited acquaintance with the subject. I am afraid that you assume I do not have a "proper knowledge" of it merely because my opinions about it do not agree with yours. (Letter of November 21, 1946)

Perhaps most notorious was Thomson's occasional habit of conspicuously catnapping at concerts he was reviewing. Outraged readers protested. Thomson didn't even attempt to cover it up, replying to one letter writer, "If I had stood through Don Giovanni I am sure I, too, should have found it sour. As it was, I had a good nap. If Miss S—— had committed grave misdemeanors about pitch, I am sure I should have waked up. At musical performances I sleep lightly, and only so long as nothing in any way abnormal, for good or ill, takes place on the stage" (letter of November 20, 1947). Kathleen Hoover goes even further: "At musical performances he seems to have listened with what psychologists describe as 'the third ear.' Nothing escaped him, and programs at which he was known to have dozed resulted in some of his most penetrating reviews."[17] What other journalist could have gotten away with it without getting fired? But Mr. and Mrs. Ogden Reid remained unflappable. The simple fact is that Thomson had become the most read and discussed music critic in the country at the time. He was an untouchable.

Many of Thomson's letters to his readers, however, do display, even better than his reviews, his genius as a lay educator, in spite of all his protestations about music appreciation. There's a music lesson in every reply to a reader, sometimes encapsulated in only a passing phrase or sentence.

When one is listening to a piece one doesn't know, the way it is performed doesn't make much difference. (November 6, 1940)

No musician is perfect, of course. Everyone is more master of certain elements than others. (November 22, 1940)

Chamber music is a test of compositional mastery because it is low in color variety. Pure line and harmony have to sustain the composition. (February 27, 1951)

Writing music is like giving parties. You make it as good as you can at the time you are doing it. Making it memorable is not the main objective. You merely try to make it interesting and worthy. (December 2, 1952)

The reviewer as
microscopic aural
examiner

Again and again Thomson has the best ear (and eye) of any critic. He hears and sees (and reports) every concert he attends as though he were an orchestra conductor hearing his players and correcting balances of ensemble, or instantaneously pinpointing a single wrong note amid a whole section of instruments. He lectures a pianist on how the ambient resonance in Carnegie Hall makes it unnecessary for that pianist to pedal as much as he did in that recital. He anatomizes the number of bow direction changes in a phrase by a single violinist. He chides George Szell of the Cleveland Orchestra, "When a musician of the first quality fails to take advantage of every occasion for bringing out metrical contrasts and irregular stresses, one is a little disappointed. One had hoped the streamlining taste in symphonic interpretation had passed from fashion" (NYHT, February 15, 1950). He notes that ex-organist Leopold Stokowski's heralded innovation of reconfiguring the seating of his strings is like pipe organ registration, and instead of meaning this metaphorically, Thomson the ex-organist explains explicitly how this is so:

His latest seating arrangement is an adaptation to orchestral uses of pipe-organ antiphony. He long ago did away with the classical symphonic antiphony of first violins on one side against seconds on the other, through both of which pierce succeeding layers of supporting woodwind, brass, and percussion. He has his musicians arranged now with all the strings massed at back center as if these were a single homogeneous body of foundation tone, like Great Organ diapasons, with woodwinds out in front, like a Choir Organ or positif, and with the brasses at the right and left downstage corners, like the heavy solo reeds of a French organ, the horns playing antiphonally on one side against the trumpets and trombones on the other. (NYHT, December 4, 1940)

240   He refers repeatedly to conductors who "force" or "push" the tone of instruments, particularly wind instruments, using a vocal analogy that he applies with a broad brush to all his critical ear testimonies. "Neither did [Pierre Fournier] at any time force his tone beyond the volume of optimum sonority" (NYHT, November 14, 1948). And similarly he notes of Koussevitsky,

> When he tries to achieve more of that weight by forcing the strings beyond their optimum sonority, the result is not so good. The sound that comes out is less loud and less weighty than that which would have come out if the point of maximum resonance had not been surpassed. . . . But at the back of every conductor's mind is a desire to make his orchestra produce a louder noise than anyone else's orchestra can produce. . . . At some time in the course of nearly every concert this desire overpowers him. You can tell when it is coming on by the way he goes into a brief convulsion at this point. The convulsion is useful to the conductor, because it prevents his hearing what the orchestra really sounds like while his fit is on. (NYHT, October 12, 1940)

When reviewing solo recitalists, Thomson also hears and tells all. He would be H. L. Mencken's dream reviewer; far from the hacks that Mencken decried, Thomson undertakes an investigation of the player's whole aesthetic approach, as in this notice of an Artur Schnabel Beethoven recital:

> No one wishes to deny the Romantic elements in Beethoven. But I do think that they are another kind of Romanticism from Schnabel's. Which seems to be based on the Wagnerian theories of expressivity. Mr. Schnabel does not admit, or plays as if he did not admit, any difference between the expressive functions of melody and of passage work. The neutral material of music—scales, arpeggios, basses, accompanying figures, ostinato chordal backgrounds, formal cadences—he plays as if they were an intense communication, as if they were saying something as important as the main thematic material. They are important to Beethoven's composition, of course; but they are not directly expressive musical elements. They serve as amplification, as underpinning, frequently as mere acoustical brilliance. To execute them all with climactic emphasis is to rob the melodic material, the expressive phrases, of their singing power. This equalized expressivity ends by making Beethoven sound sometimes a

little meretricious as a composer. His large-scale forms include, of necessity, a large amount of material that has a structural rather than a directly expressive function. (NYHT, March 28, 1944)

Whenever other critics attempt this kind of meta-analysis, it always comes out cranky or overreached. With Thomson it's as clear as Theory 101. Most critics of Artur Rubinstein wrote of his joie de vivre, his effulgent tone, his romantic grand manner; only Thomson parsed Rubinstein's way of conducting his musical traffic:

Rubinstein builds his huge climactic effects . . . by "throwing away," as theater people put it, nine-tenths, at least, of his lines. He does not obscure a minor turn or cadence, but neither does he lean on it. He treats it casually and gets on to the main thing. I should not be willing to call his manner of moving through a piece streamlined. It is too deeply aware for that. But the longest and loosest works, under his fingers, do get themselves organized and move forward. . . . In his handling of transitions, however, in getting from a faster passage into a slow one, in moving from one expressive range to another, he is alone. It is hard to know just how he does it so gracefully, because the new theme has always begun before one has quite noticed. I think, though, that his transitions are operated a little more quickly than is customary. They are not brusque, but he does not hold them back. He moves through them as smoothly as a Diesel locomotive moves in and out of a railway station. (NYHT, February 14, 1949)

He always is the objective reporter par excellence, even when from sentence to sentence his characterizations almost seem contradictory. Thus, in the following excerpt, a review of the Broadway production of Marc Blitzstein's opera Regina, he's not hedging so much as drawing fine distinctions between competing aspects of the same end product:

The musical composition is that of an incomplete opera, of one that hands over the expressive obligation to mere speech whenever the composer feels inadequate to handle the dramatic line. It contains many tuneful and well-conceived set-pieces and also a great deal of carefully composed recitative. The transitions from speech to singing are ever so

242   skillfully handled. The recitative itself, however, covers in most cases so
       wide a vocal range and is so heavily accompanied that it has to be sung
       fortissimo. (NYHT, November 1, 1949)

In his Sunday pieces Thomson would use the extra space to explore abstract nontopical issues of music (although at times he would write about a political issue such as Soviet composition). In a typical example from 1947, his premise is that the intellectual content of music is the prime criterion of artistic merit:

> It is characteristic of both Bach and Mozart to use dance meters without
> the idea of dancing being the only thought communicated. . . . The best
> concert composers . . . are those who employ the techniques of multiple
> meaning, adding thus to simple expressivity contrapuntal interest and
> the perspective effect of contradictory evocations. It is Beethoven's gift for
> working opposites in together that gives his concert music its phenome-
> nal power of suggesting drama. Beethoven has for this reason intellectual
> content to a high degree. . . . Wagner's operas have the highest intellectual
> content of any. (NYHT, April 20, 1947)

Thomson as critic was never an intellectual bully, never would pull rank as a know-it-all composer, but very occasionally, as a way of driving his point home, he would cutely betray a wink at readers that he was giving them what he called the "inside," professional view of the music world:

> Like most English composers, Elgar orchestrates accurately and compe-
> tently. Now, when a man can do anything accurately and competently he
> is always on the lookout for occasions to do that thing. In the Continen-
> tal tradition of music-writing orchestration is always incidental to ex-
> pression, to construction, to rhetoric. Many of the greatest composers—
> Chopin and Schumann, for instance—never bothered to become skillful
> at it in any major way. Others, like Beethoven and Brahms, always kept its
> fanciness down to the strict minimum of what expression needs. I've an
> idea the Elgar Variations are mostly a pretext for orchestration, a pretty
> pretext and a graceful one, not without charm and a modicum of sincer-

ity, but a pretext for fancy work all the same, for that massively frivolous patchwork in pastel shades of which one sees such quantities in any intellectual British suburban dwelling. (NYHT, October 11, 1940)

As a practicing modern composer Thomson felt that the severest test for both critics and musicians came in how they handled music of their time. Here as elsewhere, Thomson was ruthlessly fair: that it was modern, or that it was composed by a friend of his, did not mean the music would get an automatic pass from him. Of his friend John Cage:

What kaleidoscopes and arabesques lack is urgency. They can hold the attention but they do not do it consistently. The most dependable device for holding the attention is a "theme" or story, the clear attachment of art patterns to such common human bonds as sex and sentiment. . . . "Abstraction" in art is nothing more than the avoidance of a *clear* and *necessary* attachment to subject matter. It is ever a salutary element in art, because it clears the mind of sex and sentiment. Only briefly, however. Because the human mind can always find ways of getting these back into any picture. (NYHT, February 3, 1952)

And of his friend Aaron Copland's Emily Dickinson song cycle, he noted "a certain ineptitude in the vocal writing . . . less a result of the wide melodic skips, which are in themselves effective in a declamatory sense and strikingly expressive, as in the vowel sounds to which the high and the low-lying notes are set. Certain extensions of the short vowels also oblige the singer to deform these" (NYHT, November 3, 1952). Yet on Varèse's *Hyperprism,*

[Its] beauty does not require cantilena, harmony, contrapuntal imitation, or deliberate pathos. It can be made with elements commonly considered to be noise, and it does not even have to confine its sound sources to the conventionally ignoble. Trumpets, trombones, flutes, horns, piccolos, and the classical instruments of percussion give out purer sounds than flowerpots and brake-bands. Consequently they are useful. But out with their sentimental connotations! They are useful as sound sources, not as poetic references. (NYHT, January 24, 1949)

244

᭦ Thomsonian contretemps and crotchets   Thomson, though not a Marxist, made no coy disguise of his view that management was the ultimate bogeyman.

> Beneath all of management's dealings with the intellectual group lie two assumptions. One is that intellectuals like novelty and modernity. The other is that the mass public dislikes both. I think the first is true. I doubt the second. I am more inclined to believe, from long acquaintance with all sorts of musical publics, that it is management which dislikes novelty and everything else that interferes with standardization. I suspect that management's design is toward conditioning the mass public to believe that it dislikes novelty. (*NYHT*, January 15, 1950)

Management returned his animus, though it is curious why. When a critic's fame captures so much attention for music in general, would not it help the box office of the very institutions he criticizes? According to Thomson, the board members of the Metropolitan Opera Association were the most persistent demanders of his scalp, whereas the New York Philharmonic board tried the subtler tactic of getting him to join their board (it didn't work). Thomson wrote the following letter to Mrs. August Belmont, the founder of the Metropolitan Opera Guild, on February 4, 1948:

> Much more a matter of concern to me is your belief that I am "a fairly consistent adverse critic of the musical performances at the opera." Consistency is a grave charge against a reviewer, because, unless the performances reviewed conform pretty consistently to some standard, high, low, or medium, which our opera performances surely at present do not, any consistency that appears in the reporting of them, whether favorable or adverse, is evidence of prejudice. Happily, my reviews, as preserved over the last seven years in the music department files, show no such attitude. . . .
>
> My Sunday pieces, on the other hand, are often severely critical. They are not so much reports as reflections. . . . All recognize, I think, that I cannot treat so respected an institution with neglect or with easygoing tolerance. Either attitude would be discourteous.
>
> My judgment may be faulty; but I should not like to think, dear

Mrs. Belmont, that you consider me an enemy of any musical institution.   245
Perhaps criticism is useless. Certainly it is often inefficient. But it is the
only antidote we have to paid publicity.*

At one point early in his tenure the Columbia Concerts Corporation,
over which Arthur Judson, the New York Philharmonic's manager, presided,
wanted to withdraw all advertising from the *Trib* until Thomson was fired. But
Ira Hirschmann, another concert producer who was also advertising manager
of Bloomingdale's, got wind of the Columbia threat and told the paper he
would match dollar for dollar any advertising Judson would withdraw.

The music business makes for musical chairs sometimes. In 1947 Artur
Rodzinski resigned as conductor of the New York Philharmonic, alleging interference from the very same Arthur Judson. Thomson wrote a *Trib* column
pointing out that since Judson was also president of Columbia Concerts, there
was a conflict of interest. The *Trib* backed Thomson up in an editorial; Judson
swore Thomson his mortal enemy. Then Eugene Ormandy tried to propose to
Judson that he manage Virgil Thomson's conducting dates!

Thomson had bêtes noires other than institutional managers. He hated
what he called the music appreciation racket ("Can you imagine a reputable
university offering a course in the Appreciation of Surgery, for example, or
in How to Listen to Murder Trials?" he wrote in *The State of Music*). He also
tended to see music as an opposition between a Germanic style and a French
style, but went too far in finding Francophilic explanations for everything
good in music. Even late in life he wrote, "today the Germanics are in control
everywhere—in the orchestras, the critical posts, the publishing houses, wherever music makes money or is a power." [18] He claimed that even German
musicians conceded the superiority of their music as conducted and played by
French conductors and orchestras. "In Beethoven's *Fidelio* overture Mr. Paray
proved once again that the French can play Beethoven without bombast and
yet nobly. Similar treatment applied to Brahms has occasionally, as in the readings of this composer by Pierre Monteux, seemed to this reviewer highly valuable as a detergent, or grease remover" (*NYHT*, April 2, 1950). His think pieces
also display a recurrent crotchet about French rhythm being non-ictal and
thus somehow more flexible than and superior to other rhythms. "Scriabin in

---

*Later Thomson took Rudolf Bing to task for not presenting more contemporary opera at the
Met; he modified his condemnation once the Stravinsky-Auden *Rake's Progress* was produced in 1951.
But in a November 1952 Sunday piece he reverted to form, claiming the Met was not drawing the *haute*
intellectual audience.

246 Russia, Ives in Danbury, Connecticut, were no less original harmonically than Claude Debussy. What their music lacks is true rhythmic life" (*NYHT*, November 14, 1943). The rhythmic subdivisions of the phantasmagoric ragtime movements of Ives's First Piano Sonata, to take one Ives example, and the many such complex irregular rhythms and meters in Scriabin's music, clearly belie such an assertion.

Like any great sage or average joe, Thomson had his favorite flavors, though relatively few of his opinions were truly heterodox (one example: he thought Schumann a greater composer than Brahms). He had no use for Shostakovitch's *Leningrad* Symphony, then a highly touted symbol of the Allied war effort. He makes perhaps too clean-cut a distinction about composers who can orchestrate but whose inherent ideas are not interesting as music. He liked the term "landscape" composer and quirkily used it to refer to Debussy. Though never a particular worshiper of bygone musicians, Thomson did say he thought both Garden and Chaliapin had been as singing actors superior to anyone he heard at the Met during his reviewing days of the 1940s and 1950s. In a December 1943 letter, he says Lhévinne, Landowska, Horowitz, Rubinstein, Jennie Tourel, Flagstad, and Garden are "musicians whose work other musicians find it profitable to study," whereas Menuhin, Heifetz, Louise Homer, and Geraldine Farrar were primarily pleasing rather than singular or striking: characterizations that surely many critics and fine musicians could argue point for point.

His favorite conductors were Reiner, Ansermet, Monteux, and Beecham. In fact, he liked Reiner better than either Toscanini or Walter. He was critical of both Mitropoulos and Bernstein for their podium gyrations, though ready to point out their respective strengths. But his worst prediction about any musician's legacy was his pronouncement on Toscanini, the conducting idol he waxed and waned on:

> He will not loom large, I imagine, in the history books of the future, because he has mostly remained on the side lines of the creative struggle [as opposed to Koussevitsky, Monteux, Beecham, and Stokowski]. . . . He has honor and glory now, but by posterity his work will probably pass unremunerated. . . . we must enjoy him and be thankful for him and cherish him. For when he leaves there will be little left save a memory and a few gramophone records; and these give hardly any idea of his electric powers as a public performer. By a miracle we have him with us still and,

by a greater miracle, in full possession of his powers. That those powers are without peer in our time cannot be denied by anybody. (NYHT, March 23, 1947)

Pace Thomson, among musicians of the past only Caruso's recordings have been as endlessly reincarnated in reissues as Toscanini's.

In his own words: Thomson's philosophy of music criticism

The critics are conversationally either Marxian or Machiavellian. In action they are all very much alike. They have no craft union and no professional body with teeth in it. A few belong to the Newspaper Guild. Those of them who really earn their living by criticism are tied up, heart, voice, and hand, with the symphony-orchestra interests, which means the radio and gramophone interests, which means in turn the electrical-patents-and-banking combine.[19]

Just as a little teaching is good for any musical executant, and a little musical execution for any composer, a little criticism is a valuable experience too for any musician. It teaches him about audiences. . . . Composers' criticism is useful to the layman also. As I have said before, the function of criticism is to aid the public in digesting musical works. Not for nothing is it so often compared to bile. The first process in that digestion is the breaking-up of any musical performance into its constituent elements, design and execution. In this analytic process, the composer is of the highest utility. . . . The composer-critic identifies himself imaginatively with the author of any work he hears.[20]

It is a little difficult to explain briefly how a reviewer of music practices his art. One tells the truth, of course; and one tries not to state it angrily. Observance of a courteous tone sugars many a bitter pill. It is important, too, to describe the event, so that your readers can imagine what it was like. Expression of opinion is incidental and will always come through, whether one states it formally or not. A critic does not have to be right about his opinion, because there is no right in such matters. He should, however, be correct in his analysis and description of works, styles, and

248 artists' characteristics. One becomes a music critic by becoming a musician and by learning to write. (Letter to a reader, NYHT, November 24, 1948)

It has never seemed to me appropriate to display before the public my personal favorites among pieces or artists. Such preferences, anyway, are rarely permanent. Sometimes one grows to like particular works or artists, and sometimes one gets thoroughly fed up with them. In either case, one must describe them loyally in a review. I suppose doctors have their favorite diseases and operations, but they don't talk about them in public. (Letter to a reader, NYHT, September 28, 1949)

Criticism and musical journalism are also frequent sources of contributive income to composers. They seldom provide a full living. The only kind of written music criticism that really feeds its writer is a permanent post on a metropolitan daily. Musical composition seems to be quite impossible to combine with such a full-time job. (I managed it, all the same, as music critic of the *New York Herald Tribune* from 1940 to 1954.) In any case, these "major" critics never seem to write much music, not the way dramatic critics write plays.[21]

My own policy as a reviewer is to avoid the comparison of persons and to refrain constantly from recommending to managements and directors the hiring or firing of any given musician. I am engaged by a newspaper to inform the public about performances given, not to serve as an unofficial member of any board of trustees. Some of my reviews may have been influential in causing the New York Philharmonic to change its conductor five or six years ago. These reviews, however, represented no campaign on my part. They were merely a week-by-week report of what the concerts sounded like to me and what the program policy, if any, clearly was. At no point did I ask editorially that the conductor then in charge be fired or that the one who replaced him be hired. I should have considered any such behavior professionally unethical. After all, it is program policies and standards of execution that determine a conductor's value to the community. And it is the abstention from insistence on personalities that determines a critic's value. (Letter to a reader, NYHT, January 12, 1950)

Reviewing performances of familiar music takes up the largest part of a critic's week. It is also the easiest part. Reviewing new pieces is the hardest and the most important, for that is where criticism touches history. . . . The reviewer gets tired toward the season's end of hearing music, all too often the same music, and of sitting through third-class performances. The music world is incredibly full of third-class artists, many of them in first-class posts. It takes some self-control to keep one's patience with them. . . . The artist works best when his ego is big, when he feels confident. The reviewer works best when his ego is small, when he feels respect for the artist's integrity, however minor may be his interest in the artist's work. (NYHT, February 21, 1954)

Thomson's composing career while he was a critic
Thomson was able to continue his composing career while he was chief critic at the *Herald Tribune* because his duties there were fairly light. For seven months of the year he averaged two reviews per week, along with a Sunday think piece that probably did not exact of him more than minor armchair research. In the summer he skipped seven or eight Sunday articles and did no reviewing. Moreover, in 1946 the paper gave him a full five months off. For someone with a nominal full-time job in New York City, he did a remarkable amount of traveling and working elsewhere during those years. Some of the traveling was tied to reviews he wrote for the paper from various domestic and foreign points, but much of it also was guest conducting or lecturing that the *Herald Tribune* apparently felt was good publicity for the paper. Thomson himself estimated his non-*Trib* music travels took up a full one-third of his time while he worked for the paper.

Thomson's statements about his income while at the *Trib* are a little equivocal. He took the job because he needed the basic income to set up his return from war-torn Europe. But once ensconced he quickly seems to have had sufficient funds to hire a valet, a personal secretary, and various copyists, items beyond the budget of all but the most successful and famous composers. Before he became *Herald Tribune* music critic, virtually none of his music had been published; now publishers came knocking at his door. It is evident that royalties, commissions, and guest appearance fees were a substantial part of his income throughout the *Trib* period, especially during the last nine years after the war ended.* For the first four years he wrote relatively little new music, but

---

*He also published a fair number of freelance articles in such magazines as *Vogue, Harper's, Saturday Review,* and *Atlantic Monthly.*

250 after that, he composed the score to Robert Flaherty's documentary film *Louisiana Story; The Mother of Us All,* his second operatic collaboration with Gertrude Stein; and so many other works that it's no wonder he says in his autobiography he can hardly remember his last ten years at the *Trib* because they were "so little demanding of my time." [22] Thomson wrote that by 1953 "for several years I had been earning more from my music and public appearances than from the paper"; in fact, he claims in his autobiography to have been financially independent of the paper for the last ten of his fourteen years there. He tendered his resignation that spring, to take effect a year and a half later. He sums up his *Trib* job as "a post so little demanding, so honorific, and so powerful." [23] For years afterward he enjoyed a steady stream of one-year guest residencies at universities; undoubtedly his *Trib* tenure had helped his "name brand" value.

Inevitably Thomson's view of his own music seeps into his criticism, especially his think pieces. His disdain for the music appreciation racket had much to do with his disparagement of the "masterpiece" syndrome he claimed got started by Beethoven (or Gluck) and handed down through the Romantic composers, a syndrome Thomson says was unknown to Bach, Mozart, Handel, and Haydn, as well as, he might have added, himself—a composer who was voluminously productive in large part because he blocked monumental aspirations and designs from his creative mind. His partial allergy to Wagner can be seen in a similar light.

His autobiography leaves open the question of whether conductors performed his own scores because they got a good review or wanted to get a good review, because he was considered a prestige item as the *Herald Tribune* reviewer, or because they loved his music. Thomson of course socially knew many of those he was reviewing, from Copland to Stravinsky, and he tiptoed around none of them simply because he had had dinner with them. Of course, his own work was dished, too, by his critical colleagues; Olin Downes wrote in the *New York Times* of his *Symphony on a Hymn Tune* that it was "too trivial and inconsequential, too unoriginal in its material and flimsy in its structure to merit discussion." However, most of the performances he received during his *Trib* years occurred outside New York—in Philadelphia, for instance, where Ormandy played him, or in Los Angeles with Wallenstein, or abroad with Beecham. Of this question his biographer Anthony Tommasini writes:

All of a sudden, important artists whom Thomson praised in his reviews, musicians who had not previously demonstrated interest in his music, started performing Thomson's works in prominent venues, particularly conductors like Eugene Ormandy, Eugene Goosens, Vladimir Golschmann, even Arthur Rodzinski with the New York Philharmonic. . . .

Overall, the performers and orchestras performing Thomson's works could count on having him in their corner. . . . Whenever a New York concert included a work by Virgil Thomson, even when he conducted himself, an assistant critic from the Herald Tribune was sent to review it. Without exception the reviews were well considered and positive. . . . No overt pressure was applied, but no writer working with Thomson ever tested him by criticizing his pieces in print.[24*]

Thomson himself commented, in his autobiography, that upon his retirement from the *Trib*, "Minna Lederman is said to have exclaimed, on hearing of my departure, 'But how will he get his music played?'"[25]

In one or two instances, though, conflicts of interest did arise. When Rodzinski took over the Philharmonic and conducted Thomson's *Symphony on a Hymn Tune* and the suite from his ballet *Filling Station,* Thomson himself reviewed the concert. (He drolly concedes in his autobiography that "there had been tension [among the orchestra players] at the first rehearsal from their resentment over my early reviews.") When Harl McDonald, the manager of the Philadelphia Orchestra, inquired of Thomson whether the *Trib* managers would allow him to guest-conduct the Philadelphia, Thomson replied that Parsons had said sure, and besides, Olin Downes had once performed as a soloist with the Minneapolis Orchestra while critic at the *Times,* and Lawrence Gilman had been the New York Philharmonic's program annotator while working at the *Trib*.

Only a composer-critic—not a performer-critic or conductor-critic or appreciator-critic or pedagogue-critic—could have written something like this:

The composer does not think much about exact speeds or exact volumes while writing down his thought. Whatever indications he may add about these matters—and some are fanatically detailed about them—are the result of later reflection. At this later point he is merely another interpreter. And like any interpreter who is fairly familiar with a work, he is

---

*Tommasini also notes that the composer (later Columbia Records producer) Goddard Lieberson, then a stringer for the *Trib*, wrote one of the few negative reviews of a Thomson piece ever to appear in the paper, and that Lieberson's tenure at the *Trib* was (ahem) notably brief.

252 capable of giving invaluable advice about its phraseology and its basic rhythms. Unless, however, he is an experienced conductor or executant, he is likely to imagine his adagios as taking place in an eternalized slow-motion that it quite without the power of human breath or muscles to sustain and his prestos as being executed at a speed just within the ability of the human ear to follow. (*NYHT,* June 11, 1944)

ↄ *Thomson on other critics and on teaching music criticism*   Thomson regarded almost all of his New York colleagues as more conservative and less modern-music oriented than he. Of his critical confreres outside New York, he most esteemed Alfred Frankenstein of the *San Francisco Chronicle* and, to a lesser extent, John Rosenfield of the *Dallas Morning News.* Upon the death of the magazine critic Paul Rosenfeld, Thomson wrote a reader, "I did not know Paul intimately nor greatly admire his writing. He, in return, had low toleration for my music and considered me a 'crackpot composer.' I am sure that he was a valuable contributor to New York's intellectual life." He seems to have enjoyed a collegial friendship with Olin Downes. The two critics went bluefishing together on Nantucket during summers. In a September 20, 1955, letter Thomson laments, "since the death of Olin Downes and my own resignation, the profession has lost some of its brilliance," and in a 1957 article for the *Herald Tribune* with the header "Olin Downes: A Free Critical Spirit," Thomson called Downes "the last of the music reviewers to enjoy music. He consumed it with great delight and described it with gusto." Yet in an earlier May 1953 letter to Nicholas Nabokov, he had classed Downes in a grouping of music critics among the "least distinguished intellectually."

Midway into his tenure at the *Trib,* he wrote an essay for the *Atlantic Monthly* entitled "The Art of Judging Music" to codify his critical precepts. Very simply, he thought that good musicians who can write well make the best music critics, not good writers who can play music. As he had been active throughout his career in organizing professional groups for composer solidarity (the Arrow Press, the American Composers Alliance, etc.), so was he for music critics: in 1941 he founded the New York Music Critics Circle* and later was active in the formation of the national Music Critics Association. At the

---

*The Critics Circle was disbanded in 1965, after years of *poco a poco ritardando.*

annual conventions of the latter he was giving classes in music criticism as late as 1972, a practice he had started in 1941–42, early in his tenure at the *Trib,* with a graduate seminar at New York University that he cotaught with his three *Herald Tribune* colleagues Francis Perkins, Jerome D. Bohm, and Robert Lawrence—the second-string fellows who generally had to review the events Thomson opted out of covering.

In his later years Thomson's remarks about music criticism grew ever more waspish. He told a scholar in Kansas City in 1981:

> Judgment and opinion are dangerous. Any music critic or book critic who sets out to champion things is an idiot. I used to tell the people who came to work with me in the music department of the newspaper, "Nobody's interested in what you think about something or feel about something. They want to know what took place, when and where, and what it was like." You're not to help trustees raise money, or advertise standard repertory, or to form public opinion, or promote local composers, or defend the public against them, or teach music appreciation, or spread enlightenment. All these things you may do accidentally, but your main business is to report the musical life of the community.[26]

The school of Virgil: Hiring other composer-critics   When two of his staff left to join the war effort, Thomson hired prominent composers to replace them, including Paul Bowles, who in the 1940s was still working as a composer and was not yet a novelist; the Australian-born Peggy Glanville-Hicks, one of the first women and perhaps the only woman composer to work as a music reviewer for a New York metropolitan daily; Arthur Berger; Lou Harrison; Lester Trimble; and even John Cage and Elliott Carter. He helped to bring in Edwin Denby as dance critic and the following noncomposer stringers: Jay Harrison, Theodore Strongin, Allen Hughes (the latter two later of the *New York Times*), and Herbert Weinstock. He also was responsible for inaugurating a column on radio music written (until he was fired) by B. H. Haggin and a jazz column written largely by Rudi Blesh.

When Thomson tendered his resignation he proposed Bowles as his successor, but by then Bowles was a permanent resident of Tangiers, Morocco,

254 and a committed full-time fiction writer. The *Trib* eventually brought in the eminent musicologist Paul Henry Lang, who was editor of the *Musical Quarterly* and a professor at Columbia, to succeed him. In the remaining years of the *Herald Tribune*'s publication (it folded in 1966) still other composers carried on Thomson's tradition of composer-critic, though noncomposers like Alan Rich also carried the ball.

It can fairly be said that no American newspaper before or since in any city has ever had such a distinguished roster of composers as the music criticism staff of the *New York Herald Tribune*. But the tradition, alas, died with the paper.

◌ *Virgil Thomson as institution*

After he left the *Herald Tribune* Thomson continued for years to contribute freelance articles to many publications, notably the *New York Review of Books*. His composing continued unabated until late in life when his hearing started to fail. His long-awaited third opera, *Lord Byron,* was produced by the Juilliard School in 1972, and *The Mother of Us All* was revived and recorded by the Santa Fe Opera in 1976. He wrote and published his autobiography, updated *The State of Music* for a reprinting, granted interviews to other journalists, and oversaw the publication of *The Virgil Thomson Reader* in 1981.

His celebrity, if anything, grew brighter. He had always been a kind of unofficial, behind-the-scenes music czar. "A full account of the scores performed, the paintings exhibited, the books and articles published through his exertions would require a special chapter. He has sponsored candidatures, bolstered morale, adjusted problems, lent money, and by this generalized bread-casting has become involved in endless, yet often amusing, complications," wrote Kathleen Hoover in 1959.* Now in his riper years he was ceaselessly sought out as a lecturer, consultant, and general advisor on all manner of musical matters by an endless cavalcade of scholars, musicians, and broadcasters, some of whom he would kindly meet and even cook dinner for in his famous Hotel Chelsea apartment.

---

*A prime example of this bread-casting: Thomson's letter to John Marshall, an official at the Rockefeller Foundation, helped put over their support for the Louisville Orchestra's "First Edition" project: commissioning, playing, and recording new American symphonic works.

🐮 *Coda*   The man Ned Rorem has called "the most stylish music critic of the twentieth century"[27] was asked by the *New York Times* critic John Rockwell in a 1977 interview:

> ROCKWELL: When you look back at your own life, how important a place does your critical writing hold? Do you regard yourself as a composer who, in one brief moment, happened to be a critic, or do you think of yourself as a composer *and* a critic?

> THOMSON: I have to admit, when I look at my life, that I have written music all of it and performed music all of it; and that I have written about music practically ever since I was, say, twenty-five. . . . The only thing I've stuck to really is composition. You never know when you're successful in it. It isn't a thing you *do,* like teaching or playing the organ or reviewing. It's a thing you *have* to do.

9
American Music
Criticism's Second Empire
Power Brokers and
Paper Tigers

Do classical music critics sometimes shake up more than just the egos of those they review? Do their pronunciamentos, for example, ever actually affect orchestral programming or the hiring of conductors? Do their temporal championships of certain composers, conductors, and performers ever go so far as permanently to alter received opinion, canonical repertoire, and performance practice? In other words, are they only tastemakers who at best merely can sell a few more tickets, or genuine power players who sometimes can alter institutions and music history?

With the departure by 1940 of all the original players who had constituted the New York–Boston "Old Guard," Olin Downes at the *New York Times* and Virgil Thomson at the *Herald Tribune* represented the twin Gotham pillars of what might be called the Second Empire in American music criticism (Thomson's predecessor, Lawrence Gilman, was a borderline Old Guard holdover). Fading fast was the era of socializing between artist and critic. Press agents were now as firmly entrenched as General Motors. Powerful concert managers like Arthur Judson and Sol Hurok were more formidable than some critics. The golden age of opera and the cult of the prima donna that had been coextensive with the Old Guard had given way to a cult of the conductor, with its chief icons Toscanini, Stokowski, and Koussevitsky. Radio had begun to supplant live lectures as the oral means of purveying music appreciation to the masses. Phonograph recordings had replaced player pianos as the mechanical means of disseminating great music.

The musicologist Edward Downes, son of Olin and himself briefly a Boston newspaper music critic around 1940, looked back in 1961 at the changing of the guard: "I do not know a single music critic who does not deplore the exaggerated importance attached to his words by a large part of the public and for a variety of reasons by artists and their managers. The shrinking number of daily newspapers has been accompanied by a shrinkage of space available for music news and criticism. During the first two decades of this century daily criticisms often averaged twice the length they do today." Long gone were the days when critics took money for "puffs." But Downes also observed that certain hidden aspects of appropriate professional conduct for a critic were subtly changing:

> The number of European artists new to the American scene who have sent more or less expensive gifts to American critics would seem to indicate that this was at one time an accepted practice in Europe. In cases of which I had personal knowledge the gifts were always returned courteously, sometimes to the deep embarrassment of the donor. All except one, that is. This critic, who must be nameless, kept the case of champagne, acknowledged it handsomely in the opening paragraph of his review, and proceeded to "roast" the performer.[1]

And to think that Schumann-Heink once sent Henry T. Finck oranges and he felt he deserved more! *O tempora! o mores!*

With the ascent of films, radio, recordings, a less leisurely style of life, and the curtailment of space allotted for criticism that Downes refers to, the philosophical expatiation and beautiful prose style of the Old Guard, of Huneker and Mencken, were becoming things of the past in newspaper criticism. But also, with the gradual attrition of newspapers, the consolidation of power that Downes mentions frequently posed situations in which the critic was arguably more actor than commentator. Let's look at some selected episodes when American classical music critics peddled influence beyond the usual.

A case study in a music critic's abuse of power   Outside New York, music critics have tended to be bigger fish in smaller ponds than their Gotham counterparts, and have accordingly sometimes accrued more real power; the fishbowl of orchestra boards, management, and press is smaller, even in the larger cities, than in New York. Multiple-threat critics in other towns also tended to retain their many hats—music, drama, dance,

258 book criticism—later than those on New York and Boston newspapers, where departmental specialization had pretty much become the rule by the 1930s.

Perhaps the most proverbially infamous among non–New York critics for power plays was Chicago's Claudia Cassidy (1899–1996), who was music, dance, and drama critic for the *Chicago Tribune* for almost twenty-five years and Chicago's most influential critic before and afterward. Tennessee Williams credited Cassidy with paving the path to Broadway success with her early favorable review of *The Glass Menagerie* in its Chicago tryout. The fathers of the Chicago Lyric Opera are still grateful to her for her early support of their institution during its weanling years. But the lasting national reputation of Claudia Cassidy—whether she deliberately sought it or not—is that of "the Lizzie Borden of the Midwest culture circuit . . . lowering the axe on American theatrical endeavor." [2] Depending on whether you were locally proud of her or your ox was gored by her, Cassidy was referred to as either "Claudia" or "acidy Cassidy."

Cassidy, born and raised in southern Illinois on the Kentucky border, graduated from the University of Illinois at Urbana. She began her critic career in young Lenny Bernstein style when as a cub reporter and girl Friday on the *Chicago Journal of Commerce* she subbed for the paper's ailing regular reviewer one night in 1925 and thereupon assumed the triple-threat music-dance-drama reviewer job on this business newspaper, continuing until 1941, when the publisher Marshall Field hired her for the *Chicago Sun*. The very next year Colonel Robert McCormick, publisher of the rival *Tribune*, wooed her over to his ranks, where she stayed till 1965, becoming perhaps the most powerful critic in relation to the local community of any American city newspaper. After 1965 she continued actively to freelance as a writer; as late as 1983 she was still making weekly appearances on a Chicago radio program about the arts.

Cassidy had a more interesting modus operandi than most for meeting her copy deadline. Her husband, a stockbroker who would nearly always be with her at the performance she was reviewing, would accompany her to the *Tribune* office and watch her finish her review; then "we would go out and dance the night away." [3] Cassidy's prose was ornate and distinctive, a late holdover from Hunekerese, but spiked with W. J. Henderson–like barbs: for instance, the contralto Marie Powers, appearing in Gian Carlo Menotti's opera *The Medium,* had blended "Hermione Gingold's Brünnhilde with the Three Witches from *Macbeth*"; after reading this, Powers publicly threatened to punch the reviewer in the nose. [4] The stage director Tyrone Guthrie, apoplectic at Cassidy's notice of the production of *Hamlet* that opened the eponymous

Guthrie Theater in Minneapolis in 1963, referred to her in public as "that bitch."[5]

Red-haired and petite but with a resemblance to Tallulah Bankhead both in looks and temperament, Cassidy covered her triple beat in a column entitled "On the Aisle." By the 1950s "her long tenure and increasing power in the realm of opinion have given her a sense of infallibility," lamented one commentator.[6] It has been a legend for years that she singlehandedly hounded three conductors of the Chicago Symphony Orchestra out of their jobs, and it appears to be true. The first of these was the Belgian Désiré Défauw (1885–1960), a man who, having guest-conducted the NBC Symphony in the early 1940s, was a rising star at the time he became Chicago Symphony music director in 1943. Défauw personally blamed Cassidy's reviews for his 1947 exit. Thereafter his conducting career quickly decrescendoed: his next post was conductor of the orchestra of Gary, Indiana, a suburb of Chicago known for its heavy industries, not its culture.

Cassidy's next victim, Rafael Kubelik (1914–96), conducted the CSO from 1950 to 1953. Before Kubelik's first season was over, Cassidy, disliking his programming, had already begun a campaign of vitriolic reviews to get him removed from the orchestra. News of this warfare even reached the pages of *Time* magazine, where it was reported in the issue of February 5, 1951, that the *Tribune* was receiving two hundred letters of complaint against Cassidy a week. She allegedly offered to resign, but Colonel McCormick was so impressed by the number of readers to which the letter barrage was testimony that he enjoined her to stay on. Kubelik, a younger man than Défauw, went on undiminished to a distinguished international career, and some of the monophonic recordings he made with the CSO for Mercury Living Presence in the early 1950s have recently been remastered and rereleased on CD to great critical acclaim.

Fritz Reiner had no such trouble with Cassidy, but when he died in 1963, the CSO's board hired the French composer-conductor Jean Martinon (1910–76), who had guest-conducted in 1962 to enthusiastic notices from Cassidy. For the first six months or so of the 1963–64 season Cassidy's notices of Martinon were scintillating. But Martinon and the orchestra's manager, Seymour Raven, did not see eye to eye, and Raven resigned in March 1964. It so happens that Raven had been Cassidy's assistant at the *Tribune*. Cassidy had lobbied for the orchestra's hire of him back in 1960 during Reiner's tenure.

Immediately upon Raven's resignation, acidy Cassidy started in. On March 13, 1964, Cassidy had written of the Frenchman's conducting of Stravin-

260   sky, "Martinon happens to be one of the finest Stravinsky men around and this [*Jeu de cartes*] was superlative proof." In the very next review she did an about-face, sputtering disagreeably about Martinon for the first time. Her notices of Martinon got nastier and nastier until by the spring of 1965 she fairly spat on him in print: "When a man in the gallery shouted 'Bravo' almost before Mr. Martinon had finished what may have been the worst performance of 'Sacre du printemps' in history, well, perhaps the old time opera claque had found a new home in Orchestra Hall." Martinon was gone by 1968 (he was succeeded by Sir Georg Solti); though she retired from full-time duties in 1965, Cassidy continued to contribute articles to the *Tribune*.

In a column for the suburban Illinois *Hyde Park Herald* on May 27, 1964, relatively early in this imbroglio, Robert Pollak wrote of the Seymour Raven / Martinon matter, "That Miss Cassidy ever had anything to do with the choice of conductor of the Chicago Symphony or the choice of its professional management has been symptomatic of the city's immaturity in matters artistic."

Abuse by a critic or of a critic? A case of perception of power   Another cause célèbre in the annals of the alleged power of the musical press was the episode surrounding the 1965 resignation of longtime *San Francisco Chronicle* music and art critic Alfred Frankenstein (1906–81). A native Chicagoan, Frankenstein had gone to San Francisco before he was thirty. He eventually served even longer than Claudia Cassidy, his name attaining a national cachet perhaps unique among music critics outside the New York–Boston axis. He was the only non–New York City critic Richard Franko Goldman exempted by name from his 1955 blanket condemnation of American music critics as "ignorant, incompetent and illiterate." [7] Certainly the respect and influence Frankenstein carried in the Bay Area was closer to that of the Old Guard critics of New York and Boston than to that of the post-1950 critics. Editors and staff at the *San Francisco Chronicle* affectionately referred to him as "Maestro."

Frankenstein, who graduated from the University of Chicago in 1927, had three interesting formative artistic experiences as a young man before he went to the West Coast. First, he played clarinet in the Chicago Civic Orchestra from 1923 to 1930 under Frederick Stock, and "with Stock's encouragement began sitting in with various sections of the orchestra during rehearsals to sharpen his perception of scoring." [8] Second, Carl Sandburg was a personal friend of the Frankenstein family in Chicago, and young Alfred assisted the poet in preparing his *American Songbag* collection. Third, Alfred contributed some articles to H. L. Mencken's *American Mercury* and even attended a few of Mencken's famous Saturday Night Club musicales. Sandburg may have had something to do with Frankenstein's later Americanist outlook as a critic, while Mencken surely helped inspire his dislike of cant.

Like some of the Old Guard critics, Frankenstein had parallel journalistic and academic careers from the beginning; like Huneker and W. F. Apthorp, he was both a music and an art connoisseur. In 1932 he began lecturing in music history at the University of Chicago while also serving as an assistant music critic on the *Chicago American.* Then in 1934 he took the job of dual music and art critic for the *San Francisco Chronicle* and remained San Francisco–based for the rest of his life. He also was program annotator for the San Francisco Symphony from 1935 to 1965. He was a civic presence, serving for a long time on the San Francisco Art Commission and other bodies. This busy man also found time to write for *Musical America* and *High Fidelity,* taught art history courses at Berkeley, Mills, Stanford, and Harvard summer school, and free-lanced as an art curator. Frankenstein's special expertise in art history was early American painters such as the trompe l'oeil still life painter William Harnett and the portraitist John Singleton Copley, as well as much modern art. Frankenstein's zealous advocacy of American artists helped change the syllabus of art history courses; he may well have a larger place in art historiography than in music historiography.

The Maestro "frequently created an impression of preoccupied inapproachability," remembered one colleague, who, however, added that he "was almost always on the side of the underdog." Shirley Fleming recalled that he could be "blunt, unadorned, and more often than not, a little salty,"[9] as some sample quotes attest: "The proceedings began with Lalo's odoriferously worthless overture to 'The King of Ys,' which is hereby nominated for oblivion, if possible before the concert is repeated tonight." "Nothing can come after William Schuman's 'Credendum,' except an intermission."[10]

The issue that became the albatross for a great career began simply enough. In March 1962 the principal conductor of the San Francisco Symphony, Enrique Jordá (1911–96), made a surprise podium appearance to lead the orchestra in a concert at the Opera House that was supposed to have been guest-conducted by George Szell of the Cleveland Orchestra. A press release from the San Francisco Symphony offered that Szell was tired and wished to be relieved of the remaining four of the six concerts he was scheduled to conduct.

262   Then came the mischief. Word leaked out that the real reason for Szell's withdrawal was that he was aghast at the state of disrepair of the orchestra after its years under Jordá—an elegant, cultivated Spaniard who, like Dimitri Mitropoulos at the New York Philharmonic, had programmed adventurously but who alas, also like Mitropoulos, was a lax disciplinarian. Furthermore, irrespective of Jordá, the orchestra's personnel was aging; some of the veteran players who had performed during the tenure of Pierre Monteux at the SFS (1936–52) were still there, well past their primes. Frankenstein wrote a private letter to George Szell appealing to Szell to clear up the impression that his abrupt departure was an implied criticism of Jordá's years of work with the orchestra. What Frankenstein proposed to Szell in his letter as the solution was that Szell make the gesture of inviting Jordá to guest-conduct the Cleveland.

    Szell went so ballistic at Frankenstein's unabashed attempt to intervene in the matter that he wrote him a caustic letter impugning his professional integrity. Szell's letter stated that fatigue was only his "polite excuse," that the orchestra was in "the saddest state of musical affairs I have encountered . . . during almost 50 years of my active conducting career," and mentioned "your delicate dual position as Music Critic of the Chronicle and Program annotator for the San Francisco Symphony, which in itself is liable to cast grave doubts upon your objectivity." Szell sent a copy of this letter to the city's other leading music critic, the longtime *San Francisco Examiner* reviewer Alexander Fried. Complicating the unpleasantness for Frankenstein was the fact that Fried had been his close personal friend and his predecessor as music critic at the *Chronicle* in the 1930s. But by the 1961–62 season the two men in their respective newspaper columns had already become polarized in anti- and pro-Jordá positions, and Fried, even before Szell had mentioned it, had already taken Frankenstein to task in print for an alleged lack of objectivity because of his double allegiance to newspaper as critic and orchestra as program note writer.

    Fried himself may not have wanted to publish the Szell letter, but he dutifully took it to the *Examiner* editor, who printed it. Then the *Chronicle* columnist and longtime Bay Area icon Herb Caen got into the act, writing anti-Jordá, anti-Frankenstein columns siding with Fried's accounts of how the orchestra had indeed backslid. Frankenstein, already publicly humiliated by the *Examiner's* printing of the private letter and wounded by Fried's behavior, now also found himself in an adversarial position with his own paper's most famous writer. He suspected that the paper's management was against him, at one point even going to the publisher and in effect asking, "Who's music critic of this paper, me or Caen?" Jordá left the orchestra in 1963 for various European 263 posts, but Frankenstein stayed on, at first.

Robert Commanday, the choral conductor and university music professor who eventually succeeded Frankenstein for a distinguished tenure of his own as music critic at the *Chronicle* in 1965, is still a Frankenstein fan and says ruefully today, "Caen and Frankenstein got into a shouting match. Alfred used to say you can't ring the church bells and march in the procession. But he tried to do that and it hurt him. Alfred shot himself in the foot on this issue." [11] Frankenstein's son John recounts, "There seems to have been a rather strong political/cultural issue behind all this. The powers that were in San Francisco and the blue-haired set didn't like Jordá, in part because he played that awful noisy modern stuff like de Falla and Stravinsky and Rodrigo—that is to say, he tried to get away from the Golden Moldies and expand the symphony repertoire. The other part of this may have been that many people didn't accept Jordá—a Spanish Catholic—because he wasn't part of the Central European tradition, and the prejudice that arose from that was totally unacceptable to my father." [12] It was not long after both the Spanish Civil War and World War II, and some symphony supporters may have nursed some doubts about Jordá's sympathies. Robert Commanday, who knew Jordá through organizing choruses for him, recalls Jordá as a cultured, elegant, upright man to whom no political or personal opprobrium should have ever attached.

Frankenstein even began to suspect that Caen was being told what to write by the higher powers at the paper to placate anti-Jordá elements of the local music community. That was the last straw; he finally resigned as music critic in 1965, but stayed on as art critic. The incident "certainly added color to Alfred's vocabulary when he spoke of it in later years," recalled Shirley Fleming. [13] Frankenstein's friendship with Alexander Fried never recovered. Years later he was freshly outraged when the San Francisco Symphony board rejected his offer to pay out of his own pocket two thousand dollars per concert to set up a fund to engage more local talent with the orchestra. Years earlier, while still critic and annotator, he had "started a fund to have second performances of worthwhile modern pieces presented by the symphony." [14] Nothing came of that either.

No right-minded person would question Alfred Frankenstein's bona fides either in writing George Szell or in his many other good works as music critic in Bay Area musical life. He was not grabbing for power; he was merely using his pen to try to improve the musical weal of his community. Still, the

264   Frankenstein/Szell/Jordá saga remains an object lesson in how the public perception of a music critic's reach can sometimes be more damaging than the ac-
tuality of his grasp.

∾ *When music critics*
don't hail to the
chief: The Harry   Though many classical music critics have influenced
Truman–Paul   their readerships, and some have become famous in
Hume incident   their local communities—particularly in the gaslight
                          era, when a Henry Krehbiel could become something
                          of a civic celebrity—perhaps only once in American
history did a newspaper's classical music critic himself become the focus of a
front-page news story nationwide.

Harry Truman probably loved classical music more than any other president. He played the piano surprisingly well for a nonmusician, owned many
phonograph records of symphonic and piano music, which he freely displayed
during interviews for *Life* and other magazines, and told an interviewer long
after the White House years and politicking were behind him that his favorite
composition was not "The Missouri Waltz" but Chopin's A-flat Waltz, op. 42.
"No president had ever been such a frequent concertgoer in Washington,"
writes Truman biographer David McCullough. "He was a 'regular' at Consti-
tution Hall, at times, if the program included Mozart or Chopin, bringing the
score with him." [15]

Perhaps influenced by exposure to her father's tastes, Truman's only child,
Margaret, after studying and aspiring to be an opera singer for some time, began giving recitals in Washington, D.C., during her father's presidency, even
though no less than the Wagnerian soprano Helen Traubel told her she needed
five more years of study before trying the concert stage. As fate would have it,
Margaret gave a lieder recital of Schumann, Schubert, and Mozart in Washington in December 1950 on the very day after Truman's longtime friend and
press secretary, Charlie Ross, suddenly died of a heart attack. The president,
under siege with developments in Korea at about the same time that Ross died,
was decidedly on edge but attended the concert anyway.

The critic for the *Washington Times-Herald* reported that she sang "better
than ever before in her brief career." Also in attendance at the recital was Paul
Hume, a young choirmaster and organist who had been the *Washington Post*'s
classical music critic since 1946. Mr. Hume nonchalantly inked the following
words about Margaret Truman's concert:

Miss Truman is a unique American phenomenon with a pleasant voice of little size and fair quality. She is extremely attractive on stage.

. . . Yet Miss Truman cannot sing very well. She is flat a good deal of the time—more last night than at any time we have heard her in past years. There are few moments during her recital when one can relax and feel confident that she will make her goal, which is the end of the song.

Miss Truman has not improved in the years we have heard her . . . she still cannot sing with anything approaching professional finish.

She communicates almost nothing of the music she presents. . . . And still the public goes and pays the same price it would for the world's finest singers. . . .

It is an extremely unpleasant duty to record such unhappy facts about so honestly appealing a person. But as long as Miss Truman sings as she has for three years, and does today, we seem to have no recourse unless it is to omit comment on her programs altogether.[16]

The president, of course, read the review. He penned the following and sent it to the *Washington Post* himself, according to McCullough:

Mr. Hume: I've just read your lousy review of Margaret's concert. I've come to the conclusion that you are an "eight ulcer man on four ulcer pay."

It seems to me that you are a frustrated old man who wishes he could have been successful. When you write such poppy-cock as was in the back section of the paper you work for it shows conclusively that you're off the beam and at least four of your ulcers are at work.

Some day I hope to meet you. When that happens you'll need a new nose, a lot of beefsteak for black eyes, and perhaps a supporter below!

Pegler, a gutter snipe, is a gentleman alongside you. I hope you'll accept that statement as a worse insult than a reflection on your ancestry.

Though Hume (who, far from being an "old man," was thirty-four) and his editor decided it best to ignore the letter, the rival tabloid *Washington News* got hold of it and promptly printed it on page one. The incident instantly created a national brouhaha, with hundreds of irate letters to the White House scolding the president for thinking more of his daughter's vanity than the prospect of committing American soldiers to their deaths abroad. Only a minority of letter writers sympathized with the president for being edgy at the time of

266   the death of his friend and right-hand man Charlie Ross (many pundits said that, had Ross been alive, he never would have allowed the boss's note to be posted). Of course, the incident has inevitably entered the buck-stops-here folklore of give-'em-hell Harry Truman, now (but not then) considered one of our pantheon presidents.

But perhaps the most curious and important upshot of the Truman incident—when a president stooped to write a letter to a political gnat, a classical music critic—is that "the resultant furor did a lot to increase public awareness and interest in serious music," as eighty-year-old Paul Hume himself told a reporter for the *San Jose Mercury News* in 1996, some fourteen years after he had retired from his longtime job as chief music critic for the *Washington Post* and forty-six years after the notorious event.[17] In fact, Truman later dutifully responded to a request from Hume's popular local classical music radio show by naming his own choices for a poll seeking the names of famous people's favorite classics. Truman's favorites were Beethoven's Fourth Piano Concerto, Chopin's F Minor Etude, and Mozart's A Major Piano Sonata. In 1958, years after Truman left the presidency, Hume visited Truman at the Presidential Library in Independence at the ex-president's invitation. "He couldn't have been more cordial," says Hume. "He even played for me on his grand piano there—some Chopin and Mozart."[18]

There may not be any formal studies on increased sales of concert tickets or recordings in the wake of the Hume incident, but Hume was a reporter, and when he says this teapot tempest piqued public interest in classical music, he undoubtedly remembers correctly. His own prominence as a critic immediately increased, and he went on to do the local radio program that many think helped galvanize interest in classical music in the nation's capital and eventually lead to a renaissance there that included the Kennedy Center and the installation of Mstislav Rostropovich at the podium of the long-suffering National Symphony. Of presidents after Truman, only Jimmy Carter has affirmed that he was a classical music fan, impressing invited White House guest Vladimir Horowitz with his knowledge of music—a fine gesture but, alas, without the salutary aftereffects on public culture of Truman's pugilistic challenge of Hume.

A postscript: not too many years after the fact, Hume sold the original of Truman's letter for thirty-five hundred dollars to raise money to help fund a Washington concert. The letter changed hands a few more times, inflating in value, and was bought in the 1980s by Malcolm Forbes for his private collection for an undisclosed sum. In the mid-1990s Hume appeared in Dave Grubin's documentary about Truman for public television discussing the original 1950 incident.

~ *Olin Downes,
exhortationist of
the* New York
Times

As we have seen throughout this book, it was not always that the chief music critic of the *New York Times* reigned supreme over the music critic world. The first *Times* man in whom that power devolved was Olin Downes (1886–1955), who served the paper from 1924, upon the retirement of Richard Aldrich, until his death in 1955. As Downes came to the *Times* after a previous tenure at the *Boston Post* (1906–24), his career as critic is one of the longest of all. Downes's unprecedented importance at the *Times* came in part from lessened competition: the sheer number of music critics in New York began dwindling during his tenure through the attrition of the other daily papers. The *Journal* and the *American* became the Hearstian *Journal American* in 1936; Scripps-Howard merged the *Telegram* and the *World* into the *World-Telegram* in 1931, and then consolidated it with the *Sun* in 1950 to form a single newspaper called the *World Telegram and the Sun;* and the *Herald* and the *Tribune* had joined in 1925 to form the *Herald Tribune,* the *Times*'s main competitor for the upscale cultural market in New York. In those prewar years the *Herald Tribune* had slightly more artistic cachet than the *Times,* and so long as Lawrence Gilman, who had taken over for Krehbiel, was at the helm at the *Trib,* he perhaps had the cognoscenti's edge over Downes as the more prestigious critic; but with Gilman's passing in 1939, Downes—who by then had also become well known to the public by appearing on radio—emerged as monarch of the realm (shortly to become co-monarch when Virgil Thomson took over at the *Herald Tribune* the following year).

Gilman, an asthmatic, had been a somewhat delicate man of pronounced aesthetic appearance. Downes, big-boned, big-framed, blond, Viking-like, was easily the most physically robust, outdoors-looking advocate for classical music since Krehbiel. (In fact, one of Downes's great enthusiasms outside of music was professional boxing.) Downes's childhood had been unpropitious for a future music critic. He was born Edwin Olin Quigley in Evanston, Illinois, to a banker and financial speculator named Edwin Quigley. For the first few years of his childhood Edwin Jr. was raised in upper-class circumstances in subur-

268 ban New Jersey while his father worked on Wall Street. But in 1895 Edwin Quigley Sr. was arrested for shady financial manipulations. The story made tabloid headlines. Quigley pled guilty to forgery and was sentenced to fifteen and a half years at Sing-Sing. The Quigley family precipitously lost all its money and social standing. His wife not only divorced her husband but re-surnamed her children Downes, after her minister father's surname (adding an *e*).

Coincidentally, Olin's grandmother was an ardent temperance crusader, a leading member of the Women's Christian Temperance Union, and his mother (who lived until 1940 and had some influence on his musical opinions) was a Carrie Nation–like saloonbuster for a time. She had named him Olin for a well-known nineteenth-century Methodist preacher. Thus, though he never studied for the cloth as had Emerson and J. S. Dwight, Downes—by dint of the experiences of both his father's disgrace and the high moralism of his mother and grandmother—brought a strong quality of moral exhortation to his personality and work.

The aftereffects of his father's disgrace made higher education impossible for young Olin; he did not even attend school after the eighth grade. But, settling in Boston in the environs of Harvard, he became a zealous musical self-educator even as he took menial jobs for self and family support. He found the money and time to study with a series of private music teachers, and soon started to give piano lessons, accompany singers, and acquire a library of two-piano four-hand reductions of orchestral music. And he got himself hired as a music critic at the *Boston Post*—a downscale paper not serving the Back Bay readership—at the age of only twenty.*

On radio, Downes was commentator for the New York Philharmonic from 1930 to 1933 and for the Boston Symphony from 1936 to 1937; in the 1940s he ran the Opera Quiz during Metropolitan Opera broadcast intermissions. Given to frequent "ums" and "uhs" on the air, he was not as smooth a radio presence as Deems Taylor, but he joins Taylor (the narrator of Disney's *Fantasia*) as the only American music critic ever to appear in the movies, by playing himself in the 1947 Hollywood film *Carnegie Hall*. He even briefly participated in the New York World's Fair of 1939 as classical music adviser—an honor symbolizing that Downes was the de facto Mayor of Classical Music in New York. His rough-hewn quality made classical music appealing to many male

---

* At the time Olin Downes worked there the *Boston Post* had the highest circulation of any daily newspaper in the United States.

listeners of that era who normally viewed it as too effete (like Joseph Kennedy
Sr., who loved Beethoven and Brahms but would play his 78s only in private
late at night, fearing what people would think of him).[19] While at the *Times*
Downes also gave frequent public lectures in music appreciation; at Carnegie Hall in 1941 he spoke on how to "be your own critic"—a pet phrase
of Downes's which capsulizes his unique appeal to the nonaesthetic music-
loving public.

Downes had famously poor handwriting. Recalled one of his apprentices
(later a successor to the chief job) at the *Times,* Harold Schonberg,

> One of my jobs after I joined the *Times* in 1950 was to take care of
> Mr. Downes's copy. There never was copy like it. He may have been the
> only journalist in history to write his reviews in longhand and then cor-
> rect them on the typewriter. It was a mess, and only one man in the com-
> posing room could decipher it. When I worked on Mr. Downes's Sunday
> pieces, I found it much easier to retype everything and start from there.
> Mr. Downes could have exasperating work habits. But I admired his real
> love for music, his enthusiasm, his courtly manners, his gargantuan ap-
> petites. He was authentically big, in every way.[20]

As a critic Downes had enthusiasms and antipathies, but his basic style was
rah-rah enthusiasm. He was a prime drumbeater of the press cult for Toscanini. Politically left-wing, a supporter of the little man, he rejected elitism as a
music critic and was a skeptic regarding much of modern music. He liked neither Schoenberg nor Stravinsky but was especially contemptuous toward the
latter, perhaps because he resented Stravinsky's divestiture of tonality from
its classicist-romanticist emotional moorings (he called Stravinsky's music
"empty of the impulse of beauty and feeling"). It appears that Downes was musician enough to study pieces he had not previously heard by reading orchestral scores and by playing four-hand piano versions.

Downes especially disliked the music of Mahler. In 1948 Arnold Schoenberg wrote Downes at the *Times* after the critic had given a savage review to a
performance by the Philharmonic of Mahler's Seventh Symphony. His letter
and Downes's reply, fascinating documents both, are excerpted below:

> You end your review on Mitropoulos's performance of Mahler's Seventh
> Symphony with the words: "*Chacun à son goût.*" This seems to me a great
> mistake, because if once, for instance, all of you "*chacun's*" who are so

proud of your personal "*goût*" would vote for or against a work, one could perhaps make an advance poll, predicting the result of this voting. This true opinion of the majority might decide the destiny of the work of a master, right or wrong; it would include, at least, instead of the "*goût*" of only one single "*chacun,*" various opinions; and everybody would understand that in the average which it presents there are included positives and negatives, pros and cons of various grades.

Unfortunately, you are so few in whose hands the destiny of a work is laid and your authority has been bestowed upon you by people who are too modest to do this job themselves. They deem that you understand much more of music than they. But they do not expect that you are so much at variance with other, and even important, musicians, who possess greater authority, based upon their personal achievements, upon studies and upon being recognized by a multitude of even greater authorities.

If I, who would not dare always to depend upon my personal gusto, if I would look around for support of my judgment, I would in first line think of Richard Strauss, who spoke once to me about Mahler with great appreciation and with a respect derived only from his own self-respect. . . . But nothing can surpass the enthusiasm of Anton von Webern, Alban Berg, Franz Schmidt, and many other Viennese composers about Mahler's symphonies. And why do you forget Mitropoulos's enthusiasm?

One who is able to study a score need not depend upon his personal taste. He would see all these strokes of genius which never are to be found in lesser masters. He would discover them on every page of this work, in every measure, in every succession of tones and harmonies.

But all of you have the habit of criticizing a work only when it is performed, and then after one single hearing you pronounce your sentence of life and death, regardless of all experience your trade has gone through when history turned to the absolute contrary of your judgment. . . .

As I have said before: If you would study the orchestra score you could not overlook the beauty of this writing. Such beauty is only given to men who deserve it because of all their other merits. You should not call me a mystic—though I am proud to be one—because this statement is based on experience. I have seen so many scores, and I could tell at one glance how good the composition is.

Even the piano score of Mahler's symphony would have revealed
much of its beauty. (*New York Times* [hereafter *NYT*], December 12, 1948)

To which the embattled critic replied:

I have read with interest and appreciation your letter concerning my review of Mitropoulos's recent performance of Mahler's Seventh Symphony. You say some interesting things which it is a pleasure to read. I must add, however, in frankness, that some of your remarks appear to me to be illogical.

I entirely disagree with you that my sentiment of *"Chacun à son goût"* is "a great mistake." It simply means that in reviewing a work I expressed my convinced opinion, but that everyone else who listens is entirely entitled to his own opinions and tastes in the matter. It also means that, while I am frank to say, as I did say and as I completely believe, that this symphony of Mahler's is detestably bad music, others who think as you do, for example, have an equal right to their conclusions. I think this is the very essence of fair critical practice. I do not consider myself a high priest of art; I do not pretend that my values of any music are conclusive. I do not even claim that I can tell at a single glance at a score whether the music is good or bad, whether it will perish quickly or last onward into infinity.

I must ask you a question. Do you really think that a composer who states that Beethoven's Seventh Symphony makes him ripe for the madhouse is in the least intelligent or fair in this, his written judgment? The name of this "critic" was Carl Maria von Weber. Do you take seriously what Schumann wrote of *Tannhäuser,* or what Berlioz said on the same subject, or what Debussy said of Beethoven, that he was a bore? These instances could be multiplied indefinitely. I am afraid that the greatest names in the history of musical composition do not connote either balance or perspective of musical judgment. For a final illustration of this obvious fact, let me quote you what an editorial board of five of the greatest composers in Russia said when they were asked by Koussevitsky, as a publisher, whether he should publish Stravinsky's *Petrouchka.* The score was unanimously rejected by these high and mighty gentlemen as being "not music."

And then, Mr. Schoenberg, you really hurt my feelings. Apparently

272   you think that I do not read scores. I hope you don't infer also that I am incapable of this. I can even tell you the score of Mahler's Seventh Symphony has been in my library for years, while as for piano arrangements of his music, I have gone through half of his Fifth Symphony on two pianos and gotten up from the instrument, being really unable to stomach any farther such vulgar music.*

❧ Downes and Sibeliomania

By far the most publicly influential of Downes's many enthusiasms was his passion for the music of Sibelius. From his earliest days with the *Boston Post,* he had found in the music of the Finnish composer an amalgam of lean modernity with traditional emotion and epic form that galvanized him into a Sibelius boomer. As Glenda Dawn Goss, author of the splendid study *Jean Sibelius and Olin Downes,* puts it, "Olin Downes preached the gospel of Sibelius as salvation for the twentieth-century soul."[21] As early as 1911, when Downes's son Edward was born, Philip Hale reportedly said to Downes, "Well, Olin, congratulations. Is it Sibelius or Sibelia?"[22] Downes's feelings for Sibelius gradually grew ever rapter until by the time he was *Times* reviewer in the 1920s the Sibelius symphonies had become for him the lodestar of artistic deliverance amid the contemporary smorgasbord of futurists, atonalists, cacophonists, and experimentalists, all artistic flotsam bereft of spiritual meaning to Downes. He first met the Finnish composer on Sibelius's only visit to America, in 1914 to conduct his own works in New England. By 1927 Downes was corresponding directly with Sibelius, peremptorily asking the composer to send him his scores and proposing that Downes broker an American tour with Sibelius conducting the Boston Symphony. That same year Downes undertook the first of five personal visits to Finland.

During his career Downes wrote to, and received replies from, many composers: Bloch, Prokofiev, Stravinsky, Varèse, Vaughan Williams. But his correspondence with Sibelius, examined today, has a singular and almost quaint quality of hero worship. Tossing all critical objectivity to the winds, he addresses his missives to the composer "Dear Master." Downes had devoured Romain Rolland's serial novel about a fictional great composer, *Jean-*

---

* Undeterred, Schoenberg sent Downes a second letter in reply to this.

Christophe, and his epistolary style to Sibelius reads like something out of Rolland. The composer's replies to Downes are cordial but usually short-winded—probably in part because Sibelius's English was limited. Downes's letters are prolix and almost embarrassingly adulatory—or, for those post-moderns not too cynical to find them embarrassing, remarkably touching in their sincerity of direct expression, their unabashed awe of great art, their quasi-religious trembling at the foot of genius. Some examples:

> We may not be able to talk much, and since you are an older man than I am, I doubt if my company will interest you. But I have talked to you often through your music; whether we communicate personally or not is without importance. . . . there will never be walls between me and you in your music. It is the only great and *noble* music that I hear being produced today. (August 27, 1927)

> I do retain as a priceless memory the strength, the spirit and the *reality*— the marvelous *reality*—which your music, and now yourself, have for me. . . . I expect to return to Finland again, and to shake your hand, either there or when you come over here. But whether we ever meet again or not, I shall know that you are always near, and for that life will be less lonely. (September 30, 1927)

> Dear Friend and Great Master, whom I love and adore:
>   . . . God bless you, and also may He, or the Devil, or whoever or whatever produces good music, bless the new work, the great *Mystery* [Downes refers to an Eighth Symphony, never finished] which you properly keep to yourself—on which you are engaged. . . . Salute! You have made me proud to live, as I shall be proud to die. Of all the things God has given me, there is nothing more precious, more happy, than *Sibelius.* (August 9, 1929) *

At the *Times,* says Goss, "Downes was more than ever in a position to publicize his views. To his heroic image of Sibelius, Downes began to add a sanctifying essence: Sibelius was an antidote to the poison of Stravinsky's emotionlessness."[23] More problematically, Downes became a behind-the-scenes

---

* Compare Downes's worshipfulness with Sibelius's remark: "Never pay any attention to what critics say. . . . Remember, a statue has never been set up in honor of a critic!"

274   lobbyist for Sibelius performances. In the late 1920s he wrote to, then personally approached, Serge Koussevitsky—until then unsympathetic to Sibelius's
music—and persuaded him to rethink his view of Sibelius. By the end of
Koussevitsky's career the Sibelius symphonies were among the conductor's signature pieces. Downes's letters to Sibelius throughout the 1940s display unflag-
ging efforts to persuade the composer to send him more scores so Downes
could bring them to other American conductors, as well as endless inquiries
about the alleged Eighth Symphony.

Before Downes had become an outright Sibelius activist on the *Times*,
there had been relatively few performances of the composer's symphonies in
America. But during the 1930s, performances by the major American orchestras increased meteorically.[24] Suddenly Sibelius vaulted to the top of the music
public's consciousness as not just a nationalist composer but as the cosmopolitan symphonic successor to Beethoven and Brahms. Even in the 1880s
Wagner had needed the championship of a triumvirate of critics—Krehbiel,
Henderson, and Finck—as well as the performances of the conductor Anton
Seidl to put him over in New York as the "greatest" composer of the age. But
in the radio and phonograph days of the 1930s (when Koussevitsky and
Toscanini began to record the Sibelius symphonies), Downes could single-
handedly "make" Sibelius in America, even though the composer had all but
stopped composing ten years earlier.

Here was the chief music critic of the *New York Times*, no less, expostulat-
ing like a religious devotee on the one hand to his "Dear Master," and on the
other, logrolling backstage for performances like an artistic ward heeler. The
readership of the *Times* knew nothing of this behavior. Then two events put
the brakes on the Sibelius boom. First, Virgil Thomson, who was as contemptuous of Sibelius as Downes was idealizing, arrived at the rival *Herald Tribune*
in October 1940 and bestowed his imprimatur of disapproval. But perhaps
more important, Finland, fearful of Communist Russia, entered World War II
on the Axis side.

These events by no means ended Sibelius performances in America, but
the vogue for him as symphonic music's avatar started a long decrescendo that
only accelerated after Downes's death in 1955.* The final irony may be a theory
advanced by Sibelius biographer Erik Tawaststjerna: that Sibelius's long au-
tumnal creative block was due not only to the composer's uncertainty in the

---

*However, in the last few years there has been a stunning revival, both in performances and in
scholarly inquiry.

face of twentieth-century musical idioms but also to pressure he felt to live   275
up to what Olin Downes, as well as the British critics Constant Lambert and
Cecil Gray, had written of him. In other words, Sibelius was like those American baseball players who become free agents, are awarded astronomical salaries based on their great seasons, and then never again perform at their previous levels, utterly intimidated by what is expected of them. Maybe Sibelius, a
self-critical and self-doubting individual by all accounts, felt unable to live up
to Olin Downes's importuning, hero-idealizing championship of him.

*Gilman, Haggin,
Chotzinoff: The
Toscanini cultists*
That the career in America of the Italian conductor Ar-
turo Toscanini (1867–1957) received boosting from the
New York critical fraternity is a generally accepted ax-
iom and has been definitively treated at length by Joseph Horowitz in his book
Understanding Toscanini. Horowitz argues that certain (not all) classical music critics virtually canonized Toscanini as the one and only great conductor,
to the detriment of such rivals as Mengelberg and Furtwängler, who were both,
according to this theory, driven out of New York as much by Toscanini's drum-
beaters in the press as by the imperious Toscanini himself.

Toscanini's press boom, however, was not a monolith; two of his enthusiasts, Lawrence Gilman and B. H. Haggin, could not have been more different
in style as critics and personalities. Gilman (1878–1939) had originally studied
art and was for a time in the late 1890s a staff illustrator for the *New York Herald.* But a secondary interest in music eventually won him over. Gilman, although from an affluent background, did not attend college. As a musician he
was apparently mostly self-taught, though he enjoyed a notable friendship
with Edward MacDowell. Francis Perkins of the *Herald Tribune* later wrote,
"He did some composing, but a severe spirit of self-criticism limited his output. His only published works were three songs on texts by William Butler
Yeats." If Perkins is to be believed, Gilman once even wrote and scored a full-
length opera, never allowing it to be seen.*

Gilman became music critic of *Harper's Weekly* in 1901, joined *Harper's*
magazine in 1913, and became music, drama, and literary critic for the *North*

---

* Claire Reis wrote that Gilman, alone among the New York critics of the 1920s, "arbitrarily took
time for study and reflection before rendering judgment. . . . before an important premiere Mr. Gilman
liked to study new scores at home and would often ask us to send music to him."

276 *American Review* in 1915. In 1923 he succeeded Krehbiel at the *Tribune* (it became the *Herald Tribune* the following year). He also wrote program notes for orchestras and music appreciation books. A frail man of delicate health, Gilman suffered several coronaries before finally succumbing at age sixty-one. He looked almost like a New England version of Alban Berg; Perkins, a *Tribune* colleague, described Gilman as "tall and dark haired," with a "touch of shyness" and "an essential courtliness of manner." Winthrop Sargeant, in his memoir of his early years as orchestral musician, music critic, and general journalist, described Gilman thus:

> Lawrence Gilman . . . was a suave, sensitive and rather morose gentleman of extremely aesthetic appearance who wore a fur-collared overcoat, worked for hours over each carefully turned paragraph, and produced a type of elegantly tortured prose that many New York concertgoers regarded as literature. Gilman shut out the coarse sounds of the nonmusical world by wearing plugs of cotton in his ears, except when he was on the job. At concerts, he would walk quietly to his seat, bow chivalrously to his colleagues, remove his overcoat, sit, remove his earplugs, and listen with polite concentration. When he left the concert hall the earplugs would be back securely in place.[25]

Gilman wrote in the lexiphanic Old World "artist in prose" style of Huneker and Paul Rosenfeld (Olin Downes did not). Undoubtedly Gilman's most piquant concoction as a wordsmith is the phrase he imparted in 1926 to describe Webern, reprinted in Slonimsky's *Lexicon* ("a tonal glorification of the amoeba. . . . the amoeba weeps"). Upon Gilman's passing *Opera News* wrote, "Some people produce art; some people write about the art produced by others, but few make an art of writing about art. Gilman belonged to the small company of the elect. He was an artist by nature." Two of Gilman's most historically notable reviews, from the vantage of hindsight, were his misconceived pan of the 1924 premiere of *Rhapsody in Blue* ("Weep over the lifelessness of the melody and harmony, so derivative, so stale, so inexpressive!") and his unusually farsighted encomium to Ives's *Concord* Sonata, played by John Kirkpatrick in January 1939 ("exceptionally great music").

For a chief music critic on a major New York newspaper, Gilman was a strangely otherworldly fellow. Though he had been raised in part by his paternal grandfather, a Congregationalist minister, as an adult Gilman was more interested in Eastern spiritual philosophies. His colleague Oscar Thompson of the *Sun* called him "the poet and seer of his profession." Gilman was generally regarded as the dean of the profession after W. J. Henderson's suicide, though the younger Olin Downes was already in full flower at the *New York Times.* When Gilman died suddenly, he was hailed by Leonard Liebling in the *Musical Courier* as "the last of the great critics of a bygone era." Though he was more a link to the Old Guard than a member of it, Gilman was probably the last New York music critic to receive written tributes upon his passing from celebrity musicians the likes of Lotte Lehmann, Lawrence Tibbett, Albert Spalding, and John Alden Carpenter.

It is ironic that this delicate, recessive aesthete has been fingered as the cavalryman leading the charge toward Toscanini, a one-track mania, Joseph Horowitz alleges, that indirectly injured our musical life. Horowitz opines that it was Gilman more than Downes who sacralized Toscanini: "Unlike Downes, he documented Toscanini's triumphs from a height, matching Toscanini's escalating stature with escalating religious metaphor."[26] Indeed, Downes was the more go-go cheerleader type; Gilman was the canonical anointer, calling Toscanini "the greatest musical interpreter who ever lived" and announcing that "Toscanini's fame is probably without a parallel in the records of music"—uncritical expostulations that recall to mind W. J. Henderson's 1888 statement that Wagner was the greatest composer who ever lived. It can't be doubted that such numinous phraseology has its effect on public taste.

At the opposite end of the human spectrum from Gilman, but an even more rabid Toscaninist, was Bernard H. Haggin (1900–1987), who wrote principally for the now defunct *Brooklyn Eagle* from 1934 and for the *Nation* from 1936. Haggin was arguably the Ty Cobb of music critics, brooking no disagreement with his opinions, totally without self-consciousness or humor about his own megalomania. There were no sacred cows for Haggin, except possibly for the self-evident veridicality of what he himself thought about what he himself heard. An especially arrogant man even for a critic, Haggin may have been unique in his complete disregard of the amenities and courtesies of professional collegiality. He was the only critic who didn't stop at disagreeing with the other critics' opinions; he would insist (at great length in scholarly publications such as the *Hudson Review*) that the other fellow wasn't so much wrong as that he *heard* wrong; that is, the other fellow simply didn't report accurately what occurred at the concert or on the recording. He applied this very test to none other than Virgil Thomson and found Thomson wanting. Though Thomson may have had cranky opinions at times, it is unlikely that Haggin had ears superior to Thomson's. Haggin was perhaps the only prominent mu-

278   sic critic to revile the pianism of Sergei Rachmaninoff; he claimed Rachmaninoff distorted everything he played.

Haggin was a nasty critic, and nasty critics always exert a certain fascination with readers, as nasty athletes like Mike Tyson or Dennis Rodman fascinate sports fans. Notwithstanding the unimpeachable merit of such an object of Haggin's approval as Toscanini, Haggin's assumed air of superiority—at least in print—was a blight upon his profession. But he was undoubtedly influential in helping to codify Toscanini's readings as the performances of record at the time, not only through his concert reviews but through his later articles and books containing reviews of the NBC Symphony's recordings, which consolidated Toscanini's reputation for the ages.

However tastemaking and influential with orchestra management such Toscanini-loving critics as Gilman and Haggin (as well as Olin Downes) may have been, even Horowitz concedes that other prominent critics at the same time were less starry-eyed (he cites W. J. Henderson and Irving Kolodin, and later, of course, Virgil Thomson). It is true that Downes and Gilman were a uniquely powerful duo presiding over the *Times* and *Trib* in New York, but a lesser colleague ultimately was a bigger mover and shaker for Toscanini than either of them. Samuel Chotzinoff (1889–1964), born in Russia, emigrated with his family to the United States as a child and settled in New York's Lower East Side. He studied at Columbia under Daniel Gregory Mason and for a few years in the 1910s and 1920s served as piano accompanist for Efrem Zimbalist, then for Heifetz. Chotzinoff married Heifetz's sister Pauline in 1925 (Pauline had previously dated George Gershwin). "Chotzie," as he was called, reviewed the 1924 *Rhapsody in Blue* Whiteman concert for *Vanity Fair,* then succeeded Deems Taylor at the *World* from 1925 to 1931. He was critic at the *New York Post* from 1935 to 1941. Later he lectured at Curtis and wrote his memoirs.

Chotzinoff was a worthy, able, but not epoch-making music critic; he was neither a superintellectual nor a prose stylist on the level of a Gilman. But he knew everybody in the music business, and—amazingly, while still serving as critic at the *Post*—he crossed a line that none of his predecessors, even those most chummy with the artists they reviewed, had ever crossed: he simultaneously became management. In 1936 General Sarnoff engaged him at the NBC radio network as a consultant to create, and help persuade Toscanini to conduct, the NBC orchestra. Chotzie succeeded in both, and the rest is history, but it is doubtful that any news organization today would permit such a conflict of interest. That same year, in the March 7 issue of the *Post,* Chotzinoff wrote a stinging article blaming the board of the New York Philharmonic for appointing Furtwängler to be Toscanini's successor "in camera": the article's headline blared, THE PHILHARMONIC BOARD DISDAINS TO CONSULT SUBSCRIBERS OR DIRECTOR. (Needless to say, the appointment was rescinded.)

The pen may be mightier than the sword in *Bartlett's Quotations*, but deeds are more definitive in real life. Samuel Chotzinoff was unique among the powerful music critic fraternity of the "Second Empire" in being given not just a broadcaster's microphone, like Deems Taylor and Olin Downes, but real power to determine broadcast programming. The man after Sarnoff most responsible for creating Toscanini's legacy—that of his recordings with the NBC Symphony—Chotzinoff arguably had more impact on actual music life in this country than any other pre-1950 critic. Though not as familiar a name or voice to the radio-listening public as Deems Taylor or Olin Downes, Chotzinoff did more than both to enhance radio and television as media for the promotion of good music. He not only served as a radio commentator for the NBC orchestra broadcasts but also commissioned two Gian Carlo Menotti operas: *The Old Maid and the Thief* for NBC radio in 1939, and in 1951 *Amahl and the Night Visitors* for NBC television. Through these commissions and other similar projects, he created the paradigm of high-culture television from which everything from Alistair Cooke's "Omnibus" in the 1950s to PBS in the 1990s descended. He was the last music print journalist to be a de facto cultural commissar.

Unfortunately, there don't appear to be any Samuel Chotzinoffs being sought as consultants by the Ted Turners and Lawrence Tisches of television networks today.

Development and recapitulation

Olin Downes must have had an effect on Sibelius appreciation in this country; the record of increased orchestral performances during his *Times* tenure is indisputable testimony. But with the subsequent Sibelius devaluation, Downes's Sibeliomania for a long while didn't look like a permanent change in canonical wisdom—until the recent Sibelius revival. But the New York drama critic George Jean Nathan's persistent championship of Eugene O'Neill in the 1910s and 1920s secured for O'Neill an abiding place as America's premier twentieth-century dramatist (or at least a berth shared with Tennessee Williams). The consensus of critical

280   opinion has only confirmed Nathan's prescience, though lately Harold Bloom opines in *The Western Canon* that "Eugene O'Neill now makes for unsatisfactory reading."

Maybe canons are less fixed than we think; maybe the ups and downs of critical championships are more like the stock market. This card game gets especially murky when one starts to talk about the Second Viennese School's early critical boosters (such as they were in America) being proved seers. The late twentieth century has seen both a critical and a performance reversal in the stock of serialism. And what of the unique phalanx of Charles-Martin Loeffler chauvinists that commanded the Boston musical press for the first decades of the century? Loeffler (1861–1935), an Alsatian-born Frenchified German who emigrated and became an adopted Boston Brahmin, wrote much fine impressionistic music. Philip Hale and Louis Elson and company found in Loeffler not the peer but the superior of Debussy. They tirelessly promoted him as the great white hope of modern music in reviews, articles, books. For example: "Surely, if the modern school becomes permanent, Mr. Loeffler will be reckoned among its greatest exponents. He is not so purely cerebral as the bitter Vincent d'Indy and he is fully as romantic as the fawning Debussy. He is as great as either of them—or greater" (Louis C. Elson, *Boston Advertiser*, November 27, 1907). Loeffler was a critic-authenticated canonically great composer in all music appreciation materials originating from Boston for decades, cheek by jowl with the three B's. He is probably the most recent composer to have attained that status and to have been dropped from it without a trace. (Yet there are reports that even he is beginning to be attended by a revival.)

Critics sometimes influence the course of things in ways least obvious to their readers. Take Harold Schonberg, the *New York Times*'s powerful senior critic from 1960 to 1980. Schonberg was most proverbial for being Leonard Bernstein's chief press tormentor during Bernstein's New York Philharmonic years. He also authored two of the best-selling (and most lucidly written) music appreciation books in history, *The Great Pianists* and *The Lives of the Great Composers*, as well as many other books. A man feared by some—probably because after the *Trib*'s 1966 demise he wielded sovereign power in New York—Schonberg has been all too handily overlooked for his unusually forward championships of so-called Romantic performance practice and repertoire. From his earliest articles and essays in the *Times*, and later through his books, Schonberg has been on a crusade to reacquaint the musical public with the "grand manner" of piano playing of the nineteenth century and early twentieth, and to correct what he views as the scandalous neglect of Romantic repertoire and performance style by both pianists and music historians. His advocacy has had an undeniable influence on the reissue of recordings of pianists of the past, in the revival of composers such as Godowsky, and in the repertoire actually played by many concert pianists. Few other American journalistic music critics past or present can claim so substantive an effect on the actual doings of practicing musicians and musicologists. In this manner Schonberg used his bully pulpit more selflessly than many critics to render a neglected service to the art of music, but he never quite acquired public recognition for this the way Downes had for his work on behalf of Sibelius. His successors as chief music critic at the *Times*—Donal Henahan, Edward Rothstein, and Bernard Holland—have seemed to steer clear of pet causes.

Coda   Music critics in the postwar era continued to be perceived as despicable power mongers, particularly the *Los Angeles Times*'s Martin Bernheimer and the variously New York– and Los Angeles–based Alan Rich. Both critics were unusually competent, well educated musicologically, aggressive in their commentaries, and capable of provoking annoyance in their communities. In 1969 members of the Boston Symphony Orchestra boycotted concert attendance by the *Boston Globe* critic Michael Steinberg, accusing him of "personal arrogance that becomes offensive" and "insulting and unethical assaults" that had driven several of the orchestra's guest conductors away from future engagements with the orchestra. The BSO Association demanded that Steinberg be refused admission to BSO concerts until he apologized for certain reviews. One orchestra trustee wrote to the *Boston Herald Traveler* that Steinberg "had chosen to write in such tone of voice and to say things that are both unfair and rude, that major artists are reluctant to come to Boston and some have refused to come."[27]

This story has a naughty postscript.

Steinberg left the *Globe* in 1976 to become program annotator for the Boston Symphony Orchestra.

10 *Twentieth-Century Rondo*

Cutting Edge versus Neo-Con

There seems to be a general view that all forms of culture are on the right side and should therefore be praised.
—CONSTANT LAMBERT, *Music Ho!*

Forces other than musical ones go into the making of taste. . . . The role of intellectuals outside music in forming the aesthetic climate is in many ways an unexplored chapter in contemporary musical life.
—SAMUEL LIPMAN

Some forty years ago, that ageless enfant terrible of musical pantology, Nicolas Slonimsky, in the prefatory essay of his now classic 1953 book, *Lexicon of Musical Invective: Critical Assaults on Composers since Beethoven's Time,* noted a phenomenon among critics and noncritics he called the "non-acceptance of the unfamiliar." "Music is an art in progress . . . unfamiliar music impresses a prejudiced listener as a chaos of random sounds," Slonimsky nonchalantly stated. With that flourish he introduced as Exhibit A for his argument actual vituperative comments culled from newspaper reviews going back 150 years, in which reviewers flogged the then newly minted music of Beethoven, Brahms, Chopin, Schumann, and all the tonal and more or less consonant nineteenth-century immortals, frequently using the very same epithets of cacophony more recently applied by critics of our century to twentieth-century compositions.

The subtext to Slonimsky's argument was clear: insofar as it is self-evident that the unfamiliar is always at first more or less unaccepted, just so is it axiomatic that as time goes on, the newfangled is eventually accepted. Yesterday's

barnyard cacophony becomes today's retrospective masterpiece; just look
how history proves my point, Slonimsky seemed to be asserting. Why, hadn't
George Bernard Shaw himself written in 1910, referring to the fact that many
then living musicians had finally accepted Wagner's music after initially finding it "formless, melodyless, and abominably discordant," that "the technical
history of modern harmony is a history of growth of toleration by the human
ear of chords that at first sounded discordant and senseless to the main body
of contemporary professional musicians"?[1]

Slonimsky's book was itself a form of propaganda for the cause of modern music.* But soon after *Lexicon of Musical Invective* was published, exactly
the opposite thesis was propounded by ex–*Philadelphia Bulletin* music critic
Henry Pleasants in a 1955 book the title of which spoke volumes: *The Agony
of Modern Music.* Pleasants spoke disdainfully of Slonimsky's point of view as
"evolutionist," particularly poking fun at Slonimsky's assertion that there
was an actual time measure for the ripening of vintage music masterworks:
"it takes approximately twenty years," Slonimsky had written in *Lexicon*, "to
make an artistic curiosity out of a modernistic monstrosity, and another
twenty to elevate it to a masterpiece." Where Slonimsky cited as proof of his
thesis the audience reception accorded Monteux's performances of *Le sacre du
printemps* in Paris in 1913 (hysterical boos) and again in Paris in 1952 (hysterical
huzzahs), Pleasants argued him tooth and nail: in point of fact, said Pleasants,
Stravinsky's *Sacre* had had a marvelous reception in another Parisian performance only a year after the premiere, while numerous other allegedly masterly modernistic scores had failed to attain the terms-of-endearment stage of
audience reception well past the forty-year cutoff line.

Pleasants was but the most reactionary example of the many prominent
critics who not only rebelled against the perceived anti-Romantic ugliness of
modern music, but refused to shut up about it well into the century. Many
other mainline music critics tried to meet Slonimsky's time-delay criterion for
themselves and still found modernism wanting. For example, wrote Richard
Aldrich of the *New York Times* in 1915: "Music that has been veiled to one generation has often been revealed to the next as a clear and intelligible advance.
Will our grandchildren see it and smile indulgently at the bewildered listeners

---

* In a review of Slonimsky's *Lexicon of Musical Invective* in the *London Sunday Times* headlined
"Much Ado about Nothing," Ernest Newman—at eighty-five coming to the end of his more than fifty-
year career as England's most distinguished music critic—wrote, "If we were to delve into the records
with a purpose opposite to that of Mr. Slonimsky we would find that there has been considerably more
injudicious praise of mediocre composers than injudicious disparagement of first-rate composers."

284   of 1915? The question is not really important; bewildered listeners of 1915 can only listen for themselves." Eight years later, Aldrich again wrote in the *Times*: "The liberated music-maker and listener of the farthest advanced line are strangely uncritical persons. Whatever is presented to them as acrid ugliness or rambling incoherence is eagerly accepted as emanations of greatness and originality. It never occurs to them that it may be really simple, commonplace ugliness. . . . Is it only necessary to sound bad to be really good?"

Slonimsky notwithstanding, the conservatives' laments ended neither with Aldrich nor only in forty years. An Alphonse-and-Gaston dialectic between progressives and conservatives has persisted all the way into the 1990s. What had begun as a pitched battle between preservers of Matthew Arnold's High Culture and promoters of the futurists continued throughout the century with the opposing sides carrying on under new labels—the neoconservatives versus the cutting edge—with the claims of Afro-Asiatic musics and new musical vernaculars such as jazz and rock complicating the debate on both sides. Much of tastemaking and repertory was influenced by the critics who were the most prominent standard-bearers for either side. The battle royal of the revolutionist critics and the evolutionist critics has been a recurring subject throughout this century: musically speaking, a rondo. We'll examine here the careers of a few critics in depth, not because they were the only good critics to take sides on the modernism controversy, but because their ideas best distill the terms of the debate.

∾ *Huneker's heirs:*
Rosenfeld and
Van Vechten
By the time he died in 1921, James Gibbons Huneker, who had been the maverick in the turn-of-the-century New York–Boston critical phalanx, had already passed his baton on to two heirs apparent: both forward-looking, one strictly high culture and ultra-avant-garde, the other pluralistically open to high and popular culture. Of the former—Paul Rosenfeld (1890–1946)—Claire Reis says Huneker himself had said of him, "Young man, you are starting where I left off!";[2] Philip Hale wrote of Rosenfeld that he "writes about certain modern composers as if he had summered and wintered with them and been through them with a dark lantern."[3] In her memoirs Reis recalls evenings playing chamber music in New York in her Young Turk days with Paul Rosenfeld listening in; perhaps it was at one of the salons in Rosenfeld's own home where

he cooked for the artists present, artists whom he sometimes helped not only with his write-ups but with his money. But the other Huneker disciple, Carl Van Vechten (1880–1964)—like Rosenfeld and Huneker, a critic of all the arts, but music primarily—might have visited much the same memory on Reis had she been present at one of his evenings at Mabel Dodge's salon. For Van Vechten, like Rosenfeld—but unlike the word-count-enslaved wage-earner Huneker—was (after 1926) of independent means, and he not only propagandized for the moderns in print but also occasionally helped them out as a private patron.

These two remarkable men were perhaps the first notable exemplars of the avant-garde critic in American musical letters. They shook loose the term "futurism" from the vocabulary of the Hendersons and Hales and permanently replaced it with "modernism," in accord with the terminology in contemporary painting and literature.* Moreover, that they dared to fraternize with the artists they wrote about, even give money to some of them, threw out all journalistic canons of impartiality, yet resulted in the greater good of spreading understanding of the New to the Many—few if any of the ethically constrained music critics since have had nearly so much impact on the development of music and art in this country. For "it was said of Rosenfeld that, being a great friend of artists as well as a critic, he often discovered people before they discovered themselves," as Reis recalled.[4] Or as Van Vechten put it, "It is absurd to feel that you cannot dine with a singer without praising her performance. Many days in each month I dine with authors whose works I abhor. I find their companionship delightful. Should I be deprived of their society because I happen to be a critic?"[5]

Paul Rosenfeld was born in 1890 into a cultivated, arts-loving, upper-middle-class German-Jewish family in New York City. His father was a successful businessman, his mother a pianist; the family often traveled to Europe. But the mother was a chronic depressive and the father himself went into a depression when she died in 1900, whereupon young Paul and his sister were taken to live with their maternal grandmother. In 1903 Paul went to Riverview Military Academy in Poughkeepsie, where he wrote, read, and took piano lessons. His father died an emotional and financial wreck in 1908, but Paul was

---

* The term "futurism" actually originated with the Italian painters and sculptors who followed the 1910 "futurist" manifesto of Tommaso Marinetti, but for some reason the Old Guard critics adopted this term (and not "cubism") as a pejorative for dissonant or atonal new music. "Cacophonists" was another pejorative they used to describe such composers.

286 left with a munificent inheritance from his mother's family. He attended Yale, where his pursuits were more literary than musical, graduated in 1912, and then attended the Columbia School of Journalism for one year.

After graduating from Columbia, Rosenfeld spent six months as a reporter on the *New York Press* but found the work "morally distasteful." Instead, living on his private income, he decided to pursue his interests in music and art, "to show the face of expressivity to a trading society living by middle-class conventions," and spend a year in Europe. As the Great War was beginning, his trip's timing may have been inopportune, but he soon returned to New York with the avowed intent to begin his critical career with a distinctly New World tilt. He cofounded the short-lived magazine *Seven Arts* and wrote about music, as well as art and literary criticism, for the *New Republic,* the *Nation, Vanity Fair,* and other, mostly nonmusic magazines. From 1920 to 1927 he was regular music critic of the *Dial* and for many years a steady contributor to *Modern Music.* As well, he began socializing with the leading young critical lights of his time—cultural and literary critics like Waldo Frank, Van Wyck Brooks, and Lewis Mumford—as well as with artists themselves, at first not musicians but primarily painters and photographers. His most formative friendship was with the photographer Alfred Stieglitz, the husband of Georgia O'Keeffe; Rosenfeld fraternized with painters and other photographers at Stieglitz's famed art gallery at 291 Fifth Avenue and absorbed from them the raging currents in modern art.

In the 1920s Rosenfeld began publishing books that, in the manner of Huneker, consisted of recobbled versions of his magazine pieces; his first such collection, the 1920 *Musical Portraits,* was called by no less than Edmund Wilson "absolutely dazzling." During the following decade, Rosenfeld authored hundreds of articles. By consensus his most characteristic book is *Port of New York* (1924), with its profiles of fourteen American moderns whom Rosenfeld sought to establish as a stateside counterpart to the European high modernism of Stravinsky, Picasso, and Joyce: they included not only Stieglitz, O'Keeffe, and other painters and writers but also Roger Sessions, then just barely beginning his illustrious career as a composer.

From the 1920s onward Rosenfeld kept a salon going in his various Manhattan apartments, holding evening parties where poets read or musicians played. Among the musicians were Leo Ornstein, Darius Milhaud, and Edgard Varèse; among the poets, e. e. cummings, Hart Crane, and Marianne Moore. Even as he wrote his myriad articles and books, Rosenfeld was a behind-the-scenes benefactor of many young artists, either firsthand or indirectly; Aaron

Copland himself deems Rosenfeld his angel of rescue upon his own return
from Paris:

> One rather important item was being neglected—my financial setup. For
> lack of a better solution I had decided to make a living by teaching. In the
> fall I had opened a studio on West Seventy-Fourth Street in Manhattan
> and sent out the usual announcements. Unfortunately the effect of this
> move was nil. It produced not one pupil. By the time the Symphony [for
> organ and orchestra] had been played in Boston the situation was acute.
> Something had to be done. It was Paul Rosenfeld who came to the rescue.
> While still a student in Brooklyn, I had read his appreciations of contem-
> porary music in the *Dial*. The morning after the performance of the pi-
> ano pieces at the League concert, he called me up to tell me how much he
> liked them. (I couldn't have been more surprised if President Coolidge
> had telephoned me.) It was 1924; money was plentiful and art patrons
> were numerous. Through a mutual friend Rosenfeld was asked if he
> could not find a musical Maecenas to come to the aid of an indigent
> young composer. Rosenfeld said he could, and did.[6]

Shortly thereafter Copland won the first Guggenheim for a composer, but
still needed a place to write his next composition. "Rosenfeld suggested the
MacDowell Colony as a good place to work during the summer months. It was
there that I wrote my *Music for the Theatre,* a suite in five parts for small orchestra."[7] It was no wonder that Copland felt Rosenfeld was one of the very
few music critics worth respecting, even though in his earlier writings about
Copland the critic hedged his bets, calling the young composer's music "coltish." Copland was not the only American composer who endorsed Rosenfeld;
Ives issued a rare encomium: "Paul Rosenfeld had an almost immediate insight
into the larger side of music . . . a penetrative discernment into its fundamental and inner meanings." Even Stravinsky, who had given Rosenfeld an uneasy,
somewhat patronizing interview in the 1920s, endorsed him posthumously, is-
suing a jacket blurb for the 1969 republication of a Rosenfeld anthology: "This
excellent anthology of one of the very few music critics of the time is both
worth reading and readable."

Rosenfeld's circumstances became more straitened during the Great Depression; he developed diabetes, his private income shrank in the stock market crash, and many of his periodical outlets went under. But he continued
writing books and articles without stint—including translating Robert Schu-

288   mann's music criticism and starting to write the first critical biography of Charles Ives—till his untimely but poetically just death in 1946, when he suffered a heart attack while attending a movie.

∿   *The modernist champion with the euphuistic prose style*

Rosenfeld was the first prominent American music critic to write respectfully—rather than resort to the carnival freakshow approach of the daily newspaper critics—about such modernist American composers as Ornstein, Sessions, Cowell, Ruggles, Ives, Copland, Harris, and Riegger. With equal respect he reviewed the more conservative American composers such as Howard Hanson, Deems Taylor, and Louis Gruenberg, but his real innovation was bringing critical focus on the American moderns on a par with the Europeans (Stravinsky, Schoenberg, Bartók). He soon viewed Copland as better than "coltish": "The earmark of Copland's music is leanness, slenderness of sound . . . both lithe and imponderous. . . . Is Copland, struggling to handle mechanical, impersonal rhythms in a deep, exalted spirit, anything but an integral part of a movement attempting the same in practical fields?" By 1936 Rosenfeld was referring to Copland as "lofty in endeavor and accomplishment." In his 1936 book, *Discoveries of a Music Critic,* he found Ives's rhythmic and formal asymmetries to be "abrupt and nervous and ecstatic in their movements and manifestations—brought into play with a certain reluctance and difficulty, but when finally loosed, jaggedly, abruptly, almost painfully released, with something of an hysteric urgency; manifested sometimes in a bucolic irony and burlesque and sometimes in a religious and mystical elevation, but almost invariably in patterns that have a paroxysmal suddenness and abruptness and violence." No critic before Rosenfeld (save Henry Bellamann) had written anything about Ives in the 1930s, and many of the journeyman critics in the daily newspaper "chain gang" read Rosenfeld. Could it be that Lawrence Gilman of the *Herald Tribune* was influenced by Rosenfeld when he wrote his famous encomium of Ives's *Concord* Sonata on January 21, 1939?

Rosenfeld seems to have been self-educated as a musical analyst, but he did play the piano and go through piano scores. He appears to have been able to read orchestral scores. Nonetheless, like Huneker he is primarily an impressionistic critic, though Rosenfeld sometimes out-Hunekers Huneker with an Edward Dahlberg–like vocabulary replete with archaisms. Rosenfeld's

prose at its weakest reads like translated German; at its best, it comes close to   289
prose-poetry, and it is more frequently at its best. His descriptions of the urban imagery suggested by Leo Ornstein's music contain language so rich that
they could almost form stanzas in Hart Crane's poem *The Bridge:*

> The first of his real compositions are like fragments of some cosmopolis
> of caves and towers of steel, of furious motion and shafts of nitrogen glare
> become music. They are like sensitive surfaces that have been laid in the
> midst of the New Yorks; and record not only the clangors, but all the vio-
> lent forms of the city, the beat of the frenetic activity, the intersecting
> planes of light, the masses of the masonry with the tiny, dwarf-like crea-
> tures running in and out, the electric signs staining the inky nightclouds.
> They give again the alarum of dawn breaking upon the crowded, swarm-
> ing cells; seven o'clock steam whistles on a winter morn; pitiless light
> filtering over hurrying black droves of humanity; thousands of shivering
> workers blackening Fourteenth Street. They picture the very Niebelheim,
> the hordes of slaves herded by giants of their own creation, the com-
> mands and cries of power in the bells, whistles, signals.[8]

This modern-as-mechanistic, Charlie-Chaplin-in-*Modern Times* analogy
became almost a personal cliché of Rosenfeld's pen, albeit one upon which he
rang infinite changes:

> Through Debussy, music had liquefied, become opalescent and impalp-
> able and fluent. . . . But through Stravinsky, there has come to be a music
> stylistically well-nigh the reverse of that of the impressionists. Through
> him, music has become again cubical, lapidary, massive, mechanistic.
> Scintillation is gone out of it. The delicate, sinuous melodic line, the
> glamorous sheeny harmonies, are gone out of it. The elegance of De-
> bussy, the golden sensuality, the quiet, classic touch, are flown. . . .
> Indeed, the change is as radical, as complete, as though in the midst
> of moonlit noble gardens a giant machine had arisen swiftly from the
> ground and inundated the night with electrical glare and set its metal
> thews and organs and joints relentlessly whirling, relentlessly func-
> tioning.[9]

Rosenfeld did not automatically give a thumbs-up to a composer simply
because he was modern. He had some problems with Schoenberg and felt that

290 Satie's "delight in pure movement" resulted in the "replacement of feeling by surface emotions" (he wrote similarly about Virgil Thomson's *Four Saints in Three Acts*). He felt that Strauss was in decline as early as *Salome* and that Hofmannsthal was a deficient librettist. Rosenfeld also disliked Mahler's symphonies, regarding the music as inferior to Bruckner and even to Ernest Bloch.

He was not only less sympathetic but less sound a critic on composers endowed with great gifts of melody but fixed in aesthetically conservative positions, such as Rimsky-Korsakov or Rachmaninoff; Rachmaninoff's music, he wrote in *Musical Portraits*, "wants the imprint of a decided and important individuality," and Rimsky-Korsakov "lacked the voice of the people." Among American Romantics Rosenfeld derided MacDowell and Loeffler, noting sarcastically that the latter abided in "the dangerous vicinity of those amiable gentlemen the Chadwicks and the Converses and all the other highly respectable and sterile 'American composers.'" But his most peculiar critical dismissal was of Wagner, the previous generation's *summa* of advanced music; perhaps Rosenfeld, feeling what the literary critic Harold Bloom has termed "the anxiety of influence," felt the need to distance himself from such Wagnerite critics as W. J. Henderson and Krehbiel, not to mention Shaw and Ernest Newman, in order to establish a school of American modernist criticism. But he went too far:

> No doubt he is not the greatest of the artists who have made music. Colossal as were his forces, colossal as were the struggles he made for the assumption of his art, his musical powers were not always able to cope with the tasks he set himself. The unflagging inventive power of a Bach or a Haydn, the robustness of a Haendel or a Beethoven, the harmonious personality of a Mozart, were things he could not rival. He is even inferior, in the matter of style, to men like Weber and Debussy. There are many moments, one finds, when his scores show that there was nothing in his mind, and that he simply went through the routine of composition. Too often he permitted the system of leading-motifs to relieve him of the necessity of creating. Too often, he made of his art a purely mental game. His emotion, his creative genius were far more intermittent, his breath far less long than one once imagined. Some of the earlier works have commenced to fade rapidly, irretrievably. At present one wonders how it is possible that one once sat entranced through performances of *The Flying Dutchman* and *Tannhäuser*.[10]

Considering Wagner's *volk*-derived collective-unconscious underpinnings, this critique is all the stranger in that Rosenfeld elsewhere found virtue and merit in how far an artist's expression penetrated to the roots both of his culture and of his personal subconscious. He thus found Mussorgsky's *Boris* superior to Rimsky-Korsakov's operas, saying of Rimsky-Korsakov:

> Society produces innumerable artists like him, who are fundamentally incapable of becoming the instrument every creative being is, and of discovering through themselves the consciousness of their fellows. Whatever its cause, there is in such men a fear of the unsealing of the unconscious mind, the depository of all actual and vital sensations, which no effort of their own can overcome. It is for that reason that they have so gigantic and unshakable a confidence in all purely conscious processes of creation, particularly in the incorporation of *a priori* theories.[11]

In another odd inconsistency, Rosenfeld found abundant evidence in the music of the Second Viennese School, for all of the a priori contrapuntal processes of dodecaphonic technique, of this same "unsealing of the unconscious mind." One may well agree that Schoenberg and Berg's music discloses much primal emotion, yet is that to say that Rachmaninoff's does not?

Yet most of these inconsistencies can be overlooked in the sweep of what Rosenfeld accomplished. Paul Rosenfeld was one of the prime agenda-setters of modernist American music of the early twentieth century. He gave money and encouragement to the composers and facilitated performances; he raised the musical consciousness of the followers of the other arts who read his essays in the primarily nonmusical periodicals in which they appeared; and he certainly influenced the daily music reviewers who followed his articles in *Modern Music* to take a look at the new composers, especially the more forward-looking critics like Lawrence Gilman and Pitts Sanborn.

ow *Carl Van Vechten,*
dilettante ne plus Even more than Huneker and Paul Rosenfeld, Carl
ultra Van Vechten ("Carlo" to his intimates) was elaborately
multifarious—music critic, dance and drama critic,
prolific novelist, Gertrude Stein executor, white devotee of the Harlem Renaissance, and acclaimed portrait photographer. Like Huneker and Rosenfeld,

292   too, he was not just a forward-looking critic but an active discoverer of young and overlooked talent who dared to cross "that line" to fraternize with the subjects of his criticisms. Like them, he wrote about all the seven lively arts, but with an emphasis on music. Like them, he published books that were anthologies of recobbled versions of his previous magazine essays. Above all, Huneker, Rosenfeld, and Van Vechten—as no other critics of their times did—posited curiosity and exploration of the avant-garde as the duty of conscience of all artistically cultured people. If he did not venture quite so polemically into the precincts of the avant-garde as did Rosenfeld, Van Vechten went beyond him in admitting into the Western canon African-American and African-American-inspired music and art, and in this Van Vechten was uniquely ahead of his time, presaging by two generations controversies and polemics that raged late in the century.

Van Vechten was born in 1880 and raised in Cedar Rapids, Iowa, "which I loathed from the first," he told the New York Times not long before his death in 1964. "I eventually escaped via the University of Chicago and a job as a crime reporter for Hearst's Chicago American. After two years I was fired—'for lowering the tone of the Hearst publications,' I was given to understand. I later told that to Hearst, and he laughed uproariously." He moved to Manhattan in 1906, commissioned by Theodore Dreiser, then editor of Broadway magazine, to write an article about Strauss's Salome, performances of which had just been banned by J. P. Morgan. Van Vechten immediately became a confirmed New Yorker; he stayed on in a series of Manhattan apartments for almost sixty years. Later in 1906 he became assistant to Richard Aldrich, the chief music critic at the Times. Before his second marriage in 1914, to the actress Fania Marinoff (though he was homosexual), Van Vechten also wrote dance criticism for the Times, briefly served as the newspaper's Paris correspondent, and wrote drama criticism for the New York Press. He was in the audience at the notorious 1913 Paris premiere of Stravinsky's Sacre du Printemps, which event he later described in his book Music after the Great War.

Van Vechten's father was a banker and insurance agent who had provided his son, who was the baby of the family, with trust funds and inheritances that after his death in 1926 covered most of his son's needs. Art for art's sake was Van Vechten's ruling credo, and money, whether spent on himself or on other artists, was aesthetic fertilizer, a means to the end of artistic excellence. He apparently received occasional smaller subsidies before his father's death in 1926, and the financial neediness of his early married life with Fania Marinoff resembles the early married life of Huneker and his own dependence on his

wife's family. (During Van Vechten's years of genteel poverty in the 1910s his
first wife prosecuted him for nonpayment of alimony so vindictively that he
actually went to jail for a few months, becoming a newspaper item himself. He
emerged from this lurid episode relatively unscathed in reputation.) After his
stint as Richard Aldrich's assistant music critic at the *New York Times* ended in
1913, Van Vechten decided to be a freelancer for the rest of his life. Although he
did gradually begin to make some money from his writing, family help enabled
him to do a certain kind of artistic missionary work, as he wrote his older
banker brother in a 1919 letter:

> The point is that I have determined to be a writer, not a journalist or a
> scribbler but a writer. This does not as a rule make money; it usually takes
> it. . . . The kind of writing I do requires time for reflection, it requires go-
> ing about and meeting a great many people, it requires travel, and buying
> books and other expenses . . . to succeed, I am to a certain extent forced
> to keep my mind free and my pen unsullied. . . . If I were younger I might
> be able to work on a newspaper and write books too. But I am just be-
> ginning to get over the bad effects of newspaper work, i.e., the hurry pro-
> duced by the demand for copy makes one fall into routine expressions
> which eventually spoil a style. . . . My stocks serve to pay the rent and that
> is about all. . . . When Fania is working she helps a great deal but . . . within
> the month I advised her to turn down a part because I thought it would
> be bad for her career to accept it.[12]

Van Vechten's finances changed dramatically in 1926–27, when both of his
parents and his older brother all died, leaving him a million dollars in trust
funds. A writer friend, Avery Hopwood, who also died at this time, left him
money, too, though by now Van Vechten was starting to earn better income on
his own through sales of his racy novels.

Van Vechten stood with Rosenfeld and Huneker in a lone critic triumvirate writing affirmatively during the 1910s about Satie, Schoenberg, Stravinsky,
and other modern composers. (Interestingly, Van Vechten also was great
friends with H. L. Mencken.) He was the great authority of his time on Albéniz
and other Spanish composers, publishing *The Music of Spain* in 1918. Perhaps
most notably from posterity's perspective, however, Van Vechten became history's first crossover critic. With the possible exception of Rupert Hughes, he
was the first highbrow classical music critic ever to write with approval about
ragtime, jazz, musical comedy, the blues, film scores, and George Gershwin,

294   and did so at a time when the Old Guard critics were still decrying jazz as garbage.

Van Vechten's essays on music were collected in several books: *Music after the Great War* (1915), *Music and Bad Manners* (1916), *Interpreters and Interpretation* (1917), *The Merry-Go-Round* (1918), *In the Garret* (1919), and *Red* (1925). But at the early age of forty, Van Vechten gave up criticism, saying that at forty a man experienced "intellectual hardening of the arteries," which made him unfit for criticism.[13] He began writing novels that were a cross between Huneker's racy portraits of high bohemian living and F. Scott Fitzgerald's Roaring Twenties. In 1932 he published an autobiography in which "he told virtually nothing about himself."[14] Then, at the age of fifty-two he announced that he would never publish another word, whereupon he undertook his third career, portrait photography, which had been a hobby for some time. Nearly all of his subjects were arts celebrities, from Eugene O'Neill (a great personal friend) to Billie Holiday (who cried during the shoot when Van Vechten played her his records of Bessie Smith), and he did not charge them for his work. It was reported that he was up daily at 6 A.M. working in his darkroom at 146 Central Park West until the day before he died in his sleep at eighty-four.

A frequenter of artistic salons from his earliest New York days, Van Vechten met Gertrude Stein at one of them and later became Stein's de facto publicist, American business representative, and in 1946 her posthumous literary executor. Van Vechten was also way ahead of his time in promoting interracial relations; he made lasting friendships with great figures of the Harlem Renaissance such as Arna Bontemps, James Weldon Johnson, Langston Hughes, and Claude McKay. He was perhaps the first white intellectual to bring other white intellectuals to Harlem nightclubs in the 1920s and after, he made many private philanthropies on behalf of black artists, and he amassed a huge collection of documents of African-American contributions to American life, which he eventually donated to Yale.

A tall, plump man with prematurely whitened blond hair combed forward over a wide forehead, he was a caricaturist's delight: stooped, with famous teeth that looked like walrus fangs (he was careful never to pose for photographs with his mouth open), lantern-jawed, with a Maurice Chevalier lower lip, affecting idiosyncrasies of dress such as wearing bracelets—Van Vechten looked like Dorian Gray as a werewolf. An arresting figure to the end, he continued to greet new artists and intellectuals into New York's perennial bohemian subculture into his eighties. He was both one of the last of the great cultural critics who put classical music at the forefront of general artistic cul-

ture, and the first in the line of crossover critics who looked to Afro-Asiatic cultures for replenishment of the Western tradition, such as Winthrop Sargeant,
Henry Pleasants, and John Rockwell.

❧ *Countersubject:*
The agony of   Through his attentions to vernacular and African-
Henry Pleasants   derived musics, Van Vechten unwittingly begat a line
of music criticism that carried some of his ideas to extremes he may never have intended. This school of thought posited that the
true revolution of modern music was not at all taking place, as Paul Rosenfeld
thought, in art music derived from the European high art model, but rather in
popular song and dance forms that had superseded classical music. According
to this radical view, the franchise on artistic vitality and spontaneous emotion
in music had in the twentieth century been wholly ceded to vernacular music
forms all deriving from African-American influences, and all further attempts
to reinvigorate classical European art models were a doomed anachronism.
This was the point of view that held that Music—like God, in some quarters—
was dead. This was the point of view of Henry Pleasants, author of *The Agony
of Modern Music* (1955), possibly the most notorious volume in twentieth-
century American music criticism.

Ironically, Pleasants began his career as a music critic as a specialist in contemporary music. Following studies in voice, piano, and composition at the
Philadelphia Conservatory and the Curtis Institute of Music, he joined the
Philadelphia Evening Bulletin in 1930 as assistant music critic. Arthur Tubbs,
the paper's veteran theater and music editor, cared little for modern music.
The result was that Pleasants, as neophyte second-string critic, got the first-
string assignments if modern music was involved. Thus he covered such important premieres in the early 1930s as the Philadelphia Orchestra productions
of *Wozzeck*, Stravinsky's *Oedipus Rex*, Prokofiev's *Pas d'Acier*, Chavez's ballet
H.P., Louis Gruenberg's *The Emperor Jones*, and so on, along with the host of
new and experimental orchestral compositions that Leopold Stokowski championed at that time.

In 1935, at the age of twenty-five, Mr. Pleasants succeeded Tubbs as musical editor of the *Evening Bulletin* and continued in that post until entering the
army in 1942. In addition to his work for the *Bulletin*, he was a regular contributor to *Modern Music* and was an occasional musical correspondent for
both the *New York Times* and the *New York Herald Tribune*. In 1940 he collab-

296   orated with Tibor Serly on the first definitive article on Béla Bartók to appear in the United States, published in *Modern Music.* After the war Pleasants settled in Europe, writing articles for the *New York Times, High Fidelity, HiFi Stereo Review,* and books.

The thesis of *The Agony of Modern Music* was summarized in "The Argument" in the front matter of the 1955 edition:

> Modern music is not modern and is rarely music. • It represents an attempt to perpetuate a European musical tradition whose technical resources are exhausted, and which no longer has any cultural validity. • That it continues to be composed, performed, and discussed represents self-deception by an element of society which refuses to believe that this is true. • The hopelessness of the situation is technically demonstrable, and contemporary composers are aware of it. • What makes their own situation hopeless is that they cannot break with the tradition without renouncing the special status they enjoy as serious composers. • That they have this status is the result of a popular superstition that serious music is by definition superior to popular music. • There is good music, indifferent music and bad music, and they all exist in all types of composition. • There is more real creative musical talent in the music of Armstrong and Ellington, in the songs of Gershwin, Rodgers, Kern and Berlin, than in all the serious music composed since 1920. • New music which cannot excite the enthusiastic participation of the lay listener has no claim to his sympathy and indulgence. Contrary to popular belief, all the music which survives in the standard repertoire has met this condition in its own time. • The evolution of Western music continues in American popular music, which has found the way back to the basic musical elements of melody and rhythm, exploited in an original manner congenial to the society of which it is the spontaneous musical expression. • And it has found the way back to the basic musical nature of the ordinary mortal, from whom music derives, by whom and for whom it is produced, and without whom it cannot and does not exist.

The artistic godfather of "The Argument" was not Gilbert Seldes but the British composer-critic Constant Lambert; Pleasants in fact dedicated a sequel to *The Agony of Modern Music,* the 1969 book *Serious Music—and All That Jazz!,* "to the memory of Constant Lambert (1905–1951), who, in *Music Ho! A Study of Music in Decline* (1934), was twenty years ahead of any of us in discerning the new crosscurrents in the evolution of Western music in the twentieth century." In that book, Lambert had praised the innate vitality of certain forms of popular music (although he had a curious blind spot for George Gershwin), especially jazz and African-American patterns, and expounded a brilliant antimodernist argument.

Born in 1905, Lambert was a Leonard Bernstein–like prodigy who composed successful ballets, symphonic music, and vocal and chamber music; was staff conductor of the Sadler's Wells ballet and the guest conductor of many orchestras; edited and arranged music; wrote books and essays and lectured on the radio; and was called by the distinguished musicologist Edward Dent in 1946 "the best all-around musician we have in this country." An alcoholic and diabetic, he died much too soon at age forty-five in 1951. His 1934 book, *Music Ho!*, written when he was only twenty-nine, with Rosenfeld's *Musical Portraits* stands as one of the two most precociously brilliant volumes ever written in music criticism, but it is superior to Rosenfeld in its composer's "inside" insights. Oddly enough, Lambert, himself a gifted modern composer Diaghilev had commissioned to write a ballet, took a retro position almost antithetical to Rosenfeld's: that the innovations of both atonalism and neoclassicism were parlor tricks to mask an essential lack of spontaneous emotional inspiration. Lambert appealed in the introduction to the first edition of his book for "a broader and more 'humane' critical attitude towards an art which, though the most instinctive and physical of all the arts, tends more and more to be treated as the intellectual preserve of the specialist." Further on, he wrote:

> The feverish fashionable reactions of postwar Paris, the mathematical revolutionary formulas of postwar Vienna, indicate that the average postwar composer has either nothing to say or does not know how to say it— possibly both. That so many works written today depend to such an unparalleled extent on the modern adaptation of academic device is a sign not of formal strength but of emotional weakness. . . .
>
> Schoenberg . . . in many ways is the most pedantic of modern composers. He has escaped from an academic set of rules only to be shackled by his own set of rules, and this self-imposed tyranny is taken over *en bloc* by his pupils. . . . I think it in the highest degree unlikely that atonalism will ever become an instinctive and natural idiom, part of our mental background, in the way that Debussy's idiom has become so—his mannerisms now being the property of every jazz hack. "So much the better," may think the followers of Schoenberg, Berg and Von Webern, but, after

all, the vulgarization of Debussy, like the vulgarization of Wagner, is a proof of the essentially solid basis on which these one-time revolutionaries built.

Following Lambert's lead, but without Lambert's brilliant analytical powers, Pleasants's *Agony* held as its basic premise that virtually all dissonant modern music was false and objectionable, an assault on the heritage of the great masters, and thus contemporary popular songwriters were the true inheritors of the tradition of the bond between composer and public. Pleasants went so far as to suggest that George Gershwin's so-called serious compositions (*Rhapsody in Blue, An American in Paris,* the Piano Concerto in F) were musically inferior to his Broadway songs, and that, likewise, Verdi's *Aida* and *Traviata* were artistically superior to his *Otello* and *Falstaff.*

What was Pleasants's reply to the fact that the inveighing first-night critical reviews that Nicolas Slonimsky had collected did not stand the test of time in so many cases? First, he asserted that Slonimsky had manipulated the historical record: for each of the notorious cases of masterpieces initially drubbed by critics—the premieres of *Carmen, Traviata, Butterfly,* and others—second or third productions shortly afterward were great successes, the original critical pan being due to a bad initial performance or a political "intrigue." To Slonimsky's list of famous critical misses, Pleasants counterpointed a litany of examples of immediate successes of the great works from Haydn and Mozart on to about 1900, also pointing out that in each case the composer made immediate money from his work (not always true). This blissful state of affairs—of artistic excellence justly and timely remunerated (which test, need we say, could barely be passed by many great works of literature and painting)—mysteriously ceased to occur after about 1910, strengthening Pleasants's argument, in his opinion, that the classical canon had effectively died by 1910.

The second part of Pleasants's response to Slonimsky went thus: "In former times contemporary music survived despite opposition from critics and professional musicians because the public liked it. Today it languishes despite critical and professional support because the public will have none of it." Thereby did Pleasants lambaste the whole microcosmos of modern music composers, performers, critics, conductors, publishers, university music departments, and grant-making foundations, as a petulant self-styled new academy that amounted to little more than a loud and obstreperous micro-elite claque. "Under normal competitive circumstances this sort of exclusive expert sponsorship would not suffice to effect the survival of so unpopular a phenomenon as modern music. In other fields today, in the theater, moving pictures, radio, television, literature, and architecture, survival is impossible without popular interest and approval.

"Only in painting and sculpture is professional opinion a similar monopoly," Pleasants added, not realizing that he was adumbrating the thesis of Tom Wolfe's book *The Painted Word,* to be published some twenty-five years later; the Wolfe book endorsed a similarly Tory view that modern art aesthetics were in effect being kept speciously alive in a hothouse environment through the organized efforts of an influential coterie. "Only in painting and sculpture does so bad a product get so much flattering professional attention," Pleasants added in 1955, overlooking the important difference that the abstract painters and sculptors who are the beneficiaries of such tastemakers are able to profit handsomely from the sale of their wares, unlike composers.

Not only was Pleasants suggesting that dissonance, atonality, and dodecaphony were shams perpetrated by composers who lacked creative imagination, but he extended the same critique to modern music's rhythm and instrumentation. He asserted that the Stravinskyan emancipation of the bar line and irregular pulsation were the rhythmic equivalents of the Schoenbergian harmonic emancipation from tonality, and accordingly were just as factitious and artificial; older music, from Bach's dance movements to Beethoven scherzi to Schubert ländler, had regular pulsation organically immanent in its materials and was thus rhythmically more natural. Similarly, the symphony orchestra's coloristic development from Berlioz on through Strauss provided the composer with a subterfuge out of his artistic impasse: it in effect endowed him with a makeup kit for painting over and thus masking his poverty of ideas. Music was becoming more orchestrated than composed; whereas the orchestral music of Mozart, Beethoven, and even Brahms sounded equally well in four-hand two-piano arrangements, the orchestral scores of Berlioz and Strauss didn't fare so well in piano reduction because stripped of their outer garments their structural poverty was laid bare (as though orchestration itself were not a fundamentally creative act, indissoluble from invention of any other kind).

The pop counter-reformation

The real meat of Pleasants's argument, however, and the nexus joining his polemic with those of both Constant Lambert and Gilbert Seldes, was his assertion that the real musical revolution of 1910 had occurred not in Vienna or Paris but in Chicago and New

300 Orleans. Jazz, and all of its popular music by-products, constituted the real artistic phenomenon of the new century: the European art music tradition had played itself out and was now being supplanted by another continent's influence. Oddly enough, Pleasants—himself the most *derrière garde* of reactionaries—by his own terms of argument was attempting to redefine the modernists not as revolutionaries but as reactionaries, desperately trying to shore up the European tradition against the tide of the times.

Pleasants spoke of a performers', not a composers', tradition, supplanting the European one. Thus, the Romantic notion of the singularity of the artist was less important than the artist's communality with society: ironically, a throwback to the European art style of pre-Renaissance times. Pleasants likened the jazz practice of improvisational creation to performance and compositional practices in earlier serious music—jam sessions were like improvised concerto grosso, and improvised solos in jazz arrangements were no different from improvisations of cadenzas in both instrumental and vocal European art music of earlier centuries. That there might be a fundamental difference between musical improvisation and composition Pleasants apparently cared not to address.

Echoing an opinion held by both Van Vechten and Lambert, Pleasants found in motion picture soundtrack composition both the anonymous communal quality that his new era's performers' aesthetic demanded, and the last functional societal role for the moribund European tradition, "where the descriptive and psychologically articulate character of its late traditions may be turned to profitable use without the requirement of originality, and where its incapacity any longer to yield substantial forms is compensated by the form of the screen narrative."

◿ Counterpunching

Henry Pleasants   *I find Mr. Pleasants' book a mixture of some true facts and a great deal of petulant prejudice. . . . If he thinks the jam session is the answer to what he is talking about, let me, as an old jazz man, assure him that as a steady diet it can get to be a crushing bore.*
—NORMAN DELLO JOIO

Pleasants created an uproar with his book and its daringly reactionary assertions. Professor Paul Henry Lang, who presided over the *New York Herald Tribune's* music page, devoted two Sunday articles to an emotional attack on the book and allowed its author a third Sunday's column in which to reply.

Olin Downes, who could little stomach Mahler, let alone Webern, and who liked certain jazz, devoted a Sunday *Times* piece to Pleasants, cautiously but not unreservedly endorsing his ideas. The gist of the public debate over the book, as one wag had it, was whether it was Henry Pleasants or the modern composer who should drop dead.

Pleasants held on to his ideas unregenerate in the face of all controversy. The sequel to *The Agony of Modern Music*, entitled *Death of a Music? The Decline of the European Tradition and the Rise of Jazz*, published in 1961, used as its epigraph a quote from Oswald Spengler's *The Decline of the West* (a work which, unlike Toynbee's *A Study of History*, investigates the history of music): "The sign of all living art, the pure harmony of 'will,' 'must' and 'can,' the self-evidence of the aim, the un-self-consciousness of the execution, the unity of the art and the Culture—all that is past and gone. . . . What is practiced as art today—be it music after Wagner or painting after Cézanne, Leibl and Menzel—is impotence and falsehood." Later, in his 1969 book, *Serious Music— and All That Jazz!*, he broadened the spectrum of his African-American/ popular music revolution to subsume contemporary rock and roll music, including, approvingly, the Beatles.

In a later edition of *The Agony of Modern Music*, which went through several printings over twenty years and sold well, Pleasants replied to his critics. He denied that he had meant

to equate popularity with quality. I do not. But I do believe that wide acceptance of a style or idiom is proof of its cultural vitality, regardless of its quality. There is now, within the framework of the American popular idiom, a wide range of quality, just as there always was within the European idiom. Now that the standard repertoire of orchestras, opera houses, choral societies and chamber groups is concentrated upon the surviving masterpieces, it is easy to overlook the masses of trash produced within the idiom when the idiom was still contemporary, and which enjoyed more or less passing popularity. Certainly much trash is being produced today within the American popular idiom, including a good deal of jazz, and has been produced throughout the century, but looking back . . . it seems equally certain that there has been much of quality, too. Generally speaking, it seems safe to observe that the most reliable criterion of quality is survival in the affection and esteem of succeeding generations—in other words, in the capacity of a given piece of music to appeal to more than the fallible fashions of a single year or a single generation.

Pleasants was not without supportive responses from a few musical dignitaries who endorsed at least some of his ideas. Besides Downes, Abram Chasins, the pianist, author, composer, broadcast commentator, and fellow musical conservative, took up some of Pleasants's arguments approvingly in his own books. Even the composer Marc Blitzstein allegedly said, according to Virgil Thomson, "He's right, but we're not taking it from him." But musical journalists like the composer Eric Salzman and the musicologist Joan Peyser continued to write articles and books that celebrated the modernist revolution of Stravinsky and Schoenberg as uncontroverted fact and received wisdom. At length Pleasants's aesthetic expatiations on modern music were relegated to his books and ignored by newspapers and magazines, for whom he was still freelancing as a vocal music expert at the end of the century. In 1996 John Rockwell recounted this conversation with Pleasants:

> Sometime in the late 1980s I was sitting in a London pub with the critic Henry Pleasants. Henry was morose. "You know, John," he said to me, "we lost." By that, he meant that a position he had long espoused, and which I admired without fully accepting, was showing few signs of prevailing in the musical *querelles des bouffons* of the time. . . . By "we lost," Henry meant that musical modernism was showing a disturbing tenacity, and that simultaneously the traditional pop he admired had been crushed by mindless rock bellowers.[15]

℘ Winthrop Sargeant, proto-neoconservative

Pleasants was a frank reactionary. Rosenfeld was a frank ultraprogressive. But Constant Lambert heralded something in between—call it neoconservatism—and by the 1950s American letters sorely needed someone like him. Into this breach stepped another critic generally known to have a lack of sympathy for atonality, the twelve-tone school, and most of the other "isms," but also known as an ex-musician with a broad cultural gauge. This was Winthrop Sargeant of the *New Yorker*. Sargeant's review of the first edition of *The Agony of Modern Music* contributed his own exposition of the modern music problem. After paraphrasing Pleasants's argument, Sargeant proceeded airily to discount it:

> I cannot quite accept Mr. Pleasants' notion that immediate popularity is today the sole criterion of artistic importance, since by that criterion one

could obviously arrive at the conclusion that, say, the *News* is more important literature than the work of our more thoughtful novelists. I cannot agree, either, that the cultivated listener who has developed a taste for symphonic or operatic music is likely to find a modern substitute for it in the arts of Dizzy Gillespie and Irving Berlin—two entirely different arts, by the way, each of which I find ingratiating enough, but both of which seem to me to lack the emotional vocabulary and intellectual ingenuity that the experienced concertgoer looks for in serious music.

He took Pleasants to task for being guilty of the same "Hegelian determinism" of the very music Pleasants was attacking:

[Pleasants] thinks of music not as the product of free, individual composers but as a sort of uniform substance emerging from some historical sausage grinder with the laws of sociological *Zeitgeist.* It is this attitude, it seems to me, that leads him to the fairly absurd conclusion that the contemporary composer is done for. In my opinion, the prevalent notion that the musical art is the result of social forces and is under some pressing necessity to progress or evolve is precisely what is wrong with "modern" music, for it has deprived the contemporary composer of his individuality as an artist. . . . Thus, I am afraid I cannot give any more credence to Mr. Pleasants' idea that the contemporary composer is doomed to become obsolete than I can to the atonalist's idea that he is doomed to write atonally.

What made these comments noteworthy was that Sargeant himself had been the butt of ridicule for being an unenlightened middlebrow. In *Expositions and Developments* by Stravinsky and Robert Craft, Stravinsky referred cryptically to Paul Henry Lang of the *Herald Tribune* as H. P. Langweilich and to Winthrop Sargeant as S. D. Deaf, referring punningly to Mr. Deaf's favorites as all "'giants': Giannini, Dello Joio, Giancarlo Menotti." The avant-garde critic Richard Kostelanetz in the *Yale Review* in 1969 referred to Sargeant disparagingly: "If Winthrop Sargeant can write superciliously in *The New Yorker,* 'The avant-garde composers of today range a long way—from Mr. Stravinsky, the last of the great figures of the twentieth century decadence, down to men like John Cage,' he suggests that not only are those musicians no good but also that they are beneath interest; therefore, he has excused both himself and his readers from any confrontations with the difficult questions and perceptions raised by modernist music." More sympathetically, Tim Page's *New York Times*

304   obituary on Sargeant's death in 1986 described him as "an articulate and independent conservative in his critical tastes. He was a champion of such consonant, directly emotive composers as Gian Carlo Menotti, Carlisle Floyd and
Vittorio Giannini." In the same obituary longtime *New Yorker* editor William
Shawn commented, "He will be remembered . . . for . . . his steadfast belief in
tonal music and his principled, philosophically grounded resistance to musical fashion."

Born in 1903, Sargeant was trained to be a musician; in youth he played
both the french horn and the violin and studied both in America and Europe.
In his early adult years Sargeant worked extensively as an orchestral violinist,
first with the San Francisco Symphony and later with other orchestras, including the New York Philharmonic under Toscanini. In his book *In Spite of Myself: A Personal Memoir* (1970), Sargeant listed Herz, Damrosch, Klemperer,
Busch, Furtwängler, Gabrilowitsch, Mengelberg, Beecham, Walter, and Krauss
as conductors he had played under, and of these intriguingly stated, "a few
were fakes." (He did refer, however, to Beecham as "highly intelligent," to
Mengelberg as a "masterful technician," and to Furtwängler and Toscanini as
"geniuses.")

Like Olin Downes, Sargeant at first worked as a music teacher before
slowly segueing into journalism. Even while still playing in orchestras, he began writing musical criticism, first for the *Brooklyn Daily Eagle,* then *Musical
America;* then he began a notable tenure for Time-Life publications, starting at
Time magazine in 1937 and in 1945 moving over to *Life,* where he wrote profiles
on nonmusical personalities and rubbed elbows at work with Whittaker
Chambers, whom he wrote about in his memoirs. He joined the *New Yorker* as
its chief music critic in 1949 and continued writing occasional pieces after Andrew Porter took over his job in the 1970s. Like both Lambert and Pleasants,
Sargeant was also an enthusiastic proponent of the artistic values of good jazz.
His book *Jazz: Hot and Hybrid,* published in 1938, was arguably the earliest serious treatment of the subject. Also like Lambert both a professional musician
and culturally broad-minded in scope, Sargeant wrote profiles in the *New
Yorker* of such nonmusicians as the anthropologist Margaret Mead and the
filmmaker Vittorio De Sica. In his later years he also labored prodigiously
learning Sanskrit well enough to publish his own English translation of the
Bhagavad Gita.

Sargeant expanded upon his earlier remarks about Pleasants's *Agony of
Modern Music* in the introduction to his book *Listening to Music,* an anthology of his *New Yorker* articles, published in 1958. While rejecting Pleasants's

obituary of art music, Sargeant somewhat sided with Pleasants in regard to the special "coterie" argument. He went on to say that certain dicta had become dogma in the contemporary music aesthetic, among them that "Experimentation in technique is one of the composer's most important functions. . . . the position has even been held that the primary purpose of the composer is to invent and discover new sounds or new arrangements of sound. In my opinion it is better to write music which may be trivial and vulgar than to write music which is meaningless. . . . The present situation is a little like the one that might obtain in the art of writing if some relentlessly knot-headed pedant, having discovered that Hemingway writes shorter sentences than Henry James did, found in this fact the basis of a great historical trend and decreed that sentences must consequently get shorter and shorter in the interest of artistic progress. . . . In a more widely understood art like literature, this sort of thing would have been laughed out of existence almost before it got started. After all, nobody speaks of 'modern' literature in the sense that people have for at least thirty years spoken of 'modern music,' or pretends that the technical fundamentals of the art of writing have changed, in any very radical way, since the time of Homer."

Sargeant was equally unafraid of slaying sacred cows of the standard repertoire: the last movement of Beethoven's Ninth he deemed "pervaded throughout by an atmosphere of self-conscious nobility and uplift that I find highly irritating"; the "March to the Scaffold" from Berlioz's *Symphonie fantastique* was "outrageously cheap when considered as a symphonic movement"; Liszt's *Totentanz* was "one of the most awful bits of musical rubbish ever set down on paper." Sargeant had his taste crotchets. As a symphonist Bruckner was "vastly superior to Brahms." He was mixed in his feelings about Aaron Copland's music, referring to *Appalachian Spring* as merely "interesting" but essentially trivial and dismissable as ballet music. But he was never doctrinaire: he liked Alban Berg despite the dodecaphony. Among American moderns he mentioned Barber, Roy Harris, and Paul Creston favorably; he liked Menotti because, though admitting his work was not "staggeringly original," it was "undoubtedly communicative." He was curiously negative about the influence of the teachings of Nadia Boulanger: "Mme. Boulanger's ubiquitous disciples . . . seem always to have subordinated emotional content to tricks of style and, in their anxiety to avoid the clichés of Romantic music, only to have replaced them with a set of modernistic clichés of their own."

However, Sargeant faltered here as a critic in the technical analysis he used to support his intuitive opinions. Thinking Stravinsky overrated and regard-

306   ing Stravinsky's technique of changing meters as "formalist" and expressively artificial, he apparently overlooked the fact that the music of Paul Creston, a composer he liked, is itself constructed in highly complex changing meters, with polyrhythms, beat subdivisions, and asymmetrical pulsation that can be as complicated as Olivier Messiaen's music, much less Stravinsky's. Had Sargeant really inspected the scores he reviewed *sans parti pris*, he would have known this immediately; for that matter, a trained musician need only listen to Creston's work to know this.

Sargeant *was* a trained musician: he just momentarily lapsed into sloppy, wish-fulfillment thinking. He sincerely believed that the music of his time most likely to have lasting value would be that of conservatives like Hanson, Giannini, and Creston. In the ensuing twenty years his influence as a taste arbiter was overridden by other journalists, particularly by the articles published in the *New York Times* Sunday Arts and Leisure section—which became the arbiter for new music once the *Herald Tribune* folded—by Joan Peyser and others affirming the pride of place of the Milton Babbitts, Elliott Carters, and Charles Wuorinens in the *Times*'s weltanschauung of new music. When Pierre Boulez became conductor of the New York Philharmonic, the Sargeant view was pushed farther back onto the shelf. But the pendulum swung around somewhat by the mid-1980s to tonal music, whereupon there were new performances and recordings of Creston, Hanson, and other composers Sargeant had favored. The postmodern synthesis had begun, and Sargeant's writings seem more timely in the late 1990s than they had in the 1960s, although he had less influence on backstage doings in the music world during the years when he wrote than did the critics advocating what he called "formalism."

ꙮ *John Rockwell and*
crossover criticism   Toward the end of Sargeant's career, critical camps began to divide between younger writers who had grown up after World War II liking both classical and pop music, and older writers weaned during the period between the two wars. Thence began a new statement of the century's rondo of the two critical sides: on the one side, what had begun at the century's outset as the futurists, turned the modernists, turned the avant-gardists, now finally became the school of the "cutting edge." On the other side, the school that Sargeant had popularized without naming, the descendants of Constant Lambert, became musical neoconservatives. The cutting-edge critics were unabashedly tolerant and even boosters of more un-

conventional, crossover, or "cutting edge" styles, while the neoconservatives, though open-minded and unprejudiced, were highly skeptical of the apocalyptic claims of the farthest-out composers, such as Boulez and Stockhausen. While the cutting-edge group had come of age in the notorious 1960s, the musical neocons had an older connection with the Western canon and tried to subsume both modernism and postmodernism into a larger aesthetic synthesis that looked both retrospectively and reaffirmatively at older, traditional musical values. In the last quarter of the twentieth century in America the outstanding exemplars of this antinomy were the critics John Rockwell of the *New York Times* and Samuel Lipman of the magazines *Commentary* and *New Criterion.*

Rockwell is not the first ever classical music critic of the "cutting edge," "downtown" sensibility that modern music inherited from the art world of the previous generation—clearly, both Rosenfeld and Van Vechten are his artistic grandfathers and Gilbert Seldes his uncle, and similar critics, among them in New York the composer-critics Eric Salzman of the *Times* and *Herald Tribune* back in the 1950s and 1960s, Tom Johnson and Carman Moore of New York's *Village Voice* in the 1960s and 1970s, and the prolific freelance critic Richard Kostelanetz, made kindred contributions. But Rockwell was the first classical music critic employed by the *New York Times* to use that paper's stature as a culture pulpit to filibuster and evangelize in Sunday articles for the cause of postmodern crossover. Coming from the good gray *Times,* rather than the underground press, this was a sea change.

Born in 1940, Rockwell grew up in San Francisco. After graduating from Harvard he returned to the Bay Area to pursue a doctorate in cultural history at the University of California at Berkeley. After receiving his degree he began his journalism career in the late 1960s as a classical music and dance critic for the *Oakland Tribune* and then the *Los Angeles Times;* but his greatest influence started when he went to work for the *New York Times* in 1972. He wrote both classical and rock reviews for the paper, the first *Times* critic ever to have done so. In 1992 he became the paper's European cultural correspondent. He left the paper in 1994 to become the director and planner of the Lincoln Center Festival—a deluxe summer smorgasbord of cutting-edge, formerly non-"uptown" art attractions of international provenance—but early in 1998 left Lincoln Center to return to the *Times* as editor of the Sunday Arts and Leisure section.

Prior to Rockwell, the *Times* had always toed a strict line between critics reviewing classical and critics reviewing popular music. The *Times*'s John S. Wilson would write only about popular music and Raymond Ericson about

308 classical, for instance. But Rockwell's versatility, eclecticism, and genuine Whitmanesque enthusiasm for all manifestations of music, his ability to competently cover opera, symphony, and piano recitals, as well as to comment knowledgeably on jazz musicians like Keith Jarrett and Ornette Coleman, made him a unique figure in the annals of the journal of record. True, the composers Gunther Schuller and David Amram had written books about new music from a dualistic serious/pop perspective, but they were not journalistic critics.

Though Rockwell wrote myriad daily reviews of recitals and concerts over the years, it was his think pieces in which he subtly proselytized for the admission of popular forms to the academy that left his imprint on modern music journalism. In his *Times* columns and particularly in his book *All American Music* (1983), Rockwell undertook a critical approach so ecumenical that it was almost a revolution in itself in music criticism: an almost systematically panoramic approach to covering the gamut of composing styles in America, from the most serious arcana, whether accepted by concertgoers en masse or no, to light music so mass market no other classical music critic would have dared to write about it.

To some extent the liberal/neocon opposition was simply a generational thing. As the counterculture of the 1960s firmly entrenched itself ("Rock 'n' Roll Is Here to Stay," went one song), journalists like Robert Christgau in the *Village Voice* and Greil Marcus in *Rolling Stone* started applying the same kind of studied prose to rock music reviewing that classical music critics had always brought to bear on the masterpieces of Western music (though a highbrow style of writing about jazz had already been practiced for some time by such writers as Gary Giddins and Leonard Feather). The unparalleled attention the songs of the Beatles received in the mid-1960s from cultural luminaries like Norman Mailer and serious composers like Ned Rorem, and the highbrow legitimation given the new cultural value of "camp" by the intellectual Susan Sontag, also helped loosen the theretofore rigid boundaries between high and low art and repave the cultural high road with the primrose path of pop.

It was inevitable that a classical music critic of younger years would import some of this sensibility into the classical music criticism mandarinate. In *All American Music* Rockwell offered as his critical apologia that as a teenager he had been a fan of

> "Hit Parade" and other pop music as well as classical music. . . . I . . . came
> to believe that experimental music, vernacular music and non-Western
> music were important and enjoyable, too, and that a "music critic" had

no business excluding entire traditions that most of the world thought of
as "music" just because they didn't conform to his own cultural prejudices. . . . I sense a growing group of musicians, music-lovers and academics for whom the seemingly radical presuppositions that underlie this
book are already taken for granted, at least subconsciously. . . . At the
same time that classical composers, recoiling from the philistinism of the
marketplace . . . have retreated into an ever more arcane complexity, an
audience with ever more basic tastes has grown up beneath them.

Rockwell went so far as to suggest that a new type of communal creativity was
on the cusp of supplanting the lone individual creator mode of High Romanticism:

Collaborative composition is not necessarily superior to individual creation. . . . [But] as with the best rock bands, it seems that the tensions and
complementary attributes still inspire a creativity that would be impossible for the members on their own. . . . The best recent example of this
synergistic phenomenon is the Beatles, none of whom equaled on his own
what the group had been able to achieve—even when, in its last years,
every "Beatles" song was in fact composed by an individual. There was
still something about the group identity that enhanced . . . the creation.

Unapologetic in his liking for rock music and jazz, Rockwell was, nevertheless, a sometimes enthusiastic proponent of ultramodern serious composers. No Henry Pleasants he, yet Rockwell was not doctrinaire or uncritical
in his openness and could at times flail modernism with an echo of *The Agony
of Modern Music*'s critique of Eurocentric snobbism:

The obsessive knottiness of [Elliott Carter's] music suggests something
more troubling. That is the too ready equation in our culture between complexity and excellence, and between pedigree and artistic
worth. Among our academics and lovers of Europe, among those who
worry that American culture is but a poor transplant of the European
original, there is an instinctive veneration of tradition and busy ingenuity, and a concomitant distrust of the simple. These inclinations are an
intellectualized extension of the virtuoso's love for showy display. In the
absence of a sure personal feeling for what is artistically meaningful, listener, performer and composer all regress to the ornate and pedantic exposition of craft. (p. 43)

310   Rockwell unabashedly found in popular music more sheer artistic vitality than in music bred in the hothouse concert environment: "Bob Dylan's
'Blowin' in the Wind' or one of Bruce Springsteen's autobiographical laments
says more about everyday life in this country than Frederic Rzewski will probably ever know. And says it more 'artistically,' as well." Further describing the
work of the political theater/neoromantic avant-garde composer Rzewski, he
implied not only that the actual musical results of such parodistic "neotonal"
usages were artificial and bloodless, but that trying to solve the audience problem by adopting a petit bourgeois political stance to get the "little man's" ear,
as Rzewski and others had tried, was palpably absurd: "The workers *don't* want
to listen to highbrow avant-gardism, no matter how sincerely leftist a composer may believe himself to be. Given a choice—and they were, at Otto Klemperer's experimental Kroll Opera in Berlin between 1927 and 1931—workers
will take *La Bohème* over *Erwartung* any time. . . . People have always shown a
penchant for simple, clear, tuneful music" (p. 92).

An intelligent eclectic, Rockwell both beats the drum for the cutting edge
and actually joins company with the neoconservative school in criticizing the
farthest reaches of modernism—whether the chaotic school of Cage or the hy-
percontrolled school of Babbitt—as sometimes not meeting commonsense
litmus tests of musicality:

> Not all of it . . . has been very interesting to *hear:* neither "ear music" nor
> "eye music" but, perhaps, "head music," in that it seemed most interest-
> ing as ideas for pieces rather than as pieces per se. The very nature of
> Cage's esthetic discounts the importance of finished craftsmanship. . . .
> Still, Cage shows a disturbing indifference to how his music actually
> sounds, which in turn suggests a curious parallelism to Babbitt and his
> lesser disciples, in other respects so completely his opposites. The simi-
> larity has to do with a systematic pursuit of abstraction. Both Babbitt and
> Cage reject the comfortable familiarities of tonal music. For both, ab-
> straction can help jostle and expand a listener's consciousness and per-
> ceptual powers.

Accordingly, Rockwell devoted considerable space in *All American Music*
to a composer who didn't even aspire to the concert hall but rather used elec-
tronics to create everyday sound environments in public spaces like New York's
Times Square. This individual, Max Neuhaus—who may unwittingly be the
true embodiment of what Hindemith was referring to by *Gebrauchmusik*—

was quoted thus: "I'm not interested in making music exclusively for musicians or musically initiated audiences. I am interested in making music for people. We have been in an area of over-intellectualization for a long period, to the point of absurdity." Rockwell added, "All of this presupposes a populist ideology, based on an impatience with the elitism that characterizes most American composers."

~ *Samuel Lipman,*
   postmodern neo-
   Arnoldian

While John Rockwell carried the flag for innovation and non-European aesthetic values, musical Toryism still had its own standard-bearers. In his 1987 bestseller *The Closing of the American Mind* the scholar Allan Bloom devoted considerable space to lamenting what he regarded as the scandal of the younger generation's almost total loss of interest in classical music. Bloom would regard Rockwell's critical approach of equalizing the expressive claims of high and low culture as anathema, fraudulent. Bloom was an exponent of the approach to high culture first and best espoused by Matthew Arnold.

The late Samuel Lipman took a gentler approach than Professor Bloom's to propounding a neo-Arnoldian world view, but he rang other alarm bells. Lipman was notable among intellectual music critics because he was no ivory tower intellectual. Although the author of books and long articles on music for *Commentary,* the *New Criterion* (of which he was publisher), and the *Times Literary Supplement,* he was also a concert pianist adept enough in the performance of knotty new music to have given the New York premiere in 1965 of Elliott Carter's crabbed Piano Concerto. As professional literary intellectuals go, Lipman's musical pedigree was unparalleled: trained as a conservatory student, he studied piano with Rosina Lhévinne, conducting with Pierre Monteux, and composition with Darius Milhaud. He taught widely and was on the artist faculties of the Aspen and Waterloo music festivals, and his wife, Jeaneane Dowis, is a noted piano pedagogue at New York's Mannes School. Only Gunther Schuller, the pianist Charles Rosen, and the conductor–college president–*Musical Quarterly* editor Leon Botstein, among contemporary literary intellectuals writing about music, can compare to Lipman in hard-core musical training, hands-on concert experience, and scholarly erudition.

Lipman's observations on the state of modern music were unique among antimodernist critics in not being ex cathedra armchair intellectual pronouncements but rather spoken straight from the saddle of a performing mu-

312   sician who had played the stuff before paying audiences and had experienced firsthand the *frissons* of the response. In his 1979 book *Music after Modernism* he wrote:

> The evidence from concert programs and the box office is ubiquitous. . . . [there has been an] almost total failure of music written in the last generation to find a wide audience among music lovers or even practicing musicians. It is this vacuum, which has furthered the exhaustion, through overperformance, of a standard nineteenth-century repertory, and prompted the frenzied search for the new among the old rather than the new among the new. . . . A performer's career can no longer be advanced, but rather only harmed, by any association with new music. Such new music as is programmed is played either by musicians of the second level of public renown or—and then only occasionally—by stars making a quick descent into charity. No matter by whom it is performed, the new music is hastily learned and quickly forgotten. . . .
>
> The evidence for this pessimistic evaluation exists all around us. There is no audience—enthusiastic, wide, committed, and paying—for the music of the last sixty years. While performers, themselves subject to lessening enthusiasm from the audience, can make careers only by concentrating on the old and avoiding the new, composers exist only in the protective embrace of foundations, universities, and government arts funding agencies. So plain is the situation that it deserves description and analysis from more than the standpoint of those who, like Henry Pleasants (in *The Agony of Modern Music*) believe that the true musical culture of our time is popular music. (p. vii)

Lipman's world-weariness with the problematic difficulties of making the tones sound in performance clearly stems directly from battle fatigue in the trenches:

> Anyone who has had anything to do with the performance of new music knows just how tacky most of these renditions actually are, and how approximate the fulfillment of the composer's notes and performance directions. . . . While modern music is indeed hard to perform, there is no reason to suppose that it is harder for us than the new music of the nineteenth century was for the performers who first had to play it. Certainly

composers, then as now, complained bitterly about the performances they were accorded. It would therefore seem likely that such works as the Beethoven symphonies were themselves mangled on the concert stage early in their lives. . . . And yet the masterpieces established themselves.

Lipman had a view completely different from Rockwell's of the vitality of contemporary popular music as it relates to the old classical aesthetic:

It is the fashion today to see a convergence of serious and popular music, and to cite such figures as Steve Reich and Philip Glass as evidence of that convergence. Such a wishful synthesis not only muddies the facts, but also serves to hide the motives of the prophets and seers who have been dealing in the vision of these two musics growing ever closer together. While it is clear—at least to this writer—that serious music still exists as a separate and definable genre, there can be little doubt that recent years have seen an enormous growth of popular music of various kinds, and that this growth has made the largest possible inroads on an increasingly disorganized and doubt-ridden elite. The privileged young, as part of the goal of downward cultural mobility, seek to imitate the styles of assorted groups of underdogs, and the result is a pop culture based on musics at once vulgar, temporary, and corrosive. (p. 222)

For Lipman, the avant-garde, modernistic aesthetic was "a failed ideology" that "carried no audience with it," with "two . . . central preoccupations . . . : freedom—expressed internally as experimentation and externally as social provocation—and order—advocated as a means of extracting an aesthetic product from an originally anarchic insight." What led out of this impasse was a postmodernism that could be broken down into three types: the "aurally sensuous, the revolutionary-political, and the pop-hopeful."

Thus Lipman saw George Crumb and his vogue as "an advance backward from avant-gardism to impressionism." Crumb's music, "purged of all these extramusical [i.e., textual] elements . . . sounds at its best like warmed-over Debussy. . . . But at the same time it is impressionism with a difference: for this new emphasis on sheer sound is not rooted, as was the music of Debussy, in a still creative nineteenth-century musical culture." As for minimalism itself, "Whether the experience of this music is meant to substitute for or enhance

314 drug usage, the first impression a listener gains is boredom. The music goes on at great length, changes little, and achieves no noticeable climax."

Like Rockwell, Lipman clearly discerned the stylistic link between high modernism in music and abstract expressionism in the art world; talking of Stockhausen and Cage, he wrote, "the theater in which composers were now involved was much closer, in its emphasis in improvisation, to the idea of action painting as a process stemming from the painter's unconscious and performed by the body upon the canvas."

But rather than find such accomplishments estimable sheerly by dint of their daring and novelty, as Rockwell was disposed to, Lipman tended to view avant-garde techniques and procedures as not meeting the test of musicality. He even suggested that the new playing techniques were unconsciously adopted as an angry "reaction formation," in psychoanalytical parlance, to the end of the Western canon—a formulation not unlike Henry Pleasants's.

> For the avant-garde after 1945 (basing itself solidly on pre–World War II developments) new aural possibilities—pursued in the name of the liberation of sound from the tyranny of music—became, to a historically unparalleled extent, an end in themselves. . . . instruments [are used] in untraditional ways involving hitting or rubbing them in order to produce sounds, and in the case of winds and brass, singing, humming, and speaking into them at the same time as tones are being blown. For all the skill involved in the production of sound by such means, the total effect resembles nothing so much as a tuneless one-man band. . . . the whole panoply of performance techniques based upon aggression—hitting and banging instruments under the guise of using them as percussion—reflects only the widespread dissatisfaction and anger with traditional music among the avant-garde.

Lipman staked out an indictment against high modern music that was far more reasoned than Henry Pleasants's, and without Pleasants's special pleading for jazz and pop. He was also one of the few music critics of recent years to reassess the role of art music in the ecology of postmodern society: the funding structures, the government institutions impinging on music, the tastemaking apparatuses, and so on. He was scrupulously independent and free in his thinking, fearless about not following camps; in one essay he not only stood alone among highbrow critics in singing the praises of the score to Menotti's opera *Goya*, but excoriated the entire critical battalion who savaged the opera,

chiding them for their unexamined and self-contradictory prejudices about   315
Menotti and modern opera. Lipman will be sorely missed.

However arguable the case for African-American vernacular forms as the new
aesthetic direction, Pleasants perhaps made an elemental error in ignoring the
idea that great art has always been addressed to the elite—not a demographic
elite, but an elite of intellectual understanding. The litmus test of mass appreciation cannot ever sensibly be advanced as the sole criterion for greatness in
art. Ironically, Pleasants's forty-year-old argument that jazz—in its pure, original, uncommercial form—was the true art music of the twentieth century,
that the African-American aesthetic had supplanted the Euro-American tradition, took on, in the multicultural 1990s, a new, so-called politically correct
meaning that he undoubtedly never intended.

The critics both reflect the climate and help make the climate for the performance of music. What could be said to be the net result of Rockwell and
Lipman is that by the 1990s a kind of halfway point between them had been
reached in music performance. While new music pockets and ghettos still persisted and had influence, they were still ill attended by the general concertgoing public. At the same time pop crossover forms were even more ascendant.
The Kronos Quartet, a classical string quartet who played both modernist and
postmodernist, minimalist music, was actually dually marketed as a pop act in
most recordings and some concert venues and as a straight classical group in
most concert venues and some recordings. Postmodern "neo-isms" of every
stripe were ascendant, serialism and its siblings on the outs.

Perhaps, then, Messrs. Lipman and Rockwell both got it right. Perhaps the
very dialectical tensions between this century's critics of the musical left and
right have acted as a checks and balances system. The progressive critics,
through their articulate advocacy, have forced the newest musics into performance and tastemaker consideration. The evolutionist neoconservative critics,
through their countertendencies, have corrected for the excesses of the revolu-
tionists by retrieving the best non-avant-garde art.

As to the question, Where has the critical argument for a separate Afro-
Asiatic/pop/vernacular music tradition taken the classical music critic as the
year 2000 approaches—the classical music critic whose job hitherto has always been to heighten appreciation of Western classical music—that subject
segues in our final chapter.

11 *The Postmodern Synthesis*

Whither the Vanishing
Classical Music Critic?

In the arts, and especially in music, the cusp of the millennium is an age as yet without a zeitgeist. If it's the postmodern era, then what, exactly, is postmodernism? A rejection of high modernism in favor of high vernacularism, à la Henry Pleasants? A pluralistic coexistence of high with low, à la John Rockwell? A recrudescence of late Romanticism with a phoenixlike revival of tonality? Is postmodernism the gospel of the death knell to European high art? A culture of anticulture? Or is it some colloidal suspension of all of the above?

Where is the classical music critic left in this shuffle? What is the canon now? How does one write about it? How does one persuade new audiences to appreciate classical music? Where are those audiences? In fact, where are the critics?

There are far fewer newspapers today than fifty years ago in the United States, and fewer than one hundred salaried classical music critics. By comparison, in the 1930s New York City still had so many daily newspapers and so many assistant music critics that not only was there a standard textbook on the profession—Oscar Thompson's *Practical Musical Criticism* (1934)—but that book devoted considerable space merely to the problem of being a subaltern critic (for example, how to cover that umpteenth mediocre performance of Beethoven's Fifth that the first-string critic didn't have to attend). In addition to the myriad newspaper critics, each of the music periodicals of the time— *Musical America,* the *Courier,* the *Etude*—employed several full-time music critics. As recently as 1969 the *Washington Star* employed a staff of thirteen classical music reviewers, and this on but one of two newspapers in a city that is not the nerve center of classical music in America.

Albert Cohen, managing director of the Music Critics Association of

North America as of this writing, states that many newspapers in the 1990s hire a pop music critic before they hire a classical music critic. Increasingly, classical music criticism is being farmed out to freelancers; the *Los Angeles Times* does it, the *San Francisco Chronicle* does not. Cohen cites a typical 1996 New Jersey example of the fruits of such a classical freelance arrangement at a single newspaper—eight reviews, four feature articles, and four Sunday columns a month—netting twenty thousand dollars a year for the contributor (sans benefits), while a staff pop music critic at the same newspaper is paid a salary in the range of fifty thousand dollars. Of current Music Critics Association of North America members, about two-thirds are freelance, one-third salaried. Cohen estimates that there are currently about one thousand active classical music critics in this country, full- and part-time, staff and freelance.

The dumbing-down of the newspaper—emblematic historical podium for the classical music critic—is a phenomenon that has been well documented elsewhere. As previously noted, diminution in classical music listening and appreciation by college students was a prime exhibit in the 1987 Allan Bloom best-seller, *The Closing of the American Mind.* Furthermore, where stands the function of the music critic and the role of classical music appreciation in a postmodern, postindustrialized society where individuals and families are increasingly cocooned within their personal computers, Walkmans, and car stereos rather than attending live concerts, and playing synthesizers is replacing taking lessons on traditional musical instruments for America's children? A society where music appreciation is repeatedly eliminated from elementary and secondary public school budgets around the country and the NEA's very existence is under siege? In an era where the print medium, the traditional and original medium for music critics, is increasingly obsolescent, and classical FM radio stations are folding? Whither the classical music critic, indeed.

The first alternate route for music critics: Phonograph record reviewing

To be sure, in asking "whither," one cannot just lament the litany above but must backpedal to the 1930s, when newspaper critics began to review 78-rpm records. Ultimately, reviewing recorded music became almost as important as reviewing live music. The two critics most responsible for this sea change were B. H. Haggin and Irving Kolodin. Haggin published the earliest consumer guide to recordings, *Music on Records,* in 1938. Kolodin (1908–

318   88), who had been a critic and protégé of W. J. Henderson at the *New York Sun,* started reviewing records there and published *A Guide to Recorded Music* in 1941. When he went to the *Saturday Review* in 1947 he began reviewing the new 33-rpm long-playing records. Kolodin was the first critic in American history to attain a prestige equivalent to that of the Old Guard by writing more about recordings than live music (though he was also a New York Philharmonic program annotator and the author of books about the Metropolitan Opera). Trade papers like *Cash Box* and *Downbeat* also began running record reviews in the 1940s, and by the 1950s such specialized record review magazines as the *American Record Guide, HiFi Stereo Review,* and *High Fidelity* had wide readerships and impressively credentialed writers. Later, other such magazines appeared—*Ovation, Opus, Keynote, Fanfare*—but by the mid-1990s only *Fanfare* and *American Record Guide* survived as dedicated classical review magazines.

Some of the reviewers for these magazines were moonlighting salaried newspaper critics, but others were high-volume contributors who wrote copiously enough to earn semi-livelihoods from these publications, as well as attain reputations as distinguished music critics without ever needing to contribute to newspapers. A record-reviewing critic like Harris Goldsmith, who has steadily written for *High Fidelity* and other magazines since the early 1960s, has over some thirty-five years poured forth a cataract of prose more akin to the vast output of a Krehbiel, Hale, or Henderson than to any contemporary newspaper critic, not only in sheer volume but in the intricate musicianly vetting of detail. A brilliant writer and discerning musical analyst, Goldsmith, also a busy teacher, solo pianist, and chamber performer and coach, has probably heard as many live concerts in New York in the last forty years as any newspaper critic who ever lived, but has lamentably had the opportunity to write up only a small percentage of them for record review periodicals that still carry live performance reviews, such as *American Record Guide.* Critics like Goldsmith and many other fine writers for these publications are afforded the space that modern newspaper critics sadly lack, and they are carrying the banner of musical connoisseurship for a small but discriminating audience.

With the arrival of the compact disc in the 1980s, recorded classical music became an even larger share of the classical music pie; by the mid-1990s it seemed as though every composer history had forgotten had been resurrected on a compact disc reviewed in *Fanfare.* Since many of these revived works were likelier to get a hearing on disc than in live performance, record critics in the 1990s were assuming an even more powerful role, that of retro-canon-makers. At the same time, they were receding further and further from view of the mass public, who formerly encountered them in their daily newspapers and (at least in the 1930s and 1940s) on the radio.

∾ *Black classical music critics*
In a multicultural era when European art models—the source of virtually all the basic classical music repertoire—have been bashed by some as inherently elitist and antiegalitarian, it is interesting to learn that there is a history of classical music criticism in the black press. African-American-owned and -operated newspapers in America go back before the Civil War (in the North, of course). Most have been weeklies, and many had transient lives, but by the early 1900s a few—the *New York Age,* the *Chicago Defender,* the *Pittsburgh Courier*—sustained circulations in the hundreds of thousands. Integration eventually did come to the newsroom, but there still are African-American newspapers today, though fewer of them than in their heyday of the pre–civil rights, pre-integration era, when they tended to be known in that era's nomenclature as the negro press. Such negro papers as the *Oakland Post,* the *Michigan Chronicle,* the *Chicago Defender,* the *Chicago New Crusader,* the *New York Amsterdam News,* and others frequently had classical music reviews and critics.

Sylvester Russell (1860s?–1930) was possibly the first black musical journalist to write about classical music extensively. A church choir singer, college educated, he wrote both music and drama criticism for the *Freeman* of Indianapolis and the *Chicago Defender.* Russell "was a pioneer among black critics; his columns bristled with genuine critical commentary, which earned him many enemies. More than once he was physically assaulted because of his criticism, but he stoutly defended his position and refused to join the ranks of those who praised black artists no matter how poor their production. . . . He was reputed to have a private collection which listed the names of all the colored entertainers who had 'passed' for white and had moved into the white world."[1]

As early as 1902 there was a black music periodical modeled on *Musical America,* the *Etude,* and the *Musical Courier:* the *Negro Musical Journal.* The first prominent black journalist to cross over into the white classical music press was probably Cleveland Allen (1887–1953), a South Carolinian who studied at New York University in the early 1920s and wrote music criticism for the black paper the *New York Age* and, as a New York stringer, for the *Chicago Defender* and the *Freeman.* During the 1920s Allen was a regular contributor to

320 *Musical America.* After Allen probably the most significant black musical journalist was Nora Holt (1885–1974). A Harlem Renaissance personage and close friend of Carl Van Vechten (who based a character in one of his novels upon her), Holt, described in appearance as "blond creole," had a colorful life: multiple marriages, a long stint as a nightclub entertainer, and so forth. But she was also a serious classical music student and educator. She obtained a master of music degree at Chicago Musical College in the 1910s and went on to study with Nadia Boulanger at Fontainebleau. She was music critic for the *Chicago Defender* from 1917 to 1921 and, from the mid-1940s, the *New York Amsterdam News's* music critic. Holt produced a classical show on the black radio station WLIB-FM in New York from 1953 until 1964 entitled "Nora Holt's Concert Showcase"—making her in effect the Deems Taylor of Harlem.

Nora Holt was the only black member of the New York Music Critics Circle during the years of that organization, from the 1940s to the early 1960s, but she never moved over to the mainstream press. Music critics from the black press, however, participated with representatives from the national media in May 1947 in a symposium on music criticism given at Harvard University. The only African-American who was a standing classical music critic for a major urban market newspaper before the 1970s was Collins George of the *Detroit Free Press.* One of Nora Holt's protégés, the European-trained Raoul Abdul, who for a while pursued a career as a concert baritone, segued into the chief music critic position at the *Amsterdam News* in 1975.

By the mid-1970s there were several African-American critics in the Music Critics Association of North America. The black critic with the highest public profile was undoubtedly the composer-critic Carman Moore. Trained at Oberlin and Juilliard, Moore taught at various institutions and wrote music criticism for New York's weekly *Village Voice* in the late 1960s and early 1970s; he also freelanced articles for the *New York Times* and *Vogue.* Meanwhile, he was busily garnering performances of his music in avant-garde venues. In 1975 Boulez premiered Moore's orchestra piece *Wildfires and Field Songs,* which the New York Philharmonic had commissioned for ten thousand dollars. Moore might be said to be an African-American critic on the Virgil Thomson model: a composer whose prose presence in influential print media increased his renown and helped him get performances.

ᔕ *Women classical music critics*   We have already looked at the role the renaissance woman and pioneer feminist Margaret Fuller played among the New England transcendentalists as editor of the *Dial* in the 1840s: she authored articles about classical music. But in this she was not unique among women of her time. In the 1840s the *New York Herald* publisher James Gordon Bennett's wife, Henrietta Agnes Crean, appeared in print as Mrs. James Gordon Bennett. Said pianist Henri Herz in his 1846 memoirs, *My Travels in America,* of Mrs. Bennett as critic, "Into her work she often put much feeling, sometimes ingenious perception, always vivacity, and occasionally opinions which bordered on violence. For her, you were either a demigod or you were less than nothing. There was no intermediary point."

One of the most prominent Chicagoan music critics of the mid-nineteenth century, according to W. S. B. Mathews, was the vironymic Mrs. O. L. Fox. And a Bostonian contemporary of Agnes Crean's was Cornelia Walter, editor and music reviewer of the *Boston Evening Transcript,* one of that city's earliest penny dailies. She was a personal friend of the German-American composer Anthony Philip Heinrich, a forgotten creator who in pre-1850 America was popularly considered something of a stateside Beethoven. Of a June 13, 1846, concert of Heinrich's orchestral music given in Boston, the composer himself wrote that "the musicians of Boston have in their zeal and refined accomplishment nearly chopped off my head. . . . the imperfect, nay slovenly, confused execution of my orchestral works in Boston, I cannot accept." Of this same performance, however, Walter claquishly wrote, "The various compositions of the venerable artist were rendered in a manner which showed that the performers had entered into the feelings of the dreamy and enthusiastic musician, and nothing was wanted of that energy and precision which could alone carry off the peculiarities of the music. They played well because they loved the man for whose benefit they played."[2]

We have noted how the *New York Post* critic Henry T. Finck's wife, Abbie Cushman, wrote so many of his reviews that she came to be regarded as his alter ego by those few in on the secret. It was also the *Post* that engaged the celebrated pianist Olga Samaroff (1882–1948) to take over the chief music critic reins in 1926 from the British critic Ernest Newman, who had briefly replaced Henry Finck upon his 1924 retirement. At the time, Samaroff (née Lucy Hickenlooper of Texas—Olga Samaroff was a stage name) was hired not because she was a woman but because an injury to her left arm had forced her to cancel her concert engagements.

Samaroff, no shrinking violet (she was for a time married to Leopold Stokowski), engendered much controversy during her two-year tenure at the *Post* by her outright criticism of her journalistic colleagues and by her staunch refusal to write reviews of any performances that she felt were mediocre. She

322   recounted some twenty years later at the 1947 Harvard music criticism symposium:

> My failure to write about bad performances was one of the things that caused the impression of a preponderance of favorable reviews in my columns. Incidentally, it aroused just as much resentment in the neglected musician as an adverse criticism. Even the advertising manager of the Post rebuked me for it. But I stoutly refused to write about something simply because people had paid for an advertisement in the paper. I maintained that they had already received value for their money. The paper owed them no more.
>
> Mr. Chotzinoff [then of the *World*] followed a different line. His praise was reserved for things above the timber line, and it was thrown into effective relief by his well-nigh unremitting condemnation of everything else. . . . Mr. Chotzinoff once devoted considerable space in an article to what he called my "indulgent attitude." . . . I replied with some asperity in my column. . . .
>
> When the music critic whose writings are prevailing severe in the matter of censure bestows praise, his favorable review has a special value. It can make an artist. It can launch a composer. By the same token, if the critic who takes what Mr. Chotzinoff called "an indulgent attitude" writes an *unfavorable* review, the effect is devastating.[3]

Samaroff's policy of not covering bad performances was the expression of a practicing musician who knew firsthand what a roasting could do to a musician's opportunities. She also told the Harvard audience in 1947 that her reviews were persistently rewritten by somebody at the copy desk at the *Post,* stating that she suspected the culprit was someone simply ignorant of and unsympathetic to classical music; some contemporary exegetes may read in a different interpretation. Was she too outspoken? Did she refuse to kowtow to the old-boy network? While still at the *Post* she made several iconoclastic suggestions, including advocating a rotating system of guest critics from other cities so as to free long-resident critics from any taint of local power corruption. Her ideas fell on deaf ears. After only two years, but many rejections of her suggestions for improvements, Samaroff returned to teaching piano at Juilliard. A few years later, her nemesis, Chotzinoff, took over her old job at the *Post.*

Though women have always freelanced in classical musical journalism, they have never seemed as numerous in full-time staff positions as in dance, drama, literary, film, and art criticism. But their numbers have increased grad-ually. Samaroff's student Harriett Johnson eventually became music critic of the *New York Post.* Then there is Claudia Cassidy in Chicago. Later, Shirley Fleming became editor of *Musical America.* In recent years many women have been chief critics of major newspapers: the late Karen Monson of the *Chicago Daily News,* Nancy Malitz of the *Detroit News,* Willa Conrad of the *Newark Star-Ledger.* Samaroff was a fine writer and a judicious observer whose criti-cism should not be judged in any way other than for its literary and musicianly excellence. But her career in retrospect raises interesting questions about how women who practice criticism may be perceived. She seems to have received more animus for her allegedly "easy" reviews than did Henry T. Finck for his legendary "soft touch," for instance. Did her male colleagues resent her le-nience more for her femaleness or for her collegial deference to her fellow practicing musicians? A contemporary parallel to Olga Samaroff may be found in the dual career of the San Francisco Bay Area's Sarah Cahill, a concert pi-anist who is also a music critic for the *East Bay Express* and several magazines, and who, also like Samaroff, has lectured at symposiums on criticism. She writes:

> I'm afraid that some of us female critics are still battling what Virginia Woolf called "The Angel in the House." Woolf says, "You cannot review even a novel without having a mind of your own, without expressing what you think to be the truth about human relations, morality, sex. And all these questions, according to the Angel in the House, cannot be dealt with freely and openly by women; they must charm, they must conciliate, they must—to put it bluntly—tell lies if they are to succeed." Things have changed of course since Virginia Woolf's time, but I think we women are still trained in some sense to find the best in people and make only that known to others.[4]

One of the most versatile and accomplished women in contemporary classical music journalism, though not a critic, is Joan Peyser, who has been *Musical Quarterly* editor (1977–84), an influential journalist, and a biogra-pher. Peyser studied musicology at Columbia under the profession's dean, Paul Henry Lang. In the late 1960s Peyser began contributing articles both to in-tellectual periodicals and to journalistic magazines; she also commenced a twenty-year freelance career as the de facto official profile writer of new music composers in the *New York Times* Sunday Arts and Leisure section. In these ar-

324 ticles she incarnates a next-generation inheritor of the *Modern Music* mantle, with a tendency to favor the postwar "uptown" American composers of serial influence as the new academy. The wide exposure of her articles in the journal of record (as well as her 1970 book, *The New Music: The Sense Behind the Sound*) effectively disarmed the neoconservative arguments of antiserialist critics like the *New Yorker*'s Winthrop Sargeant and had an enormous impact on tastemaking among the *Times*'s upscale cultural audience. But despite her own success at the paper, she feels there is something amiss in the *Times*'s not having had a woman as a classical music critic, especially while almost every other *Times* cultural department has employed women critics (from Anna Kisselgoff in dance to Janet Maslin in film to Michiko Kakutani in books).

Peyser later became controversial for her antihagiographic psychoanalytic approach to biography in her books about Boulez (1977), Bernstein (1987), and Gershwin (1993). But a curious by-product of the books had little to do with her intent in writing them. The Bernstein and Gershwin books sold well; in fact, the Bernstein book became an international best-seller and "crossed over" into the mass market, because Peyser's warts-and-all approach inadvertently translated into "celebrity gossip," the coin of mass market publishing today. (In the early twentieth century Krehbiel's, Henderson's, and Taylor's books went into many reprintings, but none of them vaulted onto best-seller lists. Rupert Hughes's books were reprinted, too, but he didn't really make money until he went into the movies.)

As a result, Joan Peyser found herself the only serious writer on classical music since the radio days of Deems Taylor and Olin Downes to be courted by the mass media—including *People* magazine and tabloid television shows like "Hard Copy." If this unusual exposure brought classical music more to the attention of people who do not normally follow it—perhaps even creating new audience members—is it not a good thing?

ॐ *Interlude: The changing tides of canon, taste, and perception*

If critics are tastemakers, why has none blown the whistle on the concept of greatness—whatever that may be—as absolute and irreversible? Perhaps Beethoven's Ninth is trash.
—NED ROREM, *Setting the Tone*

Berlioz at the turn of the century was still adjudged minor. Even Huneker thought him "small fry," and Aldrich didn't like him at all. Elson thought Debussy was "cacophonous." But wait. To resist mincing the past through the garlic press of the present is every historian's challenge. It is very easy, too easy, to say that the Old Guard (except for Huneker) as a group got modern music all wrong and hence misread the inevitable flow of history. Yet isn't the following passage a remarkably accurate reportage of the score, though not an acquiescence in its artistic aims:

In *Elektra* of Strauss, jarring discords, the desperate battle of dissonances in one key against dissonances in another, settle themselves down into tonal delineation of shrieks and groans, of tortures physical in their clear definition and audible in their gross realism. Can you conceive of the inward scream of a conscience in the flames of the inferno being translated into the polyphonic utterances of instruments writhing in a counterpoint no longer required to be the composition of two or more melodies which shall harmonize with one another but of melodies which shall spit and scratch and claw at each other, like enraged panthers? Snarling of stopped trumpets, barking of trombones, moaning of bassoons and squealing of violins are but elementary factors in the musical system of Richard Strauss. (W. J. Henderson, *New York Sun,* February 2, 1920)

The point is, despite the chasm of history, some older critics' descriptions, read today, disclose perceptions that the music, heard today, still bears out. And some older critics' descriptions don't hold up. Compare Shaw on Brahms with Hanslick on Wagner:

Brahms takes an essentially commonplace theme; gives it a strange air by dressing it in the most elaborate and far-fetched harmonies; keeps his countenance severely; and finds that a good many wiseacres are ready to guarantee him as deep as Wagner, and the true heir of Beethoven. Strip off the euphuism from these symphonies and you will find a string of incomplete dances and ballad tunes following one another with no more organic coherence than the succession of passing images reflected in a shop window in Piccadilly during twenty minutes in the day. (G. B. Shaw, *The World,* London, June 18, 1890)

The "endless melody" is the dominating, i.e., musically undermining power in the Meistersinger as in Tristan. A little motive begins, but be-

326   fore it develops into a real melody or a theme it is forthwith bent over, broken up, raised and lowered through incessant modulations and enharmonic shifts, followed through by sequences, then patched up and contracted again, repeated or imitated by this or that instrument. With scrupulous avoidance of all closing cadences, this boneless tonal mollusk, self-restoring, swims ever on into the immeasurable. (Hanslick, 1870)

Can there be any question whose hearing of the actual music was clearer and speaks more to posterity? Yet it is Shaw whose reputation as a music critic carries to posterity and Hanslick who, Beckmesserized, is somehow confined to being "a man of his time." This observation is not at all meant as a billet-doux either to Hanslick or to critics. It is merely a plea for thinking cleared of prejudice.

The Shaw quote also puts to bed that elitist bugaboo, Were American critics hayseeds compared to their European counterparts? If European critics were always so smart, consider this quote from François-Joseph Fétis (1784–1871), the founder and editor of Europe's most influential journal of music criticism of the 1830s: "The time will undoubtedly come when the world will recognize that Heller, much more than Chopin, is the modern poet of the pianoforte."

European music journalism of the past has also differed from American in being more partisan, less objective, more frankly libelous at times in critical invectives, and less concerned with deadlines: reviewers had more time to write their reviews than overnight. It was also more overtly corrupt at a later date.

But back to the *Rashomon*-like problem of comparing critics of different eras. In matters of criminal law, contemporaneous testimony is considered more reliable than that provided long after the crime. The later the testimony, the more unreliable it is thought to be, unless it can be verified with other contemporaneous records. Not so in art criticism. Since great art ultimately must meet the test of time, there is a bias that presupposes the opposite extreme, that the original judgments must *necessarily* be wrongheaded, simply because they haven't had time to age like wine. And to be sure, it is frequently true that music critics, with the passage of time, have amended their earlier dissents about certain works that initially puzzled or repelled them. It is also true that they have frequently stayed unreconstructed in their wrongheadedness, as Slonimsky's *Lexicon* affirms. Yet to premise a total dismissal of earlier opinion on this basis is just a form of inverse bigotry, a kind of solipsism of the contemporary.

The history of opinion is still a key to understanding history, and sometimes the jury is still out. By the 1990s Bernard Holland of the *New York Times* was describing Ruth Crawford Seeger's dissonant 1931 String Quartet as "ugly" just as Olin Downes had used the word to apply to Schoenberg's Five Pieces for Orchestra in Boston in 1914. The wheel had come full circle. Perhaps it is simplistic to say that the postmodern return to tonality is but a reaffirmation of the wisdom of earlier critical opinion—the neotonalist style of today couldn't have existed without the historical intercalation of atonality—but conversely, is it fair totally to discredit earlier music critics from any faculty of discernment? We don't ask that of earlier literary critics, or even of art critics, even when they are proved wrong by history. We still read them.

In further demonstration, let's review an earlier part of our story, when American music appreciation in the early nineteenth century started and ended with church hymns. It was the early classical music critics who moved the concept of music appreciation out of religious piety to concert art music. Emersonian transcendentalism helped make that shift possible, but it was also made possible by critics who, like W. J. Henderson, both understood music as musicians and subscribed to doctrines of philosophical idealism, of artistic beauty as a philosophical good. This was their weltanschauung: "futurism" had to be experienced at first as "ugly"—which dissonance frequently is—and thus, philosophically, wrong. That does not mean that the critics could not verbally articulate the sounds they heard in ways still applicable to our ears, if not our tastes. Given that the critics of the nineteenth and early twentieth centuries had to formulate their opinions wholly without recourse to the repetitions of recorded music to refresh their memories of what given pieces and performers sounded like, their powers of verbal description sometimes seem remarkably acute and accurate even to our modern ears. In other words, there are educated people today who still agree word for word with some of the antique passages in Slonimsky's *Lexicon of Musical Invective*.

On the other hand, most late nineteenth-century critics believed tone color was not a structural element in music and thus tended to see colorful orchestration as a mask for poverty of either musical invention or structural organization. Then came Debussy and, later, Schoenberg's *Klangfarbenmelodie*. It is unlikely that many music listeners today would find Berlioz unlistenable simply because his use of tone color "masked" his "poverty" of invention or form, but such a mind-set clearly colored how the critics of that time heard, and reported hearing, the music.

328   The lesson? Some habits of hearing change, others don't; some canons of taste change, others are sempiternal. The mystery? What is it that determines which falls into which slot?

    ∾ *Trying to parse*
      concrete critical   *I sometimes think that critics do the arts an injustice by writ-*
      influence   *ing reviews that are needlessly harsh. Because audience mem-*
                          bers read that and say, "I liked the concert, and that must
                          mean that I don't know anything." And so they don't go again.
                          That's not helping create an artistic country.
                          —JoAnn Falletta

By what gauge in the final analysis can one measure what good works the critics have wrought? Readership response surveys or audience questionnaires? If Falletta, a conductor, is right, the results would not be encouraging.[5] Box office and record sales? Concerts are usually written up after the fact, and national record sales can't easily be tied to the reviews of local critics in given communities. Orchestral repertoire? The musicologist Kate Hevner Mueller compiled a list of the repertoire of twenty-seven American symphony orchestras from 1842 to 1970, plotting the performance frequencies of various composers like stocks in the market. Yes, there's a 1930s uptick in Sibelius performances that may reflect Olin Downes, but does the 1940s Sibelius downturn reflect Virgil Thomson's view of Sibelius, or Finland's position in the war? And as for critics' impact on composers? Writes Ned Rorem, "Have I ever learned about my own music through reviews of it? No, no more than through annotators who sometimes point out *trouvailles* I never knew were there. I've never altered a piece because of a critic. . . . A good write-up, alas, seems never to assure further performances."[6] The *Village Voice* critic Kyle Gann adds: "When you first become a critic, you've got a million opinions that you feel determined to express or burst. But after the first 500 or so articles, you find that those opinions don't shake the world, that music cannot be steered from its destined course to any great extent, and that, in the end, there's not that much difference between one opinion and another—each one is a little burst of hot air."[7]

    In a similar vein, the critic Peter G. Davis, writing in 1991 of the *Times*'s gifted young music critic Will Crutchfield's defection to conducting, observed, "Perhaps because music critics seldom change anything, however forcefully or eloquently they write, Crutchfield has decided to jump in and get his hands dirty by putting his ideas to practical use as a conductor himself."[8] Clearly, however, the composers and critics who contributed articles to *Modern Music* for twenty-two years thought their writings would change at least the opinions of other critics, if not the public. But did they? Even fifty years later, a cultivated intellectual like Kingsley Amis could still write, "Twentieth century music is like pedophilia. No matter how persuasively and persistently its champions urge their cause, it will never be accepted by the public at large, who will continue to regard it with incomprehension, outrage and repugnance."[9]

Looking back on the two centuries of dramatis personae encountered in these pages, one may discern certain recurrent stock types among American critics. There is, for instance, the critic-turned-manager or impresario: Samuel Chotzinoff and the NBC Symphony, John Rockwell and the Lincoln Center Festival, Eric Salzman and the American Music Theater Festival, Goddard Lieberson and Columbia Records, David Hall and Mercury Records, Will Crutchfield and conducting. It may perhaps be opined that this group—comprising some who retire from criticism and others who continue at it while simultaneously operating in arts management—have proved, by leaving their critical posts, the dictum that critics are eunuchs at the party. Or rather, it may be said that the critic-impresario types are fructifying their critical beliefs by acting out on them. Either way, this group arguably has had a more concrete effect on actual musical life than the great pontiffs of newspaper opinion like Krehbiel or Henderson.

Then there are the other types: the mass media communicators, for instance, like Deems Taylor and Sigmund Spaeth on the radio, and perhaps, indirectly, H. L. Mencken, and the rare author like Joan Peyser whose highbrow analyses cross over into the mass marketplace. They have reached millions that other critics have not. There is the sponsoring champion type, like Paul Rosenfeld and Carl Van Vechten, whose influence moved beyond the print galleys when they sought out their favorite artists in salons and occasionally assisted them, or Olin Downes, who promoted his love of Sibelius through front and back channels. There are the modernist advertisers, from Huneker to Paul Rosenfeld and *Modern Music* to John Rockwell, Joan Peyser, Eric Salzman, *Village Voice* critics like Tom Johnson, and freelancers like Richard Kostelanetz, who write about music with a tacit assumption that the moderns are the new academy; and there are now critics like Kyle Gann who write about the postmoderns as though *they* are the academy. Both modern groups tend to press agendas, while the neoconservative critics like Samuel Lipman and Terry Teachout, while intellectually no less vigorous, tend not to take stances of advocacy.

330   There are ironies on all sides. The New York and Boston critics of the 1920s and 1930s were contemptuously disregarded by Copland and the other composers who like commandos seized the presses for themselves in creating *Modern Music*. Yet decades later, the mainstream press modernist critics of the 1960s and 1970s still couldn't establish the modernist repertoire with the concertgoing public. The conservative critics had little practical influence on repertoire performed during the Darmstadt era, but they now look prescient, with formerly atonal composers themselves reverting to tonality. Does any group own a franchise on truth?

    Recapitulation   While some critical practices characteristic of earlier times such as the paid puff are deservedly behind us, there are other traditions now bygone whose abandonment has thrown the baby out with the bathwater. For one, the practicing composer-critic, and even the practicing musician-critic, is now nearly a dodo bird. At the beginning of her 1947 Harvard Symposium speech, Olga Samaroff approvingly quoted Liszt on the subject of why practicing musicians make the best music critics: "Criticism should become more and more an activity of productive artists. In regard to the objection that an artist could not easily undertake a dual activity, we assert the function of the critic would have great value for the artist because through the evaluation and comparison of the work of others, as well as the resume of decisions concerning them, every artist would inevitably gain in the maturing of his reflections and the logic of his ideas." [10]

Composer-critics have generally (not always) been the best musical analysts among our critics. Europe has always abounded in composer-critics: Berlioz, César Cui, Philip Heseltine, Reynaldo Hahn. But in America the William Henry Fry/Virgil Thomson/Deems Taylor critic type is dead, at least in large newspapers and mainstream media. To work for such organizations today a composer has to hang up his creative hat. Even such mixed types as Max de Schauensee, an opera singer who became the longtime music critic for the *Philadelphia Evening Bulletin*, are fading from view. Whatever has been gained in so-called impartiality has been lost in the dichotomy of artistic life from critical life. As a result concert music composers are on the one hand absented from a public face in the mainstream press, and on the other confined to writing for small niche publications like the *New Music Connoisseur* or *Twentieth Century Music*, where their criticism is sometimes tempered by a genteel collegiality different from the outright rudeness of *Modern Music*.

Another lamentable historical shift has been the devolution of prose style in classical music criticism. The two clichéd culprits here are the shrinkage of space available to newspaper writers, and the shrinking attention spans of readers thanks to television—both unarguable, but perhaps there are other factors, too. To reappraise every old warhorse for the Sunday think piece could try anyone's verbal chops; has the same old classical hit parade been consumed too many times and regurgitated too often for seminal new critical disclosures? Can't anyone still write like Huneker or Rosenfeld or Mencken, or even Henderson and Gilman—artists in prose who rouse the human spirit through the perfervid use of language to convey the ineffable excitement of a piece of music? Is this passé Romanticism? Or will the *USA Today* school of sound-bite prose eventually take over whatever remains of music journalism outside the scholarly journals?

Out with the bathwater of the Gilded Age has also gone the baby of the gentleman tradition of literary-musical dilettantism, the tradition that previously had seduced writers like Washington Irving, Emerson, Whitman, Longfellow, Sidney Lanier, Owen Wister, Rupert Hughes, and William Deans Howells. These writers either played classical music, wrote about it, edited for publication others' writing about it, or wrote librettos for operas and operettas. What happened to this tradition? Who are the twentieth-century American literary writers or poets associated with classical music? And what music critics in late twentieth-century America have any connection with the literary culture? With the sea change of the Gilbert Seldes/Edmund Wilson generation of arts critics, the cultural overcritic who subsumed classical music effectively went obsolete in America. Thereafter such culture critics as Dwight Macdonald wrote about culture high, low, and middle without writing about music high, low, or middle.

Cognate to the abandonment of music by cultural intellectuals as a group is the abandonment of music by mainstream journalism editors, publishers, and media producers. No one is suggesting that everybody can or should be made to love classical music. But in the heyday of radio, the 1920s and 1930s, classical music was more integrated with the bulk of entertainment fare presented to the mass listening public. Television did not replace old-time radio as a purveyor of classical music to the mass audience. Today PBS preaches to the converted, musically speaking, and no longer do the commercial broadcast networks have the likes of Samuel Chotzinoff to steer even a little cultural programming onto the tube. On radio Deems Taylor and John Erskine appeared on "Information, Please!" and on variety shows. In television, classical music

332   critics and commentators never appeared on "Hollywood Squares," nor today
are they talking heads on talk shows; nor are there TV music critic equivalents
of Siskel and Ebert, even on public television. For that matter, even newspaper
music critics today seem to have stopped bothering to assemble their articles
into books for publication, or publishers have ceased to offer them contracts.
Of the better younger critics, only Tim Page, who has worked at both the *New
York Times* and New York's *Newsday*, has anthologized his reviews in book
form in recent years.

The notion that publishers today ought to hire such writers out of a sense
of cultural duty may seem prescriptive, but what else describes what Geoffrey
Parsons of the *New York Herald Tribune* did in 1940 by hiring Virgil Thomson?
Do editors today avoid such hires because of the widespread distaste for modern music, or because the general culture simply doesn't esteem classical music today the way it did in 1940?

As we have seen in earlier chapters, small highbrow music publications
(*Dwight's Journal of Music, Modern Music*) have in the past had an effect on
mainstream American publications vastly greater than their size. No more.
What large-circulation periodical today is going to take a cue from any small
music journal? The small publications of the late 1990s that influence thinking
in megamedia boardrooms are probably techie webzines, not crusading intellectual print journals.

One bygone critical practice that is certainly problematic is fraternization
by critics with the artists they review. Paul Rosenfeld and Carl Van Vechten
were guilty of this after 1920, but the lines were not so finely drawn in the past.
At testimonial dinners of the pre-1920 era, great singers, conductors, and pianists would sit cheek by jowl with the newspaper critics who reviewed them.
Krehbiel initiated the movement to shun artists and their press agents, but
even he socialized with musicians (he played golf with the composer Horatio
Parker). Later, Irving Kolodin told Richard Freed, upon his being hired at the
Saturday Review in the early 1960s, not to befriend artists, yet Freed immediately noticed behind Kolodin a wall filled with photographs of famous musicians autographed to the critic.[11]

Perhaps that's why there were so many tributes and homages from musicians to the Old Guard critics upon their deaths—the critics in those days were
honored as constituent members of the artistic firmament largely *because* they
fraternized with the artists. The Old Guard critics weren't well paid, but they
were richly compensated by the esteem of the musical community. It is probable that no critic today in the larger cities enjoys such mutual admiration.

Regarding how in our current era to handle the problem of personally knowing whom you're reviewing, Josiah Fisk, who was from 1985 to 1995 the music critic for the *Boston Herald* and is not a professionally active musician, says he waffled a little when he knew the musician he was reviewing, but "wasn't crazy about it," while the *Village Voice*'s Kyle Gann, who *is* a practicing musician, notes, "I have frequently passed over without comment mediocre or failed music by people I know too well."[12] The critic/pianist Sarah Cahill adds, "There are cases where the fact that I know someone very well makes me feel much more qualified to write intelligently about them. . . . I don't feel any conflict of interest. . . . I believe W. H. Auden had it right: the critic has to trust his or her own instincts in each situation. You also have to feel the friendship is strong enough to withstand occasional criticism whether in public or not."[13]

∾ The real new academy

The shrinkage or abandonment of classical music coverage by editors and publishers of even likely venues for it, such as the *New Yorker, Esquire,* the *Atlantic,* and *Harper's,* attests to the fact that the Baby Boom is the first generation in American history whose mandarins are not occupied with promoting the cultural good of classical music. Their intellectual leaders feel no bonds with it as did the intelligentsias of the 1820s, the 1870s, and the 1920s, as we have seen. While philosophical idealism was the weltanschauung of Henderson and Krehbiel, rock and roll is the weltanschauung today. A generation devoted to building halls of fame to rock and roll does not see art music as qualitatively different from vernacular music; rock and roll is the official lingua franca of its culture. By comparison with media moguls of the past who promoted classical music through their mass media, from the 1840s *New York Herald*'s James Gordon Bennett to the *Atlantic* and *Harper's* William Dean Howells to David Sarnoff of NBC in the 1930s, the media managers of today are unprecedentedly philistine.

John Rockwell would not approve of this characterization, and certainly not apply it to himself. In a 1996 revision to his 1983 book *All American Music,* he wrote, "Unlike Henry Pleasants, I did not wish to consign modernism and dissonance and proudly self-referential experimentation to the dustbin of history. . . . my 'agenda' was never to replace 'serious' music with minimalism and rock & roll. . . . The idea of a true 'music critic,' one who covers all music as film critics cover all films, has yet to be validated by even one prominent American publication."[14]

334   But not all critics subscribe to Rockwell's brand of pluralism. Josiah Fisk recalls responding to a reader's letter by writing an article for the *Boston Herald* in which Fisk spoke of the "mistake of looking for 'coolness' in classical music. Classical music is not 'cool.' The David Helfgott marketing phenomenon is equivalent to standing outside a Catholic Church, waving, and saying, 'Free wine, come in!'"[15]

Rockwell, like Seldes and to a lesser extent Van Vechten, is an intellectual bestowing upon vernacular music, now including "art rock," the intellectual's imprimatur of Culture, an alternative culture perhaps, but still culture. Such writing may go back to Seldes but really took flight in the 1960s with new publications like *Rolling Stone,* when rock music critics began writing about rock music with the kind of ornate prose, intricate detail, and philosophical/aesthetic orientation that previously had been accorded only to classical music. It *was* a new worldview. There hadn't been comparable prolix, elevated prose about Sinatra and Crosby, even from Seldes. This was new.

As recently as the late 1950s, one of radio's great music appreciationists, the aging Sigmund Spaeth, himself once a great supporter of vernacular music, publicly denounced Elvis Presley as "jungle" music. Perhaps that position was analogous to Krehbiel in the 1910s supporting negro spirituals but denouncing ragtime. Today, a rapprochement between rock and classical is very much in process in "downtown" postmodern musical styles. Yet again, that nagging "baby with the bathwater" feeling comes up. It's all right to celebrate rock music. It's all right to cross over and mix and mingle forms and genres. But why is classical music therefore factored out of the syllabus? Why aren't there contemporary counterparts of the nineteenth century's George William Curtis holding forth in general magazines for classical music? William F. Buckley and Edward Said perhaps do, but they are of an earlier generation. The literati of today believe in rock music. It is the new academy and state religion.

One need look no further than the larger salaries paid to pop critics than to classical critics to see evidence all around. One of the brilliant younger critics, Alex Ross, left the *New York Times* for the *New Yorker,* where he found himself reviewing not only classical music but British rockers, thus embodying Rockwell's chimerical totalist music critic. But as time wears on Ross's articles about classical music in the *New Yorker* have appeared fewer and farther between.

The *Times* itself was not immune to these pressures and practices. The late media critic Edwin Diamond wrote:

Out of concern for its own operational comfort level, if not for reasons of flat-out financial gain, management turned to market researchers to plumb readers' cultural-news interests. Much like a modern political candidate, Arthur Sulzberger's *Times* polled target constituencies, found out what excited them or thought might excite them, and shaped its cultural campaign accordingly. Many of the changes on the arts and leisure pages in the past decade, from the decline of space devoted to classical music reviews to the prominence given the "Critic's Notebook" pieces of the *Times'* star writers, were influenced by findings of this market research. Perhaps high culture wasn't out, but it was certainly down for the count; consumerism, pop culture, and bright, smart—often, smartass— writing were in. . . . As Warren Hoge explained, the *Times* wanted to "appeal to a new generation, people whose attention spans were shorter." The market researchers, whose in-depth interviews and focus groups *Times* management was paying for, had a term for many members of the new generation: they were "aliterate"—they knew how to read but didn't read very much. . . .

Reviews of "small" recitals, cultural-news stories, and offbeat features . . . were downgraded. The critic Peter Davis, who spent twelve years as a reviewer of concerts and classical music recordings for the *Times,* remembered when he wrote up three or four recitals a week for the paper, "and that was when there were eight of us covering serious music." . . . [By 1991] the *Times* was sweeping together into a once-weekly package short, five-paragraph reviews of concert-recitals. . . . The package of short classical-music reviews appeared on Saturdays, the day of the week when the *Times* has its lowest circulation.[16]

A veteran *Times* culture reporter, Gerald Gold, added, "We do all these pieces on pop icons, as if they're important 'artistes.' In fact, they are creations of the big record companies. Yet we try to intellectualize them; we treat this material as if it is coming out of university graduate departments."[17]

The Internet and classical music commentary

The newest frontier in classical music journalism is found in newsgroups and webzines on the Internet. CultureFinder, an online site available on America

336 Online devoted to all the performing arts, until recently sported Theodore Libbey, who had previously worked as a critic at National Public Radio and the *New York Times,* as its cyber–music critic. CultureFinder also has an interactive feature, the "Classical Music Wizard," "Opera Wizard," and "Musical Theater Wizard," who are music journalists to whom site visitors can address questions about music and opera. There are also feature articles by Sarah Bryan Miller, an opera singer and noted freelance music journalist for the *New York Times* and *Wall Street Journal.* Surfers who visit the site are invited to email Miller at her AOL address. Miller is also the classical music editor of Amazon.com, the online bookstore—a job that in the next century may be more influential than chief music critic on large urban newspapers.

In addition, newsgroups like rec.music.classical afford the interactivity of bulletin board message posting to site visitors. The posts vary in musical knowledge from neophyte to sophisticate; generally, the letters to the editor of *Fanfare* and the *American Record Guide* are more on the connoisseurship level. However, the *New York Times* critic Allan Kozinn has frequently posted messages on rec.music.classical. Many classical composers have also designed their own homepages on the web and now critics are doing the same, including the *Village Voice* composer-critic Kyle Gann. And a classical music webzine, www.ClassicalInsites.com, was under construction as of this writing.

What's missing in this picture (which may well change radically in a few years) is the intermediation of editors and the supervision of authority to guide the agenda. Specialty groups of musical interest are left to post messages to themselves in the dark on the Internet bulletin boards. Communication to and education of the great mass public is left undone. The former *San Francisco Chronicle* critic Robert Commanday, speaking of both specialized websites and niche print publications like *Fanfare,* says they lack a crucial element that the newspaper critic always had. "I don't think a critic can develop authority in his writing unless he's got a podium widely established and reaches a wide readership." [18]

∾ *Finale*

Certainly classical music critics are not responsible for a weakening of interest in European art models, NEA budget cuts, the end of arts instruction in public schools, or the supplanting of piano lessons with synthesizers—all factors attenuating appreciation of classical music in our times—any more than literary critics and book reviewers, no matter how prominent or influential, are responsible for creeping cultural illiteracy or the drivel of the television medium. But, like the literary reviewers, music critics soldier on in an inhospitable climate. Perhaps the greatest seer among the critics covered in this book is H. L. Mencken. In some ways the late twentieth century is a neo-booboisie period. Synthesthetic critics of broad culture, that is, the Huneker and Mencken type, are desperately needed now. They are what is most missing in the ecology of the arts circa 2000.

For those who subscribe to the various cyclic theories of human history (Spenglerian, Viconian, etc.—though not Menckenian), it certainly is savagely amusing to learn that in the early 1830s it was the penny newspapers, not the upper-crusty *New York Albion,* that carried socially self-conscious "reviews" of opera that were mere excuses to report the doings of the beautiful people—an antediluvian example of what still runs on "Page 6" of the *New York Post* every day, an early example of the all-American propensity for sugar-coating high culture with gossip and entertainment values while at the same time promoting egalitarian appreciation of "elite" values. Fast-forward 150 years to best-selling exposés about Vladimir Horowitz and Maria Callas. *Plus ça change, plus c'est la même chose.*

From the early 1800s American classical music critics were both tastemakers and activists. As tastemakers their writings first introduced the concept of art music, then introduced the idea of well-played art music, then gradually introduced the idea of canonical art music. As activists, they tried through their writings to promote the founding of our first civic musical institutions: operas, symphony orchestras, university music department chairs. In the nineteenth century this activism was the offshoot of a general boosterism for home-growing European high art culture in the community. In the twentieth century both the tastemaking and the activist roles became more complicated. The critics had both to educate the untutored in the standard repertoire and to act as cultural ambassadors establishing an uneasy detente with the New Music. The most activist critics tended to be those boosting avant-garde music.

In all eras, our critics, at their best, have managed to champion the side of the angels, help educate masses of music appreciators, influence performance practice and programming, help rescue unjustly neglected repertoire, and overmatch and best corruption and paid publicity. At their worst, they have been bullishly wrongheaded pains in the derrière who have probably damaged worthy musical careers more often than they like to admit.

But alarm bells are ringing over classical music that have nothing to do with the critics: despite the above-mentioned similarities between music critics and book critics, people *are* still writing and reading books in great num-

338 bers, but orchestra subscriptions and endowments are dwindling harrowingly, and the over-fifty audience that is the preponderant group patronizing classical music is beginning to die out.

And the twenty-first century? What will be the pattern? And will a new Watson, Fry, Huneker, or Henderson emerge to take up the inky cloak and lead the charge once again?

Notes

OVERTURE

1. This remark was attributed by Bengt de Törne in his 1937 book, *Sibelius: A Close Up*, p. 27. Quoted in Glenda Dawn Goss, ed., *The Sibelius Companion* (Westport, Conn.: Greenwood Press, 1996), p. 230.
2. Clare Reis, *Composers, Conductors, and Critics* (New York: Oxford University Press, 1956), p. 112.
3. Ernest Newman, ed., *Memoirs of Hector Berlioz* (1932; reprint, New York: Dover, 1966), p. 80.
4. Richard Aldrich, *Concert Life in New York, 1902–1923* (New York: Putnam, 1941).
5. Vera Brodsky Lawrence, *Strong on Music: The New York Music Scene in the Days of George Templeton Strong, 1836–1875*, vol. 1, *Resonances: 1836–1850* (New York: Oxford University Press, 1988), p. xi.

CHAPTER 1

1. W. S. B. Mathews, *A Hundred Years of Music in America: An Account of Musical Effort in America* (Chicago: G. L. Howe, 1889), p. 362; the epigraphs are taken from p. 636.
2. Oscar Sonneck, *Early Concert Life in America* (Leipzig: Breitkopf & Härtel, 1907), p. 12.
3. Ibid., p. 119. This custom persisted in America well into the nineteenth century in both newspapers and magazines such as *Dwight's Journal of Music*. In Europe, Robert Schumann signed his reviews with three different *noms de guerre*: Eusebius, Florestan, and Master Raro.
4. Ibid., p. 116.
5. Mathews, *Hundred Years*, p. 57.
6. Theodore Thomas, *A Musical Autobiography* (1905; reprint, New York: Da Capo Press, 1964), p. 20. Richard Grant White, "Opera in New York," *Century* 23, no. 6 (April 1882): 869.
7. Mathews, *Hundred Years*, p. 58.
8. Lawrence, *Resonances*, p. 496.
9. Ibid., p. lv.
10. Mathews, *Hundred Years*, p. 64.
11. Frédéric Ritter, *Music in America* (New York: Scribners, 1890), p. 139.
12. Mathews, *Hundred Years*, p. 378.
13. Frank Luther Mott, *American Journalism: A History, 1690–1960*, 3d ed. (New York: Macmillan, 1962), p. 313.
14. Lawrence, *Resonances*, p. xlviii.
15. Ibid., p. 278.
16. Ibid., p. 59.
17. Ibid., p. 111.

340   18.   Ibid., p. 96.

19.   Ibid., p. 97.

20.   Ibid., pp. 185, 326.

21.   Ibid., p. 147.

22.   Ibid., p. 119.

23.   Ibid., p. 505.

24.   Charles Congdon, *Reminiscences of a Journalist* (Boston, J. R. Osgood, 1880), pp. 196–97.

25.   Lawrence, *Resonances,* pp. 373–74.

26.   Ibid., pp. 378–79.

27.   Ibid., p. 439.

28.   H. Earle Johnson, *First Performances in America to 1900: Works with Orchestra,* Bibliographies in American Music No. 4 (Detroit: The College Music Society/Information Coordinator, 1979), p. 30.

CHAPTER 2

1.   Robert Sabin, "Early American Composers and Critics," *Musical Quarterly* 24 (October 1938): 210–18.

2.   Ora Frishberg Saloman, *Beethoven's Symphonies and J. S. Dwight* (Boston: Northeastern University Press, 1995), pp. 69–70.

3.   Ritter, *Music in America,* pp. 329–30.

4.   Mathews, *Hundred Years,* p. 35.

5.   Ralph Waldo Emerson, *Collected Works,* vol. 3, p. 65.

6.   A. W. Plumstead and Harrison Hayford, eds., *The Journals and Miscellaneous Notebooks of Ralph Waldo Emerson* (Cambridge, Mass.: Harvard University Press, 1969).

7.   Irving Lowens, *Music and Musicians in Early America* (New York: Norton, 1964), pp. 261–62.

8.   Ibid., pp. 256–57.

9.   Lawrence, *Resonances,* p. 196.

10.   Irving Sablosky, *What They Heard: Music in America, 1852–1881, from the Pages of "Dwight's Journal of Music"* (Baton Rouge: Louisiana State University Press, 1986), p. 4.

11.   William Foster Apthorp, *Musicians and Music-Lovers and Other Essays* (1894; reprint, Freeport, N.Y.: Books for Libraries Press, 1972), pp. 277–78.

12.   Saloman, *Beethoven's Symphonies,* p. 68.

13.   Ibid., p. 64.

14.   Sablosky, *What They Heard,* p. 5.

15.   Apthorp, *Musicians and Music-Lovers,* p. 283.

16.   Sablosky, *What They Heard,* p. 3.

17.   Ibid., p. 5.

18.   Johnson, *First Performances,* pp. 296–98.

19.   Sablosky, *What They Heard,* pp. 55–57.

20.   Ibid., p. 12.

21.   Ibid.

22.   Johnson, *First Performances,* p. 27.

23.   *Atlantic Monthly* 89 (February 1902): 166.

24.   Robert D. Faner, *Walt Whitman and Opera* (Carbondale: Southern Illinois University Press, 1951), p. 6.

25. James Gibbons Huneker, *Essays,* introduction by H. L. Mencken (New York: Scribners, 1929), p. 417.   341
26. Faner, *Whitman,* p. 7.
27. Ibid., p. 122.
28. Ibid., p. 62, quoting from Whitman's *Uncollected Poetry and Prose.*
29. Ibid., p. 53.

CHAPTER 3

1. Nicolas Slonimsky, "The Plush Era," in *One Hundred Years of Music in America,* ed. Paul Henry Lang (New York: G. Schirmer, 1961), p. 110.
2. Louise Karr, "Musical Critics of the New York Daily Press," *Musical Leader and Concert Goer* 9, no. 10 (March 9, 1905): 16.
3. Henry T. Finck, *My Adventures in the Golden Age of Music* (1926; reprint, New York: Da Capo Press, 1971), p. 174.
4. Arnold T. Schwab, *James Gibbons Huneker: Critic of the Seven Arts* (Stanford, Calif.: Stanford University Press, 1963), p. 43.
5. Apthorp, *Musicians and Music-Lovers,* p. 6.
6. Henry Dunham, *The Life of a Musician Woven into a Strand of History of the New England Conservatory of Music* (New York: Richmond Borough, 1931), p. 220.
7. *Musical Courier,* February 13, 1901.
8. Apthorp, *Music and Music-Lovers,* pp. 289–95.
9. Joseph A. Mussulman, *Music in the Cultured Generation: A Social History of Music in America, 1870–1900* (Evanston, Ill.: Northwestern University Press, 1971), p. 182.
10. Mathews, *Hundred Years,* p. 82.
11. W. S. B. Mathews, "The Compositions of Raff," *Musician,* October 4, 1889, p. 375.
12. H. L. Mencken, *A Book of Prefaces,* 3d ed. (New York: Knopf, 1920), p. 177.
13. Philip Hale, *Great Concert Music: Philip Hale's Boston Symphony Programme Notes: Historical, Critical, and Descriptive Comment on Music and Composers,* ed. John N. Burk, introduction by Lawrence Gilman (Garden City, N.Y.: Garden City Publishing, 1939), pp. xviii, vi–vii.
14. William J. Henderson, *What Is Good Music? Suggestions to Persons Desiring to Cultivate a Taste in Musical Art* (1898; reprint, Freeport, N.Y.: Books for Libraries Press, 1972), pp. 111–12.
15. Hale, *Great Concert Music,* p. 214.
16. Daniel Gregory Mason, *Music in My Time and Other Reminiscences* (New York: Macmillan, 1938), p. 175.
17. Richard Aldrich, *Musical Discourse from the "New York Times"* (1928; reprint, Freeport, N.Y.: Books for Libraries Press, 1967), p. 284.
18. H. E. Krehbiel, *How to Listen to Music* (New York: Scribners, 1896), p. 317.
19. Karr, "Musical Critics," p. 17.
20. *Musical America,* July 10, 1909.
21. Joseph Horowitz, *Understanding Toscanini: A Social History of American Concert Life* (Berkeley: University of California Press, 1987), p. 71.
22. *National Cyclopedia of American Biography* (New York: James T. White & Co., 1904).
23. Oscar Thompson, "An American School of Criticism," *Musical Quarterly* 23 (July 1937): 434; Edward Downes, "The Taste-Makers: Critics and Criticism," in *One Hundred Years of Music in America,* ed. Paul Henry Lang (New York: G. Schirmer, 1961), p. 239.

342   24.   Downes, "The Taste-Makers," p. 239.

25.   Thompson, "An American School of Criticism," p. 434.

26.   Ibid., p. 435.

27.   Winthrop Sargeant, *Geniuses, Goddesses, and People* (New York: Dutton, 1949), p. 115.

28.   Thompson, "An American School of Criticism," p. 437.

29.   H. T. Parker, *Eighth Notes* (1922; reprint, Freeport, N.Y.: Books for Libraries Press, 1968), p. 163.

30.   Ibid., pp. 62–63.

31.   Mason, *Music in My Time*, pp. 279–80.

32.   Henry T. Finck, *Chopin and Other Musical Essays* (1889; reprint, Freeport, N.Y.: Books for Libraries Press, 1972), pp. 158–59.

33.   Finck, *My Adventures in the Golden Age of Music*, pp. 282–83.

34.   Herbert Peyser, article in *Singing*, November 1929.

35.   Ibid.

36.   Herbert Peyser, article in *Musical America*, October 10, 1940.

37.   Finck, *My Adventures in the Golden Age of Music*, pp. xv–xvii.

CHAPTER 4

1.   Channing Pollock, *Harvest of My Years* (Indianapolis: Bobbs-Merrill, 1943), p. 148; Brandes quoted in George Sylvester Viereck, *Confession of a Barbarian* (New York: Moffat, Yard, 1910), p. 157; Hecht quoted in Schwab, *James Gibbons Huneker*, p. 197; Mencken quoted in *Smart Set* 28 (June 1909): 153.

2.   Schwab, *James Gibbons Huneker*, p. 39.

3.   Daniel Dodson, introduction to James Gibbons Huneker, *Ivory Apes and Peacocks* (1915; reprint, New York, Sagamore Press, 1957), p. xi.

4.   Arthur Friedheim, *Life and Liszt*, jointly reprinted with Alexander Siloti, *My Memories of Liszt*, as *Remembering Franz Liszt*, introduction by Mark N. Grant (New York: Limelight Editions, 1986), pp. 137, 179.

5.   Mencken, *A Book of Prefaces*, p. 170.

6.   Schwab, *James Gibbons Huneker*, p. 57.

7.   Ibid., p. 83.

8.   Nathan quoted in ibid., p. 234; De Casseres quoted in the *Nation*, November 29, 1922, p. 582.

9.   Finck, *My Adventures in the Golden Age of Music*, p. 415.

10.   Schwab, *James Gibbons Huneker*, p. 44.

11.   H. L. Mencken, introduction to James Gibbons Huneker, *Essays* (New York: Scribners, 1932), p. xiv.

12.   Schwab, *James Gibbons Huneker*, p. 226.

13.   Dodson, introduction to *Ivory Apes*, p. xi.

14.   Herbert Weinstock, introduction to James Gibbons Huneker, *Chopin: The Man and His Music* (New York: Dover, 1966), pp. vii–xi.

15.   Schwab, *James Gibbons Huneker*, p. 106.

16.   Ibid., p. 181.

17.   Irving Kolodin, "Huneker's Hundredth," *Saturday Review*, January 30, 1960, p. 53.

18.   Schwab, *James Gibbons Huneker*, p. 254.

19.   Ibid., p. 197.

20. Ibid., p. 154.
21. Ibid., p. 251.

CHAPTER 5

1. Charles Fecher, *Mencken: A Study of His Thought* (New York: Knopf, 1978), p. 14.
2. Mencken, letter to Isaac Goldberg, May 6, 1925.
3. H. L. Mencken, *H. L. Mencken on Music: A Selection of His Writings on Music Together with an Account of H. L. Mencken's Musical Life and a History of the Saturday Night Club,* ed. Louis Cheslock (New York: Knopf, 1961), p. 212.
4. Fecher, *Mencken,* p. 283.
5. William Manchester, *Disturber of the Peace: The Life of H. L. Mencken,* 2d ed. (Amherst: University of Massachusetts Press, 1986), pp. 50–51.
6. Ibid., p. 85.
7. Ibid., pp. 299–300.
8. Cheslock, *Mencken on Music,* p. 34.
9. Manchester, *Disturber of the Peace,* p. xx.
10. Mencken, "James Huneker," in *A Book of Prefaces,* pp. 191–92.
11. Ibid., p. 151.
12. Cheslock, *Mencken on Music,* pp. 158–60.
13. Mencken, *A Book of Prefaces,* pp. 176–78.
14. H. L. Mencken, "The Motive of the Critic," *New Republic,* October 26, 1921.
15. Ibid.
16. H. L. Mencken, *Smart Set,* September 1919.
17. Ibid.
18. Fred Hobson, *Mencken: A Life* (New York: Random House, 1994), p. 392.
19. Cheslock, *Mencken on Music,* pp. 158–60.
20. Ibid., p. 32.
21. Anecdote recounted by a docent at the H. L. Mencken House, 1524 Hollins Street, Baltimore, Md., December 28, 1996.

CHAPTER 6

1. Mathews, *Hundred Years,* p. 363.
2. William Treat Upton, *William Henry Fry: American Journalist and Composer-Critic* (1954; reprint, New York: Da Capo Press, 1974), p. 13.
3. Lowens, *Music and Musicians in Early America,* p. 222.
4. Upton, *William Henry Fry,* pp. 140–41.
5. Ibid., pp. 136–37.
6. Ibid., p. 116.
7. Ritter, *Music in America,* p. 319.
8. Lowens, *Music and Musicians,* pp. 217–18.
9. Mathews, *Hundred Years,* p. 364.
10. Orly Krasner interview, October 10, 1997.
11. Schwab, *James Gibbons Huneker,* p. 68.

344   12.   Anna Farwell De Koven, *A Musician and His Wife* (New York: Harper, 1926), p. 240.

13.   Krasner interview.

14.   Finck, *My Adventures in the Golden Age of Music,* p. 371.

15.   De Koven, *A Musician and His Wife,* p. 176.

16.   Deems Taylor, *Of Men and Music* (New York: Simon & Schuster, 1938), pp. 232–33.

17.   David Ewen, comp. and ed., *Composers since 1900: A Biographical and Critical Guide* (New York: Wilson, 1969), p. 579.

18.   John Tasker Howard, monograph on Deems Taylor (New York: Fischer, 1927), p. 16.

19.   Ibid., p. 15.

20.   Taylor, *Of Men and Music,* p. 305.

21.   Ibid., p. 115.

22.   Ibid., pp. 44–46.

23.   Ibid., p. 220.

24.   Ibid., pp. 125–26.

25.   Ibid., p. 21.

26.   Don C. Gillespie, *The Search for Thomas F. Ward, Teacher of Frederick Delius* (Gainesville: University Presses of Florida, 1996).

27.   Taylor, *Of Men and Music,* pp. 191–93.

28.   Reis, *Composers, Conductors, and Critics,* p. 10.

29.   Ibid., p. 104.

30.   Ibid., p. 102.

31.   Ibid., p. 5.

32.   Joan Peyser, *The Music of My Time* (White Plains, N.Y.: Pro/Am Music Resources, 1995), pp. 91–94.

33.   Ibid.

34.   Ibid.

35.   Virgil Thomson, *American Music since 1910* (New York: Holt, Rinehart & Winston, 1970), p. 171.

CHAPTER 7

1.   Finck, *Chopin,* p. 175.

2.   Krehbiel, *How to Listen to Music,* p. 310.

3.   Henderson, *What Is Good Music?* pp. 120–21.

4.   Aubrey Harrison Starke, *Sidney Lanier: A Biographical and Critical Study* (Chapel Hill: University of North Carolina Press, 1933), pp. 260–61.

5.   Mussulman, *Music in the Cultured Generation,* p. 193.

6.   Ibid., p. 14.

7.   Ibid., p. 19.

8.   Henderson, *What Is Good Music?* pp. 117–18.

9.   Krehbiel, *How to Listen,* pp. 68–69.

10.   Henderson, *What Is Good Music?* p. 93.

11.   Nicolas Slonimsky, *Lectionary of Music* (New York: Anchor Books, 1989), p. 311.

12.   Josef Hofmann, *Piano Playing with Piano Questions Answered* (1920; reprint, New York: Dover, 1976), p. vii.

13.   James O. Kemm, *Rupert Hughes: A Hollywood Legend* (Beverly Hills, Calif.: Pomegranate Press, 1997), p. 117.

14. Mason, *Music in My Time*, p. 396.

15. Michael Kammen, *The Lively Arts: Gilbert Seldes and the Transformation of Cultural Criticism in the United States* (New York: Oxford University Press, 1996), p. 322.

16. Ibid., pp. 95, 117.

17. Ibid., p. 390.

18. Mason, *Music in My Time*, pp. 100–101.

19. Daniel Gregory Mason, *The Dilemma of American Music and Other Essays* (1928; reprint, New York: Greenwood Press, 1969), p. 344.

20. Ibid., p. 55.

21. Ibid., pp. 45–46.

22. Ibid., pp. 40–42.

23. Daniel Gregory Mason, *Tune In, America: A Study of Our Coming Musical Independence* (New York: Knopf, 1931), pp. xv, 11.

24. John Erskine, *The Memory of Certain Persons* (Philadelphia: Lippincott, 1947), p. 374.

25. Richard Kostelanetz, *On Innovative Musicians* (New York: Limelight Editions, 1989), pp. 240–41.

26. Kyle Gann, letter to Mark N. Grant, June 19, 1997.

CHAPTER 8

1. Ned Rorem, *Pure Contraption* (New York: Holt, Rinehart & Winston, 1972), p. 3.

2. Ned Rorem, *Setting the Tone* (New York: Limelight Editions, 1984), p. 144.

3. Virgil Thomson, *Selected Letters*, ed. Tim Page and Vanessa Weeks Page (New York: Summit Books, 1988), p. 148.

4. Virgil Thomson, *Music Right and Left* (New York: Holt, 1951), p. viii.

5. Aaron Copland, *The New Music, 1900–1960* (New York: Norton, 1968), p. 139.

6. Kathleen Hoover and John Cage, *Virgil Thomson: His Life and Music* (1959; reprint, Freeport, N.Y.: Books for Libraries Press, 1970), p. 28.

7. Virgil Thomson, *Virgil Thomson* (New York: Knopf, 1967), p. 69.

8. Hoover and Cage, *Virgil Thomson*, p. 48.

9. Virgil Thomson, *The State of Music* (1939), rev. ed. (New York: Vintage Books, 1962), p. 91.

10. Thomson, *Virgil Thomson*, p. 321.

11. Anthony Tommasini, *Virgil Thomson: Composer on the Aisle* (New York: Norton, 1997), p. 323.

12. Hoover and Cage, *Virgil Thomson*, pp. 90–91.

13. Ibid.

14. Ibid., pp. 92–93.

15. Thomson, *Virgil Thomson*, pp. 324–26.

16. Ibid., pp. 328–34.

17. Hoover and Cage, *Virgil Thomson*, pp. 90–91.

18. Thomson, *Virgil Thomson*, p. 327.

19. Thomson, *The State of Music*, p. 135.

20. Ibid., pp. 107–9.

21. Ibid., p. 106.

22. Thomson, *Virgil Thomson*, pp. 335–36.

23. Ibid., pp. 410–11.

24. Tommasini, *Virgil Thomson*, pp. 346–47.

346   25. Thomson, *Virgil Thomson*, p. 415.

26. Virgil Thomson, 1981 interview with John C. Tibbetts, Professor of Theater and Film at the University of Kansas, *American Record Guide*, November–December 1996, p. 41.

27. Rorem, *Pure Contraption*, p. 74.

CHAPTER 9

1. Edward Downes, "The Taste-Makers," p. 243.

2. *Saturday Review*, July 3, 1954.

3. *Opera News*, November 1995, p. 22.

4. Ibid., p. 21.

5. Ibid.

6. *Current Biography*, September 1955.

7. Richard Franko Goldman, "Music Criticism in the United States," *Score*, June 1955, p. 87.

8. Shirley Fleming, *Musical America*, October 1981, p. 75.

9. Ibid.

10. *San Francisco Chronicle*, June 23, 1981.

11. Robert Commanday, interview with Mark N. Grant, October 20, 1997.

12. John Frankenstein, letter to Mark N. Grant, October 22, 1997.

13. Shirley Fleming, *Musical America*, October 1981, p. 75.

14. David Schneider, *The San Francisco Symphony: Music, Maestros, and Musicians* (Novato, Calif.: Presidio Press, 1983), p. 121.

15. David McCullough, *Truman* (New York: Simon & Schuster, 1992), p. 827.

16. Ibid., p. 828.

17. "Critical Issues," Music Critics Association Newsletter, February 1996.

18. Ibid.

19. John H. Davis, *The Kennedys: Dynasty and Disaster* (New York: Shapolsky, 1992), p. 81.

20. Harold Schonberg, *Facing the Music* (New York: Summit Books, 1981), p. 20.

21. Glenda Dawn Goss, *Jean Sibelius and Olin Downes: Music, Friendship, Criticism* (Boston: Northeastern University Press, 1995), p. 57.

22. Ibid., p. 37.

23. Ibid., p. 80.

24. Kate Hevner Mueller, *Twenty-Seven Major American Symphony Orchestras: A History and Analysis of Their Repertoires, Seasons 1842–1843 through 1969–1970* (Bloomington: Indiana University Press, 1973).

25. Sargeant, *Geniuses, Goddesses and People*, p. 116.

26. Horowitz, *Understanding Toscanini*, p. 122.

27. *New York Times*, December 6, 1969.

CHAPTER 10

1. G. B. Shaw, as quoted in Nicolas Slonimsky, *Lexicon of Musical Invective: Critical Assaults on Composers since Beethoven's Time* (1953, 1965; reprint, Seattle: University of Washington Press, 1994), p. 21.

2. Reis, *Composers, Conductors, and Critics*, p. 22.

3. Hale, *Great Concert Music*, p. 295.

4. Reis, *Composers, Conductors, and Critics,* p. 45.

5. *New York Times,* December 22, 1964.

6. Copland, *The New Music,* p. 158.

7. Ibid.

8. Paul Rosenfeld, *Musical Portraits: Interpretations of Twenty Modern Composers* (1920; reprint, Freeport, N.Y.: Books for Libraries Press, 1968), p. 267.

9. Ibid., pp. 191–92.

10. Ibid., pp. 23–24.

11. Ibid., pp. 104–5.

12. Carl Van Vechten, *Letters of Carl Van Vechten,* ed. Bruce Kellner (New Haven, Conn.: Yale University Press, 1987), p. 27.

13. *New York Times,* December 22, 1964.

14. Ibid.

15. Introduction by John Rockwell to the 1997 reprint of *All American Music* (New York: Da Capo Press, 1997), p. ix.

CHAPTER 11

1. Eileen Southern, *Biographical Dictionary of Afro-American and African Musicians* (Westport, Conn.: Greenwood Press, 1982), p. 328.

2. Lowens, *Music and Musicians in Early America,* pp. 208–9.

3. Olga Samaroff, "The Performer as Critic," in *Music and Criticism: A Symposium,* ed. Richard K. French (1948; reprint, Port Washington, N.Y.: Kennikat Press, 1969), pp. 84–86.

4. Sarah Cahill, letter to Mark N. Grant, May 4, 1997.

5. Her comments are from *Fanfare* 21, no. 2 (November/December 1997): 122.

6. Rorem, *Setting the Tone,* p. 295.

7. Kyle Gann, letter to Mark N. Grant, June 19, 1997.

8. Peter G. Davis, *New York,* April 8, 1991, p. 103.

9. *New York Times,* October 23, 1995, p. B11.

10. Franz Liszt, *Gesammelte Schriften* (1885), 4:138.

11. Richard Freed, interview with Mark N. Grant, November 10, 1997.

12. Josiah Fisk, interview with Mark N. Grant, June 19, 1997; Gann, letter, June 19, 1997.

13. Cahill, letter, May 4, 1997.

14. John Rockwell, *All American Music,* 1996 ed., pp. ix, xiii.

15. Fisk, interview, June 19, 1997.

16. Edwin Diamond, *Behind the Times: Inside the New "New York Times"* (New York: Villard Books, 1994), pp. 311–13.

17. Ibid., p. 314.

18. Robert Commanday, interview with Mark N. Grant, October 31, 1997.

Selected Bibliography

Abdul, Raoul. *Blacks in Classical Music: A Personal History.* New York: Dodd, Mead, 1977.

Aldrich, Richard. *Concert Life In New York, 1902–1923.* New York: Putnam, 1941.

———. *Musical Discourse from the "New York Times."* 1928. Reprint. Freeport, N.Y.: Books for Libraries Press, 1967.

Apthorp, William Foster. *Musicians and Music-Lovers and Other Essays.* 1894. Reprint. Freeport, N.Y.: Books for Libraries Press, 1972.

Barnouw, Erik. *A Tower in Babel.* New York: Oxford University Press, 1966.

Bleyer, William G. *Main Currents in the History of American Journalism.* Cambridge, Mass.: Houghton Mifflin, 1927.

Bordman, Gerald. *The Oxford Companion to American Theatre.* New York: Oxford University Press, 1992.

Congdon, Charles. *Reminiscences of a Journalist.* Boston: J. R. Osgood, 1880.

Copland, Aaron. *The New Music, 1900–1960.* New York: Norton, 1968.

De Bellis, Jack. *Sidney Lanier.* New York: Twayne, 1972.

De Koven, Anna Farwell. *A Musician and His Wife.* New York: Harper, 1926.

DeLong, Thomas A. *Radio Stars: An Illustrated Biographical Dictionary of 953 Performers, 1920 to 1960.* Jefferson, N. C.: McFarland, 1996.

Diamond, Edwin. *Behind the Times: Inside the New "New York Times."* New York: Villard Books, 1994.

Diamond, Harold. *Music Criticism.* Metuchen, N.J.: Scarecrow Press, 1979.

Erskine, John. *The Memory of Certain Persons.* Philadelphia: Lippincott, 1947.

Ewen, David, comp. and ed. *Composers since 1900: A Biographical and Critical Guide.* New York: Wilson, 1969.

Faner, Robert D. *Walt Whitman and Opera.* Carbondale: Southern Illinois University Press, 1951.

Fecher, Charles A. *Mencken: A Study of His Thought.* New York: Knopf, 1978.

Finck, Henry T. *Chopin and Other Musical Essays.* 1889. Reprint. Freeport, N.Y.: Books for Libraries Press, 1972.

———. *My Adventures in the Golden Age of Music.* 1926. Reprint. New York: Da Capo Press, 1971.

French, Richard F., ed. *Music and Criticism: A Symposium.* 1948. Reprint. Port Washington, N.Y.: Kennikat Press, 1969.

Friedheim, Arthur. *Life and Liszt.* Reprinted in *Remembering Franz Liszt,* edited with a new introduction by Mark N. Grant. New York: Limelight Editions, 1986.

Gabin, Jane S. *A Living Minstrelsy: The Poetry and Music of Sidney Lanier.* Macon, Ga.: Mercer University Press, 1985.

Gillespie, Don C. *The Search for Thomas F. Ward, Teacher of Frederick Delius.* Gainesville: University Presses of Florida, 1996.

Gilman, Lawrence. *Orchestral Music: An Armchair Guide.* Edited by Edward Cushing. New York: Oxford University Press, 1951.

350   Gilman, Lawrence. *The Music of To-morrow and Other Studies.* 1907. Reprint. Freeport, N.Y.: Books for Libraries Press, 1970.

Goss, Glenda Dawn. *Jean Sibelius and Olin Downes: Music, Friendship, Criticism.* Boston: Northeastern University Press, 1995.

———, ed. *The Sibelius Companion.* Westport, Conn.: Greenwood Press, 1996.

Graf, Max, ed. *Composer and Critic: 200 Years of Musical Criticism.* New York: Norton, 1946.

Haggin, B. H. *A Decade of Music.* New York: Horizon Press, 1973.

Hale, Philip. *Great Concert Music: Philip Hale's Boston Symphony Programme Notes: Historical, Critical, and Descriptive Comment on Music and Composers.* Edited by John N. Burk with an introduction by Lawrence Gilman. Garden City, N.Y.: Garden City Publishing, 1939.

Henderson, William J. *Modern Musical Drift.* New York: Longmans, Green, 1904.

———. *What Is Good Music? Suggestions to Persons Desiring to Cultivate a Taste in Musical Art.* 1898. Reprint. Freeport, N.Y.: Books for Libraries Press, 1972.

Hobson, Fred. *Mencken: A Life.* New York: Random House, 1994.

Hofmann, Josef. *Piano Playing with Piano Questions Answered.* 1920. Reprint. New York: Dover, 1976.

Hoover, Kathleen, and John Cage. *Virgil Thomson: His Life and Music.* 1959. Reprint. Freeport, N.Y.: Books for Libraries Press, 1970.

Horowitz, Joseph. *The Post-Classical Predicament: Essays on Music and Society.* Boston: Northeastern University Press, 1995.

———. *Understanding Toscanini: A Social History of American Concert Life.* Berkeley: University of California Press, 1987.

Huneker, James Gibbons. *Chopin: The Man and His Music.* New York: Scribners, 1900. 2d ed., with a new introduction, footnotes, and index by Herbert Weinstock. New York: Dover, 1966.

———. *Essays.* Selected with an introduction by H. L. Mencken. New York: Scribners, 1929, 1932.

———. *Ivory Apes and Peacocks.* 1915. Reprint. New York: Sagamore Press, 1957.

———. *Old Fogy.* Philadelphia: Presser, 1913.

———. *Overtones: A Book of Temperaments.* New York: Scribners, 1904.

Johnson, H. Earle. *First Performances in America to 1900.* Detroit: The College Music Society, 1979.

Kammen, Michael. *The Lively Arts: Gilbert Seldes and the Transformation of Cultural Criticism in the United States.* New York: Oxford University Press, 1996.

Kellner, Bruce. *Carl Van Vechten and the Irreverent Decades.* Norman: University of Oklahoma Press, 1968.

Kemm, James O. *Rupert Hughes: A Hollywood Legend.* Beverly Hills, Calif.: Pomegranate Press, 1997.

Kline, Donna Staley. *An American Virtuoso on the World Stage: Olga Samaroff Stokowski.* College Station: Texas A & M University Press, 1996.

Kolodin, Irving, ed. *The Critical Composer: The Musical Writings of Berlioz, Wagner, Schumann, Tchaikovsky, and Others.* 1940. Reprint. Freeport, N.Y.: Books for Libraries Press, 1969.

Kostelanetz, Richard. *On Innovative Musicians.* New York: Limelight Editions, 1989.

Krehbiel, Henry. *How to Listen to Music.* New York: Scribners, 1896.

Lackmann, Ron. *Same Time, Same Station: An A–Z Guide to Radio from Jack Benny to Howard Stern.* New York: Facts on File, 1996.

Lambert, Constant. *Music Ho! A Study of Music in Decline.* 1934. Reprint. London: Hogarth Press, 1985.

Lang, Paul Henry, ed. *One Hundred Years of Music in America.* New York: G. Schirmer, 1961.

Lawrence, Vera Brodsky. *Strong on Music: The New York Music Scene in the Days of George Templeton Strong, 1836–1875.* Vol. 1. *Resonances: 1836–1850.* New York: Oxford University Press, 1988.

Levine, Lawrence W. *Highbrow/Lowbrow: The Emergence of Cultural Hierarchy in America.* Cambridge, Mass.: Harvard University Press, 1988.

Lipman, Samuel. *Arguing for Music, Arguing for Culture.* Boston: Godine, 1990.

———. *The House of Music.* Boston: Godine, 1984.

———. *Music after Modernism.* New York: Basic Books, 1979.

Lowens, Irving. *Music and Musicians in Early America.* New York: Norton, 1964.

Lueders, Edward. *Carl Van Vechten and the Twenties.* Albuquerque: University of New Mexico Press, 1955.

Manchester, William. *Disturber of the Peace: The Life of H. L. Mencken.* 2d ed. Amherst: University of Massachusetts Press, 1986.

Mason, Daniel Gregory. *The Dilemma of American Music and Other Essays.* 1928. Reprint. New York: Greenwood Press, 1969.

———. *Music in My Time and Other Reminiscences.* New York: Macmillan, 1938.

———. *Tune In, America: A Study of Our Coming Musical Independence.* New York: Knopf, 1931.

Mathews, W. S. B. *A Hundred Years of Music in America: An Account of Musical Effort in America.* Chicago: G. L. Howe, 1889.

McCullough, David. *Truman.* New York: Simon & Schuster, 1992.

Mencken, H. L. *A Book of Prefaces.* 3d ed. New York: Knopf, 1920.

———. *H. L. Mencken on Music: A Selection of His Writings on Music, Together with an Account of H. L. Mencken's Musical Life and a History of the Saturday Night Club.* Edited by Louis Cheslock. New York: Knopf, 1961.

Mims, Edward. *Sidney Lanier.* 1905. Reprint. Port Washington, N.Y.: Kennikat Press, 1968.

Mott, Frank Luther. *American Journalism: A History, 1690–1960.* 3d ed. New York: Macmillan, 1962.

Mueller, Kate Hevner. *Twenty-Seven Major American Symphony Orchestras: A History and Analysis of Their Repertories, Seasons 1842–1843 through 1969–1970.* Bloomington: Indiana University Press, 1973.

Mussulman, Joseph A. *Music in the Cultured Generation: A Social History of Music in America, 1870–1900.* Evanston, Ill.: Northwestern University Press, 1971.

Parker, H. T. *Eighth Notes: Voices and Figures of Music and the Dance.* 1922. Reprint. Freeport, N.Y.: Books for Libraries Press, 1968.

Parks, Edd Winfield. *Sidney Lanier: The Man, the Poet, the Critic.* Athens: University of Georgia Press, 1968.

Peyser, Joan. *The Music of My Time.* White Plains, N.Y.: Pro/Am Music Resources, 1995.

Pleasants, Henry. *The Agony of Modern Music.* New York: Simon & Schuster, 1955.

Reis, Clare. *Composers, Conductors, and Critics.* New York: Oxford University Press, 1956.

Ritter, Frédéric. *Music in America.* New York: Scribners, 1890.

Rockwell, John. *All American Music: Composition in the Late Twentieth Century.* New York: Knopf, 1983. Rev. ed. New York: Da Capo Press, 1996.

Rorem, Ned. *Pure Contraption.* New York: Holt, Rinehart & Winston, 1972.

———. *Setting the Tone.* New York: Limelight Editions, 1984.

Rosenfeld, Paul. *Discoveries of a Music Critic.* 1936. Reprint. New York: Vienna House, 1972.

———. *Musical Chronicle, 1917–1923.* 1923. Reprint. New York: Blom, 1971.

———. *Musical Impressions: Selections from Paul Rosenfeld's Criticism.* Edited by Herbert A. Leibowitz. London: George Allen & Unwin, 1969, 1970.

352   ———. *Musical Portraits: Interpretations of Twenty Modern Composers*. 1920. Reprint. Freeport, N.Y.: Books for Libraries Press, 1968.

Sablosky, Irving. *What They Heard: Music in America, 1852–1881, from the Pages of "Dwight's Journal of Music."* Baton Rouge: Louisiana State University Press, 1986.

Saloman, Ora Frishberg. *Beethoven's Symphonies and J. S. Dwight*. Boston: Northeastern University Press, 1995.

Sargeant, Winthrop. *Geniuses, Goddesses, and People*. New York: Dutton, 1949.

———. *Listening to Music*. New York: Dodd, Mead, 1958.

Schneider, David. *The San Francisco Symphony: Music, Maestros, and Musicians*. Novato, Calif.: Presidio Press, 1983.

Schonberg, Harold. *Facing the Music*. New York: Summit Books, 1981.

Schwab, Arnold T. *James Gibbons Huneker: Critic of the Seven Arts*. Stanford, Calif.: Stanford University Press, 1963.

Seldes, Gilbert. *The Seven Lively Arts*. Rev. ed. New York: Sagamore Press, 1957.

Slonimsky, Nicolas. *Lectionary of Music*. New York: McGraw-Hill, 1989.

———. *Lexicon of Musical Invective: Critical Assaults on Composers since Beethoven's Time*. 1953, 1965. Reprint. Seattle: University of Washington Press, 1994.

———. *Music since 1900*. 5th ed. New York: Scribners, 1993.

Sonneck, Oscar. *Early Concert Life in America*. Leipzig: Breitkopf & Härtel, 1907.

Southern, Eileen. *Biographical Dictionary of Afro-American and African Musicians*. Westport, Conn.: Greenwood Press, 1982.

Starke, Aubrey Harrison. *Sidney Lanier: A Biographical and Critical Study*. Chapel Hill: University of North Carolina Press, 1933.

Sullivan, Jack, ed. *Words on Music from Addison to Barzun*. Athens: Ohio University Press, 1990.

Taylor, Deems. *Of Men and Music*. New York: Simon & Schuster, 1938.

Terrace, Vincent. *Radio's Golden Years: The Encyclopedia of Radio Programs, 1930–1960*. La Jolla, Calif.: Barnes, 1981.

Thompson, Oscar. *Practical Musical Criticism*. New York: Witmark, 1934.

Thomson, Virgil. *American Music since 1910*. New York: Holt, Rinehart & Winston, 1970.

———. *The Art of Judging Music*. New York: Knopf, 1948.

———. *Music Reviewed, 1940–1954*. New York: Vintage Books, 1966.

———. *Music Right and Left*. New York: Holt, 1951.

———. *The Musical Scene*. 1945. Reprint. Westport, Conn.: Greenwood Press, 1968.

———. *Selected Letters of Virgil Thomson*. Edited by Tim Page and Vanessa Weeks Page. New York: Summit Books, 1988.

———. *The State of Music*. 1939. Rev. ed. New York: Vintage Books, 1962.

———. *Virgil Thomson*. New York: Knopf, 1967.

———. *A Virgil Thomson Reader*. Introduction by John Rockwell. Boston: Houghton Mifflin, 1981.

Tommasini, Anthony. *Virgil Thomson: Composer on the Aisle*. New York: Norton, 1997.

Upton, George P. *Musical Pastels*. Chicago: McClurg, 1902.

Upton, William Treat. *William Henry Fry: American Journalist and Composer-Critic*. 1954. Reprint. New York: Da Capo Press, 1974.

Van Vechten, Carl. *Letters of Carl Van Vechten*. Selected and edited by Bruce Kellner. New Haven, Conn.: Yale University Press, 1987.

———. *Music after the Great War and Other Stories*. New York: G. Schirmer, 1915.

Index

Abdul, Raoul, 320
Adams, Franklin P., 110, 220
Adams, John: and Salzman, 192
Adams, John Quincy: on Beethoven *Welling-
ton's Victory*, 53
Adorno, Theodor, 184
African-American music: Dwight's views on,
51–52; and Krehbiel, 86; Mencken's views
on, 154–56; and Pleasants, 315; Pleasants's
views on, 295; and Van Vechten, 292
African-American press: classical music criti-
cism in, 319–20
The Agony of Modern Music (Pleasants), 283,
295, 296, 298, 301
Ainslie's, 209
Albéniz, Isaac, 293
Albion (New York), 337; early arts reviews in,
10–11; and Watson, 16; Watson's writings
in, 18–19, 29
Alboni, Marietta, 56
Aldrich, Richard, xvii, 94, 98–99, 267; on
Berlioz, 99; on Huneker, 126; on Krehbiel,
81, 82–83, 84, 85; on modern music, 283–
84; and Van Vechten, 292
All American Music (Rockwell), 308–9, 310–
11, 333
Allen, Cleveland G., 86, 319–20
American Art Journal, 21
The American Language (Mencken), 133, 136
American Mercury, 210; Frankenstein's writ-
ings in, 261; and Mencken, 133, 134, 136,
144, 158; Thomson's writings in, 180, 232
American Music Journal, 6
American Music Theater Festival (Philadel-
phia): and Salzman, 192
American Musical Magazine (New Haven), 33
American Musical Magazine (Northampton),
33
American Musical Times, 17
American Record Guide, 224, 318
American Scholar, 223

America's Coming of Age (Brooks), 211
Amis, Kingsley, 329
Amram, David, 308
Anderson, Marian, 227–28
Anglo American, 16, 28
Anschutz's German Opera Company, 168
Ansermet, Ernest, 246
Antheil, George, 158, 190
antimodernism, of Lambert, 297
Apthorp, William Foster, 68–72, 196; on Bee-
thoven *Pastoral* Symphony, 71; on Brahms
Symphony No. 1, 69–70; on critics, 72; on
cultivation of taste, 65; on Dvořák *New
World* Symphony, 71; on Dwight, 41–42,
44, 46; on educating audiences, 71; on
Lanier, 200; on MacDowell *Indian* Suite,
71; on musical knowledge of critics, 63; on
Strauss *Death and Transfiguration*, 71–72;
on Strauss *Don Juan*, 67; on Wagner, 71;
writings in *Atlantic Monthly*, 203; writings
in *Scribner's*, 204
Arnold, Matthew, 153, 311; and American music appreciation, 196–97; and concept of
"high culture," 196, 284; *Culture and Anarchy*, 196
art criticism: by Huneker, 125, 128–29
ASCAP, 177, 178
Astor Place Opera House, 8, 21–22
Astor Place Riot, 19
Astor Place Theater, 19
Atkinson, Brooks, xv, 96
Atlantic Monthly, 202; Apthorp's music editorship of, 69; Apthorp's writings in, 70–
71, 200; contributors to, 203–4; decline in
classical music coverage, 333; Thomson's
writings in, 252; White's writings in, 197
Auden, Wystan Hugh, 245*n*, 333
audiences: in Chicago, 74; concept of highbrow, middlebrow, lowbrow, 197, 212–13;
early reviewers and, 15; and fashion, 7–9;
lack of sophistication of, 36, 51; Mason's